P9-DGO-700

9/99

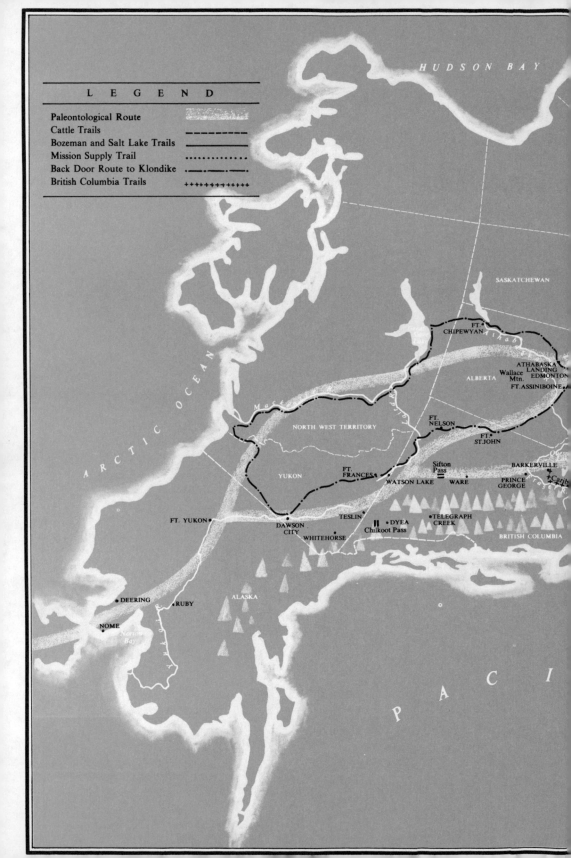

HUDSON BAY

SASKATCHEWAN

FT. CHIPEWYAN

ATHABASKA LANDING
Wallace Mtn.   EDMONTON
ALBERTA
FT. ASSINIBOINE

ARCTIC OCEAN

Mackenzie

NORTH WEST TERRITORY

FT. NELSON

FT. ST.JOHN

BARKERVILLE

YUKON

FT. FRANCES

Sifton Pass

WATSON LAKE   WARE

PRINCE GEORGE

Carib

FT. YUKON

DAWSON CITY

TESLIN

DYEA
Chilkoot Pass

TELEGRAPH CREEK

WHITEHORSE

BRITISH COLUMBIA

DEERING   RUBY

ALASKA

NOME

Norton Bay

Yukon

P A C I

P

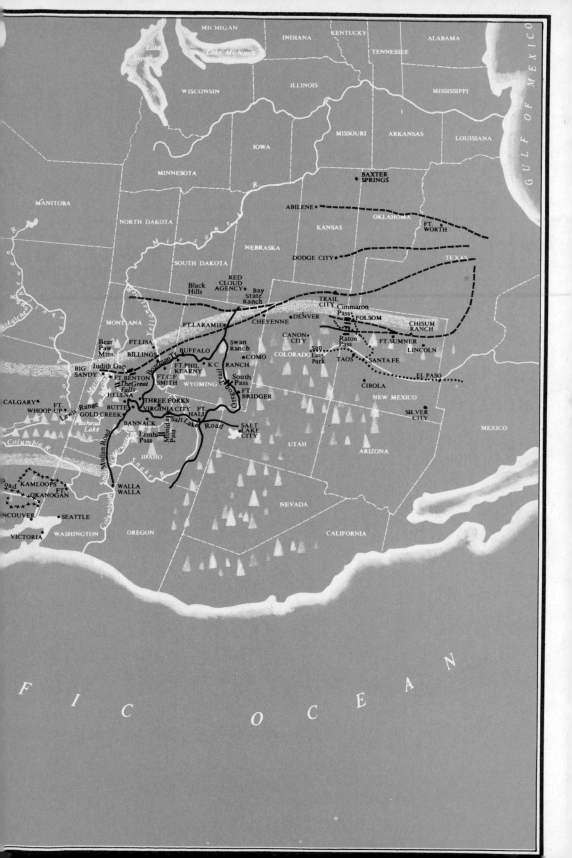

THE GREAT NORTH TRAIL

Books in The American Trails Series

THE GREAT NORTH TRAIL
by Dan Cushman
America's Route of the Ages

THE GATHERING OF ZION
by Wallace Stegner
The Story of the Mormon Trail

THE DEVIL'S BACKBONE
by Jonathan Daniels
The Story of the Natchez Trace

THE OLD POST ROAD
by Stewart Holbrook
The Story of the Boston Post Road

THE GOLDEN ROAD
by Felix Riesenberg, Jr.
The Story of California's Spanish Mission Trail

THE CALIFORNIA TRAIL
by George Stewart
An Epic with Many Heroes

WESTWARD VISION
by David Lavender
The Story of the Oregon Trail

DOOMED ROAD OF EMPIRE
by Hodding Carter
The Spanish Trail of Conquest

SUBJECTS IN PREPARATION

The Santa Fe Trail by William Brandon
The Erie Canal and Iroquois Trail by Carl Carmer

THE
GREAT
NORTH
TRAIL

AMERICA'S ROUTE
OF THE AGES

by Dan Cushman

McGraw-Hill Book Company
New York   Toronto   London   Sydney

e-1

CONTENTS

TRAIL OF ALL AGES

Chapter 1

For millions of years the continents of Asia and North America were connected. As recently as 10,000 years ago, when large volumes of ocean were sucked up to form the ice sheet, animals walked from the Siberian East Cape to the Seward Peninsula of Alaska. Grass grew where today roll the cold waters of Bering Strait, and the headlands were low hills. The bones of ice-age caribou can be traced up the Yukon and through the low mountain passes into Canada—and, by their flints and ancient campsites, the tribes who hunted them.

During the glacial age much of the North had summers little cooler than those of today. Even when the bleak sheet pushed southward as far as the Ohio River and the highest peaks of British Columbia were islands in grinding rivers of ice, much of Alaska had forests and June flowers. South of the ice was a desolation of muck and water, but the parched sands and glaring soda sinks of today's Southwest were dotted with lakes.

As in the North, men followed the herds. There is evidence that men lived in the country between Texas and California as long ago as 35,000 years. This is not to say the Indians are their descendents. It is not known that these first American men survived. A long stretch of time empty of their bones and campsites indicates they were unable to match their numbers against the immensity of the continent. But beginning 10,000 to 12,000 years ago, at the height of the glaciers, men seemed to find America to their liking.

Kills and camps, dating to that age, appear in abundance. Starting along the Texas–New Mexico border, men spread from the Atlantic to the Pacific and into South America; cave remains from that period have been found even at the cold extremity of Tierra del Fuego.

The paradox of men increasing so prodigiously at what should have been a period of extreme hardship is puzzling. The origin of these people has been sought unsuccessfully in southern Asia, Oceania, and Africa. The barrier of the ice sheet seems to preclude the possibility of entry from the north, although flint weapons of the same age discovered in Alaska indicate a single culture for both. Did the tribes somehow find their way through the great ice, opening a trail that would seem to be the marvel of the ages? Apparently they did. But their route was not new. The same general course had been followed long before. It was followed by creatures antedating man, and antedating, in fact, all the land animals on the face of the earth. There are proofs that it has existed for 200 million years.

Two hundred million years, even to geology, is a long while. In 200 million years the continent can erode, and rise, and be eroded, and rise again, and portions of it undergo a far more complex history. It might help in comprehending such vast periods to note that a mountain peak in the Alps or the Rockies becomes lowered by erosion by about one foot in a thousand years. Mountains such as the Lewis Range of Glacier National Park might be reduced to a rolling upland in about 4 million years. The rate slows as the peaks are worn down, but it can be seen that two hundred million gives a good opportunity for change. Yet the route has remained. Generally speaking the oceans have been oceans since the beginning of time, the continents continents, and the Rocky Mountain highlands have been highlands. The route has been part of those highlands. It may, geologically, be much older than the time stated. But a route implies something to follow it, and before two hundred million years ago no animal had yet divorced itself from the mother sea. Amphibians had crawled up on the shore, and there were the reptiles, but both were tied closely to the water. The first successful travelers by land were warm-blooded, able to carry their eggs within their bodies and bring forth their young in an advanced stage of development. In a sense they made their own climate. They were not so dependent on the sun. Cold made them active whereas the reptiles became sluggish. The first warm-blooded creature marked a revolution in animal adaptability.

The original was probably a tiny thing which evolved in Texas during Permian times. On the other hand there is a claim that it originated across the bulge of the globe in Mongolia. Trailwise the precise location is not very important. The species seems to have made its appearance in Asia and America at almost the same instant, as science reckons the past. Barring an odd chance that it evolved in those widely separated places independently, one must conclude it migrated, one way or the other. The path, as seen on a globe, is the most direct possible. It lies up the eastern front of the Rocky Mountains, across Alaska, the sea of Bering Strait and St. Lawrence Island, and the Stanovoi highlands. The bones of ten thousand species have marked it, and the Indian, or his ancestors, have left it strewn with his flints and camping sites. In modern times it has been used by the cattle herds and gold-seekers. One portion of it was the Bozeman Trail,

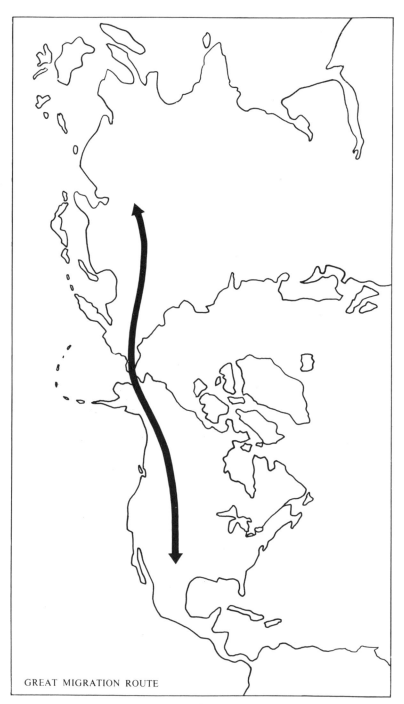

GREAT MIGRATION ROUTE

scene of the bloodiest Indian fighting of the West, another segment was the whisky trail to Whoop-Up, and in World War II it was followed by the builders of the Alaska Highway. The most ancient known passageway of all ages, one can think of no better name for it than the Great North Trail.

Conventional history first knows of it in the annals of New Spain. Coronado followed the Trail northward when he reached present-day Kansas hoping to find gold. Later a part of his route became the Spanish Mission Trail to Santa Fe, and another part the Chisholm Trail of cowboy fame to Dodge City and Abilene. To the north the fur traders of Montreal and St. Louis came by boat for the most part and established their chief Western posts where it forded the Saskatchewan, Missouri and Yellowstone rivers. Yet neither those early ones who traveled it nor those who built to utilize its traffic were aware of the Trail's grand pattern. This was not the discovery of pioneers or explorers, but of scholars, and it came about through a curiosity regarding the strange appearances and disappearances of the American horse . . .

Although by the nineteenth century wild ponies ranged the West and the Indians of the Plains were a cavalry, it was known that not a horse had existed in all America when the Spanish landed on the coast of Mexico. Nothing in the animal world, not even the ice-age rise of the buffalo, with numbers estimated at sixty million, was more remarkable than the increase of horses in the West. In the late 1860s, when paleontologists started digging in the fossil-rich chalk beds of Kansas and riding the new Union Pacific into Nebraska and Wyoming, the bones of primitive horses in stage after stage of evolution were found to be so plentiful that America was acclaimed as their true homeland. Soon, however, European scientists were showing that each American stage had been duplicated there. Obviously there had existed through many ages a migration route. Professor

Othniel Marsh of Yale, who had recently enjoyed his first national publicity for exposing as a fake the Cardiff Giant, made news again mapping the entire length of the Trail, from Siberia down to Mexico, and even into South America, a grand geological and biological concept; in doing so he caught up all the Indian, Spanish and fur-trade fragments in its course. His map, drawn with a generous sweep as befitted a man who dealt with the ages, later was proved surprisingly correct in detail.

To English-speaking Americans, the idea of a northern entrance to the continent was quite novel. Settling along the Alantic coast, they had always looked at the land from east to west. They followed the setting sun. "Westward the course of empire," said Bishop Berkeley in his poem on the prospects for learning in America, and one of Thoreau's most famed passages had man's natural bent to the west. Their wagon roads ran westward, as did their chief railroads and even today's airlines. However, they did not conquer America for humankind because the Indians were there already. The only mammal, in fact, which can be shown to have spread across North America from east to west was the Norway rat, introduced by the Vikings. One has to go back to the reptiles before a westerly migration becomes the major one. During the Mesazoic era, 150 million years ago, when the continents became so eroded it seemed that the seas would wash over the entire globe, there appears to have been a shallow zone across the North Atlantic by which the dinosaurs came from Europe to America. Making their way across the mid-American sea they attained along the shores of Wyoming a size and fanged ferocity unique in history. From there they traveled to Alberta and on to Siberia.

The Great North Trail, starting at the Seward Peninsula, crosses to the Yukon and, during most of its history, seems to have traveled along the northern shore of the river. At Fort Yukon, where early fur traders built a post, the most important one in interior Alaska, a strand winds off, crossing to the Mackenzie, but later it rejoins the main cord at Edmonton. Another strand unwinds south of the famed Klondike to fray out into the Pacific plateaus and valleys. East of the mountains the main route was marked in part by the Old North Trail of the Blackfeet. These swashbucklers of the Indian world already knew the Trail north to the Land of Little Sticks—the barrens where only shrubby trees could grow. When Spanish horses fell into their possession by capture and trade, the Blackfeet adventured far southward. Sometimes they came back only after years, with silver ornaments, and tales of strange men who lived near the River of Hot Sand, the Rio Grande.

Today the Asiatic homeland of the Blackfeet, and of the Athabascan tribes which followed, has been cut off by 26 miles of gray stormy sea at Bering Strait. After 200 million years it might seem that the Great North Trail had finally been ended. However, with only a minor buildup of ice in the polar regions the seas would drop sufficiently to make a passage. Also, recent igneous activity has moved areas at the base of the Seward Peninsula, while across in Siberia stands the active Anadyrski Range. A small continuance of mountain actions east and west would again bring the passage up from the sea.

It has already been shown that the Trail has existed repeatedly for past eons because of recurring continental geology. It might be well here to go ahead and discuss the grand geological balances of the earth in more detail.

In the distant past, when the earth solidified from gases and molten rock, the continents came into being. Characteristically they are of granite, with a specific gravity of about 2.6, while the oceans are basaltic and heavier, about 3.2. The difference is not great but seems sufficient for the granites to rise, on average, 3 or 4 miles higher than the ocean floors. Not only do the lighter rocks make up the continents, any traveler can see that the lightest, hardest granites form the highest mountain ranges, while soundings indicate that the heavier basalts sag to form the deeper ocean floors. Throughout the ages the Mississippi Valley has been lowland or shallow sea. It is thickly covered by sediments, but its few exposures of igneous, once-molten rock and some deep bore holes indicate a medium basalt below, making it an in-between piece of the earth's crust.

In all periods the sea and atmosphere have worked at leveling the continents. Repeatedly they have almost succeeded, but always the shifting weights of sediments, products of erosion, have destroyed the equilibrium, and they rose again. Perhaps the earth's age of 4½ billion years is only a few hours in the order of time, and the elements yet may succeed, but there is little present evidence that they will. The continents of today are as high as they ever were, the oceans as deep. They are, if anything, higher and deeper. Our age follows the Cretaceous when, as already noted, it seemed that the last land was about to be covered by sea. To any intelligence then existing it would have seemed that the earth had reached old age, a final stability. But the shifting weights only seemed more profoundly to violate the balances. The Sierra Nevada rose. Erosion attacked it and the clays of its feldspars filled the California Sea. Then the Cordillera, for 10,000 miles from Tierra del Fuego to Alaska, was thrust up in an almost-solid chain. Along the coast of South America the 20,000-foot range of the Andes is fronted by a belt of coastal troughs which reach depths of 24,000 feet. It is theorized that the troughs are a result of the great weight of the Andes which have sagged and pulled down the ocean floor at their feet, but still the climb continues. In the United States the new Sierra outran itself and settled back on its base, pulling the surrounding rocks down so that Mount Whitney, highest point in the West, and Death Valley, lowest on the continent, are found only 80 miles apart. Inland, the mountains are still climbing. At Aspen, Colorado, faults encountered in the mine workings shortly after the silver rush of 1879 have shown upward movement almost continuously since, while the glacial marks of the ice age form a datum plane on which the fault movements of the past 12,000 years can be gauged. The

Mosquito Range, site of the celebrated mining camp of Leadville, is a block being pushed upward along the planes of four main faults. The San Juan region of southwestern Colorado is a rising dome with ever-deepening canyons, and the Sawatch Range, with altitudes already exceeding that of Pikes Peak, is climbing to new record heights.

In Alberta and Montana one of the scenic wonders of the continent was created when deep granite, pushing from the direction of the Pacific, lifted a mountain block of shale, quartzite, and limestone—all products of a sea antedating the known life on earth—and pushed it across the younger rocks of the Great Plains. This major break in the rocks is known as the Lewis Overthrust Fault and the mountains which were raggedly chiseled into the elevated strata the Lewis Range. Both are named after Captain Meriwether Lewis of the Lewis & Clark expedition, the white man who first recorded seeing them. Surely there exists few visual experiences as awesome as this range, with its cliffs like battlements, its summer snow and peaks shouldering the clouds, rising like a wall of the giants. Standing a measured 8 miles from their parent strata they have been called "the mountains without roots." The main fault, one of the most famous in geology, can be seen as a rusty line around the base of the mountain ridge to the north by anyone who cares to stop at the summit of Marias Pass on the Roosevelt Highway. Also, the break is marked by Trick Falls between the Two Medicine lakes, and it is responsible for more and more bold escarpments as one travels north. Foothills lie at the base of the mountains. The foothills are also the result of the Lewis Overthrust. Pushed forward like a giant bulldozer it crowded the rocks of these hills into hundreds of tight folds and smaller faults, fittingly called the Montana Disturbed Belt. Farther to the east, and generally giving no hint of its existence to the casual viewer, the whole central chest of Montana has been lifted into a formation known as the Sweetgrass Arch. Of vital interest to oil and gas exploration, the arch has been mapped across an area 200 miles long and 60 wide. The Missouri River, passing its crest, descends about 500 feet in a few miles, a steplike descent forming the Great Falls.

The Great North Trail runs along the high ground, bounded in the west by the mountains. In many previous ages it was bounded in the east by the sea. The Disturbed Belt and the Sweetgrass Arch are today typical of the formations underfoot, and the Lewis Overthrust is its typical western wall. In all times travel north and south has been relatively easy, due to the primeval geology. That from east to west has generally been difficult. Yet, openings in the mountains do exist, and trails of apparent antiquity make use of them. It is interesting to observe that these, also, have their origins in geology.

Perhaps the most interesting of the east-west trails is the one followed by the Nez Percé Indians from their homeland on the Columbia River through the Rockies to the

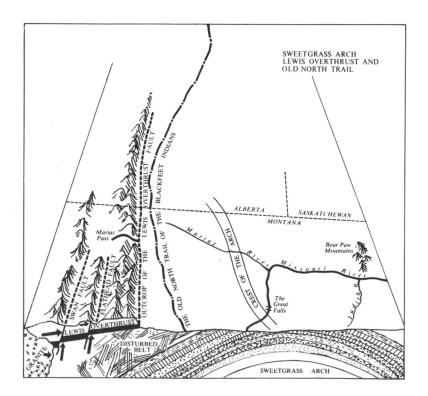

buffalo hunting grounds of the Missouri. It runs atop the
Osborn-Bearmouth Fault from Spokane to the Deer Lodge
Valley of Montana, a distance of about 250 miles. The
Osborn-Bearmouth is the western part of a much longer
fault, or series of faults, called the Osborn-Bearmouth-Lake
Valley Fault Zone. This major break, a plane of adjustment
in the earth's crust, can be traced for about 500 miles, termi-
nating in southeastern Montana, but it is sharply revealed
by the typography only in its western half. The Mullan
Wagon Road followed the fault—and the Nez Percé's trail—

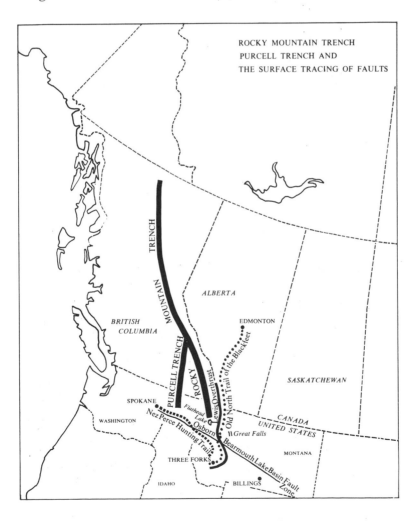

offering a route alternate to the Oregon Trail in the 1860s, and today the same course is followed by railroads and highways. It is believed the trail far antedated the Indians found using it. The first white men reported that stretches of it had been worn two feet deep into the forest cover. The Nez Percé were famed for the quality of their bows. No bow of Nez Percé ever fired an arrow more strongly and accurately than their trail bore through the mountains, following the Osborn-Bearmouth Fault.

A dozen other trails, many of them now marked by rail lines or highways, can be seen to follow other structural breaks of the earth. Some of the most interesting of these run from British Columbia down into northwestern Montana. There a series of northerly-southerly faults of the Lewis Overthrust kind have pushed up ranges of mountains and have resulted in some amazingly long, straight trenches—and passageways. Most remarkable of these is the Rocky Mountain Trench, a depression in many parts only a few miles wide, which starts at Flathead Lake in northwestern Montana and continues through British Columbia, a north-westerly course, a straight 800 miles, terminating only at the Liard Valley near the boundary of Yukon Territory. A second, shorter depression, called the Purcell Trench, begins south of Bonners Ferry in Idaho and runs more directly north, joining the Rocky Mountain Trench near the peaks of Jasper Park. Both were hosts to mountain branches of the Great North Trail which frayed off the main cord near Klondike.

Professor Edward Salisbury Dana, in his bible of mineralogy, has listed ice with a hardness of 1½ on the Mohs scale, a specific gravity of .9, and crystallizing in the hexagonal system. Ice then is clearly a mineral and the ice age a petrological phenomenon. We have already touched briefly on its relation to the Great North Trail and the sudden appearance of men in America. Whether the Trail is considered in its broadest sense, biologically from the view of the rise and fall of species, or as a narrow path, the track from Asia, one has to understand the ice age, its rise, growth, and the cataclysmic effects of its disintegration.

Only a few decades ago, scientists believed they lived on a dying globe. The earth, born in fire, was steadily cooling. Coral had been found in the polar sea, and dinosaurs wallowed through the marshes of Alberta where temperatures of 60° below are now recorded. The ice sheet was deemed proof of an encroaching arctic. Many geologists believed that mountains were caused by a shriveled globe, its skin grown too large for the body. "Like the skin of a withered apple" was a figure they were fond of. Soon the temperatures would lower until only the hardiest moss would survive anywhere; the oceans would freeze, and, all animals dead, locked in the lifeless cold, the world would fly through space forever.

Later it was found that there had been ice ages as far back as the Cambrian period, when the first tiny life forms appeared in the sea. Also, the earth was far older than had been supposed. Early scientists had hit on an age of about 100 million years; study of radioactive decay has placed it at 4½ billion. And as far as cooling is concerned, there is evidence that it has attained a balance capable of producing as much heat by friction, pressure, and radioactivity as its insulating cover of rock allows it to give off.

Although there are a number of currently favored explanations for the ice age, the cooling of the earth's interior is not one of them. Ice ages seem to have coincided with times of high mountains. Temperatures decrease about three degrees for each thousand feet of altitude. Central Wyoming, which has been bulged to 6000 feet by the pressure of the Rocky Mountains, is for that reason alone eighteen degrees cooler than as a shore of the Cretaceous sea. Small differences in average mean temperatures reflect profoundly on climate. Eighteen degrees, for instance, is the difference on average between Milwaukee and Fort Reliance in the Canadian Arctic.

The ice age came at a time of the greatest mountain-building in the recorded geology of the world. In all latitudes mountains crystallized moisture into snow. The seas shrank from the withdrawal of water and created a still greater comparative relief. (There is a fallacy in computing altitudes from sea level. It is like measuring with a rubber ruler.) Toward the poles—not where it was necessarily coldest, but where snowfall was heaviest—the ice built up to the thickness of mountains, adding to the total relief. One thing led to another. Snow reflects as much as 75 per cent of the sun's heat. This increased the cold; the ice sheet gathered more snow, and by its own settling weight flowed outward. In so doing it covered more of the heat-absorbing soil and churned up the forests. Everything seemed to add to the cold. It even got closer to the Gulf of Mexico, chief source of its snow. But finally the Gulf diminished in size through the withdrawal of water, and other forces contributed to a dissolution which, once started, built on themselves in a manner which will be considered later in this chapter.

There have been four major ice advances in the past 600,000 years. The last one retreated from the Great Lakes region of the United States only about 7000 years ago. It was in the time of the last Rameses pharaohs of Egypt that the present drainage of the Great Lakes to the Gulf of St. Lawrence was established, abandoning the ice-age outlets via the Mississippi and the Hudson rivers. In another two thousand years, by A.D. 986, southern Greenland had become so warm that Eric the Red was able to establish a colony whose chief subsistence was dairying. It hung on for about four centuries, but the warm cycle came to an end and the chief product became walrus ivory; and finally, at about the time of Columbus' discovery of the New World, the colony died out, abandoned to the returning cold. Small fruits and quick-ripening vegetables mature in Greenland today, but there is no talk of the island becoming self-sufficient. Its weather observers, soldiers, and miners depend on the outside world for food.

Evidence in Greenland and elsewhere has led some glaciologists to believe that a fifth ice advance is even now under way. Various expedients, such as spraying coal dust to absorb the rays of the sun, have been suggested to stay the next ice sheet and avert the destruction of Canada and the northern United States. Perhaps the ice will retreat still farther. In other words, Greenland may emerge, its cap and the other large ice accumulations of the world melting to add their water to the oceans. This would wreak havoc, too. If all the ice of the poles should melt, as it has done frequently in the geologic past, the oceans everywhere would rise approximately 100 feet. This would be sufficient to cover Florida and much of the Atlantic seaboard, and turn the lower Mississippi Valley into a shallow sea.

During the last ice age the oceans lowered by about 300 feet and much of the Gulf of Mexico was dry land. Scarcely more than 200 miles of sea separated Florida from the Yucatán Peninsula. The southern coast of North America ran eastward from Corpus Christi, Texas. What is now sea bottom was covered by grass and shrubs, the home of roving elephants. The teeth of elephants have also been dredged up nearly a hundred miles off the coast of New Jersey.

A narrower strip of the continental shelf appeared off the coasts of California and Oregon. Some maps of the ice age show the flat ground continuing up the coast past Alaska, and it would be seen at a glance that a highway was there provided for migrants from Asia, but the coast from the Alaskan Peninsula to the Straight of Juan de Fuca was fronted not by mountains of rock but by mountains of ice. A layer of ice had formed in central British Columbia, of unknown depth but probably higher than all but the highest mountains. Some of it lay quiet, but most of it moved as glacial rivers. It flowed slowly, grinding through the passes. In the south it reached the Columbia. Westward it pushed far out, digging deep channels in the floor of the Pacific. Today, where the timbered mountains of the Inside Passage rise from the sea, ice moved in rivers thousands of feet thick and its cliffs broke and thundered into the ocean. Passengers on ships look at the crenelated coast of British Columbia and imagine they see the channels of mighty rivers, drowned when the land sank into the sea. The mountains of British Columbia, like those of Aspen and the Lewis Overthrust, are still climbing, but the sea has risen much faster these past few thousand years, and the channels were caused not by rivers of water but by rivers of stone and ice. The Finlayson Channel of British Columbia was dug to a depth of 2559 feet under the sea, and Alaska's Chatham Strait reaches a depth of 2860 feet. All along the coast rivers reach the sea through glacial channels so the largest ships can now steam as far as 100 miles into the mountains, greatly to the advantage of the provincial timber, mining, and tourist industries. Even more impressive reminders of ice ages are the Sogne Fjord in Norway, 4000 feet deep, and the Meissier Channel of Patagonia, 4250.

Across the Pacific the ice pack sealed off northern Asia as completely as it did America. The Asiatic continent, however, having no coastal mountains to compare with the Canadian Rockies and a less abundant rainfall, was not impacted very far inland. Kamchatka enjoyed brief summers. In fact, as a peninsula, Kamchatka did not exist. Withdrawal of water to the ice domes removed the sea of Okhotsk so its floor was level land where stone-age hunters followed the reindeer. Withdrawal of water also left a land passage all the way to Japan. The Great North Trail of that age, ice notwithstanding, could truly be called a trail of all continents. South Asia had land connections with Sumatra, Java, Borneo; joining Alaska and Siberia was a plain 50 miles wide.

On land the ice sheet left its mark in many ways. The U-shaped valleys of the West, with broad bottoms and cliff sides over which the streams of the upper drainage spurt in waterfalls, are the mountain reminders of rivers of ice. Hills of mixed boulders and gravel stacked with characteristic lack of regard for the local drainage are signs of glaciers. Reaching its limits, the ice sheet melted and cold Mississippis cut across the land. For thousands of miles along the Canadian boundary with Montana, Dakota, and Minnesota there were lakes where gray breakers rolled against cliffs of ice. Lake Agassiz, named for the pioneer ice-age scientist, formed an area larger than all the Great Lakes combined and lasted for 4000 years. The Missouri in Montana, blocked by ice and moraine, formed a lake over the Great Falls, and motorists today can look above and see the ancient beaches rimming the prairie hills. For a time the Missouri's waters poured around the northern toe of the Highwood Mountains, forming a deep, level valley famed in stagecoach days as the Big Sag. Glacial Lake Missoula was formed where a lobe of the British Columbian ice pushed down the Purcell Trench, damming the Clark Fork, and glacial water lay a thousand feet deep over Hell Gate and the Nez Percé hunting trail. Another lobe, moving down the Rocky Mountain Trench, came to a stop north of Glacial Lake Missoula, dumping rocky hills which remained after the ice was gone, and Flathead Lake backed up behind them.

The former channel of Flathead River is now a dry valley a few miles wide called the Big Draw; the river, diverted to a more easterly channel, has carved its steplike way, forming a succession of potential of power sites. In their most grandiose plan, the would-be developers of the river once proposed a dam which would raise the level of Flathead Lake and inundate the city of Kalispell (pop. 12,067) but only to a shallow depth. Other plans call for more modest downstream dams and lakes, which would cover much of the area's scanty agricultural land, and dispossess the bison from the best of their range which lies just east of the river, at the mouth of the Jocko. Partisans of cheap public power argue that Montana's industrial development would be given a big boost, more than compensating it for such annoyances as smog and pollution. Others oppose such moves, maintaining that the area's natural beauty is a valuable asset, and anyhow the Upper Columbia development will merely turn the state into a storage reservoir for the benefit of Oregon and

Washington. Leading the opposition is the local private power company, which wishes to develop the sites in a smaller way; and some elected officials who campaigned with power-company support on a platform calling for new industry have been placed in the embarrassing position of sounding the drum for industrial development while opposing the only thing which could conceivably bring it about. The ice sheet was responsible for the political Donnybrook of another day when it constructed the Grand Coulee of Washington. The Grand Coulee is the huge watercourse which carried the ice-age Columbia River and enclosed what has been called the greatest waterfall of all time.

Although the ice sheet led to some cooling of the southern latitudes of North America, the chief change was in the rainfall it brought. The deserts of the Southwest were then lake-spattered grasslands abounding in game. The Great Salt Lake of Utah is a shrunken remnant of Lake Bonneville, whose shoreline can be seen winding around the mountainsides. At its maximum it reached 1000 feet in depth and overflowed to the northwest, emptying into Snake River. The outlet remained to form Red Rock Pass, a route for the fur traders and emigrants of a later day. Lake Lahontan in Nevada had a meandering length of 300 miles and was in one spot an estimated 866 feet deep. Salt and soda flats which glare like caustic snow in the desert sun, and seasonal lakes all across the basin area of Utah and Nevada, are reminders of a time when the climate was like that of Minnesota.

The Great Lakes are believed to have been scooped out by the rock-weighted ice of Canada on its several journeys southward. During the time of melting they were much larger, connected with the ocean, and they breathed with the tides. Whale remains of recent date have been found in southern Michigan. Another imposing residual is Hudson Bay, a sag caused by the main ice dome. The total sag was about 1000 feet in depth, but the ancient granites of Canada started rising as soon as they were relieved of the weight, and the Bay now averages only about 210 feet. As the earth's crust reveals itself to be an elastic rather than a plastic medium, it continues to rise and the Bay to shrink, with the result that the land area of Canada increases several square miles per year, and it is estimated that in another ten thousand years Hudson Bay will be reduced to a marshy freshwater lake.

The drowned mouth of the St. Lawrence is also attributed to subsidence under glacial weight. It, too, has been rising since being relieved of its ice. The Gulf of St. Lawrence slowly warps to the northwest. Marine strand lines indicate sizable areas near the mouth have risen above the sea within historic times. The rise of the St. Lawrence–New Brunswick–Québec area will have the effect of turning the Great Lakes drainage southward, and Lake Michigan might deepen sufficiently at its southern end again to seek an outlet through Illinois to the Mississippi.

The Missouri River once flowed to the Arctic north of Hudson Bay. It was turned southeastward by ice, hunting a new course from one of its tributaries to another, some of which it turned around and made to flow upstream, cutting through divides and forming what would seem a senseless course through the Dakotas.

Chief evidence of the ice sheet throughout most of the country consists of the refuse it left behind. Ontario granite is found as far south as Missouri. Native copper from Upper Michigan has been found from Ohio to Missouri. A mass of native copper weighing 200 pounds was found in the glacial drift near New Haven, Connecticut. It is not known whether the material for the copper artifacts and ornaments repeatedly found in Indian mounds of the Midwest and South came from early copper mines of Michigan or whether it, too, was carried by the glaciers. Widespread occurrences of diamonds in glacial drift have given people reason to believe that one of the great diamond deposits of the world may be located in Canada. In 1876 a yellow diamond of 15 karats was found by a well-digger 40 feet below the surface near

Eagle, in Waukesha County, Wisconsin. Somebody bought it for a dollar, thinking it to be topaz, but it was correctly identified by Tiffany & Co. and later became part of the J. Pierpont Morgan collection, and was left by him to the American Museum of Natural History, New York. The Eagle diamond was later in the news when on the night of October 29, 1964, it became part of a haul including the far more famous Star of India sapphire taken from the fourth-floor display cases in an acrobatic burglary deemed one of the most remarkable of the century. On January 8, 1965, the Star and most of the other gems were recovered from a bus depot locker in Miami, Fla., and the thieves, Florida beach boys, one of whom bore the name of "Murph the Surf," were brought to the bar where they confessed. The Eagle diamond at this writing has not been recovered. Authorities expressed the opinion that it passed into unknown hands and was cut up into smaller, less recognizable stones.

Although the Eagle was America's most famous stone, it was exceeded in size by another from Wisconsin weighing more than 21 karats. This was found near Kohlsville, between Milwaukee and Fon du Lac. Both stones came from glacial detritus believed to have originated in Ontario above Sault Ste. Marie. A number of smaller gray-green stones have been found near Eagle and at Plum Creek in Pierce County. A 6½-karat white diamond was found near Saukville. The moraines of Illinois have yielded hundreds of small diamonds, most of them coming from near Macomb in the west-central part of the state. One found near Ashley in the south weighed 8 karats. Numerous stones have been found in Indiana, chiefly while washing for moraine-borne gold. The discovery of so many diamonds in comparison with the continental thickness of unsorted glacial rubble makes it obvious that the total weight of undiscovered diamonds would measure in the tons, or the hundreds of tons. Each year new bonanzas of gold, copper, and nickel are found under the moss of Ontario. Are diamonds to come?

Turning from the very small to the very large, the carrying power of glaciers is attested by a quartzite block near Calgary, Alberta, weighing 18,000 tons, whose parent stratum has been located 50 miles to the west. There is little doubt that the ice had power to grind off whole mountains, but most of the rock was quickly shattered and churned to fragments. The churning action of glaciers can be seen in Maine, where rock has been deposited at altitudes half a mile higher than its bed of origin only 15 miles away. Such deposits also indicate the minimum depth of the ice. The tops of the Adirondacks are strewn with glacial rock at altitudes of more than 3000 feet. Again, in Alberta, George Mercer Dawson, of Dawson City fame, found rocks that had been transported for a thousand miles and lifted a vertical distance of 5000 feet.

The greatest thicknesses of glacial dirt in America have been found in the West. Glacial dirt has been measured at depths of 1450 feet in the Spokane Valley of Washington. Glacial gravel was found even deeper in the lower end of the Rocky Mountain Trench in Montana. Oil seepages detected in the Big Fork–Creston area of the Flathead Valley by ranchers in water wells encouraged a wildcatter to set up rig and drill, but he gave up after reaching 1475 feet without even coming to bedrock. The valley had been scooped out by the glacier to that depth, and for an unknown depth beyond; he was in gravel all the way. In Ohio there are layers more than 700 feet thick. In the Seneca and Onondaga valleys of New York, drift lies in depths of more than a thousand feet. More impressive than such maximums are the breadths of deposits. Wisconsin is covered by a layer of Canada 40–50 feet thick. Over Michigan and Minnesota it lies much the same. Minnesota's lakes are due to a haphazard dumping of rubble by the melting sheet. Most of Illinois, Iowa, and Indiana are covered to depths of around a hundred feet.

The channels of the British Columbia coast and the denuded rock face of Canada bear testimony to the ice sheet's scraping action during the centuries of its youth. The power of its disintegration can be read in the layers of mud and windborne dirt southward to the Gulf of Mexico. Icebergs floated on the Mississippi, which was a moving sea a hundred miles wide, and some of them dropped ton-size rocks in Missouri.

Water came not only from the face of the ice sheet. The heat of the earth increases by one degree for each hundred feet or so in depth. Any gardener in a northern climate knows his perennials are not so likely to winterkill in winters of heavy snowfall, and the arctic Indian buries his fur bed as deeply as possible in snow. The ice sheet grew warmer as it approached the earth, and it was not many centuries before it started to melt along the bottom. The water, under the pressure of billions of tons of ice, sought outlets. Finding one, the underice rivers blasted forth like hydraulic giants, carrying rock, sand, and all the unassorted detritus of a continental glaciation in front of them. One can imagine the force of such jets by the evidence of their work. In places rocks of boulder size were driven with a velocity that heaped them into hills now standing as high as 400 feet. Sands, muds, and smaller rocks all were carried by the currents to form reefs and beds at greater distances. Upon the release of pressure, expansion of the water, already at the freezing point, caused new ice to form. The outlets were turned into basins and eventually became dammed, so new ones were continually hunted out. Wide fans of sorted material were sometimes formed, and these, subsequently covered by soil and cut through by the streams of later times, have presented the partial cross-sectional appearance of ancient rivers and are occasionally so mapped.

The worst blight was not flood, however, but mud and dust. As the ice receded and the lakes disappeared, a desert of glacial muck gathered in a zone hundreds of miles wide and more than a thousand in total length. Trees took root, flourished for a few seasons, and were extinguished by moving dirt and sand. With nothing to check the winds, the seasons were violent. In winter this desert was as bleak as the great barrens, and snow was carried across it in savage blizzards. In the summer it fluctuated between dust and quagmire. As with all deserts, it had the faculty of encroaching. The finer material, a rock flour, minutely ground by the ice, was transported by the winds. Some was so fine it was carried around the world, but most of it settled within a distance of 300 to 500 miles. In the Mississippi Valley it is typically a yellowish silt. It holds up well in cuts and forms low cliffs or cutbanks. One celebrated exposure is at Council Bluffs, Iowa. Glacial dust today forms a belt across America from Pennsylvania all the way to Colorado. At their height the dust storms must have been immense. Dust thickened the air, obscuring the sun for weeks at a time, and when rain fell it reached the earth as blobs of abrasive mud. Devoid of life, even of the roots of plants, the glacial dust that settled on Kansas alone totals 50,000 cubic miles.

At a glance it would seem impossible that men could have traveled from Alaska down to the temperate southwest during any of the long centuries of the ice sheet. Yet both North and South America appear to have received their first widespread human penetration at that time, not merely during the ice age but when it was at its height, and somehow they got here from Alaska. The most obvious route is implicit in the maps of the glacialists. The Hudson Bay ice dome pushed out in all directions, particularly to the south and west. In the West, on reaching Alberta and Montana, it became shallow enough so the low mountains of the plains were left as islands. In certain places and periods it pushed into the Rockies, but for the most part it barely reached the foothills. The British Columbian dome was more confined. It was directed southward by the deep rift valleys, or through the passes to the sea. Little British Columbian ice found its way eastward. Apparently it was walled in by the mighty mountains of the Lewis Overthrust, of Yoho, Banff, and Jasper. From the town of Choteau, Montana, northward is a narrow finger of ground never touched by the ice sheet. In places it shrinks to little more than a mile. In others it widens to ten or fifteen. It passes into Canada. Fort Whoop-Up, which figures in a later chapter, stood near the end of this glacier-free strip. The Old North Trail of the Blackfeet ran along it. Did indeed the trail go on and on, and offer, at least part of the time, a narrow and hungry passage to the first American Indians? No one knows. But it must be remembered that the greatest barrier was not the ice or the cold. The great barrier—and destroyer—seems to have been the floods, muck, black blizzards, and sudden variations in climate which attended the break-up.

Not only did men spread over America during the high years of the ice age, but game also abounded. The continent had four species of elephants, two of which exceeded the largest African elephants in size. The imperial mammoth found its central range along the Great North Trail and stood almost 14 feet in height. Herds of mastodons ranged the land, becoming extinct so recently that their fresh bones kept explorers in hopes of finding them roaming the West until the days of the covered wagons. Woolly mammoths were numerous all across Alaska. There were seven species of bison, one with a horn spread as wide as the outflung arms of a man. There were horses and camels, and a variety of more peculiar animals such as the giant ground sloth, which attained elephantine size, the saber-tooth tiger, and the fearsome dire wolf. All passed to extinction.

Man, too, had some lean years after his phenomenal spread across the land. He seemed to reach a high point about 9000 years ago, and then fall back. By 5000 B.C. the signs of human habitation, cave ruins and hunters' camps, almost disappear. The few which have been found yield the bones of no large game. Apparently the once mighty hunter of the elephant and the giant bison was forced to survive on birds and rodents, and his flint weapons, which had been long as the hand, shrank to tiny points. Why the beasts of the land should survive and even flourish during the height of the ice advance, only to disappear on its retreat, has inspired a number of explanations, the most likely of which seems to be that they vanished when their food supply was destroyed by recurrent floods and black-mud blizzards, and when their southern lake-dotted grasslands dried to deserts. Later, about 3000 B.C., the grass of middle America came back. A single species of bison had hung on through the hungry years. It multiplied and spread abundantly through the belly-deep grass that grew from the North Saskatchewan to the Rio Grande. The Great North Trail became central to its spring and autumn migrations, and the Indians, tuning their lives to its movements, awaited only the horse to become the wild hunter, the noblest savage of all romance, the ideal of a free man in an unfenced, unending, abounding wilderness.

THE FAINT TRACKS
OF AMERICAN MAN

Chapter 2

North America, particularly the Trail area along the Rockies, has been for a century the world's foremost bone quarry, its richest storehouse of vertebrate paleontology. In no other place has been found such an abundance of animal remains or such a perfect succession of species. Many animals, such as the camel and the ancestors of the kangaroo, were represented in Montana and Wyoming to a degree that that part of the globe has been deemed their prehistoric homeland. The lemurs, frequently put forward as the ancestors of the higher primates including man, once were common. Considering all this it seems strange that no transitory form of man, no *missing link* in the popular interpretation of the term, has ever been found in the Americas. For all the digging, few human bones more than a thousand years old have been found, and none shows a single primitive (evolutionary) characteristic. They have been old Indians and nothing more. There are signs of men —camps and weapons—dating to 23,800, 29,650, or 35,000 years ago, depending on the type of evidence, sometimes conflicting, which one cares to accept. The oldest human bone ever turned up in the hemisphere has an age of 12,000 years.

Some attribute the paucity of American human bones to the custom of burial in the open, often on platforms, instead of under the floors of caves. Many of the best European examples of primitive man were entombed accidentally in swamps or buried under landslides. If there were American counterparts of Neanderthal or Swanscombe men, how they escaped similar fates has never been satisfactorily explained. Men buried in desert countries are often transformed by desiccation and heat into mummies. American mummies, particularly in Peru, are plentiful but not very old.

Although the bones of early American man have been scarce, his artifacts have been plentiful. Mounds, particularly in the southern and middle United States, have been treasure troves of arrowheads, stone tools, and utensils. The antiquity of the mounds was, until recently, much in question. Archeologists, studying the problem of the age of the American Indians, had little to go on. The time of their arrival in America was generally estimated at between 3000 and 4000 B.C. Starting in the middle 1920s a series of discoveries, most of them in the southwestern United States, pushed this estimate back.

The little New Mexico town of Folsom is located in the northeastern corner of the state, a short distance from Raton Pass, where one of the main branches of the Great North Trail crosses between the Sangre de Cristo Range and the Ratons on its way to the upper Rio Grande Valley. In 1925 the attention of archeologists at the Colorado Museum of Natural History was drawn to the town when some ancient bones were found in a gulch which ran down from the mountains. Excavation started the following year. Soon unearthed were the bones of a large extinct bison, and an extinct member of the deer family. Neither caused much excitement. They were not old, dating no farther back than one of the recent ice ages. The Colorado archeologists would probably have departed had not some curious flint cutting tools shown up in the diggings. Folsom was already known to arrowhead hunters. From time to time the rock shelters of the nearby mountains had yielded flints and pieces of pottery. The new ones, however, were of a different type. They were examples of a very refined technique, minutely chipped to give a keen edge, as sharp as deckled glass. Large ones were about 4 inches long and 1½ inches wide. Their most distinctive feature was a concave middle, where a handle of bone or wood had once been installed. Mounted in such a manner, with the handle ground down to continue the contours of the flint, a smooth knife was obtained, strong where it needed to be strong, and sharp where it needed to be sharp. The shape of this and other Folsom blades rendered them ill-suited to deep penetrations of animals, and they have turned up mostly at camps and butchering spots.

Since the Folsom flints were associated with extinct animals and buried in from 4 to 15 feet of clay and gravel, the discoverers were in no doubt that they had the oldest hunters' site yet found in the Americas. Some attempt was made to correlate the barren overburden with the blown dirt of the last glacial retreat, but nothing conclusive was determined. The glacial dating of that time seemed to give the Folsom flints a minimum age of 13,000 years. In 1928, when that phase of the digging stopped, it was generally thought that the first Indians had come from Asia no more than 5500 years before. The Colorado scientists decided to add only about 2000 to that estimate, a compromise with the orthodoxy of that time.

Since the days of the first traders, white men had been gathering arrow and spear points. When the Folsom flints were seen, similar ones were found in the existing collections. Most of them had come from gravel wash, or from blowouts—places where wind had carried away the fine material, leaving flints and pebbles; no depth horizon could therefore be assigned to them, but at least collectors knew what part of the country they came from, and the occurrences soon were traced up the Rocky Mountain front from Texas to Montana. At Clovis, a New Mexico town near the Texas border about halfway down the state from Folsom, some points were found at an old mammoth kill which were regarded by experts from the Texas Memorial Museum to be older than any discoveries made by their Colorado colleagues. The Clovis points were similar to Folsom, the chief difference being in their workmanship, which was not so delicate, and in the fact that they were grooved for only about a third of their length. To some archeologists this meant Clovis points were Folsoms in a stage of evolution, their makers having the idea of grooving them partway but not all the way. Others termed this nonsense, saying the Clovis was made stronger because it was intended as a spear point instead of a knife. Another discovery of Folsom-type artifacts was made at a cave in the Guadalupe Mountains in the southern part of the state. These were associated with a prehistoric species of musk ox, leading some to believe them to be of the ice age, and estimates even in excess of the more extreme 13,000-year datings at Folsom began to be heard. Blades without any grooving at all but otherwise similar to the Folsoms turned up in Yuma County, Colorado, and were named Yuma points. Major discoveries were made near Fort Collins, Colorado; Scottsbluff, Nebraska; Angastura, South Dakota, and Plainview, Texas. Others were found, particularly in caves, across the Southwest to California, and a scattering in the East. But the great area remained the Rocky Mountain front.

For a time it was believed that none of the Folsom and Yuma types would be found in those areas which had been covered by the Great Ice Sheet, or if found would rest in disturbed deposits, thus proving them older. This belief was destroyed when they turned up in Montana and Alberta, well inside the reach of the giant ice scraper, lying atop glacial lake deposits. They were next found in Alaska. In Alaska, the most abundant area of the ancient flints was on the Seward Peninsula, steppingstone of the old land bridge to Siberia. The Seward archeological sites have produced artifacts related to Folsom, Yuma, and Clovis. One limestone cave near Deering on the north side of the peninsula has yielded, layer on layer, the evidence of each culture from the modern Indian and Eskimo down to the paleo-Indian age of Mexico. An upper layer contained unusually fine ivory carvings, judged older than the Eskimo and related to artworks of Asia. Next to these were found a number of rusted iron blades dating to the early Chinese age of iron. Another important discovery was made across the peninsula on Norton Bay. A stratified deposit, it was followed downward until, at the very bottom, more than a thousand flint artifacts were counted, many of which identified with the Folsom and the Yuma peoples. Of greatest single interest was a blade known as an "oblique Yuma," heretofore believed a Southwestern departure in technique. Some experts consider it possible to correlate the Alaska flints with ancient cultures in Siberia, also.

With the advent of radiocarbon dating, the Folsom site was given an age of 10,000 years, upping by 2500 the accepted Colorado estimate of two decades before.

Unfortunately, for all of the treasures no skeleton of the makers was found. Writers, however, had for years been referring to Folsom Man, by implication placing him with Cro-Magnon and Neanderthal Man of Europe. Digging went on, and his skeleton was expected momentarily. Filling in until the skeleton turned up, artists pictured him as hairy, bowlegged, and squat, with very large hands and knees, a slanting skull with a heavy ledge of bone over the eyes. His women were correspondingly ugly and durable. Such skeletons were not forthcoming. A skull found in Mexico by geophysical methods was hailed in the field as an American missing link and named Tepexpan Man. Cooler heads at the

museum ascertained it to be just a very old Indian. In 1953 a
pipeline welder at work near Midland, Texas, found sixty
bone fragments which fitted to make a narrow skull, but it
also was similar to our present-day Indians. It is difficult to
test uncharred bones by means of radioactive carbon meas-
urement because so little carbon often remains, the fate of
bones being to be opalized by contact with the silica of the
earth. The Midland skull was, however, subjected to a
fluorine test which indicated it was also about 12,000 years
old. The 12,000-year extreme has turned up again and again.
One of the most publicized archeological sites of the continent, Danger Cave in Utah, contained stratified cultural remains which bottomed at 12,000 years. Fishbone Cave, one
of a series of ancient shelters near Winnemucca in northwestern Nevada, has produced charcoal and an extinct horse
dating back 11,000 years. Gypsum Cave near Las Vegas has
relics of a thousand years later. The oldest remains have always been in the West. There seems little doubt that early
man arrived there first. Thence he spread southward into
South America, where the oldest dating, the Palli Aike Cave,
is about 8500 years. Modoc rock shelter in southern Illinois
is the most famous archeological site of the Mississippi
country. A great bulk of the Modoc deposits date from 3000
to 6000 years, but extreme readings of 11,500 have been obtained at the very bottom. Russell Cave in Jackson County,
Mississippi, yielded a cultural complex dating from the time
of Columbus to about 8500 years ago.

A number of more extreme datings have come from the
West, not from caves but from hunters' camps. Most famous
was in the Las Vegas Wash of southern Nevada. There, in
the early days of the century, archeologist Fenley Hunter,
exploring for the American Museum of Natural History,
found accumulations of ancient bones, the hardened remains
of campfires, and some primitive flint and bone artifacts. Although many were convinced of the site's antiquity, there
was no proof of it until the advent of modern dating, when
some of the charred bones gave an age of 23,800 years. Some

mammoth bones, caught up in a charred rock layer on Santa Rosa Island off the coast of California, gave a reading of 29,650, but only a single flint artifact has been found associated with them and there is no agreement that it is genuine. An age greater still has been attributed to some firepits near Lewisville, Texas. These have been dated at 37,000 years, but certain disparities in the associations have cast this estimate in doubt. Anyhow, it seems certain that human beings, for a time at least, lived in the area of the southwestern United States about 25,000 years ago, and this falls at a time when the ice sheet was at a maximum, apparently blocking off entrance from the north. The search goes on.

Although from the first nearly all serious investigators have believed that North and South America were settled by Mongoloid peoples crossing from Siberia to Alaska, there are evidences of other peoples and, of course, other routes.

One of the most persistent beliefs is that a European colony was long ago established in America, took Indian ways while keeping its blood intact or nearly so, and could be found living somewhere in the interior.

During his early travels in the Americas, Baron Alexander von Humboldt, the celebrated German naturalist, detected what he believed to be European strains in many of the Indian tribes. He noticed that whole villages tended toward blue eyes, light skins and Caucasian features, and decided that the tendencies must far antedate the European conquest. He saw a number of such "White Indian" groups in South America as he sailed along the coast and explored the river mouths. Humboldt also noted the peculiar incidence of blue eyes in Central America and Mexico, but was not struck fully by the phenomenon until he saw the Tuscarora Indians of the Eastern seaboard.

The Tuscarora originally numbered about 5000 people and lived in South Carolina. Observers long before Humboldt had noticed their white characteristics and had called them the white Indians. Others referred to them as the

Welsh Indians. Jonas Morgan, a Welsh expatriate, reported that in 1685 he alone of a party captured by Tuscarora had escaped death because of his ability to make himself understood in Welsh. When the French arrived in Nova Scotia the coastal Indians were already used to the sight of white men. The French had hoped to locate a sea route to India. Tales of white men led them to hope they were merchants to Cathay who had come from the West. Later they learned that it had been common, perhaps for centuries, for European fishermen to take cod in American waters and dry their catch on shore.

When hints of Welsh strains in the Atlantic coastal tribes crossed the Atlantic, the scholars of the old country got to searching and turned up a couple of ancient manuscripts concerning a King Madoc of the time of William the Conqueror. It was set down that in 1170 Madoc launched an expedition to the West, and returned to tell about discovering a land of immense size and abundance, a land burgeoning for harvest. He gathered ten shiploads of colonists, but after sailing into the sunset no more was heard of him or any of them until, after 500 years, the reports from the Carolinas. The people of Wales, and of all England, were profoundly moved that their countrymen had maintained themselves, their race, and their language throughout all those centuries.

As exploration pushed over the Alleghenies and around the Great Lakes, a great mass of Welsh-in-the-New World evidence was gathered. Signs of fortifications and European-type villages were found along the Ohio River. Daniel Boone and George Rogers Clark both were convinced that white men had preceded them into the Ohio wilderness by centuries. For a time it was believed that the Arikara, often called the Ree Indians, of Dakota were descendents of the Welsh. They were known to have moved Westward within historic times, and there was some reason to believe they had moved up the Missouri from the Ohio. The Arikara built villages on high bluffs overlooking the river, reminiscent of the forts of Europeans with their stockades and dry moats.

The houses seen by the fur traders were of mud brick and earth, circular in shape, but the houses of earlier villages were found to be square or rectangular. They were an agricultural and trading people, staying near the river for reasons of both fortification and commerce. They prospered in their early years and at their height held as many as thirty villages of about one hundred houses each. They raised corn, squash, beans, pumpkins, and tobacco. The tobacco culture, brought from the East, provided their most valuable item of trade. They were skilled makers of baskets and pottery. In their later years they bought and sold horses, becoming middlemen between the southern and northern tribes, and were believed to have established the trading fair, or rendezvous, with the Kiowas, Arapahoes, Cheyennes, Apaches, and Sioux near the Black Hills. They rose to the apex of their power about 1760, whereupon they commenced to have trouble with the westward-moving Sioux, but they stood their ground for almost three quarters of a century, and, resenting competition, were the most troublesome Indians the St. Louis fur traders had to deal with until they reached the land of the Blackfeet.

Houses, fortifications, and trading culture notwithstanding, the Arikara were certainly not Welsh, so the Welsh-Indian legend moved farther, to the Mandans, their neighbors to the north. They too lived in fortified villages on the river and engaged in agriculture and trade.

Pierre Gaultier de Varennes, Sieur de la Vérendrye, ruler of the far lake regions, old soldier, adventurer, and last of the great fur traders of New France, was the first white man known to have seen the Mandans, reaching their villages from the region of Winnipeg in 1738. "Their women," he wrote, "are extremely beautiful, especially those who are white, some of whom have lovely fair hair. Both men and women are very industrious and work with a will. Their lodges are big and spacious; they are divided into several rooms by partitions of thick planks. Nothing is left lying about untidily; all objects are placed in large bags and suspended from the posts. . . . The women do not look in the least Indian. . . ." Also, the first trader from St. Louis, Jacques D'Eglise, returned in 1792 and reported them as light as Europeans. George Catlin, the American lawyer, ethnologist, naturalist, painter, and idealist, was forcibly struck by the Mandans' ease and elegance, and remarked on the diversity of their complexions, hair, and eyes. "I am fully convinced," he wrote, "that they have sprung from some other origin than that of other North American tribes, or that they are an amalgam of natives with some civilized race." Among the women particularly he saw skins which were almost white, and many had gray or blue eyes.

If American explorers were convinced that a tribe of Europeans lived on the Missouri, the people in England could be excused for believing it also. In 1791 a man named William Bowles decked himself out as an Indian chief and arrived there as living proof of the white Indians. Bowles was lionized by the literary set. Soon money was raised to send a representative to America who would re-establish the home ties. Chosen was John Evans, Welsh, twenty-two years old, religious and stubborn. He got to St. Louis in 1793 and was jailed by the authorities. St. Louis at that time happened to be Spanish territory, and he was thought to be an English or American spy. Finally gaining his freedom and traveling upriver, young Evans failed to find anything in the least Welsh about the Mandans, physically, culturally, or linguistically. But faith in the white Indians died hard. Missionaries were impressed when they found the Mandans already holding a belief in the virgin birth of God and His death as an act of redemption. The Mandan story of the creation in some ways paralleled that in the Bible, although in their version man attained more dignity, lifting himself from the lower worlds through his own efforts, by means of a vine. They treasured a sacred picture, which was carried in an ark. They believed in a personal devil, represented as a childless man, totally black, who roved the world seeking recruits for the underworld. Had they been visited by missionaries long before the first Jesuits from Montreal? At one of their village sites near Mandan, North Dakota, a Catholic silver medal was found at a depth of three feet among habitation remains that far antedated any known white penetration. The village itself had been abandoned at the time of a smallpox epidemic in 1764.

The Mandans are believed to have resided at one time in Ohio. Their own legends tell of a more remote history. They were, according to these, once of the Eastern seacoast. Catlin thought they might have entered the continent by way of the Gulf. When Prince Maximilian of Wied lived with the Mandans during his historic trip up the Missouri, he found them treasuring adornments made of seashells. In 1837 they were practically wiped out by smallpox. In 1838, only 32 could be counted. In 1859 their number had increased to 50, but even these few succumbed to the cholera which moved West with the gold rush to California, and the fair-haired Indians, who in manners, traditions, appearance, and even speech struck a familiar note with so many white travelers, ceased to exist.

This, in brief, is the story of the Welsh Indians. Norse Indians also have their partisans. Norse blood has long been suspected among the Eskimos of Baffin Land, Labrador, and Ungava Bay. In Massachusetts, the English colonists realized almost from the start that the Vikings had preceded them. When a skeleton in what seemed to be a suit of armor was dug up from a sandbank at Fall River in 1862 Longfellow composed his "Skeleton in Armor," making the man a Norseman who antedated Columbus. With him came a blue-eyed bride, and she became a mother. Through Longfellow, generations of American schoolchildren became accustomed to the idea of the early arrival of Norsemen, their descendents staying on in the new land. In view of this, the opposition encountered by a more recent Norse emigrant, a farmer of Douglas County, Minnesota, who dug up a far more convincing evidence, seems peculiar:

In 1898 Olaf Ohman decided to clear some of his land for

a garden plot. The ground was covered with aspens, not a particularly resistant tree, but one of them showed great reluctance to be uprooted. He had to dig the stump out, and when he got down 10 inches he saw the cause of his trouble. The roots had grown around a stone which by later measurements proved to be 30 inches long, 16 inches across, and 7 inches thick. It looked like a gravestone. After cleaning it off he discovered it was covered with inscriptions. He had seen runes, the ancient writing, in the old country, and this seemed to resemble them.

Ohman called to his neighbor, Nils Flaten, who came over and helped him speculate about the stone, how it got there, and what it said. Both men noticed how the roots of the tree had shaped themselves into a rectangle, exactly fitting it. Obviously it had been there a long time, because the aspen, while not a tree that attains much age, was a mature one. Later it was estimated by farm experts to be at least forty years old. This was to be an important point, because it was not long before people started to say that Ohman had carved the stone himself. Forty years before, when the stone would have had to been placed, he was three years old, living in Helsingland, Sweden. He had resided in America for seventeen years, and this was the first time he had been accused of being a crook.

In the succeeding months crowds came to examine Ohman's stone. Professor O. J. Breda of the University rode over from Minneapolis on the train. Breda acknowledged that the inscriptions all looked like runes of one kind or another, and they formed words which were a mixture of English, Norwegian, and Swedish. He translated it: "We, a number of Swedes and Norsemen on a journey of exploration west from Vineland have camped one day's journey north from this stone. We fished one day; when we came home we found red men had killed our companions. Our boat is on the ocean one day's journey from this island." Breda, however, pointed out many inconsistencies in the find. He didn't think it was genuine. The stone, however, had its local partisans. They sent it to Northwestern University at Chicago. There an expert on runes and ancient Scandinavia went Breda one better and pronounced the stone "a clumsy fraud." It went back to Kensington, where Ohman picked it up and hauled it home. Disgruntled by its academic reception, he used it as a doorstep to his henhouse.

However, interest was not dead. He allowed it to be taken to Alexandria, the county seat. After a time the geologists had a look at it. They did not pretend to know about runes, but they understood the weathering of minerals, and attested the age of the engravings. One of those willing to stake his reputation was Professor Hotchkiss, Wisconsin state geologist. Interest grew until the stone was sent to the Smithsonian Institution and there, by more exact tests, the age was again verified and set at about 500 years. Officially, then, the Kensington Rune Stone might be described as a clumsy fraud perpetrated before the voyages of Columbus.

Then in 1930 there was another find. Near Beardmore, a small place about 50 miles north of Lake Superior in Ontario, James Dodd, an employee of the Canadian National Railways and part-time prospector, unearthed a cache of Norse weapons while blasting. These were identified by the Institute of Archeology in Toronto as the type used by the Greenland and Vineland Vikings. Their age seemed to square with the Kensington stone. The blond Indians, therefore, may have had Norse rather than Welsh blood. It has been pointed out that Indians along Lake Michigan had a legend, long before the first French trader arrived on the scene in 1623, that ships with cloudlike sails once cleaved the big waters.

And there are other proofs of early white men, not only there but also in many other parts of the Americas. At the time of Pizarro priests inscribed lists of South American Indian words which were obviously derived from the Latin. Subsequent scholars have noted similarities between the Indian tongues and ancient Greek. A Spaniard in 1750 compiled an extensive vocabulary of Inca words which were related, he said, to ancient Hebrew. The upper-class Incas were surprisingly fair, hence perhaps descendents of the Lost Tribes of Israel. Mormon scholars have long held that the Lost Tribes of Israel roved America, and see archeological proof at Chichen–Itzá in Yucatán, where legends of white gods persisted to the days of the Spaniards.

Scholars in Peru found evidence of emigration from both East and West, printed lists of Polynesian-Indian words and symbols, and pointed to the fact that the ancient cry *"Hailla!"* with which the mighty of the land were greeted might easily have derived from the Germanic *"Heil!"* The languages of early Mexico have been seen by some scholars as having come from Middle Africa. Others deem this preposterous and point to the strong similarities between Aztec words and Egyptian. A Phoenician influence has been detected in some tongues of the pampas, and this is backed up by a Phoenician counterpart of the Kensington Rune Stone which turned up in 1899 near Rio de Janeiro. And one writer attributed the civilization of the Incas to the Greeks, having the lost fleet of Alexander the Great sail all the way to Peru in the the year 336 B.C.

Although most people were satisfied that the Indians came from Asia across the Great North Trail just as scientists from the 1860s on said they did, a recent piece of biochemical evidence seems to have made it certain. In 1954 in Caracas, Venezuela, physicians were faced with a problem in treating an erythroblastotic infant. The child's malady was one which involved the blood, and had as its chief manifestation an overabundant production of the red corpuscles. Unable to isolate the factor believed to be responsible for the infant's disease, Dr. Miguel Layrisse forwarded samples of its blood, together with those of the parents, to Dr. Philip Levine, director of the Division of Immunochematology, Ortho Research Foundation, in Raritan, New Jersey. Dr. Levine succeeded in determining that antibodies in the mother's serum reacted with those of baby and of her husband, but did not react with two hundred random samples out of group O. He labeled the sample "Diego," naming it for the Venezuelan family of the child, and laid it away, believing it to be only another of the private or "family" groups which sometimes turn up.

Back in Venezuela, Dr. Layrisse decided to engage in further investigation. The Diego family happened to be a numerous one. He tested 33 of them and discovered the antigen in 10. He also sampled 266 other residents of the area, and was surprised to learn that, although they had no known blood ties with the Diegos, the factor was present in 6 of them too. He thereupon was able to inform the foundation that the factor was not a family group after all.

Dr. Layrisse noticed during his testing that the Diegos and the nonrelatives who were positive reactors all looked as if they had Indian blood. Inquiry proved this to be the case. He thereupon extended his investigation to Indian groups in the hinterland. He found the antigen present in a high percentage. Another doctor found the Diego antigen in 54 per cent of the members of one tribe in Brazil. Pure Caucasian stock meanwhile tested zero, except those, like the Diegos, who were suspected of having Indian blood. Negroes also showed a minor number of positive tests, but in every case they proved to have one or more Indian ancestors. It seemed at that point that Dr. Layrisse had discovered an exclusively Indian blood trait. Then he decided to test a group of pure Japanese and Chinese. Here again it was found to be relatively high. The antigen then was very old, perhaps as old as the Mongoloid race itself, and carried into South America with its first humans thousands of years before.

Dr. Bruce Chown of Winnipeg tested a group of Eskimos in northeastern Canada but found them free of the factor. It had been assumed that the Eskimos were of Asiatic origin, but that seems seriously in doubt. Investigations also delivered a blow to a recently developed theory that American Indians settled the islands of Polynesia. If this were the case, the Diego antigen would be present in at least a small percentage of that population, but an English doctor, Hermann Lehmann, found no trace of it in investigating 92 New Zealand Maoris of Polynesian origin. Eighty Polynesians of the eastern islands were also tested, and none had the factor.

Although blood testing seems to have proved the relationship which has long been assumed between the American Indians and the Mongoloid races, it does not necessarily indicate that the Mongoloids came *to* America. Some loyal American theorists have seen the migrations proceeding in the other direction. They point out that there is no proof that Peking Man, Neanderthal Man, and Cro-Magnon Man are links in a chain, and that one led to another and all to modern man. Any of them might only have been a mistake of evolution and become extinct. Modern man, they have argued further, perhaps evolved from some still-undiscovered type, and the cradle of the human race may be in Texas. In that event he migrated up the Great North Trail and then back again like the early hippus, and the Chinese and Japanese whom Dr. Layrisse tested in Caracas may have returned at last, after many vicissitudes, to their prehistoric homeland. The thesis has thus far caused little excitement in anthropological circles.

Chapter 3

After the ice retreated and the lakes vanished, a desert moved up from Mexico through the Southwest and the Great Basin. In Utah, Lake Bonneville shrank, losing its outlet over Red Rock Pass and concentrating the dissolved salt and sodium sulfate of Utah into the small remnant of Great Salt Lake. To the northwest, the redwoods which had formed lordly forests never came back, the new forests consisting of Douglas-fir, cedar, pine, larch, and hemlock, with aspen and birch in the valleys. To the west of the mountains, from northern Saskatchewan to Texas, the loess and moraines were worked over by surface agencies making a thin but fertile topsoil, and grasses sprung up which the first white men described as a green and yellow sea, flowing in the wind. Of the grazing animals known in the pre-mud-and-loess cataclysm, few remained. The horse, elephant, and camel all were gone, and with them the large predators which preyed on them. The bison, however, had survived and was on the increase. He was the massive bison of the West, the buffalo, the charging ton of meat described by the Western pioneer, but still a small relative or descendent of the giants of glacial time. Into the waiting sea of grass he spread rapidly, taking over the heart of the continent. At his zenith he went beyond the prairies and ranged middle America almost from the Atlantic to the Pacific.

The American bison is the *Bison bison* of Linnaeus. Actually there were two subspecies in America. The woodland bison, which ranged from the Montana–Alberta border north to Great Slave Lake was *Bison bison athabascae.* It was somewhat larger and darker of coat, with more delicate horns, and occupied the foothill woodlands; a few still remain in the Lake Athabasca country. If the woodland bison is *Bison bison athabascae,* a subspecies, the common bison, the buffalo of the frontier, becomes *Bison bison bison.* In Europe the similar *Bison bonasus* lingers on in small numbers in a few Russian preserves. Whether the American buffalo descended from the giant bison of the early ice ages or whether both the European and American species descended from a common ancestor which migrated along the Great North Trail is not known. The European beast is almost identical to the American, its only noticeable difference being that in the summer months its shoulders lose the shaggy hair which the American species keeps, more or less, the year round.

The bison has hollow horns growing unbranched from protuberances of bone from the skull, not horny sheaths or cores which are shed at certain periods. In North America their hollow-horned relatives are the musk ox, the Rocky Mountain goat, and the bighorn sheep. All are unknown in South America.

The bison is a large wild ox. Its stomach is complex and it chews its cud. Some of its dorsal vertebrae are large, projecting upward at the shoulders to produce the characteristic hump, the meat which was so prized by prairie gourmets. The cows are smaller than the males and distinguishable by their darker color, but all are brownish-black in the forequarters and cinnamon behind. Under the long guard hairs is a dense, woolly coat. A female buffalo runs about 1000 pounds in weight, but a big bull weighs a ton and stands as much as six feet at the shoulder. They ate grass for the most part, but also they browsed, and during hard winters could subsist on bark. They moved south in the autumn and north again when the green grass showed. Many small herds moved but little, wintering in protected valleys.

Observation in today's buffalo preserves indicates that the bulls are polygamous, although Audubon, who early wrote of them, thought differently. Their calves are born in May and June. Many early accounts tell of the bulls forming circles around wobbly legged calves to protect them from the wolves which followed the herds. According to early accounts, the buffalo was, in hair-shedding time, the itchingest animal ever known, rubbing off its winter coat on trees which were polished to waxy smoothness. In later times buffalo disrupted telegraphic communication by rubbing the poles down. Buffalo also denuded themselves of itching hair by rolling in gumbo mud which, drying in cakes, fell and carried hair with it. In the early days, thousands of mud-flat lakes gathered a greenish scum of buffalo hair. Many beasts were mired and the depths became layered with their bones. Buffalo wallows of the West became one of the features of the land. Even dry, the wallows were an obstruction to travel, for they baked rock-hard with the deeply molded prints of buffalo, a banging nightmare to wagon wheels and both dangerous and fatiguing to the feet of horses.

The height of the buffalo population has been variously estimated. The guess finding most frequent acceptance is sixty million. This is generally offered for the Western range only. In earliest times buffalo ranged far to the east. In 1727, while surveying the North Carolina–Virginia boundary, Colonel William Byrd recorded the occurrence of buffalo in the clearings of the Piedmont. Pioneers pressing into Kentucky and Ohio found herds of the beasts and remarked them as being stupid, near-sighted, and easy to kill. Kill them they did, the easiest game available and with the greatest weight of meat. People used to eating beef were glad to get buffalo instead of venison. It was similar, and some considered it superior. There was a belief that nobody could become sick on buffalo, it was so easy to digest. Early observers report Indians gorging themselves on as much as 25 pounds of buffalo at one sitting and suffering no discomfort. Indians also ate buffalo in a highly fragrant condition. They retrieved swollen carcasses from the rivers and considered the flesh a tender treat. Fresh-killed, it was one of the easiest meats to preserve. No salt or smoke needed, it was simply cut in strips and hung in the sun.

Although buffalo had for decades vanished east of the Mississippi, Paleontologist O. C. Marsh in 1869 found buffalo so abundant in Kansas that the possibility of their extinction did not seriously occur to him. Yet Marsh was an authority on horse evolution, and he could see how the American herds had vanished only a few centuries before.

Many accounts describe great numbers of buffalo. The largest herds exceeded the power of the eye to appraise. Northeast of present-day Regina, Saskatchewan, witnesses reported a herd on the move which stretched in each direction as far as one could see and, counted at several hundred a minute, required 24 hours to pass. They estimated its numbers at 1,000,000. In the Cypress Hills, near the western boundary of the province, a party told about riding 20 to 30 miles per day for 7 days through a single herd. Paleontologist Marsh, a meticulous observer, reported the buffalo in Kansas so abundant that a single herd darkened a valley 12 miles long and from 6 to 8 miles wide, and he computed their number at 100,000. His rival scientist, Edward Drinker Cope, coming through a year later, also commented on the almost incredible abundance of buffalo, yet the total number then was scarcely a third of the 60,000,000 which ranged the land slightly more than a century before. The herd centering in Kansas was then estimated to number 4,000,000.

The mortality which the American bison took in stride is also interesting. One observer in 1867 reported 2000 of a herd of 4000 engulfed in a stretch of quicksand on the Platte River. Alexander Henry, the fur trader, found dead buffalo an actual hindrance to travel. In his journal of May 1807 he said, "The number of buffalo lying along the beach and on the banks passes all imagination. They form one continuous line and emit a horrible stench. I am informed that every spring it is about the same." Another observer, noticing the great numbers of drowned buffalo, spent an entire day counting and set down 7360. As this was the toll for only one stretch of river, and the rivers of the northern range totaled an estimated 20,000 miles, the deaths from ice and mud must have been enormous. Prairie fires sometimes left blackened stretches a hundred miles wide from which the stench of burned and rotting buffalo turned the traveler away. Dakota blizzards were believed by later naturalists to have taken greater toll of buffalo than the Indian hunters.

Seldom had the entire culture of a people been so based on a single animal as was the Indians' on the buffalo. The buffalo furnished his fresh food in summer and his preserved food in winter. The buffalo provided him with his house, his clothing, his sport, and often his religion. Scarcely a part of the buffalo carcass went unused. In addition to its flesh and fat, which were staples, its purine-rich organs were eaten raw for their health-giving qualities, particularly as an aid to the hunter's virility. Its gall was a favored dressing, particularly as an addition to broiling meats. Sausage was made by pounding sun-dried meat, fat, and chokecherries, stuffing the mixture into the small intestine, and smoking over a willow fire. Fat, mixed with the dried sap of the box elder tree, was a candy. Although most Indians preferred antelope skin for garments, the buffalo-calf robe was a standard material. Cow hides were favored for the making of tepees, and the size of the dwelling was known by its number of skins. An eleven-skin tepee, with two more for the wings which were moved to keep the fire drawing, was an average for the home of a prosperous Plains Indian. The bull hides found use as shields, moccasin soles, and the heavy parfleshes which have been likened to small trunks. The hide of a buffalo could be eaten if it was steamed long enough, and many Indians survived the hungry moons by cooking and eating their homes. The pericardium, carefully removed from around the heart, formed the only nursing bottles that Indian infants ever knew. Bladders were buckets and pontoons. The brains were eaten as food, and when dried and rubbed on skins furnished an oil with unparalleled softening qualities. The tongue and nose of the buffalo were its greatest delicacies, and its hoofs were most proletarian. "We are having tongue tonight, so I'll be unable to come," said a snobbish Assiniboine belle, but when spied on, her family was found dining on boiled hoof.

The hair of the buffalo was braided into rope and used for saddle paddings, and its tendons were split for thread. Children slid downhill on sleds made of its ribs. Its paunch was used for buckets and stewpots. The thick hide of the bull buffalo's neck was boiled for glue. His scrotum, dried, loaded with pebbles, and mounted on a handle, was a favored rattle. The horn found many uses. Steamed, it could be bent and formed into spoons, ladles, and small utensils. It was used to carry smoldering dung, the Indians' matches. The dung, or chips, were standard fuel and cooked many meals for the emigrants to Oregon and California. Well-rubbed dung sprinkled on a pipeload of tobacco would afford an even start. It was also blended with the tobacco in amounts of about 5 per cent to improve the burning qualities, and early sojourners in the tepee attested its richer flavor and more pungent bouquet. The bones of buffalo were cracked and boiled for grease. When feasible the blood was caught, later to be boiled in the animal's stomach, where it was thickened by the natural rennet to make a transparent pudding, rubbery when cold.

Rawhide had numberless uses. The horseman made his bridle of rawhide and he covered the frame of his saddle with it. Scraped thin and dried over the hoop of a drum, it responded with a strange, submetallic musical tone and remained taut for a lifetime. The shrinking of rawhide can break stones and its bindings were unmatched for holding the heads of stone hammers. The beard and tail tassels of buffalo decorated lances, and attached to the heels of moccasins they stirred the grass as the warrior walked.

In the prehorse days, Indians crept up on buffalo with bows and arrows and undoubtedly had a hard time bagging one. They got them in deadfalls dug in the trails, penned them in blind canyons, and drove them inside heavy log-and-stone enclosures to be killed with spears or simply run around and around until they fell and were trampled. Buffalo in deep snow could be approached on snowshoes. The favored way, and one of the best means ever devised for getting a large amount of meat in a short time, was the *pish-kun,* or buffalo jump. Favored cliffs and cutbanks were chosen and when a herd was found properly situated it was stampeded over the edge. Wing fences of stone were used to guide the victims to the proper spot. The pishkun was a communal effort, with everyone taking part. Sometimes the kills were gigantic. Only a fraction of the meat and hide could be saved. From the pishkuns rose a perennial stench unequaled on the Plains, and they became gathering places for wolves and feathered scavengers.

North and east of Loma, Montana, the Missouri River was turned by the ice sheet to cut deeply through the flanks of the Bear Paw and Little Rocky mountains, one of the continent's best grazing grounds. The gorge it formed is in many places a thousand feet deep, and the canyons and coulees which today rapidly dig their way back into the benchland offered numberless buffalo jumps. Probably only a small fraction of the kills have been found. In the two to two and a half centuries since their abandonment erosion has moved most of the cliffs back so all evidence lies under tons of dirt and rock, suspected only when a seasonal stream cuts through a layer of bone and rusty hair, or when arrow points show up in the clean-washed pebbles.

Large pishkuns have been screened by arrowhead hunters since the 1890s and still yield a harvest. The bones and blood-iron of buffalo form layers many feet under the surface, and the rich loam of their decomposition, minutely pulverized and screened by the arrowhead searchers, provides an incomparable fertilizer for the author's flowerbed.

> *I sometimes think that never blows so red*
> *The Rose where some buried Caesar bled. . . .*

The Great Spirit, offended by the awful slaughter of the pishkuns, warned that if the slaughter went unchecked the buffalo would go away. The earth would open up, His prophets said, and all the buffalo would walk into it and disappear forever. When this in fact seemed to take place during the late 1870s, it was logical to believe that the Great Spirit had acted, and the Ghost Dance madness came as an attempt to appease Him and bring the buffalo back again.

It was the horse and not wholesale carnage which spelled the end of the pishkun. When Spanish horses moved up through their prehistoric domain, the Indian mounted himself and was no longer obliged to wait for the buffalo. He went out to look for the herds and follow them. With the aid of horses, entire villages moved across the land. Many observers of the nineteenth century have written of the speed with which an Indian village of skin lodges could be taken down, packed, and set moving. One hour and there would be a teeming community with men and women, children, barking dogs, horses, and clouds of flies, and the next only the empty creek bottom and quiet hills, the dust of passage diminishing across the prairie. But portable as the lodges seemed, without horses they were not movable except for a mile or so. An average eleven-skin, eighteen-pole buffalo-skin lodge was cargo for three horses. Not packsaddle cargos, but cargos for the *travois*, skids made of the poles, butt ends fastened to the horses' sides, small ends dragging the dirt, in form like a letter *A*, making wide, wagonlike ruts through the sod, double-trailing the prairie. Squaws used dog travois until recent times, and probably they were used for light hauling even before the time of horses. (Old Indians, in fact, referred to the prehorse time as the "dog days.") They were of questionable utility, however, dogs having an ungovernable propensity for chasing rabbits. They would do it travois and all, and leave some poor woman's possessions scattered over a mile of the country.

Indians of the dog days lived in villages which were much more permanent than those later on. Sod and poles were the favored materials rather than buffalo hide. Particularly in the eastern part of the Trail country, in Dakota and Kansas, they were agricultural, raising maize, squash, beans, and tobacco. Some of them fused pottery of the glacial clay using an open fire for a kiln, the ash acting as a flux which more or less glazed the surface. The Indian never was much of a potter, and those of the northern Plains forgot what skill they had when the horse arrived. Earthenware was too cumbersome and easily broken to be moved from place to place, so the squaws learned to cook and carry liquids in skin containers. The tepee was adopted, and the old, permanent huts were constructed only for ceremonial use. The Cheyennes, for example, continued to plant gardens, but they did not remain in their home territory, then in South Dakota, to till them. They picked up and left for the buffalo trails, returning in the autumn to harvest what happened to grow. This was probably very little, but if the horses were laden with jerked buffalo, who cared? The Crow Indians, who by 1800 occupied a position of strategic importance where the Great North Trail crossed the Yellowstone River in southern Montana, are a good example of the change which came about when a tribe in the buffalo range obtained horses. The Crows had been an agricultural people of the Midwest. There they lived a rooted village life and made pottery. Moving west, they became buffalo hunters. By the time the first white men came they had so completely lost their old skills that only a few of the old people had a memory of them.

Although the tribes had a variety of horses, large and small, all of them seem descended from the stock brought over by the Spaniards. Explorers brought them north of the Rio Grande in the 1540s. They escaped from the sizable herds which were driven as a *remuda* and in a hundred years wild horses were running the hills of the Southwest. By 1680 the Pawnees owned horses they had captured, stolen, or traded for in the South. In the next thirty years tribe after tribe to the north procured horses, the Shoshones of the Three Forks country first appearing mounted and warlike in about 1710. With horses the Shoshones became a scourge, driving their old Blackfeet enemies off the southern end of the Old North Trail, even beyond the Great Falls, and they were a danger on the Saskatchewan.

With survival at stake, the northern Indians would do anything to get horses. A flourishing trade developed up the trail from Mexico. The Arikara, whose European-type houses and fortifications were previously marked on the bluffs of the Missouri, established a trade fair in the Black Hills area and became one of the most wealthy and powerful tribes in the West, continuing so for more than a century until they fell before the Sioux.

The Spaniards, careless with horses, made sure that firearms did not fall into the hands of the Indians. But the French traders coming by way of the Great Lakes had no qualms about guns or anything else that would bring in the beaver skins. By 1760 the Sioux in Minnesota owned an estimated 2000 guns of various descriptions. When they obtained horses also, nothing in the Minnesota–Black Hills country could stand against them. With their allies the Cheyennes they controlled the prairies of the North, and were broken only after Crook's campaign following Custer's defeat at the Little Big Horn, in the late 1870s.

At that time the white traders were not yet competing for the furs of the upper Saskatchewan. The British hardly stirred from their posts along Hudson Bay. They found it easier to supply the Crees who occupied a gigantic section of the North, and who became middlemen, trading with the still half-known tribes farther on. Cree traders got guns to the Blackfeet in good time, just when the well-horsed Shoshones were pressing them from the south.

Many of the Blackfeet owned guns when the first white men visited them in the 1750s, and by that time they were well supplied with horses. With guns and horses both, the Blackfeet turned on the Shoshones and recaptured their old domain. Although the Blackfeet could not have secured their first horses much before 1720, Anthony Hendry of the Hudson's Bay Company (who arrived among them in 1754) described their horsemanship as amazing. Hendry, who had traveled from Hudson Bay, through The Pas, and up the Saskatchewan River, found the Blackfeet in possession of many fine riding horses about fourteen hands high. They picketed them on buffalo thong, used hobbles in turning them out to graze, and had learned to make saddles. They had become seminomadic in their hunting range. The younger men would no longer consider such "squaw methods" as the pishkun, the pound, or the surround. Hunting had become the chase, and it was done on horseback. A fine buffalo horse was an Indian's most valuable possession. The herd was still stampeded, but the Indian was now in the thick of it, his horse running free of the bridle, on his own or guided by pressure of the rider's knees, across ground which might be rendered dangerous by badger and gopher holes, bringing the huge running beasts into close arrow range.

Many tales are told of the strength of the Indian's arrow shot, and there seems little question he was able to drive an arrow out of sight between the animal's ribs. Some report Indians able to drive an arrow all the way through at close range, but this may have been through the abdomen or through the breast of a young animal. Buffalo were also killed by lance thrusts from horseback, but the bow and arrow, the frontier's repeating weapon, was preferred. Even when they obtained guns, the bow was better because after one shot the gun required considerable time in reloading. A good bowman with a string of trained buffalo horses might make several runs through stampeded buffalo herds in a day and his kill total a dozen of the beasts, a tremendous tonnage. It would be food, clothing, and a home for the year, and some to give to the poor—who, since the end of the communal killings, were caught up in a new order. With the horse added to the buffalo economy, the rich became richer, the brave braver, and the poor, in goods and in spirit, so much the poorer. It was the bold buffalo runner of the Plains, feathered, with his lance, shield, and bow, his high-boned face and eye of an eagle which so captured the fancy of the white man, and holds it still.

The trails of the Indian and buffalo were shifting and numberless, but if all were drawn they would coincide with the broad north-to-south sweep of the Great North Trail, from the Peace River country of Canada to New Mexico. Other animals were plentiful in the trail country also, but their signs are pounded under the trample of buffalo. Of these the most important was antelope.

George Bird Grinnell, who probably knew more about the Plains and Rocky Mountain West than anybody else, estimated that there were more antelope than buffalo, but they went little noticed because of their color. Their prairie tan blended with grass, and their bellies with the sage, so as to make them almost transparent in bright sun, and only when running away, with puff-white tails up, were they easy to see. An antelope will leave its fawn and run with its tail on display, but turn invisible when coming around side-view or front-quarter-forward after a circle of several miles. The curiosity of antelope is legendary. White men have hunted them by mounting red flags on hillocks and lying in ambush, waiting for them to come and investigate. Indians used what they called "antelope arrows" which performed

the same function as red flags. Antelope arrows were standards bearing feathers, tufts of fur, patterns of willow leaves,
inscriptions on aspen bark, and bright bits of stone and
metal. Frequently some man in the tribe would specialize in
the luring of antelope, but he would keep his medicine secret. Many stories were told of men who could go out alone
and return with antelope, having attracted them by arcane
means. When the cattle herds moved from Texas up the
main line of the Great North Trail to Wyoming and Montana to occupy the range vacated by the buffalo, antelope
were still plentiful, and many a camp cook, flying a red flag
over his chuck wagon as a guide to the point riders, driving
hell-bent in advance of the dusty herd to pick a camp spot
and get supper going, found his banner an irresistible lure to
the curious antelope, who would come close, provided they
were not watched or thought of. Camp cooks recalling the
early days were always positive on the point that wagons,
flag-equipped, would attract no antelope if sent out ex-
pressly for that purpose. But take a cook when he was busy
trying to mix quick-bread or prepare a batch of son-of-a-
bitch-in-a-sack, the cowboy's haggis, and thinking only of
getting finished before the hungry men, the dust, and the
bawling were on him, then he was likely to look up and find
an antelope with its head practically in the mixing pan.

Wild sheep were plentiful. They were the most gentle
and approachable of animals, with the result that they are
rare today. Sheep were particularly numerous in the badlands which offered their chief security. Deer were taken by
snares in the woods. Often a simple rawhide loop hung over
one of their runways was sufficient. A loop worked better if a
log was placed for the deer to leap over. A male was often
caught by the antlers and eventually escaped. Hence the
does were the chief victims. There were also snares of more
refined construction, making use of a bowed tree which was
released by a triggered thong. They could be made to react
with the power of a medieval catapult and lift a deer, or
some unsuspecting man, off his feet to hang helpless, to

strangle or freeze, a danger to all who traveled the forest. Particularly in the Lake country and Canada, one hears of men hanging in the loops of deer snares. Even moose were not too large for the snare. There is a record of Ojibwas snaring 2400 moose on Manitoulin Island, in Lake Huron, in the winter of 1670, but far indeed from the domain of this volume. Few snares were used along the trail short of the Far North. There, beyond the range of buffalo, Indians snared snowshoe rabbits in large numbers, thus gathering a large part of their food, clothing, and bedding. Salmon have been called the coastal Indian's buffalo. The same might be said of the rabbits of the Arctic. Rabbit is a poor food, drying thin and gray rather than thick and black as buffalo did, and it gave little sustaining power to those who ate it. Its skin also was fragile. The only superb rabbit product is the famous rabbitskin blanket. Loosely crocheted from the endless strips of rabbitskin, they have been acclaimed by travelers as the best of beds, many preferring them even to eiderdown sleeping bags. The pelts are uncured, however, and perishable. They need the deep cold of Northern winter to keep them from putrefying. Northerners joke about being able to find one's rabbitskin bed in the dark. Springtime odors in an Alaskan lodge where the past year's catch of salmon and the past winter's rabbitskin blankets have both come to life have stunned many a visitor and caused him to reel from the doorway.

Hungry Indians passed up few foods. Prairie dogs, a terrestrial squirrel with a body as much as eleven inches long, and gophers, which grew to a plump and juicy nine inches, were snared or drowned out of their burrows, to be eaten in time of want. Gopher stew was specified by many white men as the dish most characteristic of squaw cooking, but how common it was is a question. Indian and gopher bear the same relationship as Negro and 'possum. Indians such as the Sioux, who had recently come from the Lakes, sometimes caught fish, but there were few fish to be had in the land of the Trail. Skunks were prized as food and easily caught at night. Indians made little use of small furs until the traders came, but skunk tails were a valued decoration. Eagles were taken for their feathers. The recognized means of getting eagle feathers was from a baited, slat-and-dirt-covered pit on top of a hill. There are tales of Indian boys, ambitious to obtain their first eagle feathers, crouched and waiting to grab one of the big birds by its legs. The largest eagles have wingspreads of almost 8 feet. Golden eagles carry off fawns and pigs, and even kill young colts. There are tales of eagles carrying off the Indian boys who tried to capture them. Not true, perhaps, but both ways it was a sporting proposition.

Indians utilized many plants growing along the Trail, knowing them for food, medicine, dyes, and chemical reagents. White men often used hot coals from their fire to purify and clear their drinking water. The Indian method of boiling it with the joints of cactus did the same job better. Hemp and peyote were used as opiates. Hemp is a native hashish which can be either brewed or smoked. Peyote is a small cactus growing for the most part south of the Rio Grande, but the northern Indians obtained it through trade. One bush furnished the Indians an excellent tea, and syrup came from the box elder tree. The shoots of young cocklebur plants tasted like licorice. The most famous root was the camas, but it grew only in the foothills and mountains. A native tobacco was grown in many places along the Trail, but most of it came from the East through trade. This is only the start of his larder and pharmacopoeia, which could make a book in itself. How much was developed by any single tribe and how much was borrowed from its neighbors is a question. It is probable that history came upon the Indian of the Trail at a happy moment, at a high point in his culture, just after the horse gave him a far-ranging mobility, a view of strange things and distant places, a desire for adventure and change.

PRAIRIE GOLD
AND MOUNTAIN SILVER

Chapter 4

In 1527, powerful, raw-tempered, one-eyed Pánfilo de Narváez gained from the Spanish crown a concession to colonize the little-known peninsula of Florida and exploit the deposits of gold which were believed to lie in the mountains of the interior. This expedition, three fourths of the continent away, became a chain of misfortune and hardship unique even in the annals of New Spain, but its survivors were the first Europeans known to have set foot on the Great North Trail.

Narváez, already storm-beaten and lost, put his expedition ashore near Sarasota. He headed inland around Tampa Bay, then north. There were no mountains. He was caught in jungle quagmire. There was nothing to do but go on, and at last he got the remnants of his party to salt water at the mouth of the Apalachicola. They built boats, hacking out the frames with their swords and covering them with the hides of their surviving horses. They believed themselves only a few days' sail from Mexico. They set out surviving weeks of thirst and the pitiless sun. Then a storm came, and one might almost say put a merciful end to them. But not quite. Narváez and most of his men were never heard of again, but four were cast up on the coast of Texas, somewhere in the vicinity of Galveston Bay. One of these was a representative of the King who had been sent to make sure the royal treasury was not cheated of its share of gold, a man known to history as Cabeza de Vaca. Two were soldiers. The fourth was a Moorish slave, a Negro named Estéban.

After six years as captives of a coastal tribe they escaped and struck out for the West. They came to the Rio Grande and followed it deep inland, to the region of old San Saba and to the rough country of the Concho River. Their subsequent route is uncertain, but it seems likely they found the natural passage which later became the Overland Mail road to El Paso through the Guadalupe Mountains. Now on a branch of the Great North Trail, what was later to be the Spanish Mission Supply Trail, they headed toward Santa Fe. They probably did not reach that ancient center of Indian life, but they had no doubt they were on a mainstem of travel.

De Vaca and his companions wandered for two years. They found the desert tribes more friendly than those along the Coast. De Vaca convinced them he had magical powers. They believed him to be the child of the sun, his two Spanish companions lesser children of the sun, and Estéban a black child of the sun. De Vaca afterward admitted using his learning to good effect, actually performing cures and prognostications bordering on the miraculous. Accounts of the visitors traveled ahead, and they gathered a retinue that numbered at one time an estimated four thousand. Unable to assume native garb because gods, they went naked, and de Vaca later claimed to have responded to the sun's rays by shedding his skin like a snake. Gifts were borne to them in unending abundance but little could be carried along and when at last they reached the Spanish settlements of Mexico they had little to show for their years as gods, only a few Spanish coins obtained by selling the last of their Indian followers into slavery. But they were rich in information.

They had visited pueblos described as fortified towns, of little interest except that they were obviously the desert counterpart of much greater cities in the more temperate and well-watered lands farther north. Among the gifts they told about and perforce left behind were metals—copper, silver, and gold. One of the groups who visited them were Indians from far to the north, and de Vaca marked their surprisingly fair, European appearance. They were a graceful people, he reported, and wore clothes of soft leather and woven cotton. Their arrowheads he identified as emerald. They had no horses, but told of large herds of animals which ranged the grasslands. Their land was called Cibola. Agriculture was practiced, and gold was too plentiful among them to be considered valuable. They gave de Vaca to understand that their ordinary drinking vessels were made of gold. None of these had he seen. He was not deliberately lying. Embellishing, perhaps, but he *believed*. His communication had been mostly through sign language. And Indians always tried to tell white men what they longed to hear. The taller stories he discounted. Only if he saw proof, or if a thing was told to him again and again, in one village after another, or repeated by several travelers were they regarded as fact. One so authenticated told of a fertile land to the west and north, and another, oft-repeated, the coast of a western sea. Pearls were described, and silks, and things of an Oriental nature that no desert Indian could have thought of on his own.

At that time the Pacific north of Mexico was little known, most of the maps showing it bent westward, the Asiatic and American continents being one. People who sailed far into the Pacific did not thus prove contrary facts of geography. They had merely sailed across a vast bay. The Pacific then, and for more than a century thereafter, was generally considered to be at least half-surrounded by the American and Asiatic continents. The land of Cibola was believed

by some to lie on the coast and be in fact China, while others
considered it an American land, separated by the Strait of
Anian from China. A third saw both to be in error, saying
China and the land of pearls were on the coast, while Cibola
was in the mountains. They placed it about where Santa Fe
was later founded. About one fact all agreed, however. The
land of Cibola had seven rich cities, always seven. Through
repetition they became fixed in the Spanish minds as an abso-
lute of the land to the north.

In Mexico City the travelers caused a wonderful excitement. The silver mines had not yet started to pour out their
deep treasures. Parties looking for El Dorado, the Golden
Man and his fabulous lake, had gone into the Colombian
mountains to die of palm adders, poisoned arrows, and a
hundred exotic fevers. The tales of gold in the jungles of
Florida and Guinea led men to a green hell of vines and
swamp. The country up the northern trail, however, was
different. It was to all accounts quite like Spain. Soon it was
not a question whether an expedition would be launched to
the Seven Cities, but whose expedition it would be.

Would de Vaca, the Viceroy asked, like to go back as
commander of an·expedition? De Vaca parried this. He
wanted to visit Spain. He was homesick, he said. Actually
he wanted not only to captain an expedition but to be Viceroy
of the new lands.

The Viceroy in Mexico City then acted on his own,
sending out his own Cibolan expedition under a Franciscan
religious, an adventurer formerly with Pizarro, named
Marcos—"Fray Marcos" to history—with Estéban as guide.

Estéban had particularly extolled the north. His geography and projected location of the Seven Cities exceeded even
de Vaca's for exactness. He had found his life as a black god
much more congenial than it had been as a Negro slave, and
he could hardly wait to resume that happy condition. According to the tales that have survived, Estéban was particularly drawn to the young women of the tribes who had
offered themselves one after another hoping to become im-

pregnated by the child of the sun. He did not fare well the second time around. Returning with Fray Marcos he got in trouble over a woman, was taken captive, and tried to win his freedom by showing a "sacred" rattle. The rattle was recognized as a charm belonging to an enemy tribe. Poor Estéban was put to death, and so were the Spanish soldiers who had accompanied his guide party. His bones today lie somewhere close to Gallup, New Mexico. He was killed in the pueblo of Hawikuh; the Indians were Zuñis.

The expedition crossed over one of the mineral-rich districts of the globe which one day would boast such mining camps as Tombstone, Bisbee, and Morenci, but nothing of value was found except some crudely cut turquoises. It returned a failure. In Spain, de Vaca saw the King and gained an appointment as Administrator, but of the Province of Rio de la Plata in South America. After some swashbuckling explorations there he was sent home in irons. He finally regained the royal favor and ended his life as a judge in Seville. Long ere this the task of exploring for the Seven Cities fell to others.

De Vaca and his men had escaped from captivity in 1534. Estéban died in 1539. In 1540 Coronado—Francisco Vásquez de Coronado, grandee of New Spain and Governor of New Galicia—left Compostela near the Pacific coast of Mexico on a full-scale expedition to the north to occupy Cibola and take charge of its treasures. Although the Franciscan Marcos had failed and black Estéban was dead, the reports left little doubt that the Seven Cities existed and that their wealth was on the scale of the Incas'. The cost of the expedition therefore seemed justified. Coronado headed 250 horsemen, 70 Spanish foot soldiers, a number of priests and brothers with their servants, and several hundred Indian stock-tenders, servants, and laborers. He had a thousand horses and numerous baggage mules; for food, a herd of cattle and a flock of sheep. Coronado was forty years old. He had the best record as a soldier and administator of any man in New Spain. Few doubted that he would succeed.

Chief impediment proved to be the sheer size of the expedition. The stock had to graze along the way. Huge masses of supplies made progress slow, particularly on the approach to the Sierra Madre. The Spanish wore armor or coats of mail, or at least carried it along. The weapons included artillery in the form of wheeled cannon. At last Coronado, impatient, set out ahead with a hundred picked horsemen. He led the way through the coastal range of Sinaloa, across the pass where Rio Fuerte flows westward to the Gulf of California, and north along the Yaqui and Sonora rivers, choosing the mountain rather than the plateau route which was later the supply trail to El Paso and Santa Fe. Coronado crossed into U.S. territory at the southeastern corner of Arizona, where the low Sierra de San Jose and Chiricahua mountains rise from the desert near Douglas, then went northward to Zuñi, where it was believed the Seven Cities of Cibola would be found. There were only some pueblos of baked mud and rock. So he turned eastward to the headwaters of the Canadian River, passing the site of Santa Fe. He in fact followed the future Santa Fe Trail, as it was known to Missouri wagoners of another time. His interest had now shifted from Cibola. He had heard of a new land called Quivera. Quivera was ruled by a prince who owned silk, and hence had some contact with the Orient. Gold was so common and easily won from the streams that Quiverans used it not as money or jewelry, but as a ready substitute for brass. Gold was so plentiful in Quivera that it was annealed and beaten into kitchen utensils.

The man who told them of this was a Pawnee who had been taken south by other Indians as a slave. He encouraged them to search for Quivera because he wanted to get home. He spoke no Spanish or any of the southern Indian tongues and had to converse through sign language, so there is doubt that he actually told them all these things, but the Spanish interpreted him in the manner which gratified them most. It pleased them to regard him not as an Indian but as a Turk.

Their "Turk" took them into Kansas by a route which in little more than three hundred years would be followed by Texas cattle on their way to Dodge City. They crossed the Arkansas River and almost reached the future site of another famed town of the cattle trail, Abilene. Grass waved in the wind endlessly—future gold of the cattlemen—but it was a desolation of Spanish hopes. The Quivera they reached was a Wichita Indian village of dirt-leaking sods little better than wolf burrows in the bottoms of the Smoky Hill River. There they tortured their poor guide to make him confess his lies, and then they strangled him. The Wichitas knew the way south and guided Coronado and his men back to the Rio Grande.

Half a century after Coronado, an adventurer named Gaspar de Sosa took a party north as far as Santa Fe. The trail he followed, later to be known as the Spanish Mission Trail, would have taken him on to the San Luis Park country of Colorado, and to South Park, Middle Park, and North Park, a remarkable chain of level lands within the mountains. Sosa's colonizing endeavor did not have the blessing of the Viceroy, and soldiers were sent to evict him. Eight years later a colony was formed under the leadership of a Don Juan de Oñate who chose to locate north of Santa Fe where the Rio Grande, flowing from its sources against the Continental Divide, channels its way between the Sangre de Christo and the Valle Verde mountains. The place proved lacking in pasture, however, and vulnerable to surprise attack, so in 1610 the main Spanish post in the north was moved down to the location of an ancient Indian settlement and named Santa Fe.

A more ideal spot could not have been found. Santa Fe's altitude made it cool in the summer and there was abundant fuel, pasture, and water. Game and Indian agriculture were sources of food. Most important for control of the country, it stood at the crossing of many trails. One of them led westward to the Zuñi villages, later the wagon road to Prescott,

Arizona, and Beal's Crossing of the Colorado River. The Santa Fe Trail, or trails, led east, and of course there was the trail to San Luis Park and middle Colorado.

Santa Fe was never very important to New Spain, although it did serve as a mildly effective outpost against a western penetration by England and France. It later became the center of a rich cattle region. There were vast ranches in Mexico, but the herds and flocks were a poor second to its mining industry. Commencing with the Spanish conquest and continuing to the present, Mexican mines have produced two thirds of the silver of the world. With this gigantic wealth so close to home, the rich and powerful of the land took little interest in Santa Fe once it was certain the Seven Cities and Quivera did not exist. There was little to be made in the hides, furs, blankets, wool, piñon nuts, and slaves which were its chief exports. Few merchants sent trading caravans. The only regular supply was the one sponsored by the Church. Six months was required for the heavy wagons, loaded with two tons each and pulled by eight-mule teams, to make the journey down the Rio Grande to El Paso, across the desert plateau to Parral, Durango, Zacatecas, and Mexico City. Later Santa Fe was supplied by American traders from Missouri who made the trip in about sixty days.

Officially the explorations from Mexico ended at Santa Fe, the Grand Canyon, and California. How much farther some adventurous Mexican prospectors pushed through the mountains is a matter of speculation. Evidence which came to light in the last century indicated they traveled very far indeed. Silver hunters from Mexico perhaps traveled the Great North Trail in its mountain branches to the 49th parallel or beyond. That section of the main Trail from southern Wyoming into Montana generally referred to as the Bozeman Trail, after the gold miner who mapped it for wagon travel, had a number of ruins believed to be the remnants of Mexican habitations. There are also some signs of early mining in Montana. Much of the evidence is inconclusive, but for what it is worth, here is the case for Spanish exploration up the

Trail, starting with the situation in Mexico which forced those without political connections to turn their backs on one of the richest treasure troves of the earth:

The Crown recognized no poor man's bonanzas. From 1516, when mining started, until 1821, all subsurface rights in New Spain were deemed the King's property. Spanish subjects could work mines only under a special license. One of the conditions was that the King's treasurer received two thirds of the profits. He seldom got it, but no matter, the average citizen, the soldier sent across the ocean, the minor official stood little chance of getting a license, and the poor Indian or halfbreed miner none at all. Under the *Real Cedula* and *Ordenanzas de Mineria* mining concessions were granted to favored persons only. If any ordinary miner went out and discovered a rich outcropping his only chance was to keep it secret and find a patron in some official. In time the *Ordenanzas* liberalized the regulations somewhat, and the two-thirds rule was rescinded in favor of a 20 per cent gross royalty, but only because the operators of the richest silver mines, worked by slave labor, part of whom were set to raise corn for food, protested hard times and that the ore barely met expenses.

Because of the monopolies, prospecting proceeded on an outlaw basis, and the discoverers of new silver mines worked them clandestinely. Later they organized into independent outlaw communities and fought off the soldiers and the concessioners as long as possible. Mining districts such as the one at Guanajuato, discovered in 1550, might sport a city with a provincial society imitating Madrid, but the fringe of exploration was a lawless region. Military men enlisted soldier miners and struck out to establish themselves on the mining frontier, generally with the most questionable authorization. Then there were white swashbucklers, renegades, criminals escaped from Europe, soldier deserters, mestizos, bandidos, runaway slaves—mulatto, Negro, and Indian—all pushing into the mountains and deserts, knowing they could have only what they were able to hold and accounting life very cheap indeed. Even the Church, when its converts led it to silver deposits, was loath to share with the authorities. They mined themselves, not advertising the fact, and there are still legends of mines hidden by the religious, too well hidden, still luring treasure seekers, some not only equipped with old maps and journals but also with the latest geological detecting instruments.

In the North, independent miners ranged to Santa Fe and beyond, but records of their explorations and discoveries seldom became a part of the colonial archives. Some tales have them penetrating the Rockies as far north as Alaska. That they reached Wyoming and Montana there seems little doubt. During the Mexican war one Father Ortiz was taken prisoner trying to carry dispatches through General Stephen W. Kearny's lines, and while in custody proved himself well versed in Western geography, volunteering that the Spanish from Santa Fe had a hundred years before made settlements seven or eight hundred miles to the north. He spoke of the Big Muddy River, probably the Missouri rather than the Platte, and said the Spanish had built stone houses as well as arrastres for crushing gold and silver ore. Metal and furs both came down from the northern land in quantity, Father Ortiz said, but the settlements were abandoned because of the warlike Indians. Little more was thought of the tale until General Conner's Big Horn expedition of 1865 came across a stone house of considerable age at De Smet Lake in northern Wyoming, on the Bozeman Trail. The following year ruins of an old Spanish-type arrastre was found over the Big Horn range to the west, and other stone houses, at least foundations and ruins, were found by General Miles' expedition in the Big Horn late in 1874. In 1866, miners driven from the Rosebud Mountains of Montana by Indians came upon evidence of a canal and placer workings of great age, as well as traces of iron tools eaten away to shells by exposure. Iron rusts out in that manner in about forty years and so might not antedate the fur traders, but no early fur trader ever came out with more than small amounts of gold, and none was known to carry on any systematic mining. When ranchers came to Wyoming the discoveries of rusted-out tools were reported from many localities.

In 1887, near Racetrack Lake high among the mountains of the Flint Creek Range in southwestern Montana, prospectors from the silver camp of Philipsburg came across a mine tunnel about two hundred feet deep which, by its rotted timbers and the weathered nature of its dump, was judged to be at least fifty years old. Those familiar with such things identified the timbering as one with the Spanish antiguas of the South. The end of the tunnel was caved, and no record exists that it was ever cleaned out. The vein it followed was spotty and subsequent prospectors were content to do some test-pitting farther up the slope, but the workings did yield some relics—a crude charcoal drawing of a woman and a handmade silver drinking cup. The cup was found amid the rock rubble of the drift, and it was deemed strange by its discoverers that the miner had not on leaving taken it with him. They speculated that he might have fallen victim to Indians. Another possibility which did not occur to them, apparently, was that he might lie buried beneath the fallen rock at the end of the drift.

The story was carried in the press, and a year or so later a man named Miguel Martinez and several Spanish-speaking companions arrived in Philipsburg equipped with a treasure map from Mexico, and the legend of a lost mine of fabulous wealth. It did not take them long to see that Racetrack Lake had no such resources. Fate took them again south to the old El Salvador mine in Wyoming. There, later that fall, prospectors came on the bodies of poor Miguel and his entire party, murdered. Some previous operators of the El Salvador, it was reported, had been trapped by deep snow and starved ten years before.

THE LONGKNIVES

Chapter 5

Coming the hard way, by lake and river
and many portages across the shield of
America, the French and English were
more than two centuries in reaching the
Great North Trail.

In 1534, the year Cabeza de Vaca
set forth as a child of the sun, Charles I,
King of France, sent navigator Jacques
Cartier to establish a northern route to
the Orient. He believed he had found it
in the Gulf of St. Lawrence. It was not a
clear passage. He was on a river, blocked
at last by rapids, but he learned to his
satisfaction that a passage did exist. He
had reached the Indian city which became Montreal. The Indians took him to
the top of an eminence which he named
Mount Royal in honor of his King, and he
was able to look across a country stretching westward into the mists where a lac-
ing of water shone in the autumn sun,
leading, they told him, to seas where the

surf rolled with a power which smashed the largest canoes, and where the far shore was beyond the sight of an eagle. There were a number of such seas, one after another, each becoming larger, and the last was the largest of all. It was the Gitche Gume, the great water. No man had ever set foot on its far shore because it was said to have none, but to thunder over the outer edge of the world. He asked if its waters were salt. Indians who had traveled far across the seas and had met men from even farther, told him yes, they were. So Jacques Cartier returned and told his King that the Pacific lay approximately 500 miles to the west. Lake Superior encountered at Sault Ste. Marie is indeed almost that exact distance from Montreal.

In Europe the religious wars diverted French attention from a sea passage through America, so it was 1603 before another explorer, Samuel de Champlain, returned to the St. Lawrence. Champlain was a skilled navigator and had visited Mexico. He had speculated on the feasibility of building a canal across Panama. If America narrowed there to only a few miles it might do it again in the north. When Hudson Bay was discovered he believed it to be the Arctic Sea. But, like Cartier, he believed the Pacific to be closer through the lakes.

Arriving at the western shore of Lake Ontario or the northern shore of Lake Huron was like reaching an ocean. The French set out to explore the big waters, but they were handicapped by a lack of suitable vessels. It was necessary to move by stages along the shore, and a lifetime could be spent hunting out the bays and sailing around the islands of northern Lake Ontario alone. Even the Indians, skilled canoe navigators, had only vague notions of their shape. In time Lake Superior, the western "salt sea" of Cartier, was reached, and Indians brought Champlain a piece of native copper from the mines on its southern shore. Later he saw nuggets of native silver, and silver and copper half and half, both so pure they could be hammered into foil like gold. He believed that the lakes were bordered by the Spanish silver lands. The fiction of Cibola, with China close beside, was not dead, and tales of strange men in rich garb and great vessels with sails encouraged the French to drive on and on.

Although nothing like the Orient was ever found inland from Lakes Michigan and Superior, the land was not without its treasure in furs. Within a short time the Winnebago, Ojibwa, and Sioux of the forest were obtaining knives, guns, and other wonders of the age of steel in exchange for beaver skins.

It was now the middle 1600s. The Indians of the Plains still lived in the dog days, taking their buffalo in the deadfall, pishkun, and surround. Their first guns and horses were still fifty to seventy-five years away. Yet all was not the same. The Arapahoe, living in the Milk River country of the Montana border, the Kiowa and Commanche in the Montana–Wyoming lands later held by the Crows, and the Crows, then in eastern Dakota, all felt the unsteadiness of change. A new force was developing in the more easterly tribes. The Sioux and Cheyennes commenced moving west, falling back from the power of the Ojibwas along the Lake. The Assiniboins in the north were also pushing to new hunting ground. One always thinks of such the westward movement to be Indians falling back from the white men, the superior culture making room for itself, occupying land and turning it with the plow. All that would come later. In the middle 1600s the white numbers were but a handful, their farms a few acres fronting the St. Lawrence. The Indian flux was caused by a few tons of goods that the white men had brought—the knives, hatchets, guns, and kettles possession of which gave one tribe an instantaneous superiority over the next, not only in war but also in its power to dominate the hunting environment.

Consider what they had had to work with. The difficulty of cutting up a moose, bear, or some other large, tough-skinned animal with nothing except a sharpened rock can hardly be imagined. To obtain a knife, or even the poorest piece of sheet metal from which one could be fashioned, the Indian hunter would pay any price, and did. Iron, first in the form of knives and sheet metal and then guns, revolutionized the complex tribal balances of the Lake country, and from there, passing like a wave, disrupted them all across America. The Hurons, placed nearest the supply, obtained what they needed and became middlemen, a position of power, and the Iroquois to the south waged the longest and most merciless of Eastern wars to even the balance and drive out the French suppliers.

The Iroquois struck in 1649, and swept the Hurons from the Lakes. For four years no fur flotilla reached Montreal. Champlain had been dead for fourteen years. In his place the chief power had fallen on The Company of One Hundred Associates. Actually there were 120 and they had been granted the whole of New France, with certain obligations which were never fulfilled. They were to develop a French Catholic colony, but all they were interested in was beaver. So long as the beaver came in the most trifling expenditure was resisted by the partners. However, after several seasons of meager returns, the hard-pressed partners, and the governor, took action. They sent out with wide powers, and in an independent trading position greater than any had had before, an explorer and wilderness man, Médard Chouart, Sieur de Groseilliers. He is always associated with his wife's half-brother, Pierre Esprit Radisson, and because it was Radisson who wrote the accounts of their journeys, they are Radisson and Groseilliers.

Traveling, threatening and shaming the Huron chiefs, Groseilliers, a tireless and at times bitterly violent man, managed to get some of them back on the lake routes. He traveled far, farther than any Frenchman had gone before, into Illinois and perhaps reached the Mississippi. He saw Indians in possession of Spanish trade goods, and believed their lands were close to the south. Hearing tales of the Missouri, he confused it with the Colorado or, as it was generally called, the River of the West. With Radisson he then turned toward the northwest and Lake Superior.

By all accounts Superior was the ultimate sea, but it was not salty and had no tides. They hoped it was a freshwater arm of the ocean. No Indians could tell them of its far shore. By sail and paddle they went west, keeping to the red cliffs of the southern shore because the waters of the deep, cold lake could roll in storm like the Atlantic. They passed the indentation near Marquette where the specular iron of the shore pulled the compass needle, saw mountains rising wooded in the mists, sailed around the peninsula where copper was dug, and built winter quarters behind the sheltering islands of Chequamegon Bay.

It was a cold winter and the snows came very deep. They had traded for a large treasure of furs and finally, in the locked cold of March, they were forced to the extremity of boiling and eating some of the poorer pelts to prevent starvation. But no matter, the fur country was endless. They had opened whole new nations, Sioux, Cree, and Assiniboin, to the trade of New France. Returning with this news and a rich haul of beaver, Radisson and Groseilliers expected to reap both wealth and gratitude. Instead the governor levied taxes and fines against them, taking away almost half their profits for two years of work. They had opened a large new beaver country which the Montreal Company of One Hundred, without thanks or payment, now proceeded to exploit.

Smarting under their treatment, Radisson and Groseilliers sought redress in France. None was to be found. Their words about the great fur country beyond the Lakes and northward to Hudson Bay occasioned no excitement. Rebuffed, their next stop was London. They had ended their wilderness trek at about the time Charles II was making his triumphant entry into London after the death of Cromwell and the fall of his successors. They found the country still in a fine state of optimism. England had no shortage of men with daring and capital willing to reap a beaver bonanza across the seas. And to counter the French control of the St. Lawrence and the Lakes the partners presented a novel idea. Instead of attempting to reach the fur country by way of New York and the Iroquois lands, why not enter from the north, by way of Hudson Bay? Their conversations with the Crees had convinced them that the Bay extended deeply south and west, and was, perhaps, the long-sought Northwest Passage. At any rate it would be a whole season's travel closer to Europe than the Lakes via Montreal.

The British were enthralled. It was a chance to outflank the French from the north, and perhaps the Spanish also. And to do it by sea! The project received semiofficial backing. In 1668 the partners returned, this time under the British flag, sailing north through Hudson Strait, and down across the choppy, cold waters of the Bay. By early 1670 they were trading with Indians at the mouth of Nelson River. In the meantime the English company was completed, sponsored by Prince Rupert, brother of the King, its full name, The Governor and Company of Adventurers of England Trading into Hudson's Bay.

If Radisson and Groseilliers had been given sole direction of the Company it would have exploited its advantages in position to push south toward Lake Superior and wrest all the beaver land of Ontario from the French. Although this was the patriotic empire-expanding thing to do, the two Frenchmen were held in check by their British partners who saw no need for such an expensive effort so long as the furs and the profits were rolling in. For in the North the Company had set up among the Crees, a vast tribe willing to carry the trade to far places. What the Hurons had been to the French the Crees were to the British. They were in fact farther-ranging, more shrewd and aggressive, and in a few years the knife and musket were available, at a staggering price in furs, even to the Blackfeet in their home against the Rockies.

The French were at first hardly aware of the new company. Around them the forest, lake, and river country reached apparently without end. Generations were to pass before competition developed more important than some wandering Cree with a few articles of the superior English steel. The Montreal fur merchants were little more interested than the H.B.C. partners of London in extending the

French power, in fortifications, exploration, or anything else that might take money without yielding a quick profit, but there were adventurous and restless individuals, men such as La Salle, who explored the Mississippi; Duluth, who pushed beyond the tip of Superior, opening up the country toward Lake of the Woods while following a will-o'-the-wisp of a salt sea, the Northwest Passage; and Vérendrye, who established New France at Lake Winnipeg, was first to see the remarkable fair-skinned Mandans, and whose son Louis-Joseph is credited with being the first of his race to see the Rocky Mountains north of Colorado.

These men had official sanction. They represented the authority of New France and made reports to the mother country. Their explorations are hence a matter of record. There were others, however, who traveled even farther. These were the *coureurs de bois,* the outlaw traders, the men without sanction. No matter where the frontier was, they were beyond it. They lived with the Indians, became more Indian than white in their culture, and raised families of halfbreed children. They hung onto their French tongue, but it became violent and explosive with a wild metallic twang in its nasal sounds, the "Coyotie French" of Dakota, Montana, and the Canadian plains.

How many *coureurs de bois* reached the Great North Trail, and followed it with their adopted people, can only be guessed. The first certain claim would be that of Boucher de Niverville, trader and explorer from the outpost at Lake Winnipeg. In 1751 Niverville made his way up the Saskatchewan River, stopping only when the last tributary came pouring from the mountains, a range which rose from the foothills like a wall of the gods. He was made welcome at a village of Blackfeet. It was a large village at a ford of the river, and there were many travelers from the north and south who told him of wonders scarcely believable. It seems probable his camp was at today's Calgary. At any rate, he was the first white man known to have attained the mid-reaches of the Great North Trail.

Almost a century had passed since the establishment of the Hudson's Bay Company. In 1690 Henry Kelsey a young employee at York Factory had set out for the West to find the Assiniboins, get them to make peace with the Crees, and bring their furs to the Company. He traveled through The Pas, found the Assiniboins, and, joining one of their parties, emerged from the forest and lake country on the Great Plains. He described much of his journey in poetry. How far he went is a matter of speculation, some even believing he glimpsed the Rockies. He probably was far short of the Rockies, but he learned of their existence. He returned, but the Company regarded his to be a sporting achievement and little else. Not until the French started to establish posts on the Saskatchewan did the English partners stir themselves into really penetrating the West.

A couple of years after the return of Niverville, and 64 years after the explorations of Henry Kelsey, the Company sent out a stout and intelligent young clerk named Anthony Hendry to see what there was beyond the prairie, and to determine whether the resources in beaver made a western expansion advisable. Hendry's visit with the Blackfeet has already been mentioned. His stay was longer then Niverville's. He had a good look at the people, and the country. He traveled with the Indians to the Milk River. He saw hills deep in conifers where a hundred streams ran steplike from beaver ponds. He heard of the three rivers where the Missouri was born, and the thunder water, its five falls.

On his way west Hendry had met the Assiniboins, the Gros Ventre, and the Blackfeet. All were powerful, warlike tribes. The Blackfeet had traveled farthest and were best versed in geography. Their journeys, however, were from north to south, not east to west, making them dependent on Gros Ventre, Assiniboin, and Cree for iron. Why not, asked Hendry, trap the beaver which abounded and carry them downriver (the Saskatchewan) to the H.B.C. posts near Hudson Bay? Unfortunately the Blackfeet did not build canoes, only round boats of buffalo hide used in crossing from bank to bank of the largest streams. And such boats were the craft of squaws, for an Indian man in his pride rode horseback. In crossing a stream he did so boatless, swimming and holding his horse's tail. Even at best the journey east and the equally long return would consume the travel seasons of two years. The chiefs, smoking native leaf blended with the white man's Virginia tobacco, thought hard of this and said *no*. While not discouraged at the prospect of longer journeys to the south by horseback, they rejected the idea of doing it by water.

If the Blackfeet would not journey east, then the Company should move West, and Hendry said so when he returned in 1755. The partners were not yet ready for such a major effort. Such things had to be done by degrees. Besides, the days of New France were drawing to a close. At the time Hendry was in the West, British forces were reported moving across the Appalachian Mountains into the Ohio Valley. The Governor of Virginia had sent a young officer named George Washington to drive the French from Fort Duquesne, but he was defeated. General Braddock went back next year and fared no better, but the pressure on the French continued to increase. The British were too numerous, too well supplied, and they controlled the seas. In 1759 Quebec fell, Montreal a year later. In 1763 Canada was handed over officially to Britain.

If the Hudson's Bay Company expected things to improve with New France gone they were in for a surprise. The competition from Montreal continued, only worse. It was British now, and hence London was unable to favor one side over the other. And to the Montreal competition was added the Colonial fur trade headquartered at Albany. In a few years the Colonial trade would become independent with the United States, and a worse influx of freebooters the frontier never saw. Two of the latter were violent Peter Pond of Connecticut and Alexander Henry of New Jersey. These men, moving from the Lake country to Canada, were responsible more than anyone else for establishing the North West Com-

pany, from 1784 until 1821 (when the two companies amal-
gamated) the bitter competitors of the Hudson's Bay for control of half a continent.

When the North West Company moved into the Athabasca region the partners found themselves at a severe dis-
advantage to the salt water-based H.B.C. By lake and brigade,
it required two years of effort to deliver trade goods to those
remote parts, and a comparable time for the furs to reach
Montreal. A few years earlier Captain James Cook, an explorer sent out by the British Admiralty, had sailed into a
deep inlet on the Pacific coast at approximately Lake
Athabasca's latitude. It was named Cook Inlet, and was believed to be the mouth of a river large as the Columbia. Indians had told Peter Pond, the Athabasca partner, about a river
whose waters moved like a sea flowing from Great Slave
Lake. If the Northwest Passage started at Great Slave Lake,
then the Company could, with a Western headquarters at
Cook Inlet, match the Hudson's Bay, more than match it, for
it would open the Oriental trade and span the continent.

At fifty, Pond did not himself leave to explore. He sent
his second in command, young Alexander Mackenzie, who
traveled around the edge of Great Slave Lake, just breaking
up from winter, and down the gigantic flood of the river
which took him not to the warm Pacific shore, but to the gray
ice floes of the Arctic. It was quite a setback to the dreams of
Peter Pond, but he was a tenacious man. Still believing in
Cook's river, he turned toward the mountains and the gap
where the Peace rushed forth. Again he sent Mackenzie, who
portaged through the Peace River gorge, followed it to its
headwaters, and portaged over to the Fraser. After a terrible
journey, during which his boats smashed in the canyons, he
struck out overland across the mountains and reached tidewater on the Bella Coola, one of the deepest of the glacial
fjords which slice inland from the sea. His journey to the
Arctic Ocean took place in 1789. He reached the Pacific at
Bella Coola in 1792. Important historically as were his ac-
complishments, it spelled the end of a dream for Peter Pond.

Following Mackenzie, the great figure of Canadian exploration was David Thompson. Thompson was a product of the poorer streets of London who had had little formal education. He had come to America as an apprentice with the Hudson's Bay Company as a boy of fourteen, and had taught himself astronomy and mathematics. He left the Hudson's Bay Company, the Northwesters offering greater scope for his talents. They had resumed pushing toward the Pacific, and the prospects interested him.

In 1807, Thompson crossed into the Rocky Mountain Trench through Howse Pass, where the headwaters of the Saskatchewan River rush down from the mountains of what is now Banff National Park. He took his halfbreed wife and three small children with him. The river he found was the Columbia, where it flowed north. Later it doubled back around Warsaw Mountain at the northern end of the Cariboo Range, but he did not know that. He started south and built a post called Kootanae House on a long lake under the summits of Coppertown and Farnham Mountains of the Purcell Range. The next summer he resumed his journey, following the Kootenai River over the U.S. boundary. In 1809 he built Kullyspell House near the eastern outlet of Pend Oreille Lake, northern Idaho, and Saleesh House at Thompson Falls, Montana.

Although Thompson explored the two prehistoric trails of the Rocky Mountain Trench and the Purcell Trench, neither was suitable for the purpose of trade with the Pacific. They were too far west, and much more difficult to the traveler than one would suppose on seeing them contoured on a modern map. Through most of their length they were made difficult by timber, brush, and rock, there was scanty grazing for pack animals, and, beyond the lake areas, the swift drop of the streams necessitated numerous portages. A better route came to the Northwesters inadvertently through the efforts of a trader in the employ of John Jacob Astor, who, reviving the old dreams of Peter Pond, had beaten them, temporarily, to the mouth of the Columbia. David Stuart, for a while the companion of Thompson in the Snake River country, turned north and established an American post where the Okanogan flowed down from Canada into Washington and joined the Columbia. He then went north, finding generally easy terrain and abundant grass for pack animals, into the central British Columbian Plateau. He was on the main mountain branch of the ancient migration trail, followed by tribe after tribe in their movement from Asia and Alaska south to Washington, Oregon, and California, the mainstream of Pacific-coast migration turning south from the Great North Trail. He traded through the winter and next year sent Alexander Ross north to establish a post at Kamloops—"Cumcloups" of the early journals—meaning The Meeting of Waters where the North and South Thompson rivers join. Four thousand Indians were there to barter their beaver at a rate in trade goods which amounted to about 10 cents per skin, but the War of 1812 and the subsequent abandonment of Astor's Oregon outpost forced him to relinquish the rich area to the Northwesters. By horse and canoe brigades the Montreal traders then made the British Columbia–Washington area one of the most traveled in Western America.

In 1762, not knowing that the French territory along the Mississippi was being dealt off to England and Spain, a pair of merchants from New Orleans, Pierre Laclède and Gilbert St. Maxent, obtained an exclusive franchise to trade with the Indians of the Missouri River. They set out with trade goods in 1763, intending to locate somewhere on the Illinois shore, but news of the treaty which gave that side to the British and the other to Spain left them in a quandary. They eventually decided to go to the Spanish side; shortly after the first of the year 1764, Laclède chose a post below the mouth of the Missouri, sending his stepsons Auguste Chouteau, twenty-four, and Pierre, fourteen, with a party of workmen to build houses and a stockade. Although the post for many years was known as Leclède, its official name was St. Louis, in honor of the patron saint of Louis XV.

A French settlement called Cahokia stood where East St. Louis is today, and immediately after the Chouteaus' arrival most of its residents moved across to the new town, which soon had 40 inhabitants. In eight years, when Spain got around to sending an administrator, it had 500, two-thirds of them French, the remainder mostly Negro slaves.

In 1763 King George III had issued an order strictly forbidding "on pain of our displeasure, all our loving subjects from making any purchases or settlements" in the region west of the Appalachians. The order came late for quite a number of his "loving subjects" who were already there. Soon the vanguard reached the Mississippi, crossed over to Missouri, settled on the free land without inquiring much into sovereignty, and in a little while St. Louis was shipping flour and lumber and molding its own bullet lead.

With St. Louis as headquarters, traders—most of them French, but a few Spanish and American—started pushing up the Missouri. Joseph Garreau got as far as the Arikara villages in 1787. In 1792, Jacques D'Eglise reached the Mandans, stopping for a time at the mouth of Knife River, which winds from the Montana border lands where Theodore Roosevelt was later to have his fling at ranching in the Wild West. It was a wilder West in the 1790s because the Sioux were occupying large sections of the country, moving westward from Minnesota. At the Mandan villages, D'Eglise met white men and halfbreeds who had journeyed from the North with trade goods, some of them independents, and some owing a nominal allegiance to the Hudson's Bay Company, or the North West. One of them had started a more or less permanent trading post.

Little news of this reached the East, where the American colonies had only recently launched forth as an independent nation but about that time Alexander Mackenzie, backing the old Western dream of Peter Pond against the more conservative stay-at-home partners in Montreal, attempted to win support in England by publishing a book of his travels. It had little effect there, but it found a more than casually in-

terested reader in America. This was scientifically and geographically minded Thomas Jefferson, and as soon as he
licked Aaron Burr for the Presidency in 1801 he did something about it. He knew that Congress could not follow his
thinking into the larger spheres, but the members could understand money, so he convinced them that a quite profitable
fur trade could be diverted to U.S. merchants if they could
wrest the Missouri River country from the slackening hands
of Spain. He procured an appropriation of $2000 for an ex-
pedition to go to those parts and look around. To disguise its
true purpose he called it scientific.

For the task he chose his secretary, twenty-nine-year-old
Meriwether Lewis, a studious and to many an unapproach-
able man, who had seen frontier service serving as a militia-
man in the Whisky Insurrection. Lewis, being solidly realistic,
knew there was a good chance he would not come from the
dangers of the journey alive, so he chose a co-leader, his old
Army friend, thirty-three-year-old William Clark, "a youth of
solid parts and brave as Caesar," brother of the frontier hero
George Rogers Clark.

Things went well from the start. The expedition was
competently planned and equipped. Clark knew what to take
along—and, a more difficult problem, what to leave behind.
When they arrived in St. Louis the need for subterfuge had
ended. The whole of Louisiana Territory had been purchased
from Napoleon. To the Rocky Mountains they were to explore their own nation; all claims beyond, Russian, British,
and now American, were as misty as the Pacific forests.
There was no white settlement in all the miles between
Russian Alaska and Spanish California.

They set out in the spring of 1804, wintered at the
Mandan villages, and reached the Great Falls in time to celebrate the Fourth of July. They reached the Three Forks on
July 27. Much time was spent in the passes of the Bitterroot
Range, but that autumn they dropped down on the Columbia
and spent a sodden winter near tidewater of the Pacific. They
returned the following year. It was then Captain Lewis on a

northern trip of exploration saw the range of mountains which would be named for him. Of greater impact historically, was his encounter with a party of Blackfeet who tried to steal some of his horses. They fought and two of the Indians were left dead. By that autumn Blackfeet all up and down the trail, from the Three Forks to the land of the Sarsi north of Edmonton, knew of the white men who came from St. Louis and that they were enemies. Many in future years were to suffer for it.

The Blackfeet were the most powerful people on the Great North Trail. They held its central region, the best of the buffalo country. The Blackfeet are of Algonkin stock whose relatives are spread across Canada from the Kootenay River of British Columbia to the Atlantic Coast. Traders becoming proficient in the Algonkin tongue had little trouble being understood as they moved from one tribe to another above the forty-ninth parallel. On reaching the Blackfeet they heard what seemed to be a different language. Scholars, however, found it to be Algonkin in a basic sense but that it had developed in a manner which set it far apart. Since the tribe was set squarely on the Great North Trail and had tribal legends of a northern home, The Land of Little Sticks, it was thought they might be the last of their linguistic group to arrive from Asia and that perhaps the Blackfeet dialect was closest to the Asiatic original. Somewhere in Siberia or Mongolia might be found a tribe speaking Blackfeet. No such Asian mother tribe has been found.

The Blackfeet Land of Little Sticks is now occupied by the Chipewyans. These people also have a legend of tribal movement—eastward from the Mackenzie River country. The Chipewyans are an Athabascan linguistic group. Blackfeet regions excepted, the Athabascan people held the Trail all the way from the Seward Peninsula to the Rio Grande. Starting in the north the Khotana and Kuchin tribes occupied central Alaska and to the Mackenzie, with the Yellowknives and Chipewyans down that river to Peter Pond's old post at

Lake Athabasca. In middle Alberta the Sarsi, an Athabascan tribe of only a few villages, met the Blackfeet and became allied with them, taking their ways, exchanging wives, and joining in their sun dances. Early whites believed they were a branch of the Blackfeet, but their Athabascan language indicated the truth. Athabascan speech reappears in the South with the Apaches. All came pushing down the Trail from their Asiatic homeland, and with the arrival of white men they still occupied it. The British Columbian branches of the North Trail were the homelands of Sikanis, Beavers, Carriers, Babines, and others, all small tribes of Athabascan origin; still others can be traced by language as they frayed out by further wandering along the mountain and desert routes to Oregon and California.

We have already seen how the Lewis Range and the continuing mountains of its overthrust form a wall with the Old North Trail of the Blackfeet running along it. When the big cattlemen came to the country, driving their longhorns through the Judith Gap to the Sun and Teton river regions, they found the Indian trail easily recognized by the travois marks dug deeply in the sod. "They drove a broad-gauge wagon," the cattlemen said, marking the fact that the wheels of their chuckwagons would never fit the ruts, but always rode with one side higher and bumpier than the other. There are places where the old travois marks are visible still, if viewed from a distance, as grass-filled depressions, or they can be detected as gullies running counter to the natural erosion patterns of the land. The Old North Trail was also marked by stone monuments, by writing on stone, and by Indian burials. Tepee rings—stones laid around the edges of tepees to hold them down—may still be found at old camping spots along the trail. The midpoint of a tepee ring is usually a pile of stones, which was the fireplace. People have scattered many tepee rings, homesteaders clearing their claims for the plow have loaded them in wagons and stacked them at the fence corners, and the stones of others can be found overgrown by sod. People are often surprised to find tepee rings on the crests of ridges in what appear to be poor camping spots, far from drinking water, and in the full blast of the wind. They speculate whether the camps were so placed as a precaution against surprise attack. Old Indians said such locations were chosen in the spring when the ridges poked high and dry and many snow freshets were close by.

In Alberta the Old North Trail is followed, approximately, by Highway 108, but it turns from the ancient course near the U.S. boundary. A number of Indian trails pass downward into Montana and it is no longer possible to determine which was the Old North, although best guess seems to be that it crossed the international boundary at a point about 20 miles east of Chief Mountain in the northeastern corner of Glacier National Park. It can be located about 10 miles to the east of Babb, Montana. It crosses the Hudson Bay Divide by a depression caused by the head of Hall Coulee where, in the spring, water can be found flowing toward Hudson Bay and the Arctic and toward the Gulf of Mexico from opposite ends of the same ponds. It crossed the North Fork of Milk River, and, continuing in almost a straight line south, crossed the Middle Fork, Dry Fork, Livermore Creek, and the South Fork, always avoiding their deepening valleys and staying to the bench. In the southern sector of the Blackfeet Reservation a number of ridges run east from the precipitous mountains of Glacier Park. Highway 87 turns the flank of Lookout Mountain and heads straight across, but the old trail skirts them on the east and descends into the swampy lowlands of Willow Creek a short distance west of the town of Browning.

Another old Indian trail became a wagon road through Emigrant Gap, a small sag in the hills above the north fork of Milk River. The Gap is about 6½ miles to the east of the main trail. Still another, much used by outlaw traders as well as by the Indians, lies about 5 miles farther to the northeast, and passes through a depression called Whisky Gap. Both gaps, like the sag of Hall Coulee, cut through the Hudson

Bay Divide, although little in the monotonous rolling country indicates so mighty a geographic schism.

The Park-to-Park Highway which runs through Dupuyer and Choteau to Sun River is sometimes considered as following the Old North Trail, but actually the trail ran miles to the west. The Indians, needing ready supplies of wood and water, skirted the mountains as closely as their travois allowed. Today the ranch-to-market roads run down the stream valleys from west to east, and hence only a few jeeps follow the Old North Trail in that section. Farther south, this changes. The Helena–Fort Benton stage crossing of Sun River was said by old freighters to be on the trail. Ruts believed to be ancient travois tracks can be found near the town of Augusta well to the west. The road most nearly following this segment of the Old North Trail is Montana Highway 33 from Choteau to Augusta and Wolf Creek. The trail can be accurately placed in the narrow canyon of Prickly Pear Creek, between the town of Wolf Creek and the Helena Valley. Much of the trail was utilized by the first emigrant wagons in the canyon. It was tough going. The wagons had to be stripped of their more topheavy superstructures, and finally, on the steep banks, to roll along precariously on two or three wheels while being secured by ropes to the trees above. It was then a route to the Montana gold fields for argonauts who came to Fort Benton by river steamer and for the intrepid souls who crossed the prairie from Minnesota. The present highway deviates from the old route in favor of a steep mountain grade. White men find that miles saved in this manner are generally hard come by. New multilane plans promise to erase much of this foolishness and return to the Indian trail exactly.

The trail emerges onto a broad valley near Helena and follows the Missouri River southward. Much of the land thereabouts is lake bed of tertiary age, with slight bulges from the alluvial fans which come down from the Elkhorn Mountains, and nothing to confine a trail to any one place.

The early travelers went according to their whim, or as dictated by grass, water or game. The old mining camp of Radersburg stands near the trail as it swings some miles from the river, passing to the west of the Lombard Hills, making a cut-across the Three Forks, birthplace of the Missouri River.

When Louis Joliet and Père Marquette discovered the Mississippi Joliet wanted to name it the Frontenac for the Governor of New France, while Marquette insisted on Conception because of a vow he had taken to the Virgin, an intransigence which helped save its Indian name. The three rivers which join to make the Missouri had a less happy fate. Lewis and Clark named them for President Jefferson and for Madison and Gallatin, his Secretaries of State and Treasury. As with Sault Ste. Marie, crossing place of the Great Lakes and Cahokia at the mouth of the Missouri, no tribe was permanently in possession of the Three Forks. The place was at all times common ground, or at least battleground. Lewis and Clark found it a corner for the domains of Blackfeet, Crows, Shoshones, and Flatheads.

From Three Forks trails ran in all directions. There was the Old North, and the trail eastward to Yellowstone by which the Crows received trade goods from the Mandan villages and St. Louis, their survival at stake against the Blackfeet. A branch of the Yellowstone Trail, turning before it crossed the Bozeman and Bridger passes, led to the Great Stinking Water of Yellowstone Park. The park area was not a favored hunting ground, but Indians went there, braving its devils, to get sulphur, which was used as a medicine, orpiment and realgar, the sulfides of arsenic, for their brilliant pigments, and obsidian, one of the prized arrowhead materials of the continent. Another major trail went up the Jefferson, turned southwestward on the Beaverhead, and passed over a gently climbing but high divide to the Snake River country and to the Great Salt Lake.

Another favored meeting place of Indians and their trails was near the present site of Twin Bridges, Montana, where the Beaverhead, Ruby, and Big Hole rivers converge within a distance of 4 miles to form the Jefferson. Here again Lewis and Clark busily named the streams, this time with less lasting effect. Although leaving the name Beaverhead unchanged because of Beaverhead Rock, an eminence which bore, perhaps, some vague resemblance to a beaver's head, they changed the Indian names of other streams to the Wisdom, Philanthropy, and Philosophy after what they deemed to be President Jefferson's cardinal virtues. The early trappers, however, named them respectively Big Hole, Willow Creek, and Stinking Water. The Stinking Water, named for numerous hot springs effervescent with hydrogen sulphide gas, was elevated to "Ruby River" by the regional promoters of another day.

Geography made the Blackfeet natural customers of the British. Their trail ended at Three Forks, and their power ranged much farther, being felt in Wyoming and Idaho, but the center of their domain was above the Montana–Alberta boundary. From the days of the Cree traders their source of trade goods was down the Saskatchewan River. The Missouri was the supply line of their enemies. The Missouri's main tributary, the Yellowstone, ran into the heart of Crow country. Lewis on his way out of the country had killed Blackfeet, while Clark, though not making friends with the Crows, had passed safely through their lands and let them steal his horses. Then the St. Louis traders set up business in Crow country, supplying them with arms to kill Blackfeet. This was the Blackfeet point of view. Yet the St. Louis men could not understand why the Blackfeet distrusted them. They blamed it on the British lies and intrigue. They came to regard the British and the Blackfeet to be allies.

Of these "allies" the British were not so sure. Hendry gave a good report on the tribe in 1755, but seventeen years passed before Buckingham House was built at the edge of their country. The expected quick reward in beaver failed to materialize. Then when the trade was being built up to size, a calamity befell the tribe. In 1871 a war party of Piegan

Blackfeet, on its way up the Bow River, sighted a Shoshone encampment near Three Sisters Peaks of what is now Banff National Park. All was quiet, the buffalo-skin lodges arranged without watchmen against the magnificent setting, horses without herders ranging belly-deep in the river grasslands. It seemed all too easy for the wary Blackfeet. The main groups of the Shoshones had been driven far to the south, yet this camp was placed deep in the very heart of Blackfeet domain, and unwatched, apparently defenseless. However, even the most careful scouting revealed no flanking force; the village and all the horses seemed there for the taking, and an attack was made at dawn.

Not a hand was raised against them. The tepees they found to be occupied only by the dead and dying. They were elated. They believed that the powerful medicine possessed by one of their own number had wrought a miracle, striking down the hated Shoshones, rendering them unable to lift a gun or a bow to protect themselves. They sacked the village, killed those still living, took everyone's scalps, and, laden with plunder, driving the Shoshone horses, they returned to their own village located about midway along the trail between Calgary and Edmonton, and staged a gigantic celebration.

About three days later the Piegan war party were struck down by frightening pain and fever to a man. According to the stories of survivors, the blow fell suddenly, and on all at almost the same hour. Soon the entire village felt the plague which turned men black, with grotesquely swollen faces, blind and dying. It was passed on to the other Blackfeet tribes. Terror of the deadly affliction became so great that many fled to the woods; others, feeling its first symptoms, committed suicide. The following year, after the epidemic had run its course, the Hudson's Bay traders estimated that about half of all the Blackfeet had perished.

Smallpox was first recognized in America when a Negro slave with the troops of Cortez came down with the disease, setting off an epidemic which raced through Mexico, exterminating whole tribes, and killing, during the next few years, an estimated 3,500,000 people. Later, the plague was transmitted to the Indians of Massachusetts by the English, and there were other severe outbreaks. Although white populations suffered mortalities of about 25 per cent, the disease was far more virulent among the dark-skinned races. Negroes, Chinese, and Indians, particularly when penned up in their noisome quarters of the time, were in instances cut down almost to the last man. Some Indian tribes managed to escape with only 30 or 40 per cent losses, but the village dwellers such as the Mandans almost always lost more than half their population. The plague had been unknown before the white men and Indians accounted all such afflictions the work of evil spirits, they considered smallpox the white's supreme religious incantation.

At its most deadly the hemorrhagic papules of smallpox blacken the skin. Hence black is associated with the disease, and in declaring smallpox-infected areas taboo, the tribes, as in Africa today, posted warnings in soot and tar. When the religious arrived garbed in black robes the Indians jumped to the obvious conclusion—they had control of smallpox and hence were men it was unwise to offend. The priests did not trade on this power attributed to them, but many were amazed at the wholesale number of their conversions. Their trouble started when they tried to explain Christianity. The idea of loving an enemy did not register at all. Neither did sin and monogamy. When the Blackrobes refused to use their powerful medicine to strike down the Crows and Shoshones the Blackfeet were disappointed. It seemed poor payment for their hospitality. They did not kill the missionaries as some tribes did; they merely lost interest.

Although the priests did not use their supposed smallpox medicine to frighten the tribes, traders were not so ethical. Traders from St. Louis threatened to loose smallpox on Indians who treated them with hostility. When this had the reverse effect of making the Indians take their furs elsewhere, traders on the Missouri spread word that the Canadian posts were infected, that the British had deliberately brought the plague of 1781 in order to kill all the Blackfeet and bring in the Crees, their allies.

The Blackfeet came back strongly from the epidemic. They were a virile people. Food was plentiful. They were well supplied with trade goods, better than any other tribe in the West. Guns, knives, and all manner of other things came not only from the H.B.C. up the Saskatchewan but also from the North West traders of the Athabasca. In 1799, the North West Company built Rocky Mountain House close to the mountains north of Kicking Horse Pass, where the Clearwater River flows into the North Saskatchewan. By the time Lewis and Clark came up the Missouri, the two companies had at least one hundred white men established in various trading posts to the north.

None of this meant that the British could assume Blackfeet friendship. Even after 25 years, when establishing posts they were careful to build on easily defensible promontories, with one side protected by the river, and to surround themselves with ample fortifications. On arrival it was common for them to unload their cannon first and point these outward through temporary cribworks; only then would permanent stockades, gates, and blockhouses be built. When the fort was finished, trade was customarily conducted through iron-barred trade windows, and at all events no more than a limited number of Blackfeet were ever allowed inside at one time. It was a great deal of trouble, but the Blackfeet controlled the greatest remaining beaver resource west of the mountains, and the trade was worth it.

In 1806, when the Lewis and Clark Expedition was on its way home and had passed the mouth of the Yellowstone, two trappers were met coming up the river. These men, named Dixon and Handcock, wanted to know whether there were many beaver in the mountains. The answer was yes, beaver abounded. They were told that everywhere the streams descending from the mountains came steplike because of the brush dams and beaver ponds, each with its colony waiting for the taking, and that the furs were particularly glossy, thick, and fine, some of a chestnut hue and others with the color of pinchbeck gold. A member of the expedition, young John Colter, was particularly enthusiastic. He asked permission from the commanders to join Dixon and Handcock and became the first of the great mountain men.

The trio's trapping expedition was successful. They escaped the notice of the Blackfeet, and next spring Colter, alone, set out by dugout canoe with a cargo of furs for St. Louis. He was not yet to reach civilization, however. On his way he was met by tough and foxy Manuel Lisa, Spanish trader from St. Louis, who had decided to make a foray into the Blackfeet country after talking to Clark. Lisa knew he was lucky to find Colter with an extra season's experience at the headwaters, and he did not let him get away. There is no record that Colter gave him much resistance. He accepted one of the partnerships in the endeavor, and turned around to serve as Lisa's guide.

By this time the Three Forks was known as the center of the best trapping country and the Yellowstone as the best way of reaching it. A portage was required. One left the Yellowstone where it turns sharply south and crosses the pass where Bozeman now stands, but it was no more arduous than portaging the Great Falls, and one avoided the gorge south of the Little Rockies and Bear Paws. Most important, one also avoided the Blackfeet. It was the Blackfeet trade Lisa was looking for, but he could see the wisdom of advancing by degrees, first placing himself at the edge of their country rather than in its heartland.

The journey by keelboat had been a long one. Lewis and Clark in their first season reached only the Mandan villages. Summer waned, turning the cottonwood bottoms of the Yellowstone a golden yellow. It was too late for the Three Forks that year, so, reaching the mouth of the Bighorn, which flows in from the south, they stopped and built some log huts, calling the place Fort Lisa. It was Montana's first white settlement.

From many viewpoints it was a shrewd location and probably one of the alternatives recommended by Clark. It was at a meeting of the rivers, and of the trails. The Yellowstone Trail, which started at the Three Forks, ran eastward past the mouth of the Bighorn. The main sweep of the Great North Trail came down from the northwest and crossed over, heading up the valley to the Little Bighorn with a long view of the bare hills where Custer would fall, toward the stone houses and foundations which perhaps were Mexican, the future Bozeman Road and cattle trail, and a succession of historic sites then yet to be. So Lisa set up business at the crossing of the trails, and he sent Colter out to drum up business.

Colter traveled toward the south and located a large band of Crows on Wind River in west-central Wyoming. They received him well and were glad to hear about the fort. Falling in with them, he crossed over the Grand Teton Range to Pierre's Hole, near which it was his fortune to distinguish himself fighting off an attack by Blackfeet. He was recognized as a white man, and later identified as one of those at Fort Lisa. If any more proof of American enmity had been needed, this supplied it.

After recovering from a leg wound, Colter headed north and was the first white man known to have viewed the steaming and sulphurous wonders of Yellowstone Park. Colter, a truthful young man, gained the reputation of being one of the world's great liars when he subsequently told about it. Word of the region had in fact found its way out before. Brigadier General James Wilkinson, when posted in St. Louis, had heard tales of the Yellowstone as early as 1805. Late in that year he sent a Captain Stoddard with some Indians to visit President Jefferson and with them went a buffalo hide on which was mapped the Missouri "and Rivers Plate and Lycorne or Pierre Juane . . . among other things a little incredible, a volcano is distinctly described on the Yellow Stone river."

Traveling across the park toward the northeast, Colter found few Indians except the "diggers" who inhabited the area. It was not favored by Indians, probably because of its canyon-cut and extremely mountainous character, or because it was the home of fire-breathing devils, "the place where the Great Spirit had not finished building the world."

It remained Lisa's purpose to establish at the Three Forks. In the spring he sent Colter and John Potts to trap and look for a suitable location. In July they were discovered by a band of Blackfeet. Potts was killed but Colter they took captive. To amuse themselves without giving him too much chance, the warriors stripped Colter naked and set him free like a rabbit to the hounds, the fastest runner to have the privilege of killing him. Colter estimated that he ran 6 miles. He ran until blood spurted from his nostrils and he had outdistanced all but one of the Indians. About to be overtaken, Colter stopped suddenly, wrestled with the warrior, and killed him with his own weapons. Then, making it on to the Jefferson where it flowed deep and cold under a pack of driftlogs, he jumped in.

He recovered while lying among the driftwood with only his nostrils showing. The Blackfeet, enraged, hunted the river and the brush shallows. He reported that at times he could feel them joggling the logs under which he lay. Finally night settled and he crept out. Naked, shivering in the 40-degree chill of the mountain night, he headed eastward. He took to the hills south of the Three Forks and crossed the Gallatin Range. After seven days, unable to get any food except frogs, insects, and green berries, he staggered into the fort on the Bighorn.

When it became clear the beaver of the Three Forks were not to be obtained through trade, Andrew Henry and Pierre Menard, shareholders in Lisa's company, built a fort and put a party of their own men to trapping. The yield was good.

Although they had arrived late in the season, it was estimated that as many as 300 packs could be taken before the furs went out of prime the middle to the last of May. A pack weighed 100 pounds and contained an average of 80 pelts.

Prime beaver at that time was worth $600 a pack, and hence the expected take would have a value of $180,000, a very large reward in those days when St. Louis merchants hired clerks for about 10 cents per hour. But these happy expectations were not to be realized. On the twelfth of April, just when the beaver were being harvested in good numbers, the Blackfeet struck. Five of the trappers were killed and their outfits taken. The others were afraid to leave the post except in large groups, and this interfered seriously with the number of beaver taken. One man alone can trap out a dam as easily as a dozen. Menard tried to make contact with the Blackfeet to tell them he would gladly start a trading post in their country, perhaps at the Great Falls, and bring them many guns to use against the Crow, Flathead, and Shoshone, but no council took place. The Indians remained in the locality.

Trapping impossible, there was nothing left but to abandon the post. Henry decided to go south and try his luck over the Snake River divide. It was the land of the Shoshones, enemies of the Blackfeet. He led his party to the Madison headwaters, and over either Red Rock or Raynolds Pass. On his way a number of horses were stolen by the friendly Crows. He passed the lake which bears his name, and dropped down through a wide, almost flat coniferous forest. He left the forest and came out on the plains, the edge of the vast lava fields that cover much of southern Idaho. There he built a post and waited for the Shoshones to come to trade.

His location in one sense was good. The main north-south trail from the Beaverhead to Salk Lake ran past his door. Half a century later the first wagons would pull that route from the California Trail to the gold camps of Montana. To the east was the Indian trail to Pierre's Hole and the Teton Pass to Wyoming. But in winter the place was a bleak survival. Only 60 miles away, at West Yellowstone, a temperature of 71 degrees below zero has been recorded. Nothing stopped the wind as it blew through the leafless cottonwoods and the sagebrush. There were fewer streams and fewer beaver than in the north, and the Snake was not famed as buffalo country. Henry sent out and found the Shoshones and suggested they trap to earn guns, power, and ball to protect themselves against the Blackfeet. The Shoshones wanted guns, but they considered the capture of small furs squaw's work. In the spring Henry left and returned to St. Louis, his men scattering to become the first independent Mountain Men of the West.

Henry went east in 1811. The War of 1812 soon closed the Mississippi, ruining the beaver trade. A mining industry was just getting started southwest of St. Louis, supplying the West's brisk demand for bullet lead. Henry went there and tried his luck. His luck was not great except for making the acquaintance of William H. Ashley . . . Ashley, brilliant and enterprising, became interested in the beaver bonanza, and the two men were in the field in 1822. Failing on the Missouri because of Arikara and Blackfeet opposition, they pioneered an east-west route which would later become the Oregon Trail. The northern route, after Henry's experience of 1810–1811, fell into disuse. The Hudson's Bay Company and the North West consolidated, and with their allies the Crees, Assiniboins, Gros Ventre, and Blackfeet held the north. Jim Bridger, a footloose blacksmith's apprentice, went to work for Ashley (who had become the leading partner) and discovered the Great Salt Lake, heretofore only a half-credited Indian legend. By 1827 Jedediah Smith had explored a frightening mountain route to California. Starting in the country south of Yellowstone and moving south, the company's main activity was first on the Green River and later centered in northern Utah. In five years the beaver of all that vast area were harvested. A few pelts still came, but in numbers hardly enough to bother with. It was time for the more adventurous again to look up the Great North Trail to the lands of the Blackfeet.

In St. Louis Ashley's success was not unnoticed. The trading and financial king at that time was Pierre Chouteau, Jr., grandson of city-founder Auguste Chouteau. A man of cultural attainments, polished and witty, fluent in French,

Spanish, and English, he nonetheless had spent much time in the wilderness and could be as ruthless as the fur trade demanded. With John Jacob Astor and others he had already taken over the trade of Minnesota, the southern Great Lakes, and the lower Missouri. Now his American Fur Company looked to the Rocky Mountains. He sent trappers to the Ashley rendezvous, the yearly conclaves at which the Mountain Men secured trade goods and sold their furs, their purpose being to spy out the best beaver lands and if possible set up a competing rendezvous. He also moved up the Missouri to the edge of the Gros Ventre–Blackfeet country, and established a post called Fort Union at the mouth of the Yellowstone.

Some of the Blackfeet chiefs were asked to visit Fort Union as guests of the management. They sampled the United States brand of firewater and pronounced it far stronger then the 10 per cent rum the British provided. Following this, Mr. James Kipp, a talented trader from Fort Union, was able to travel upriver and complete a trade for no fewer than 4000 beaver pelts, as well as many smaller furs, a rich harvest. Soon the company was allowed to move into the Blackfeet country and establish Fort McKenzie, named for the kingly Kenneth McKenzie, head of the upper Missouri division of the company, near the mouth of the Marias River just across a wedge of bare dirt hills from where the village of Loma, Montana, now stands.

It was not easy to find men willing to accept company employ in the heart of Blackfeet country, and to Fort McKenzie was sent a man of violent temper and unmatched physical prowess named Alexander Harvey. He was described as being six feet tall and weighing about 170 pounds, not tremendous, but no man could stand against him. He was reasonable when sober, but he had a taste for whisky and, as this formed the chief trade item at McKenzie, he had at hand an abundant supply. Drunk, he terrorized Indians and whites alike. Finally, so many complaints reached St. Louis that Chouteau decided to discharge him. Fearing to leave him in the country to wreak vengeance, he summoned him by letter to St. Louis. The letter arrived shortly before Christmas, and he set out alone with his rifle and a large dog on whose back he packed his sleeping robes, and two and a half months later he reached St. Louis. He had walked almost all the way. Chouteau was so impressed he decided to keep him on. Harvey forgave no one. Returning to his old domains, he hunted out, one by one, all the men he considered responsible for his near downfall and revenged himself using fists, gun, and tomahawk.

Harvey's lust for revenge, although in a different context, caused Fort McKenzie's abandonment. One cold January afternoon a party of young Blackfeet, the hoofs of their horses laced in rawhide to protect them from the snow which gathered thin but harsh on the prairies, crossed over the ice-locked Missouri River to the fort and asked admittance. They were not bent on trade, they had no furs, their journey had been of a predatory nature aimed at the Crows, but as their people had received repeated assurances of undying brotherhood on the part of the American Fur Company, it never occurred to them that they would be left out in the snow instead of being invited in for food and a few drams of liquor. (The Blackfeet, unlike other tribes, had come to believe that liquor was strictly a convivial potion, given away by the traders rather than purchased, the British to the north having made it a policy to distribute liquor as a good-will gesture before the trade.) However, Alexander Harvey and his associate in command, Chardon, kept the gate barred and offered their visitors no hospitality whatsoever. In retaliation, the Blackfeet stole a pig which had been turned out to forage near the river. Domestic animals were highly valued in the upriver posts, and when the white men saw their pig being carried off squealing, they gave chase. The upshot was that the pig was butchered, and the Blackfeet, waiting in ambush, also knocked off one of the pursuers.

White men were being killed by the Indians all the time. A few years later a census was compiled of all the white men killed by Indians in Chouteau County, the area compris-

ing about an eighth of the territory of Montana where Mc-
Kenzie was located, and it looked like the voter's registration
rolls, with nobody pretending that more than half the victims were included. But the cruel and impudent execution
of their pig left Harvey and Chardon intent on revenge. An
opportunity of sorts was presented about a month later when
a party of Piegan Blackfeet arrived to trade. They were obviously peaceful, and had their women and children along.
While they waited unsuspecting at the gate, Chardon and
Harvey had the cannon loaded with pellets; then, ordering
the gates flung open, it was blasted waist high into their
midst. Ten Piegans were killed outright. The others fled and
escaped, but most of the wounded were overtaken and
hacked to death with hatchets. The Chardon-Harvey forces
scalped all the victims, and their revenge was celebrated by
whooping revelry far into the night.

This massacre was not calculated to help the fur business. Fort McKenzie had to be abandoned. Kipp was again
called in. He built a small post on the banks of the Missouri,
opposite the mouth of the Judith. It was generally called Fort
Chardon. Later its location was moved to Brule Bottom.
Both locations were unsuccessful.

Before any of these events, and as early as 1832, when
the first permanent post was built at the Marias, there were
signs that the beaver trade was on the downgrade. In the
summer of that year, even while the cottonwoods were being
squared for the walls of the fort, Astor in Europe was writing,
"I very much fear beaver will not sell well very soon unless
very fine. It appears that they make hats of silk in place of
beaver." From the south, traders were moving into the Blackfeet country as far as the Judith Gap, following the main
route from the Yellowstone and the Bighorn to Great Falls,
while Bridger and others trapped cautiously in the Beaverhead. No post was ever established permanently at the Three
Forks in the years of the Blackfeet power, and indeed the
tribe was never wholly won over or defeated by the whites. A
second smallpox infection, this one carried by passengers on

an American Fur Company steamboat, laid waste the tribe, as it did most of the tribes of the Northwest. Roving, some Blackfeet still reached the Three Forks, but most of the weakened tribe pulled northward along the edge of the mountains where their reservations are found in the United States and Canada today. Their unconquered state is even, in a sense, recognized legally. The Blackfeet are unique in that they have a constitution ratified by Congress acknowledging what is termed "sovereign state powers," and the tribe to this day stands up against efforts to diminish it.

When beaver fell in importance, the chief income of the Blackfeet lands was derived from buffalo hides. These were salted and baled and ran to large tonnages. The St. Louis traders, with steamboats and the mighty Missouri at their disposal, now had an insuperable advantage over their rivals to the north. Steamboats were tried on the Saskatchewan, and some of them plied its dangerous currents all the way to Edmonton, but downstream there was no St. Louis to receive them. Buffalo hides could be taken to Hudson Bay, but it was an expensive operation.

Fort Benton became the great buffalo port of the West. It was the head of navigation on the Missouri, about 25 miles downstream from the last of the Great Falls. Later it became an outlet to the Montana gold fields, and to prairie Canada via the Whoop-Up and Fort Walsh trails.

Chapter 6

When Martin Van Buren, who had been both President and Vice-President of the United States, sent the newspapers a letter opposing the annexation of Texas, he lost the support of many fellow Democrats, enough to cost him the party nomination of 1844. The two-thirds rule then governed the convention. It had been used once before to insure Van Buren's nomination. This time it worked against him. Many delegates pledged to Van Buren found this Texas stand distasteful, and these were glad to continue with a rule which was sure to defeat him. The other leading candidate, Lewis Cass, one-time Governor of Michigan Territory and recent ambassador to France, could not even come close to the two thirds, so the convention, left in a stalemate, chose a dark horse—the first in American convention history—James K. Polk, a defeated Governor of Tennessee, of whose Texas and general expansionist attitudes there was no doubt. The platform adopted by the convention said that U.S. title to the whole of Oregon was "clear and unquestionable." No portion of it, it said, should be ceded to England or any other power; "the reoccupation of Oregon and the reannexation of Texas at the earliest practicable period are great American measures, which the Convention recommends to the cordial support of the Democracy of the Union." (By re-occupation and re-annexation the Convention referred to the fact that John Jacob Astor had established Astoria before the arrival of the North West Company in Oregon, and that Texas was assumed to be an original part of the Louisiana Territory.) All this was backed by Polk without qualification, and he went much further, first in private and later in public utterance.

In the preceding election, won by the Whigs, a brilliant catch-phrase was introduced in "Tippecanoe and Tyler Too." This time the Democrats stole the fire with "Fifty-four Forty or Fight," demanding Oregon to a latitude which would include all of the Fraser and Columbia drainages. Against Fifty-four Forty the Whigs with Henry Clay were left with nothing better to shout than "Hooray for Clay." Clay was a popular personality and Polk was neither well known nor well liked, but Polk had the popular point and was elected by a narrow margin.

What the shrewd Polk really had his eye on was neither Texas nor Oregon, which would fall to America through force of colonization anyway, but California. He said little about it because Texas and Oregon nicely balanced slave and free; but after annexing the Texas Republic and fighting the war with Mexico which was its inevitable consequence, he saw to it that California and the Southwest were taken first by military force, than "purchased" for $15 million. Oregon was divided between the United States and Britain at the Forty-Ninth parallel, the long-established northern boundary which had been mapped in the East by David Thompson, although Polk still wanted to insist on 54 degrees 40 minutes, and might well have bluffed England into agreeing.

There was no unanimity about Polk's wisdom in purchasing California. The price of 15 million was branded ridiculous for a coast that would be forever inaccessible beyond mountains and deserts, no more a natural part of the nation than a piece of the moon. Then his critics subsided: Gold was discovered. The rush to California was on.

The celebrated nugget of moderate size which James Marshal picked from the millrace at Coloma was by no means the first gold discovery in the West. For twenty-five years wagons had been hauling Yankee merchandise to Santa Fe and coming back with native gold and silver, but there had been no rush to discover the mines. In 1804 gold was discovered in Colorado somewhere near the later camps of Florence and Canon City by a lost trapper named James Purcell. Later it was well known in fur-trading circles that gold existed in a wide area near the headwaters of the Platte, the later Cherry Creek diggings beyond Denver. No great excitement was generated, at least not for another twenty years. But gold in California stirred the emotions and set off the greatest transcontinental movement known in the annals of mankind.

There were a number of reasons for this. The California deposits were rich and extensive, but that was not known until later. The human tidal wave was well along before they were proved greater than those of Colorado or New Mexico. Probably the main reason lay in the fact that the war and the recent expansion of the national boundaries had renewed the Americans' interest in distant places. Then, California was a storied land. It was foreign and strange tales had been told about it. It was a tropical land beyond the highest mountains. It was Spanish, a word that always stood for treasure. And the administration in Washington, looking for vindication, made much of the discovery to show how quickly the expenditure of 15 million would be recovered with profit.

The movement to California rose and became a wave across the Plains, around Cape Horn, and by sea and land via the Isthmus of Panama. It was so great that, in 1852, after being admitted as a state, California cast more votes for President than did Missouri. The gold rush came from all sections of the country and drew from all classes, slave and free. Many a master came with his black man who, on reaching California, was likely to become his partner. It was so representative of the nation that when the Presidential candidates Franklin Pierce and Winfield Scott split 53 per cent and 47 per cent nationally, California turned up with that exact proportion, so it could have been truly said that, instead of Maine, "as California goes so goes the nation."

California was no flash in the pan. Its gold region kept extending with new discoveries until it reached from Mariposa County, in the middle of the state, to the Trinity River inland from Humboldt Bay, a distance of nearly 300 miles. The Trinity River deposits, while seldom rich, were so gigantic in size that they have kept men working them until the 1950s, when the fixed price of gold lagged so far behind rising costs that further mining was rendered unprofitable. In the south, ancient stream gravels were found capped by lava flows and mined by drifting. Deposits too low in grade to dig manually were washed down by giant blasts of water, so whole miles of ground, in depths to a hundred feet, were carried over the new farm lands, and the fine clay of the Mariposa slate could be detected far out in the Pacific. But chiefly the mother lodes were found. In many ways they were more remarkable than the placers.

The Mother Lode proper was not a single vein but a series of linked veins in a strip about a mile wide running north and south straight across the foothills through Mariposa, Tuolumne, Calaveras, Amador, and Eldorado counties, a distance of about 130 miles. Similar, less obviously defined systems of veins were the Serpentine Belt, 70 miles long, and a belt through Placer, Nevada, and Sierra counties passing through Washington and terminating near Downieville. And there were camps phenomenally rich in gold quartz associated with none of these systems at Grass Valley, Ophir,

Nevada City, and elsewhere. But gold in quartz and under the torrents of the hydraulic giants was big business. The poor man's bonanzas soon were gone. By the late 1850s there were jobs to be had working in the new, heavily capitalized mines, but California had attracted fortune-hunters, not job-seekers. Men fanned out through the forests and mountains following the gold streaks north until they disappeared under the Oregon lava beds. The high Sierra and the deserts to the east were not encouraging. The Comstock silver excitement was still a couple of years away. Then gold was reported on the Fraser River of British Columbia.

The timing was perfect. Also, the geography of British Columbia was right. It seemed arrestingly like that of California. The Fraser, like the Sacramento, flowed south-ward through tremendous mountains and turned sharply westward to the sea. Both had famous canyons. The bars of both were rich in gold, the Fraser significantly reported to be the richer. With loud hosannahs, large segments of the California population pulled stakes and set out for the Fraser.

British Columbia had only recently been severed from Oregon Territory by the ambitious Polk administration. England had interested itself enough to dispatch some naval units to that part of the globe, and a colonization scheme was under way, but the real authority rested in the Hudson's Bay Company and its head man in the West, big James Douglas. Douglas had been sent to the Fraser by Dr. John McLough-lin, the famous chief company factor of Oregon. When Mc-Loughlin decided to remain in the newly created U.S. terri-tory, Douglas became the Company's leading representative on the Pacific Coast, his headquarters at Victoria, on the southern tip of Vancouver Island.

British Columbia, after the first years when sea otter were in abundance and the beaver bonanza taken, was not particularly productive of furs. Douglas had a more immedi-ate problem than lack of furs, however. The Company's transport was set up to use the Columbia River and the ocean port at its mouth. Now the international boundary sliced directly across the old route about 25 miles south of Okanagan Lake. According to the treaty signed June 15, 1846, the Hudson's Bay Company retained its property south of the line and was protected in its rights to navigate the Columbia. Douglas knew it was necessary to isolate the area from its dependence on Oregon, or it too would be lost to the Americans. Soon the authorities in Oregon started levying duties. Immigrants poured in and the Indians rose up and there were reports of a massacre at Walla Walla. Douglas thereupon sent out one of the Company's last pathfinders, Alexander Anderson of Fort Alexandria, to hunt a new route across the mountains from east to west. After several trials and failures, a way was found by way of the Coquihalla River, a stream cutting west and south through the British Columbian Cascades to join the Fraser below its near-impassable canyon. A post called Hope was built there, and the new brigade route was named the Hope Trail.

Douglas now had a trail which could be used at least during the summer months, a river route suitable for steamboats reaching 80 miles into the interior, and a bastion at Victoria from which he could control both the entrance to Fraser River and Puget Sound. But just when he felt safe against a new push of Americans, gold was discovered in California.

Douglas was a realistic man. He knew there was nothing he could do about the gold rush. If the excitement moved to his domain it was bound to injure the fur business. However, it presented some opportunities also. The Company had a coal mine, a lumber mill, and a store, all on tidewater. He had been saddled with a colonization and agricultural experiment by the Colonial Office in London. Even the farms might pay off. The market was even better than he expected. There was no need to take his goods to California; the merchants of San Francisco, desperate for almost everything, came to him. There was a not unexpected problem: most of his employees left. "Tales of the wondrous stores of wealth discovered in the new El Dorado have captivated all minds and disgusted them with the moderate rewards of common-place industry," he wrote the head office.

Douglas made out by using Sandwich Islanders and Indians in place of the French Canadians who had gone south. Then he had to face a new problem—there was gold on the Fraser.

It was not news to Douglas. Employees of the Company had been coming in with small quantities of gold even before the rush to California. There had been a discovery in 1855, at Fort Colville, across the boundary in U.S. territory, where the Pend Oreille River plunged into the Columbia, a place now submerged beneath the waters of Grand Coulee reservoir. A rush started, but the district was not rich, so a number of the miners moved on, some of them to the Thompson River in British Columbia. At the same time Douglas' old employees began showing up, not to work for him again but to jawbone supplies and go prospecting the Fraser. Soon there were reports of strikes on both rivers, and in the summer of 1856 the Company records showed 115 pounds of gold arriving at Victoria. The total for British Columbia was undoubtedly much larger, however, because many of the miners were trading down the Okanagan Trail or at the post in Colville. By 1857 the miners from the Thompson country were meeting those from Victoria in the Fraser Canyon, and there, in the deep holes and the bars revealed by the falling waters of late summer, the first bonanza finds were made. It was then that the news reached California.

Although in 1857 Douglas wrote the Company in London that he had no doubt many gold-seekers would arrive next season for the Fraser, no one could have foreseen the immensity of the human wave which washed up from the south. It was estimated that 40,000 left California. Additional large numbers came from Oregon and from the Eastern states, while the Empire and foreign lands sent contingents by sea. To little Victoria the rush came with a sudden impact. It was a bright, peaceful morning and the residents of the town were just coming from church services when they saw a sternwheel boat, its decks jammed with passengers and heaped with equipment, churning in from the Sound. It tied up at the dock and roughly garbed men poured ashore, dragging their outfits, armed against their neighbors and the wilderness. The town's Sabbath quiet was filled with strange accents and the clump of heavy boots. Quickly their boat, the *Commodore,* took on fuel and set out for San Francisco and another load. The new arrivals fell to buying out the local supplies of several commodities on a rapidly rising market. They looked for transportation to the mainland. Although by the map Victoria was far closer to the Fraser than any other port, it was still inaccessible across the unquiet waters of the Strait of Georgia which separates Vancouver Island from the mainland. Anyway, the river was not navigable at that season. Even had riverboats been available they would have been forced to wait for the ice to clear and the spring floods to subside. Meanwhile more fortune hunters arrived—and more.

Douglas managed to feed his new residents and keep them under control, but nobody worried about the thousands who made landfall in the region of Seattle. Dumped at some sawmill dock, or on any handy shore, they found themselves marooned by estuaries, rivers, salt flats, and forest, with perhaps only the rudest notion as to where the Fraser lay. All the lumber of the region was quickly snapped up by boatbuilders. Steamboat captains expecting to take on payloads of lumber for the return voyage found not a stick to be had. When they tried to return empty they were unable to round up crews, all their men having jumped ship to join the stampede. Such boats perforce had to carry passengers to the Fraser or go out of business. Many parties came overland from Oregon, even from California. They came on foot or with packtrains, and some got their wagons through as far as present-day Tacoma. There a lumber mill, earlier burned by Indians, had gone back into business, sawing planks for boats capable of making the journey up Puget Sound to the Fraser, a distance of 125 miles. The huddle of Fort Steilacoom became a city of tents as men built boats and rafts or sought other passage northward. Indians with canoes became temporarily wealthy, and one of them traded boats for whisky, started a saloon, and claimed to be the only Indian in the vicinity of present-day Seattle who had corrupted the whites with alcohol.

On Vancouver Island the experimental farms started showing a profit. All the H.B.C. enterprises except furs were in good shape. Douglas had a hard time keeping labor at the coal mine and sawmills, but everything he had went at high prices. Waterfront and business locations sold early. A governor had been sent over from England in 1849, but left after a couple of years when no provision was made to establish his administration. Douglas was then named Governor of Vancouver Island. When the gold rush came he named himself Governor of British Columbia also, and began charging each miner a monthly license of one guinea, slightly over $5. The Americans were very bitter about paying this, but Douglas succeeded in collecting from about 10,000. Getting the following months' fees from prospectors scattered throughout the wilderness proved a bit more of a problem, but the initial $50,000 was a welcome addition to his treasury.

Daily there were reports of gold discoveries up the river. They indicated that the wealth of the Fraser was likely to exceed even the most optimistic expectations. A number of bars beyond the post at Yale were already said to be paying miners at the rate of $75 a day, with added riches coming in sight with each hourly drop of the river. At the river mouth, where the steamboats waited for navigable water, the passengers clamored to leave but the captains refused. Reports kept arriving. One strike in the canyon itself was said to be paying its discoverers $1000 per man per day. "Wages"—run-of-the-river diggings—were reported to exist everywhere and to yield about $25 a day.

At last the boats set out. The strikes at the foot of Fraser Canyon proved not all fiction. Hill's Bar, for example, looked for a while like one of the major gold discoveries of all time. As the river fell, nuggets were actually picked out of the moss. The first boats arrived just as Hill's Bar was displaying gold in its greatest prodigality. Stampede madness then reached its height. At Yale, head of navigation, the Indians who had quit hunting and trapping to wash gold found they could make still more money packing supplies. They received an initial 40 cents per pound for a task that the Company had for decades expected them to perform for their board and keep. The price rose to 70 cents, then a dollar. Farther into the wilderness were Indians who neither mined nor packed but spent their time raiding the miners, or, offering their services as guides, fabricated tales of gold and led their charges into ambush, or simply stole what they could and left the whites to their fate. One group was driven inside a cave and kept there starving for more than a month, living on stray porcupines. A favorite trick of the British Columbia Indians was to capture white men, rob them of all they had, and turn them loose naked. Some of the Californians who had been charged $5 a month for the privilege of mining in British Columbia claimed that the Company was purchasing back from Indians the outfits it had sold in the first place, thus keeping its stock up.

By July, these difficulties notwithstanding, miners were at work all along the river. Color was everywhere, but one dug deeper and found nothing. This was a baffling thing. In California, when the river bars showed good color, one dug down from 4 to 60 feet and found major concentrations at bedrock. In California the gold was so heavy it worked its way into the bedrock itself, so that sometimes it formed an ore, and nearly everywhere in the placers the rock crevices were rich enough to justify the labor of breaking up the top few inches and washing it through the sluices. But Fraser River gold stayed topside. A large bulk of it was taken from a layer of fine sand or a dense sandy clay, less than a foot beneath the surface gravel.

Much of the Fraser gold was an illusion. Gold, while soft, is a tough metal and lends itself to almost limitless division. Gold-beaters are able to thin it until it flutters in air. Flakes of gold worth as little as one-thousandth of a cent are easily recognizable to the naked eye. With the aid of a 50-cent hand lens, one can see colors worth no more than one ten-thousandth of a cent. At Gold Beach in Oregon miners had captured colors running 600 to the cent, but they used mercury to amalgamate it. There grew a belief that the Fraser gold was of a different composition than that of the South, lighter and hence unable to work its way down through the gravel or even to sink readily to the bottom of a pan. Many an early-day miner in Idaho and Montana, veteran of the Fraser fiasco, maintained to the end of his days that the stuff was not gold at all but a gold-colored mica, a scaly brilliant vermiculite common in the region.

Anyone fortunate enough to win a mosshide poke of the Fraser metal could show that it weighed just as heavily as the California variety. In time, the unwillingness of British Columbia gold to gravitate to the bedrock of streams became understood. About the time of the Fraser rush, a Swiss biologist and part-time glacialist, J. L. R. Agassiz, was studying the geology of eastern North America, correlating its ice-age phenomena with those noted in Europe and locating its dome of origin at Hudson Bay. Dawson and others in the Canadian Geological Survey later traced rocks carried by the Hudson Bay dome to the overthrust wall of the Rockies in Alberta where it met, or came within a few miles of meeting, the outpouring rubble of the British Columbia dome, and (as already mentioned) there are the layers of rock in the Flathead Valley and at Spokane, and the unknown depths which scatter the floor of the North Pacific, all British Columbian in origin. Much of the gold went with it, and can be found, traces to the pan, churned and diluted in miles of barren rubble. Like the diamonds of Ontario, the gold of Fraser River was found sprinkled everywhere, but seldom in concentrations of much persistence. Given time, a geologic age or two beyond our present, British Columbia's drifts and moraines may be re-sorted, the bulk of its gold again concentrated at bedrock. Had man come along 10 or 20 million years later in the earth's history he might have found it a true rival of California. But in the mid-nineteenth century there were only the near-surface, mudbar skiffs of color, brought down little by little by the yearly floods of the Fraser. They still come, and to this day miners with pans, rockers, and a device peculiar to the region known as a grizzly, recover it.

Nowhere in the West had so much gold been seen and so little recovered as that first season of the rush to the Fraser. When mining got under way, people everywhere had small amounts of gold, but only a few had very much. It was rare to find anyone with a claim which yielded more than $5 per shift. Prices of staples, however, were very high. Beans and flour ran from 50 cents per pound upward. Before the close of summer, disappointed miners flowed out of the Fraser by all the trails they had used to get in, and by several others discovered in the meantime. An estimated 4000 returned to San Francisco by mid-August, denouncing the Fraser. Bitterly angry men gathered in Victoria, and Douglas had to call on a British naval unit to put down a riot. Many without money for passage home got as far as Puget Sound and shacked up there in the stampede towns, attempting to survive on game and quahogs. Feeling ran high against James Douglas, the company he represented, and Great Britain. It was said that Douglas had perpetrated a hoax, spreading false reports of Fraser gold in order to collect license fees and sell merchandise. The winter before, anticipating a small rush, Douglas had stocked heavily. His action had probably prevented widespread famine; now his foresight was pointed to as proof of treachery. During the summer, miners' meetings had assumed the rude and direct administration of justice in the river camps. Since nearly all the camps were dominated by U.S. citizens there was a cry for a military force to come up and establish the Stars and Stripes. Fifty-four Forty could become a reality. But nobody on the U.S. side paid heed.

As for Douglas, he had no time to answer American charges. He kept count along the Fraser, and knew that although large numbers had left the country, many thousands remained. News from the interior indicated that some had penetrated the land to great distances, prospecting the headwaters of the river to Fort George, end of the cut-across trail which connects mid-British Columbia with the Liard. He knew the travelers had been too busy hunting gold to hunt anything else. Hardly any of them had laid in such Indian larders as meat and fish. Supplies were moving up the old Indian trail through the canyon, but at great cost. Beans worth 10 cents per pound at Yale had now increased to a minimum of 80 cents per pound at the upper end of the canyon. White men who watched the Indians in their job of transport considered a charge of 70 cents per pound cheap. At some of the cliff passages the old trail rose as high as 800 feet above the water. Often there was no trail at all, and fronts of sheer rock were crossed by means of suspension bridges. An Indian suspension bridge consisted of a long, slim, and limber pine trunk hung on ropes. Fifty-odd years before, tough old Simon Fraser, miserly with words and possessing scant sympathy for man's weakness, was so appalled at the canyon passage he was moved to write:

> I have been for a long period among the Rocky Mountains, but have never seen anything like this country. It is so wild that I cannot find words to describe our situation at times. We had to pass where no human being should venture; yet in those places there is a regular footpath impressed, or rather indented upon the very rocks by frequent traveling. Besides this, steps which are formed like a ladder or the shrouds of a ship, by poles hanging to one another and crossed at certain distances by twigs, the whole suspended from the top

to the foot of immense precipices and fastened at both extremities to stones and
trees, furnish a safe and convenient passage to the natives; but we, who had not
the advantage of their education and experience, were often in imminent danger
when obliged to follow their example.

A mule trail had been built, but it necessitated fording
the river, and many animals were swept away with their cargoes. At best the canyon supply line barely kept up with day-
to-day needs. And very little could be expected to get
through after the first big snow. So, starting shortly after the
middle of July, Douglas enlisted the assistance of the men he
found along the lower Fraser, about five hundred of them,
and laid out a plan for a freight route which would commence at Harrison Lake, about sixty miles up the river from
its mouth, and provide a boat and packtrain route to Lillooet,
main camp at the upper end of the canyon.

Working long hours, their willingness increased by the
fact that they were engaged in a mission of mercy, Douglas'
volunteers put through what became known as the Harrison
Trail at the rate of around five miles a day. Boat-builders preceded them, and the freight was right behind. With the first
snow flurries it was done. The Indian packers at Yale were
outflanked, their lush times vanished, and the price of flour
down from a high of $1.60 per pound to a mere 40 cents, or
even lower.

That winter and for the next season, it appeared that
James Douglas had licked the problem of supply to the gold
fields of British Columbia. The population was thinning out
as more and more gave up and looked toward the diggings of
Washington Territory. The miners learned to shift for themselves and devote part of their summer to hunting and fishing. Some of them had married squaws, a great aid in the
struggle for survival. But it was only a lull.

That first year some of the miners got as far as Fort

George, at the main forks of the Fraser. The year following they prospected down those forks to the headwaters. One group, on reaching the Columbia–Fraser Divide west of the mountains of Jasper, started back for a winter's grubstake at Lillooet, crossing the range of low mountains someone had named the Cariboo. The way was blocked by Quesnel Lake, a long, branching body of water shaped something like a ginseng root. They decided to build rafts and pole their way around its shallow edge. . . .

Lake Quesnel is 50 miles long. The land about is not rugged, there are swamps and thick overburden. It is obviously unfavorable for gold. But color can be found almost everywhere. Not a great deal, but a few fine flakes. Late as it was, some of the men that first year were encouraged to follow a stream to the south. Rich color was found near Horsefly Lake. It lay just under the gravel surface, against a layer of dense blue clay. They needed no hard-to-get mining equipment. Working with a pan and a shovel, one miner recovered $100 worth of gold in a single day.

The autumn freeze was upon them. A meeting was called and men selected to go outside for supplies. They were admonished against breathing a word about the Cariboo, but it was impossible to buy in winter quantities without letting the gold be seen, and the Cariboo gold didn't look like Fraser gold, or have the same value. They told a few of their friends, and, as always happened, these told some of theirs, and before freezeup the rush to the Cariboo was on.

At first it did not cause Douglas much concern. The men were mostly from the Fraser. The new find in east-middle British Columbia did not seem attractive to the once-bitten men from California or from the new camps in Idaho. In mid-America a great many people were disrupted by hard times and the border fighting in Kansas; they were up and rolling, but they had *Pikes Peak or Bust* painted on their wagons and couldn't have reached the Cariboo had they wanted to. Not until news of the find got to more distant shores did the real rush commence.

The gold of Quesnel Lake was first hunted as it had been on the Fraser. Men panned the bars or dug down, at most, 2 or 3 feet. Fair results. The big strike came in the Humbug Creek area, a stream so named because its elusive gold colors, everywhere apparent, refused to gather along the bars. Humbug had been sampled by hundreds of prospectors, nearly all of whom gave up and moved on. One team of miners, Ed Stout and Billy Deitz, built a cabin and proceeded to dig deep holes, ignoring the advice of their betters, the old-timers of the Fraser who had arrived four years before and now were the elder geologists of the northern gold fields. Stout and Deitz did not quite explore the bedrock in making the first big strike on Humbug Creek. They did, however, reach a layer of dense blue clay, a formation called by California men a false bedrock, which in this instance served the same purpose, and would, in the normal course of geological change, have become a stratum of shale. They found coarse gold in quantities which clogged the sluice riffles. Six thousand men rushed to Humbug Creek, renamed it William's Creek in honor of Billy Deitz, staking all of it as well as the smaller streams nearby. What Deitz and Stout had discovered was an island in the British Columbian glaciation, a place where the ancient gold concentrations had not been greatly disturbed.

On the Cariboo all the gold orthodoxy of California applied. Everyone went to bedrock looking for the paystreak. Those who arrived too late for the gulch diggings looked to the sidehills where the ancient floodplains were left high by erosion. When the gravel was too deep for simple stripping and excavation, the Cariboo miners operated in the best deep manner, sinking shafts, running drifts along bedrock to the limits of their claims, and retreating as the pay was mined out, timbering where they had to, and letting the worked-out ground cave. Miners in too great a hurry timbered too lightly and were caught under the buckling posts and cap pieces, or were drowned when the soft muck came loose and ran in tons through the lagging. Most of their bodies were recovered because they fell in the pay. In its first year, the Humbug area produced $2½ million worth of gold. A town sprang up close to a mine belonging to a Cornishman who had jumped ship at Victoria and was named for him, Barkerville. Sprawled amid the tailings heaps which continually threatened to engulf it, Barkerville became one with all the wild, jerry-built camps of the era—wealthy, drunken, lawless. At its height it contained perhaps 2,000 residents, and was headquarters for twice as many more. Flour rose to $2.50 per pound, higher by a dollar than it had ever been at the high point of the Fraser. The Harrison Trail provided passage for less than half the way. It required many loadings and unloadings, and gold-happy Barkerville demanded many items in a hurry. Mule drivers got busy and fixed up the Indian trail through Fraser Canyon. By mule train straight up to Quesnel from Yale, the trip to Barkerville could be accomplished in about a month.

Far to the south, at the edge of the Nevada desert, the Comstock Lode was at that time mounting to its full production, and salt was needed in large quantities to reduce some of the more complex silver sulfo-salts to a chloride for subsequent amalgamation in what was to become known as the Reese River process. Salt was found in good quantity over toward the middle of the state, but it lay across the desert, and the loaded wagons proved unwieldly vehicles when their wheels sank into the sand. To overcome the problem somebody had the idea of importing a herd of camels. Hearing of this innovation and that the camels were great travelers, able to carry half a ton, one of British Columbia's leading pack-train operators, a man named Laumeister, went south and purchased a herd of the beasts from one of the salt merchants who happened to be oversupplied. Consternation greeted Laumeister's camels when they appeared on the mountain trails of British Columbia. They were large brutes with two humps, long of hair, selected to withstand the rigors of the North American winter. The first people who saw them thought they were dehorned caribou. Others maintained that

Laumeister had succeeded in training a number of cow moose.

Many Indians believed that the white men had consummated an allegiance with the evil spirit, and they named the camels the English equivalent of "devil-elk." Some Indians called them stink elk and gave them wide berth. In Nevada they were in charge of their native drivers. They were so ill-tempered that few in British Columbia wanted to work with them. Hard feelings erupted when the horses and mules of the other packers were stampeded by their smell. It was true they could carry upwards of half a ton, were possessed of re-markable endurance, and could, of course, go a long time without water, useful in the dry area of British Columbia or where, amid canyon torrents, one might travel for days within sight and sound of water without being able to obtain enough to make the evening tea; but their usefulness came to an end when their large, padded feet, so perfectly suited to desert sand, were cut to pieces by the rocks. Laumeister freed his camels in the desert back of Thompson River. There they ran wild and were still to be found in 1897, when a Kamloops merchant suggested them as substitutes for mules on the long, rigorous journey to the Klondike. No appearance of camels on the Klondike has ever been reported, however. The last of the herd is believed to have died in 1905.

James Douglas had long since given up any thought of preserving British Columbia as a fur-producing wilderness. The gold trade was proving, anyway, far more lucrative. He wrote the Colonial authorities in London that it was his purpose to "push rapidly with the formation of roads during the coming winter, in order to have the great thoroughfares leading to the remotest mines, now upwards of five hundred miles from the seacoast, so improved as to render travel easy, and to reduce the cost of transport, thereby securing the whole trade of the colony for Fraser's River and defeating all attempts at competition from Oregon."

Not waiting for an answer, which was likely to be of a

procrastinating nature, Douglas set to work. He decided to build a road suitable for wagons all the way to the Cariboo. He proposed to start on the west bank of the Fraser at the mouth of the canyon and follow the old Indian trail. At Spuzzum the river could be forded during low water, and there was a cable ferry for use when it was too high. A bridge was to be built at Spuzzum, and the road, crossing to the eastern shore, would travel north to about the mouth of the Thompson River, thence to swing northwestward and find easy going in the rolling hills and dry plateaus of central British Columbia.

Americans, particularly those who had come up from the Colville region, could scarcely believe their ears when they heard about Douglas' foolhardy plan to get up Fraser Canyon. They were quick to point out the advantages of several southern routes. If men were needed to show Douglas one of these superior paths for his road, a number of U.S. miners expressed their willingness to lend themselves to that project.

For this offer they received no thanks. Big James needed no American placer miner to tell him about the trails of southern British Columbia. He had been over them himself as early as 1826. In that year he had traveled the Okanagan Trail, established six years before as the main route down the middle of British Columbia, from Fort George to Kamloops and south to the big bend of the Columbia, now in Washington, thence to the river's mouth. It had been with much reluctance that the Company had decided to abandon such a natural route and buck the grain of the country westward to Yale. Recently, he had heard that a man named "Okanogan" Smith was building a trading post on the trail at a point just inside U.S. territory, on the southern end of Osoyoos Lake.

(Like Kootenai, which it is on the U.S. maps, Kootenay in Canada—although the tribe is sometimes called the Kutenai, but also Kootenae, Kootanae and Kootanie—Okanogan Smith spelled his name with an *o;* or at least it is so written today. Had he been located north of the boundary in Canada he would be Okanagan Smith, as the name goes on the maps there. At an earlier time the name was more commonly spelled Okinakane, though it was to Okanikane City that one bought his ticket when he detrained from the early Northern Pacific Railroad near Ellensburg and took the stage northward along the Okanogan Trail. It was also Okinagan and Oakinachen, some geographers shortening it to Oak Lake, and a bit of Old Erin crept in when early maps showed O'Kanagon Mission on the shore of the lake. The name came from a band of Indians occupying the river mouth on the Columbia.)

Okanogan Smith, besides engaging in trade, had planted a huge apple orchard and was busy digging irrigation ditches. He was also U.S. Land Commissioner, and Douglas was suspicious as to whose land he had designs on. As yet, however, Smith was handicapped by the fact that he had no road, not even an easy trail to the coast. When elected to the Washington legislature, he reached the capital at Olympia by traveling north into British territory, across to Yale on the fur route of 1850, down the Fraser by riverboat, and to his destination by ferry. Transportation to the eastern United States was soon to be an easier matter. The U.S. Army was completing a road from Fort Benton, at the head of steam navigation on the Missouri River, through the Rockies to its counterpart the Dalles on the Columbia. A branch of the road was to connect with Fort Walla Walla. Another could just as easily swing north from the Spokane region and reach the outpost of Okanogan Smith. If the Cariboo Road were now built to Kamloops there was every chance the trade would drain off to the south for the benefit of U.S. merchants. Next the miners would be calling for troops, and central British Columbia would go the way of Oregon. So Douglas left Kamloops, the old natural trade center, bypassed. The Kamloops road down the Okanogan Trail would be built, but long after the mines and trade of the Cariboo had diminished to minor importance.

Today's road up the Fraser is universally admired for its stunning scenery. Its magnificent vistas and declivities were less appreciated by the men who first built it as the Cariboo Road. Miles of it had to be hacked and blasted from the rock walls. Log cribbing held much of it, and some was supported by trestle. Douglas' bridge at Spuzzum came to be considered the engineering marvel of the North. The contours of the stream and the volume of its floodwaters rendered impracticable the standard rock-ballasted log piers of the frontier, and a suspension span was called for. It proved impossible to haul cable of a size and length necessary because of the weights of the coils. The builders therefore had a choice of splicing shorter lengths of cable or bringing in the individual wires and twisting their own. They chose to do the latter, and did it so well that years passed without a strand giving way.

Beyond the bridge the scenery became less immense, and likewise the scope of the road job. This was grassland, with pines on the hills. To the north the rolling land went on and on to Summit Lake, at the divide where the waters flowed toward Hudson Bay. Douglas still had a big job because of the distances, but he had stopped bucking the country and was going with it. He was on the main course of the north-south mountain passage. Had he continued to the north, the route would have taken him over the Liard Divide to the mainstem of the Great North Trail. South the trails of the Rocky Mountain and the Purcell Trench led to the Flathead Lake and Coeur d'Alene countries. Or, as noted, the main plateau brigade route of the fur trade, to the Okanagan, and the new road connecting the Missouri and the Columbia.

The great accomplishment of James Douglas was not that he discovered or used the prehistoric trail in building the northern part of the Cariboo Road. That part of it was dead easy. Douglas' great achievement was turning the traffic and administration of his province away from it, taking it through mountains and canyons in a geographically preposterous route to the sea. In bringing this off in opposition to all forces of nature and economics he saved British Columbia for his company, and for the new union of Canada. Had a man less resolute than Douglas been in charge at Vancouver Island, the traffic to Cariboo would have gone as a matter of course up the Okanagan Trail through Kamloops. Freight destined for the Cariboo would have appeared on the docks at Fort Benton, and the banks of the United States would have traded in its gold. Without Douglas, the Harrison Trail supplying the upper reaches of Fraser Canyon would probably have remained unbuilt, and the gold fields together with the heart of British Columbia would have been lost by the summer of 1859.

The Canadian hold on eastern British Columbia had another shaky period. This came when farmers moved into the rich land near Kamloops, and had no way of marketing their crops. They looked to the south and the projected Northern Pacific Railroad. It had been surveyed to follow the famed Nez Percé hunting trail to a high point at Spokane, where one of the best traveled branches of the Trail came down from the north. Crossing the Columbia River plateau, it would, had the original survey been followed, have come within two days' wagon travel of the mouth of the Okanogan. But, although its charter was granted in 1864, the N.P. did not reach Spokane until 1883. The Dominion government had meanwhile started a transcontinental line of its own. Some of this was built in 1871, but it, too, suffered reverses. Private financing allowed the Canadian Pacific's completion in 1885. By its link the farmers of central British Columbia established outlets east and west through the mountains.

Whether the position of Canadian farmers was as good as that of their counterparts in the United States is open to question. A complaint over the years has been that they receive lower prices for their produce while being charged more for the manufactured things they have to buy. Canadians who travel south to buy in the United States have had their money discounted while being faced with signs in the supermarkets reading WE SELL ONLY U.S. BEEF. A campaign for Canadian trade goes on, while the same chambers of commerce pressure Washington to raise the tariff barriers without, apparently, comprehending the ambiguity of their position. Despite a boundary which has been made artificially troublesome by both sides, every year the north-to-south pull becomes stronger. Spokane has long advertised itself as center of the "Inland Empire," a region between the mountains including not only northern Washington and Idaho but southern British Columbia as well.

Old James Douglas would undoubtedly flinch at the treaty recently signed providing for the development of the Columbia River system which rises and flows without regard for the international boundary. The resulting hydroelectric power will most certainly provide for a California-size expansion of industry in Washington state. As this region becomes more heavily populated and industrialized it will provide a market of preëmptive demand for the farm products and raw materials of the north.

Canada on the map is larger than the United States, and at a glance would seem to have a land mass which lends unity. It is in fact a narrow strip of a country, clotted here and there to its southern boundary, a chain of provinces without much of mutual interest to tie one to the other. Severed by a dissident, proud, and recalcitrant French-Catholic minority, English-speaking United States-type Canada often longs to immerse, or at least dilute, this problem in the complexity of its southern neighbor. "There is such a thing in this State of Louisiana as the Napoleonic Code," said Stanley Kowalski in *A Streetcar Named Desire,* occasioning mild interest among U.S. audiences, but ringing like a gong through the theaters of Canada, for it showed how the more populous country could contain a French culture. In one district after another along the Canadian boundary there is a greater feeling of unity with the people to the south than with those in the province east or west.

The Stateside citizens of Montana and Washington, living in a region closely tied to their northern neighbors by roads and economic interests, give little thought to dispensing with the international boundary. In Canada, however, it is a perennial issue. Television viewers in the northern United States got their first inkling of this when they started tuning in on CBC, where the programs are likely to be less commercialized and of better quality, and found that the political panel discussions had a way of getting around it before the night was over. A poll conducted by one TV program showed slightly more than 50 per cent of Canadians favoring union with the United States. The opposition, however, is bitter.

When the U.S. President and Canadian Prime Minister in 1964 met in Great Falls, Montana, to give final approval to the Columbia River Treaty, both men made short addresses. On that occasion nothing ruffled the calm current of the Presidential rhetoric; he gave no more thought to the boundary than to the horizon which reached at every quadrant and was always taken for granted. Not so the Prime Minister. Knowing his words would be heard at home, he felt obliged to put more metal in his voice and point to the boundary as a wall, one that had to be kept built up in good repair.

The problem is not one likely to be settled politically. James Douglas saved British Columbia with his Harrison Trail and Cariboo Road, and Canada it is likely to remain. Yet its interior is part of a larger province, that of the intermontaine West. In all geologic times the pull was north-to-south. The forces exert themselves more and more. The same is true east of the mountains where the wartime Alaska Highway (subject of a later chapter) has not been abandoned, as many Canadians may have wished, but will at last be paved, returning it a step closer to its ancient preëminence as part of the Great North Trail.

The Cariboo Road of James Douglas was 385 miles long. It was not all road at first—for a year Douglas had to be content with steamboat navigation for a 50-mile stretch near Quesnel. Although the road had some narrow passages, most of it was kept to a minimum of 18 feet. Much of the work was done by Chinese. The total cost was only a million and a quarter dollars, but Douglas turned over segments to contractors who paid themselves by collecting tolls. Before the road's completion Barkerville was reached by pony express. Later the express coaches made two trips weekly between Barkerville and Yale. Horse changes were at intervals shorter than in the States because of the steep grades. Many a passenger closed his eyes on the canyon passages, but swift schedules were maintained. An armed cavalry at first accompanied the gold coaches, but later the usual shotgun guard sufficed. Neither experienced trouble from bandits. Some have marked this as tribute to the mettle of Canadian stagecoachmen. Perhaps so, but the bandit of the Cariboo Road would have been faced with an unusual problem: after robbing the coach he would have had no alternative but to ride down the same road and probably get caught. There was no road but the Cariboo.

THE GOLD TRAILS
OF MONTANA

Chapter 7

In the 1850s the U.S. Army of the West found itself faced with a gigantic problem of transport, particularly to Washington and Oregon. To remedy this a number of roads were actively promoted and some of them explored, mostly by Army men working on small budgets. Congress did nothing until the Mormons added their hostility to that of the Indians and the two together threatened to sever the Oregon Trail. An alternate northern route was deemed imperative, and a young Army engineer, Lieutenant John Mullan, was sent out to survey a road for which he had been plugging, one designed to allow wagon passage from Minnesota across the high plains and through the mountains to the head of steam navigation on the Columbia. As finally surveyed it more realistically started at Fort Benton, which could be reached by Missouri River steamboats, rather than Minnesota. Mullan set forth on his survey in 1858; the road was completed in 1863, a speed due in part to the genius of the young officer and in part to the fact that he was astute enough to follow one of the oldest trails of the West, the hunting trail of the Nez Percé, running along the cleft of the Osborn-Bear-mouth Fault from Spokane to Deer Lodge Valley.

When young Mullan passed along the the Clark's Fork of the Columbia in 1858, three men were busy at one of the tributaries sinking a prospecting shaft. They were the Stuart brothers, Granville and James, and a partner, Reese Anderson. The men had been to California without making a fortune and then wanderers of the mountains as traders, explorers, and prospectors. On their most recent journey they had come north over the Red Rock Pass, in Alexander Henry's old country, to the Beaverhead and thence north to the Deer Lodge.

The Stuarts had known for quite a while that the region was gold-bearing. On an earlier trip they had met a halfbreed Indian called Benetsee, also with California experience, and seen a bit of gold worth a dime that he had picked up from one of the creek crossings on the Nez Percé trail. Benetsee had prospected since, winning a few colors from the bars. The Stuarts, with more ambition (or know-how), decided to sink a shaft to bedrock, but the lack of tools stopped them. They went away, and another man appeared briefly in history. This was Henry Thomas, known in the land as "Gold Tom," who had been living with the Indians a couple of days' travel to the north. Tom sank 30 feet through lumpy gravel and built a sluice of hollowed logs.

Tom's diggings netted him a dollar or so per day. He had located on a drift of glacial gravel that had been shoved down from the Flint Creek range about 10 miles to the west, and while the drift was rich as such things went and miners have since made attempts to work it, there had been no opportunity for the values to concentrate at bedrock.

Returning, the Stuarts brought in some light equipment

for mining, and Mullan saw them in the springtime of their hope. Soon the road gangs arrived, with immigrant wagons close behind. The Stuarts then laid aside their shovels and started a store. A town called American Fork sprang up. Wagoners stopped, built shanties, and tried their luck along the creeks. Flakes of gold were washed almost everywhere, and there were several hopeful-appearing strikes. When they started trading gold for supplies Granville wrote a third brother, Thomas, who was in Colorado and having a lean time of it. "Drop everything for the Deer Lodge," he said. Tom showed the letter widely, with the result that he did not come alone. This was wise. The course he chose was through some of the worst Indian country of the West. Accompanied by a group of Pikes Peakers, he eschewed the old Oregon and Mormon routes via Fort Hall for a short cut through present-day Wyoming. By luck, or after inquiry, he chose the main route of the Great North Trail east of the Big Horns, then between the Yellowstone and the Gallatin, past the Three Forks, and to the Deer Lodge Valley by way of Pipestone Pass.

Upon arrival, Tom Stuart and his Coloradans immediately "turned the color." They occupied a small stream south and west of the previous diggings, named it Pikes Peak Creek, and went to mining by rocker and, when there was sufficient water, by means of a small sluice. Later bar diggings along the head of the stream, most notably a strip of hillside below the now-abandoned camp of Yam Hill, were to yield as much as $140,000 worth of gold in a single season, but the Pikes Peakers of 1862 saw at best $10 per day. Most of them shoveled into the sluices through the rest of the season to recover barely enough metal for a winter's grubstake.

Moderate returns these were, but the name Gold Creek didn't sound moderate, and it got to the outside world. Far away in St. Louis was heard the name of another, more important, discovery. Prospectors moving down from the Fraser had struck it rich on the Clearwater River of Idaho, and the steamboat owners, throttled by the Civil War which was then in its Shiloh stage, advertised the Missouri and Mullan's Road as the best means of reaching it. HO! FOR THE CLEARWATER AND THE GOLD MINES OF IDAHO! read the placards of the steamboat owners recruiting customers for the Fort Benton run.

The gold deposits of the Clearwater were the richest yet found outside California, but few boats reached Fort Benton until June. There was next a problem in getting outfits ready for the road, and when they set out Mullan's construction was not what the travelers had been led to expect. It was all right for about a hundred miles southward of Fort Benton, all rolling and prairie country, but when the road entered the mountains they were in trouble. Mullan had built a road, but nobody had kept it up. Much of it had to be rebuilt as the travelers went along.

It made small difference anyway. Even had they started a month earlier, their way would have been blocked by the torrential streams. Particularly was this true on the western side of the divide. The wagons crossed by Mullan Pass, jouncing over the uninteresting flat end of famed Last Chance Gulch to get there, winding over the bonanzas of Sevenmile Creek as they climbed the penultimate pitch to the summit and everyone cursed the delay. But the brooks of the Pacific side, which were placid and filled with the darting shadows of trout when they reached them in midsummer, would a month before have had the floodpower to sweep away whole tandem wagons and six-horse teams of work stock.

Gold Creek was now their destination. By the Fourth of July forty-five people, Indians not counted, were on hand to celebrate. Several saloons set up business. By August American Fork had a bawdy house, or tepee, and monte sharpers. Three horse thieves arrived from Idaho, a posse in pursuit. One of the thieves, a man by the name of Spillman, surrendered at Stuart's store. The other two were surprised while gambling. One of these—Arnett—sat with his Navy Colt in his lap. This model pistol, a cap-and-ball piece of 36 caliber, was the standard sidearm of the mining frontier. His partner,

Gehrigman, cried "Look out!" and dived for cover. Arnett was dropped by a charge of buckshot. When the smoke cleared he was dead with his monte cards clutched in his left hand and the Colt in his right. Neither could be pried loose, and he was buried both hands full, and so lies today near the Clark Fork River, close beside the Northern Pacific tracks, the exact location a matter of speculation. Gehrigman and Spillman were tried by a miners' court for horse-stealing. Spillman was hanged, the first of quite a number to suffer that fate, and American Fork became known as Hangtown all along the frontier as a result. Gehrigman, who claimed he had been picked up along the way, was banished.

· With its first shootings and hangings, Gold Creek showed signs of becoming one of the most exciting camps in the West. Soon, however, it was overshadowed by much bigger doings in the Beaverhead and up from the Stinking Water, the long trek back from the Fraser having brought the main army of prospectors to those mountain shores.

Four years had now passed since the Stuart brothers and Reese Anderson started their first prospecting shaft near Benetsee's old diggings and since the stampede to British Columbia. In 1860 when Gold Tom came to look around before starting his shaft in the dollar-per-day moraine, several thousand men, disappointed by the Fraser, had come down the trails into Washington and were learning the hard way that the Cascade Range, for all its wilderness grandeur, was mighty poor shakes as a gold country. News of the Cariboo would have depopulated Washington all over again, but in the late summer of that year, when the Cariboo miners were rafting their way along the arms of Quesnel Lake, Washington miners were testing some bars at the mouth of Peshastin Creek on the Wenatchee River; and when the Cariboo men were going to the Fraser for supplies, one of the discoverers of Peshastin was precipitating a rush from Seattle. The Wenatchee diggings were nothing like the Cariboo, but there were other discoveries close at hand, and they *sounded* as good. The one at Blewett Pass sounded even better. There the placer discoveries were backed by lode mines whose near-surface ores were "rotten with gold," many tons of which were pounded in hand mortars, a solid promise which encouraged farmers from the Cle Elum area to build a road over the Wenatchee Range seeking a cash market for their grain, dairy products, and vegetables.

The Blewett Pass lodes did not prove a northern Mother Lode. Poorer ore was found which had to await a more sophisticated treatment than was available at that time, and the placers of the gulch were even more quickly exhausted. The Washington miners might still have joined the Cariboo rush when the deep workings of Barkerville were reported, but over to the east, on the Clearwater River of Idaho, hard by the place where Lewis and Clark came down through early blizzards on the Lolo Trail, Captain E. D. Pierce, California man and Indian trader, made the first major strike of the U.S. Northwest. Soon such camps as Pierce City, Orofino, Florence, and Elk City were to render Barkerville of second importance. Barkerville's wealthy first season amounted to only a fourth of the value poured out by the Clearwater camps the same year. Pierce City alone had a population of 7000.

Washington men arriving too late for the Clearwater prospected southeastward along the Snake and met Coloradans coming northwest. Oregon immigrants, lost and hungry, were said to have found some heavy metal which they used as fishing sinkers. All that had been a long time before, and the immigrants—learning their sinkers were gold nuggets—returned, but were never able to find the place. A party hunting the Lost Sinker Diggings discovered the Owyhee placers, and later the silver mines of War Eagle Mountain. Stellar finds of gold were made in the Boise Basin by 1862. Some of the greatest excitement was caused by the diggings at Florence near the Salmon River canyon. They were not the most important, but they caused the wildest stampede. Colorado men, hearing of the Florence strike, tried a short cut by way of the upper Salmon, thinking they were on legendary Mormon Trail. The Mormon Trail led only to Fort Lemhi, a settlement started by one of Utah's schismatic sects and by that time abandoned. The trail, reputed to slant northwestward through the heart of Idaho's mountain forests, existed only in the imagination, but so firmly was it rooted that the maps of the time all showed it solid to Lewiston, and it was a dream of the later railroad builders, the Northern Pacific once considering it, as did Marcus Daly, the copper king, when he planned his railroad from Butte to the Pacific in the 1890s.

Finding the country impassable beyond Fort Lemhi, the first arrivals—like those at American Fork Pikes Peakers from Colorado—found a quantity of grain the Mormons had buried, and, so supplied, decided to remain and prospect. It was good gold country, and still is, but when the initial paystreaks played out, they turned their wagons toward Gold Creek. An Indian trail led them eastward, and they followed it along much of its sidehill course by putting both hind wheels on one side and the front wheels on the other. The pass was called the Lemhi. It led them to Horse Prairie Creek and to the Beaverhead River. Others followed them, or hunted out passes of their own, and before the autumn of 1862 people had crossed the Beaverhead Range through passes which they christened the Bannack, the Whisky Spring, the Deadman, and Bloody Dick's. The wagons rolled down Trail Creek and Bloody Dick Gulch and over Horse Prairie, not suspecting that gold lay under the ground, and came out on the little hills above the Beaverhead River. They tried their luck in a dozen gulches, handicapped by lack of water and by the sniping of the Bannock Indians, a Snake tribe who resented the encroachment on their hunting grounds.

Gold was widespread in the Beaverhead country, but many of the miners headed out for Gold Creek for supplies. One party found its way to a creek they named the Grasshopper, and there John White was credited with the first major discovery of the Beaverhead area. Bannack City, named for the Bannock Indians but misspelled, came into existence. Gold turned up in a dozen prospecting shafts in abundance and of a deep bronze color and softness scarcely ever seen before. News of the find reached American Fork on the twentieth of September, and next day the place was deserted. Gold Creek had bench gravel just as rich as any at Bannack, but its discovery awaited another day. Colonel G. W. Morse later of New Chicago recalled that that autumn, when he visited the district, only two miners were at work, the rest having gone to Bannack. Even the Stuarts departed, temporarily, taking all their goods to start a store and butcher shop in the new El Dorado.

Among these who left with the Stuarts for Bannack was a young Georgian named John M. Bozeman. He had joined the Cherry Creek rush to Colorado in 1859 and was among the Pikes Peakers who accompanied Tom Stuart to Gold Creek. He had claims on Pikes Peak Creek and later on the Grasshopper, but he was not a natural gold miner. The hills rather than the gulches, the open air rather than the dripping darkness of the drifts appealed to him. So, after spending the cold months in Bannack, and noting the severe hardship, time, and expense experienced by the freighters bucking the desert and mountain trail from Salt Lake City, he decided to open a road of his own, a good part of it to follow the trail taken by the Stuart party from Colorado. He remembered it as being well supplied with water and grass. There were no steep grades or difficult river fords before the Yellowstone was reached, and nothing insurmountable thereafter. And best it was a short cut, at least for those coming by way of the Oregon Trail. For those coming to Montana via Fort Laramie it meant a saving of a good 250 miles.

In Gold Creek, Bozeman had made the acquaintance of a frontiersman named Jacobs who had been employed by Mullan in building his road and who was, furthermore, a squawman, deemed an advantage in the wild country to the south. Jacobs was enlisted as a partner in the enterprise, and the coming spring they set out to map a road. On this journey they were accompanied by Jacobs' eight-year-old half-breed daughter. A party of Sioux found them on Powder River and took their horses, guns, and supplies. On foot they continued into Wyoming and survived because that summer had produced a large hatching of grasshoppers, which they ate raw. Undismayed by the ordeal, Bozeman traveled eastward along the Oregon Trail, promoting his road, and succeeded in getting a wagon train together for the journey north. The Sioux and Cheyenne were already alarmed by the heavy traffic on the Oregon Trail. When they saw wagons rolling directly across the heart of their hunting ground, they came out fighting. The train succeeded in escaping back to Fort Caspar, (now spelled Casper) but Bozeman himself drove through.

In the north, Montana Territory had come into being, and the capital quickly moved from Bannack to the diggings at Alder Gulch. Here indeed was the biggest of them all, larger and richer than anything north of California. Nobody bothered to count, but there were probably twelve thousand miners in Alder Gulch, centered at the new metropolis of Virginia City. The entire gulch above and below Virginia, 10 miles long and from an eighth to a mile in width, was solid with claims, the gold country extending toward the summit and up many of the gulches tributary to the Stinking Water. Nobody doubted that this was only a start. Silver mines were already producing high-grade ore at Rattlesnake Creek near Bannack and there were reports of silver, gold, and copper in the quartz veins near Virginia. It was only a question of time, people thought, until large cities would grow where streets of dugouts and shanties now lined the gulch. Bozeman quickly found backing. The legislature chartered the Bozeman City and Fort Laramie Wagon Road and Telegraph Co. There were also charters issued to the Hell Gate & Deer Lodge Wagon Road Co., the Bitterroot & Kootenai Wagon Road Co., The Little Prickly Pear Co., The Prickly Pear & Virginia City Co., and the Missouri River & Rocky Mountain Wagon Road & Telegraph Co., while others were in the process of promotion. The last-named, capitalized at $800,000, was backed by a number of budding gold and freighting kings. It was projected from Virginia City through the Gallatin Valley to the head of navigation on the Yellowstone River. Toll gates were to be erected every forty miles, and the following rate schedule applied:

> *$2 Wagon & 1 Team*
> *$1 Each Odd Team*
> *$1 Man & Horse*
> *25¢ Each Pack Animal*

An express company was formed to operate between Virginia and Walla Walla, using pack horses, but it failed, as did another which secured a mail contract. Both hoped to maintain a two-week schedule, but the mountain route was too rough and unpredictable because of snow, flood, and—as Montana was approached—Indians. Most of the freight and mail came up on the Salt Lake Road. Connections existed there with the Overland Trail, the Oregon Trail, and the road to California, but the camp was for long periods isolated. With gold the only thing it had in true abundance, the prices of flour, sugar, and other commodities rose to speculator's heights. In Jeff Davis Gulch down toward the Bannack Pass, young red-headed W. A. Clark took time off from his placer mining and his job as recorder of claims to travel westward and meet the packers coming in with the winter's supply of chewing tobacco and bring off the first merchandising *coup* of his spectacular career. Clark guessed rightly that tobacco ranked above liquor and food as a necessity. Before winter was over, the pole walks were torn up in Bannack to get the cigar butts which had fallen beneath, and the ultimate price Clark got for a twist of tobacco will never be known. Although he went on to become the American copper king and a U.S. Senator, with a son who was the main support of the Los Angeles Philharmonic, the old-timers in the Bannack of the author's youth still thought of Clark in connection with chewing tobacco. "At $50 a plug," a man named Ashworth said, "you'll chew your tobacco until it spits the color of cabbage."

In Virginia City similar corners involving flour and sugar led to near-riots, seizure of stocks, and rationing. It was obvious that a great deal of money could be made from freight, express, and communications, and in the spring John Bozeman was again in the field. Soon, Sioux and Cheyenne notwithstanding, wagon trains were using his route. In 1864 one caravan moved northward consisting of 150 wagons, 637 oxen, 79 horses and mules, and 461 persons. It was too large to tempt an Indian attack, but smaller groups were not so lucky. Bozeman never did collect any tolls or erect any road to speak of, but he served as a guide, and his route became deeply rutted in the prairies. It followed, as closely as a road could, the central course of the ancient passageway through Wyoming.

Bozeman's road left the Oregon Trail near Douglas, crossed the North Platte by ferry at Shawnee Creek north of the Cedar Hills, then, climbing to the top of the bluffs, it headed northwestward. The first town which now lies in its path is Buffalo, but its route can be traced on a map by the abandoned forts and the locations of Indian battles. From Buffalo north to Sheridan it is followed by today's Highway 87. A Wyoming road marks it to the village of Dayton. It again finds Highway 87 briefly at the Montana line, but the highway continues north to Billings, while the old road swung west to Fort C. F. Smith on the Big Horn. Farther along, the town of Pryor stands close to the trail. It paralleled the Yellowstone River, staying 10 or 15 miles to the south to take advantage of good ground at the edge of the Beartooth uplift, and finally dropped down and crossed by means of a ferry west of Big Timber. Those looking for the original trail can travel some of it almost in its freight-wagon condition from Springdale, Montana, to Hunter's Hot Springs and back to Highway 89, a distance of about 14 miles. Hunter, a physician, heading for the mines in the 1864 migration, discovered the springs and some years later returned to build a cabin and bathhouse with a mind to founding a spa. It was a famous stop in the early years, not because anyone cared to drive 14 miles northward for a bath, but because in turning that way they happened to avoid some bad going where the Yellowstone looped around a knob of ground called the Buffalo Hump. When an Indian agency was built east of Livingston in 1869–1870 the road was moved to the south side of the river. For a time it used a ferry at the mouth of Shields River. This crossing can easily be seen from the new Livingston Municipal Airport. Parts of the road are followed by Highway 10 through Bozeman Pass.

Jim Bridger, who had been up and down the country before Bozeman was born, considered any road east of the Big Horns to be madness. The Sioux constituted the greatest Indian power in the West, calling on a well-mounted and fairly well-armed cavalry all the way to Minnesota if need be. No route they seriously challenged could become dependable and make a profit. But the Sioux were not likely to worry much about a road on the other side of the range, and so he mapped a road of his own, leaving Casper for the west and north just about where Highway 20 now runs, touching or coming close to the present towns of Thermopolis, Worland, and Greybull in Wyoming and Bridger, Montana, north of which it joined Bozeman's. He went east along the Oregon road trying to get business, and guided a number of emigrants through but, although his road was safer and had better grass, it was too difficult ever to attain popularity.

Little would have happened to Bozeman's road, either, had not the federal government taken a hand. To understand the interest in Washington it might be well to look at the gold bonanzas from a different point of view—that of national finance.

In 1849 the nation had little money in circulation; little was needed. That year there were fewer than a million wage earners in all the United States, and they made a total of 237 million, about a dollar per working day. The country was predominantly agricultural. A typical farm family raised nearly all of what it ate, and bartered for most of its other needs. Perhaps it saw $50 in hard money per year. Huckleberry Finn said, "Steamboat captains is always rich, and get sixty dollars a month." The Panic of 1837 was precipitated when the U.S. Treasury demanded that specie payments be made for inflated banknotes during the height of a speculative boom in land. The total circulation of the watered notes amounted only to 149 million, but there just wasn't enough hard money around to pay off at face value. Twenty or twenty-five million was enough to meet the entire expenses of the federal government, Army, Navy, and everything else in those simple times. Then, into that all-but-moneyless economy came an avalanche of California gold. From 1850 to 1856 the gold production of California amounted to just under $100 million per year. Soon there was so *much* gold that its value fell in relation to silver; or, to put it another way, silver commenced to rise, and it rose so far that the Treasury had to cut the amount of white metal in its coins to keep people from melting them down for bullion.

If there was any doubt about what all that new monetary medium could be used for, it ended with the start of the Civil War. The federal government needed all the gold it could get, and soon it was forced to suspend specie payments and issue greenbacks. These fell in value until at one time gold was worth, greenback price, $63 per ounce. President Lincoln was glad, therefore, to welcome Nevada, with its Comstock, as a state, and grant territorial status to gold-rush Idaho and Montana, dispatching governors who did not know where their territorial boundaries lay and were obliged to gather some sort of governmental organization from hastily called conventions of surprised miners, many of whom were inclined to give three whoops and a roar for Jeff Davis.

When the war ended, the need for gold continued strong. The Treasury moved to retire the greenbacks and was forced to slow down when it was feared that a shortage of money would halt the expanding economy. The Comstock was adding ten million a year, California gold was coming at a pace that would bring the state's total to a billion dollars by 1872, and Alder Gulch was getting toward the hundred-million mark, but the country's demand was even greater. In that situation it was plain that no Indian cavalry must be allowed to hamper metal production. Anyone with a map could see that the most direct route to the Montana gold fields, and to the promising new silver mines, lay through Wyoming by the Bozeman Trail. It was decided that a couple of permanent Army posts, with patrols and summer camps during the danger times of summer, would be sufficient to keep the Sioux and Cheyenne in check. The forts were built on the Bighorn River in Montana and near the Spanish ruins of De Smet Lake in Wyoming. When these bastions were believed secure, the Army laid down for travelers rules designed to insure their safety en route. No parties of fewer than thirty armed men were to travel in the hostile areas. The parties were to have a military organization, with elected officers. Violators of the regulations were to be taken into custody, or sent back.

The system seemed excellent. As more and more people came into the country, the Indian menace was expected to abate. Unfortunately, however, it was decided to economize. Fewer than the full contingent of troops were sent. They did not overawe the Indians by appearing on the road with guns shining and flags flying but instead felt themselves obliged to stay close to their forts, and to survive rather than risk all for the travelers. These people, without Army prompting, had already been banding into large parties. They were on the whole better armed than the Army, most of them having Henry repeating rifles, a potent gun firing fifteen metallic rimfire cartridges in .44 caliber as fast as the lever could be worked, while the soldiers were too often armed with muzzle-loading Springfields, their officers opposing the repeaters because they feared a waste of ammunition and consequent complications in supply.

It was not long before the posts were in a virtual state of siege. Worst afflicted was Fort Phil Kearny, about 35 miles south of the Montana boundary, picturesquely located near 13,000-foot Cloud Peak at the edge of the Big Horns. By late autumn of 1866, Fort Kearny was so beleaguered that not even the weekly mail could get through.

Isolation rather than violence weighed heavily on the men. Particularly afflicted with cantonment fever were the young officers, many with brevet ranks from the Civil War, men who considered themselves majors reduced to the pay of lieutenants, and anxious to render their demotion as temporary as possible. After facing the tough organization of the Confederate forces throughout the war, the Indians seemed to them a mere rabble. They believed that one blow in full force would put all the Indians to flight, break the siege, let the mail get through, place the feather of victory in their hats, raise them in rank, and get them transferred to more civilized surroundings where a man could have his brandy in a decent club.

The leader of this group of impatient officers at Kearny was Captain William J. Fetterman. Fetterman had arrived in November and by his dash and charm had won instant popularity. He laughed at the idea of hiding from the Sioux. One quick blow, he said, would be sufficient to establish order and put them in their place. "A single company of regulars could whip a thousand Indians," he said. "A full regiment could whip the entire array of hostile tribes. With 80 men I could ride through the Sioux nation."

As the weeks went by and an iron cold settled across the bleak country, the task of holding Fetterman and his partisans in check became increasingly difficult. For this reason the commander, Colonel Carrington, let them engage in a number of apparently foolish forays which, he hoped, would serve to work the edge off their impatience. One night Fetterman and a group were allowed to hobble a number of mules and leave them in the bright moonlit snow along the creek and wait hidden in the brush ready to jump the Sioux when they came for them. No Sioux appeared, so, after several hours, the chilled party returned to the fort. While the soldiers were warming themselves the Sioux sneaked down and chased off another herd one mile away. The fiasco was a severe embarrassment to the officer and his friends, laying ground for the debacle which followed.

The winter had set in cold, and it was not long before Fort Kearny was faced with a serious fuel problem. The wood at hand along the bottoms of Piney Creek was deciduous growth considered useless except for kindling. Conifers grew on the mountain slopes, but the civilian woodcutters had to travel some miles to get to them, and the Indians waited. It was possible to work only behind the guns of a military escort. On the morning of December 21 a courier rode in with word that the Indians had moved down from a ridge and attacked in force. The woodcutters and their guards had taken refuge in a circle of fuel wagons and were holding off the attack, but a rescue party would be needed to get them home.

Colonel Carrington instructed a Major Powell to put such a force together, but before he could leave Fetterman asked for the command himself. Carrington acceded, but with a warning that he was merely to relieve the wood train and report back to the fort. Under no circumstances was he to pursue the Indians over the nearby ridge because the chances were that any Indian retreat would be for the single purpose of leading him into an ambush.

Fetterman set forth shortly before noon. His force numbered 81 men, just one over the number he had once judged sufficient to ride through the Sioux nation. Soon the woodcutting party fought its way free and returned to the fort, but they had not even caught sight of their relief. This was an alarming development. Even more alarming were the sounds of a distant, sharp engagement, followed by silence. Later, all eighty-one in Fetterman's command were found dead— beyond the ridge. He had pursued the Indians and been led into ambush. His name was immortalized on the maps when, the following July, Fort Fetterman was built on a windy eminence above the mouth of La Prele Creek on the

North Platte, a winter–summer situation which gave it the worst of both seasons. Officers and men regarded it a disciplinary assignment, one of the worst in the West.

From Kearny the wagons were sent back, not for wood but for the stiff-frozen dead. It was twenty below zero. Despite the cold which generally brought quiet, clear weather, a blizzard swept down from the Yellowstone River country. Back at the fort there were drifts as high as the stockade, and shovel details were kept busy all night for fear it would pack hard and make a ramp, rendering the wall useless. Although the blizzard was undoubtedly worse for the shelterless Indians, an attack was expected at any moment. The loss of Fetterman's force had left the post dangerously undermanned. Colonel Carrington could count only 119 defenders, including civilian employees. Ammunition was down to only twenty rounds per man. Plans were even made to place the women and children in the powder house, there to be blown to bits as a final resort to keep them from falling into the hands of the Indians. The fort's situation was as precarious as had been that of the beleaguered wood train except that now the closest relief was Fort Laramie, 236 miles away. In this extremity, Colonel Carrington asked for a volunteer to run the Indian barrier and found his man in John "Portugee" Phillips, who had been engaged at various times on the water wagon, the wood crew, and as a mail carrier. A civilian employee, he had been born thirty-four years before in the Azores.

Phillips was severely affected by the grief of Mrs. Frances Grummond, whose husband, young Lieutenant Grummond, had been killed that morning. Phillips gave her as a parting gift a wolfskin robe which was his prize possession, asked the use of the colonel's valuable charger, filled his pockets with biscuits, put a bag of hay behind his saddle, and announced himself ready. "May God help you," said Colonel Carrington, shaking hands with Phillips as soldiers unchained the gate. For a while they could hear the thud of hoofs as he rode into the stormy dark, then all became quiet.

"Good," said the Colonel, "he has taken softer ground at the side of the trail." They were not for weeks to know whether he made it through.

Phillips was glad when the storm closed around him. He managed to slip through the thousands of Sioux and Cheyenne warriors to the open prairie. He rode all night, and rested through the day. The blizzard slackened, but only with an increase in cold. Stations along the Oregon Trail reported 40 degrees below zero. An Indian war party glimpsed him and gave pursuit, but he was able to take refuge on a rocky hilltop and hold them off until dark, when he slipped away again. At least he had the wind at his back. After four days, at eleven o'clock on Christmas night, he rode up to the parade ground at Fort Laramie. His horse fell and died as he dismounted. "Beldam," the officers' club, was aflame with light. A ball was in progress—the glittering Christmas levee. Phillips, his beard frozen to the collar of his coat by a mass of frost, was allowed inside with his dispatch. He had completed the greatest ride of Western history, and summoned aid in time to save Fort Kearny. After his death, the government refused assistance to his widow because Phillips had not been a U.S. citizen.

Such forts as Kearny, Reno, and C. F. Smith did not make the Bozeman Trail safe for travel. There was scarcely a time when they were even sure of their own survival. All winter they lay isolated in a bleak desert of cold and snow. Food shortages were common. Horses and mules died of starvation and many soldiers suffered from deficiency diseases. Veterans recalled nights when they stood in the cold and listened to wolves claw at the stockade posts. Only when summer came, and with it the wagon traffic, did the soldiers feel safe to stir far from their enclosure. One group strayed too far from Fort Kearny, were attacked by Cheyennes, and saved only by the timely arrival of a wagon train.

John Bozeman continued as a guide and a road promoter, but in 1867 his luck ran out. He was camped on Yellowstone River, a few miles southwest of Hunter's Hot

Springs, near the point where its valley narrowed and ran sharply around the Buffalo Hump. With him was a prospecter and frontiersman, Tom Coover, who four years before had been in on the discovery of Alder Gulch. Seeing a party of Indians and believing them friendly Crows, Bozeman offered them food and was shot for his hospitality. His murderers were renegade Blackfeet from Canada. Coover managed to escape into the bushes. Bozeman was buried where he fell, but later his body was exhumed and moved to Bozeman City which had been named for him. Another early customer of the Bozeman graveyard was Henry T. P. Comstock, one of the discoverers of the Comstock Lode. Both men in failing had left their mark on the West. Comstock, after going broke in Nevada, came North to try for a second fortune in the new silver mines, but he despaired and died by his own hand.

Shortly after Bozeman's death the government concluded a peace treaty with the Sioux, and the country from the Yellowstone to the North Platte was for a time given over to them. The trail forts were vacated. Quite a number of people had settled nearby and taken up farming. With the abandonment of Fort C. F. Smith they moved and their places were burned by the Indians. The conquest of the Sioux and Cheyennes waited until the campaigns of 1876, the most famous of which was Custer's last.

None of the companies founded to construct long transportation and communication lines succeeded; they were on the whole ahead of their time. However, some of the more modest ones paid their investors. One group built a wagon road through Little Prickly Pear Canyon near Helena, claiming an expenditure of $60,000—a figure never given credence by the freighters who used it—and was repaid in tolls after two years. Several stretches of the Salt Lake Road were taken over by individuals, often without franchise, and stretches of grade and bridges were built, but for the most part the entrepreneurs were regarded as bandits and pushed out of the way, or they were outflanked by the terrain which afforded too many alternatives.

The Salt Lake was too important a route for tolls to be tolerated for long. Although much heavy freight and many passengers came and went from Fort Benton by steamboat, the season was unfortunately short, limited at most to five months per year. Long and difficult though it was, the Salt Lake Road was the most dependable route to the Montana gold camps. From Last Chance Gulch to Salt Lake City it was 534 miles long. When the Union Pacific was built, its termination became Corinne, Utah, and 60 miles was cut off its length.

Although there was a Salt Lake stage line by spring 1863, the northern gold communities were all but isolated for long periods of the year. Snow came very deep in the upper Beaverhead, along the Centennial Valley, where the road swung eastward and climbed toward the Continental Divide. On the Idaho side the snowfall was less, but the cold winds swept unimpeded over the barren lava plains. Trains of freight wagons, loaded with supplies worth a fortune at gold-camp prices, would climb Monida Pass and become impacted in the snows of Centennial Valley, there to remain for months unless expeditions came to rescue them. However, the greatest problem posed by the road did not involve getting supplies in, but transporting the gold out. It has been estimated that 320 tons of the yellow metal were washed from the gravel of Alder Gulch alone. Some estimates run as high as 700 tons; about 165 tons can be substantiated by gold buyers' ledgers and similar means. The production at other diggings was also high—not so high as that at Alder, but running to a total of several hundred tons. About the only way of telling how much gold was produced in those years is by ascertaining the amounts secured by the Treasury, the banks, and the jewelers and guessing its origin. The local records would mean little even if complete, which they were not, because so much of the gold was smuggled out of the country. It was the only way to get it past the highwaymen.

The first who came across the Bitterroots and Beaver-heads were honest miners, but as soon as the news of the Grasshopper diggings got out, the most footloose in the Idaho camps immediately responded. Many were criminals who had already been run out of California. In Montana they found neither law nor organization of any kind to hamper their activities, and the remoteness of the camps, with their trails winding endlessly through forest and rocky defiles, was ideally suited to ambush and robbery. It was estimated that 200 men were murdered by the lawless element in 1863, the first full year of the Montana camps. Bandits—calling themselves "road agents"—constituted a greater danger on the Salt Lake and Walla Walla trails than did Indian warriors on the Bozeman, and parties wanting to leave the country had to organize as if for passage through the land of the Sioux.

Their problem was often more difficult because the wagon trains of the Bozeman Trail at least knew they had no Indians in their number, while there was always a danger in a country of new acquaintances that some of the party would be road agents who had joined to decoy them into a deadfall. Later, when wagon trains were hauling silver ore down the Salt Lake Road, gold was hidden in the sacks; it could even be distributed through barren vein material, later to be separated by panning, but little ore was shipped until the arrival of the Union Pacific in Utah. Even as late as the 1870s the owner of the Black Friday mine at Radersburg raised potatoes on the side, pretending to earn his living thereby, so the gold-quartz ore picked from the upper bonanzas could be hauled as tubers to Helena. Many of the early miners took a year's stake from their claims, sold, and left for home, smuggling their gold out by pack train under the pretense of setting out on prospecting trips. Some went over the Bozeman Pass to the Yellowstone, or northward to the Missouri, and built mackinaw boats for the long journey east. Attacked by Indians or victims of snags and rapids, quite a number of such craft went down so that gold in the amount of several tons lies today in the mud of the river, frequently searched for but never recovered. Some miners got the better of road agents by caching their gold and spending it little by little as they needed to. Mamie French of the Beaverhead area told of attending college with the two granddaughters of one of Bannack's pioneers who took with them a small fruit jar full of the "heavy yellow" to defray their expenses. It had been in the family cellar for fifty years. In the pint size, fruit jars full of gold weigh 18 pounds each.

When James and Granville Stuart started their store at American Fork, one of their customers was a well-formed, well-spoken, handsome man of about twenty-eight named Henry Plummer. He had a shotgun which needed fixing and the Stuarts did the job for him. He was not a professional gambler, although much at the tables. He had the facility of moving in all classes of society, the best and the worst, and convincing them all that he was one of them.

Plummer was first heard from in California in 1852. In Nevada City he operated a bakery and engaged in other small business enterprises. It was not long before he established a reputation as a man of nerve, adept with firearms. He took on the job of town marshal. He had an eye for beautiful women, and women were in their turn flattered by his attentions. It led to trouble. He killed the husband of a woman with whom he was having an affair and was sent to prison, but influential friends went to Governor John B. Weller, who gave him a pardon. He returned to Nevada City and more trouble, wounding a man in one gunfight and killing a man in another, and he became suspected of highway robbery. Jailed again, he escaped with the aid of two pistols which a friend smuggled in to him, and headed north to the gold excitement of the Clearwater. His approachability and charm quickly won him the best of friends—and the worst. Dabbling in the hotel, saloon, and gambling business, he became acquainted with the slothful and desperate bunch which the camps always attracted. Proving himself their superior in force of character, intelligence, and connections, Plummer quickly gave order to their depredations while shielding them from what little law the Clearwater had.

Plummer was well known in Walla Walla, Lewiston, and Orofino. He was a prominent citizen, consulted on civic matters, and there was nothing in the ambiguity of his role which he seemed to consider strange. He was and would remain peculiarly loyal to both societies. When his gun got him in trouble at Orofino and his true activities were a matter of common gossip, he joined the rush to Florence, but things quieted down and he was able to go back again, entering the freight-station business with two "shebangs" (way stations), one between Lewiston and Orofino, the other west on the Walla Walla road. With the aid of these he instituted quite an efficient system for relieving travelers of their money and livestock. Choosing those who lacked the backing of large parties or of local friends, and in possession of good outfits, he fabricated bills of sale and sent fast horsemen to be at the freight station on their arrival. Faced with such evidence and the threat of hanging as horsethieves if they raised a fuss, most of them were easily convinced they had better give up their property. With care this might have gone on for quite a while, but some of Plummer's men became too bold, and the Clearwater vigilantes hanged several of them. Nothing clearly pointed to Plummer, but he was involved in another shooting, so he decided to sell out and visit the East. He traveled to Fort Benton in company with a man named Reeves, but they arrived too late for the season's boats and returned to American Fork. At Stuart's store, Plummer ran into another of his Idaho friends, a brawling, bullying desperado named Jack Cleveland. The two decided to winter up the Benton road at Sun River Crossing where some pioneer ranches were located. The attraction was probably a girl named Electa Bryan whom Plummer had met on his journey to Benton. Cleveland was attracted to her also. The friends quarreled, and when Electa would make no choice between them, they decided to leave the country together. She was not just one of the many women in Plummer's life, however, as future events were to prove.

Winter had already set in. Cleveland and Plummer crossed the passes to Bannack and found there a town of five or six hundred living in huddles of dirt-roofed cabins, wickiups, and caves in the hillsides, prospecting through the frozen gravel to bedrock and whipsawing lumber for sluices.

Despite the freezing weather, considerable gold was being produced, but Plummer and Cleveland experienced hard times. Plummer remedied his situation by renting saloon space for a card game. Cleveland used the more direct approach. Finding a lone victim on Buffalo Creek, the Grasshopper's chief tributary to the southwest, he rode up and shot him while his hands were lifted. At least that was the assumption when the poor fellow's body was subsequently found with a bullet hole under the armpit and frozen blood around it. The impoverished Cleveland, reappearing, now had money to carouse the camp.

Here was a situation readymade for the adroit Plummer. He saw a chance to stand up for common justice while ridding himself of a potential danger. He was playing cards in one of Bannack's long, low, winter-dim saloons when Cleveland came in, still on his haroo. A former acquaintance was there, and Cleveland started a bellicose argument over an old debt. After this had gone on in louder and louder tones for some time, Plummer rose from the table, announced he'd had enough, called Cleveland a suitable name, drew his Navy pistol, and opened fire.

The first shot went wild but the second dropped Cleveland on folded legs, clutching his groin. "Plummer, you wouldn't shoot me while I'm down!" he pled. "No, you son of a bitch, get up," Plummer answered, and shot him over the heart.

The camp did not hold it hard against Plummer that he rid it of Jack Cleveland. Although only a gambler at present, he had been ranking law officer in one of California's leading camps, and a freight-station owner in Idaho. Hank Crawford, the sheriff, gave succor to the dying Cleveland, and afterward he tried to make something of the affair, as though Plummer might not have acted as a good citizen. Many of the residents said Crawford was jealous. When the two men got to gunning for each other, the sheriff had less support from public opinion than might otherwise have been the case. Few cared to take sides. It was assumed that both men could take care of themselves.

Crawford, in addition to his duties as sheriff, operated a butcher shop. One day when he walked from the door of his establishment, Plummer was facing him in what appeared a threatening attitude across the street. They exchanged shots, Plummer missing and taking one of the sheriff's bullets in his right wrist. Both retreated from the field, Plummer to be bandaged and practice the draw with his left hand, Crawford to sell his meat market and depart for his old home in Wisconsin.

Bannack was without a sheriff and remained so for a couple of months. The spring thaw was at hand. The gravel which had been mined through the winter months at last could be put through the sluices. A great deal of gold had been won already by pans and rockers, but this was the flush of Bannack's bonanza. Although the claims situated on creek level had water enough to sluice most of the year, those on the benches, where paystreaks had been left by Grasshopper Creek in its prehistoric meanderings, could be worked only when the tributary streams flowed for a few weeks early in the season. Some Bannack claim owners were forced to wait years until the lower placers were worked out, or until companies were formed to bring in the water from creeks far back in the hills.

A miner's meeting was finally called for the twenty-fourth of May 1863. A poorer time could hardly be imagined. Placering was then at its height, with muddy water spilling from the tails of a hundred sluices and being caught in dams to be reused. Men who left their claims for a day were likely to have their precious sluice water channeled away from them; nor did they dare leave their sluices without shutting off the water and making a cleanup for fear that someone else would do it for them. As a result, only about five hundred of the several thousand in the Beaverhead area attended the meeting. A sheriff was selected for the entire Beaverhead country chiefly by the residents of Bannack, and instead of being a true miners' meeting, it was dominated by the business people and the denizens of the saloons and gambling dens.

Plummer was chosen sheriff. Already most of his old Idaho cohorts had followed him over or come in the general rush to the Beaverhead and found him there. He was their natural leader. He named some of them his deputies. They were men he thought he could trust to establish his power, but it is not so clear that his true ambition was to be a bandit king. He was out for easy money, as he had been in Idaho, but only incidentally to a position of true leadership in the new and growing country. He conducted himself in a manner which held the respect of most of the merchants, budding freight kings, and professional men. He made an effort to suppress petty crime, and hunted out and hung the horse-thieves with whom he had no connection. He got married, going over to Sun River for Electa Bryan. The sacrament was performed by the priest at St. Peter's Mission, on the trail 18 miles to the south. He arrived in Bannack with his wife and her possessions in a borrowed Army wagon and received congratulations from the best people in the community. After a couple of months with the dashing and personable sheriff, Electa left on the Oliver & Co. stage for Salt Lake City, and thence to the East where she had relatives. Plummer stayed on, intending to join her later in the year. In the meantime the gold country was expanding in a manner to surprise even the most optimistic.

A week before the meeting which put the sheriff's badge on Henry Plummer, a prospecting party organized by James Stuart started for the Yellowstone country. A smaller party went to the Deer Lodge to secure horses but, being delayed, they failed to make an intended meeting and fell into the hands of Indians near the present Livingston. One member, Bill Fairweather, was credited with saving himself and his companions when he pulled a rattlesnake, alive and lashing, from under his buckskin shirt where he had been carrying it for just such an emergency, and, holding the reptile aloft, pronounced himself big medicine, able to call down a curse of all the devils, including smallpox, if harmed. The Indians were sufficiently impressed to spare the white men's lives, but not enough to return the loot they had taken from them. So, short of supplies and riding some castoff horses, they headed back the short way across the Beaverhead-Madison divide, along an alder-filled gulch, and there they stopped to camp for a night. While some of the boys were preparing supper, Fairweather tried his luck panning at a place where some low rimrock broke the bench gravel above the stream and was rewarded with the first colors of the "richest gulch in history."

They needed supplies and tools. It was necessary to get them in Bannack. Secrecy was sworn. However, they whispered to a few of their friends, and word got around. How far it got around they learned when, after leaving quietly in the middle of the night, they looked back along the Beaverhead Valley and saw people strung out for miles, in wagons, on horseback and on foot, and there were spies watching them from the hills to make sure they didn't make a run for it and get away.

It was estimated that five hundred followed them to Alder. Even Bannack's brand-new territorial governor left, packing his papers and seal of office and thereby moving the capital to the new camp of Virginia City (named not for the Nevada town but as a compromise, Confederate partisans having first called it *Varina* City, honoring Jefferson Davis' wife).

Although not a plank section of sluice was whipsawed and in place before mid-summer, Alder was so rich that twenty-three tons of gold were produced the first year. It seemed a windfall to Plummer. The new district had no organization, but since nearly everyone on the ground had been resident of the Beaverhead it was a simple matter for him to extend his authority. However, complications arose. The men he had posted in Bannack as his deputies, or as agents to keep watch for treasure cargoes along the Salt Lake and Walla Walla trails, had been welded into the tightest organization possible, with secret signs and passwords, special beard trims, necktie knottings, and similar hocuspocus to awe them and promote secrecy; but they were drinking men and not really the kind to be entrusted with secrets. It further complicated things that not all of his deputies were crooked. He had at least one honest one, his chief deputy Dillingham, who had received his appointment after serving as chairman of the meeting which had named Plummer sheriff in May. When Dillingham learned that two of his fellow deputies planned to waylay a miner and rob him he gave warning and the miner escaped. This cost Dillingham his life.

At least in retrospect, it would seem that Plummer was entirely culpable. How much true control any man could exercise over so far-flung an organization is a question. Men such as his deputy Ned Ray had a proud arrogance which brooked control from no one. He must have realized that things were getting out of hand. The country was growing, with new mining camps springing up in a dozen gulches, and these were electing sheriffs of their own. His secret club continued, but there are indications that Plummer wanted to get out from under. His men, murdering and robbing for a few ounces of gold or some livestock, could hardly have put much profit in his account. He was seen less at the gambling tables and courted political favor, aspiring to be U.S. Marshal for the Territory. He talked a number of influential men into supporting him.

In wondering how Plummer maintained his position in spite of all that was known about him, it must be remembered that all sheriffs, indeed all law officers, are said by many to be dishonest. And the growth of the gold country helped. Men were too busy trying to find a piece of pay gravel, or otherwise establish themselves in the new country, to worry about cleaning it up. Once a claim was staked the first problem was protecting it against claim jumpers. No valuable claim could be left unguarded day or night, and as a result the miners had to work as teams, or, more often, they banded together in larger groups, and even then some rival group might move in to take at least partial possession. Sluices and ditches had to be guarded too, and small wars were fought over water rights. After they got a stake of a few thousand dollars was time enough to worry about getting out along the road. Hence it was autumn before it became apparent to the larger group that the road agents, organized and unorganized, held them in siege.

On Thanksgiving day Plummer brought in some turkeys from Salt Lake City and served a dinner which, not only because of the cuisine but also because of the guest list, became celebrated in territorial history. Among them was Plummer's true nemesis, Colonel Wilbur F. Sanders, lawyer, Republican from Ohio, young, fearless, and undeceived. It is not recorded that any of the choice viands and liquors stuck in his throat, but there seems little doubt that he was already measuring Plummer for his final collar. The showdown came not with Plummer, or even a man who was undeniably a part of his forces, but a free soul and errant highwayman named George Ives.

Ives was a tall and dashing adventurer from Wisconsin, a fancier of fine horses, charming and amenable companion when sober, violent roisterer and bully when drunk, who already had had quite a career as gold miner, gambler, Indian fighter, and highwayman behind him when he rode over from Idaho in the summer of 1863. Horses seem to have been his main passion, and he set up a ranch, or custom pasture, where the better-fixed stampeders could leave their stock for herding and protection against white thieves and Indians. It was believed he served as a lookout for the Plummer gang, but the chief thing which caused resentment around Virginia City were his drunken escapades. He liked to ride down the sidewalks and back his horse's rump through windows which had to be freighted all the way from San Francisco. Or he would ride into the saloons and demand that his horse be served as well as himself. Short of cash, he negotiated loans at the point of a gun. But he had many good citizens as friends, and a large following among the roughs.

In the summer of 1863 Henry Clark and George Burtchey came up with a wagon outfit from Colorado to locate at Summit, the mining district at the head of Alder Gulch, beneath 9800-foot Baldy summit. Their horses and mules were beaten out from the journey, and it seemed the wise thing to turn them over to Ives to pasture on the good grass of his claim on Wisconsin Creek, about two miles north of present-day Sheridan. Clark and Burtchey had no need for the stock until early in December, when they sent a young employee named either Tbolt or De Bolt to bring back a certain pair of mules. Nothing more was heard of him until a couple of weeks later when a grouse hunter found his body, bullet-pierced and multilated by animals, hidden in some underbrush at the side of Wisconsin Gulch. The hunter, a saloonkeeper from Nevada City, the next camp down Alder Gulch from Virginia, attempted to get help from Ives' ranch in loading the body in a wagon, but nobody there would stir to assist him. Why get so excited about a dead man, they wanted to know? Dead men turned up every day.

Alone he rolled the frozen body in a blanket, got it in the wagon, and started back to camp. Mines and sluices were solid along the gulch, with clutches of miners' cabins, and all along the winding road men gathered to view the body and attempt an identification. Tbolt was finally recognized and taken to Summit for burial. In a couple of days a party numbering among them his employers, Clark and Burtchey, together with X. Beidler and Nelson Story, famed in the annals of law enforcement and business enterprise, respectively, set out for Ives' ranch and took him and a couple of his men prisoner. They were brought in to Nevada City, camp closest the murder, and locked in a warehouse.

When the prisoners were brought in Colonel Sanders

happened to be in town taking care of some legal business. Just as he was about to board the Oliver line stage to Bannack, he was approached by the arresting group to take over the prosecution. There were several local lawyers, but all of them had been retained by Ives' friends. It was not the sort of a task courted by a man who wished to stay alive, but Sanders agreed.

Nevada City had no building large enough to accommodate the miners who came to attend the trial, and attend they must, all who wished. There were no regular courts, no judges. All authority derived from the miners in free meeting assembled. Today mining property worth uncounted millions bases its title on the rules laid down by miners' meetings which were the law of the frontier from 1849 until 1865. In this instance it seemed for a while that no lawyers would be allowed to participate in the trial, so bad was their reputation for the obstruction of justice. However, Sanders spoke on behalf of the profession and won their acceptance by narrow margin.

The crowd grew until an estimated 1500 were gathered on a shoulder of mining claim between the Main Street of Nevada and the gulch. It was obviously too large to hear the testimony, so a jury of twenty-four, twelve each from the mining districts nearest the scene of the crime, was selected. This left the Fairweather district unrepresented, and as it was the most populous, containing Virginia City, the Ives partisans saw an opening. One of them, Constable J. B. Caven, who owed his appointment to Henry Plummer, got busy and made a list of twelve men from the Fairweather district, and, mounting a wagon which served as the official platform, moved that these be added to the jury, making a total of thirty-six.

"Perhaps you have something to say against the character of these men I have named," Caven cried, shaking the list in Sanders' face. Sanders answered that he did not personally know any of them, but if what he had heard of some was true, he had no desire to make their acquaintance. "I will hold you personally responsible for that remark!" Caven said, but Sanders was not swayed by the threat. In his own words, describing the scene later, he accused Caven of attempting to advertise a courage he did not possess and that he would be available after the trial should Caven wish to come looking for him. This heartened the miners, who now saw they had a real prosecutor; the Fairweather jurors were rejected, and the trial went on.

The court, counsel, and prisoners were seated in the wagon, the twenty-four jurors on benches moved from a hurdy-gurdy house around an open fire, and the posse, with reinforcements, in a circle with shotguns to guard against escape or rescue. It was a long trial, the crowd forced to stand for hours on the frozen ground, and the defense made every attempt to make it longer, hoping that the crowd, which was antagonistic to Ives, would go back to their claims, leaving the preponderantly lawless camp residents in charge. Nothing of the sort happened. Sanders pursued the prosecution relentlessly, and was helped by a volunteer counsel, a country-style lawyer named Charles Bagg, who owned a mining claim nearby and spoke with good effect in the vernacular of the land.

The trial recessed at night and resumed in the morning, the crowd returning. William Palmer, the Nevada City saloonkeeper who found Tbolt's body, gave confidence to the proceedings when he testified, not a small thing when one considers that he would have to face the vengeance of the Ives and Plummer men after the miners went home. Later witnesses appeared and left no doubt that Ives was a road agent, and had been one in Idaho, but the key witness was one of his employees, "Long John" Frank, who told how young Tbolt had come for the mules and paid for their keep from a buckskin poke containing a pound of gold. "That was a fine team of mules," Ives had remarked. "It's a shame we can't keep them and the gold, too." The men flipped a coin to see who would bring them back, and the task turned to be Ives' own. He examined the cap and ball loads in his pistol and rode after Tbolt at a gallop. The men in camp heard a distant shot. Returning with the mules a short time later, Ives said it seemed cowardly to shoot a man in the back, so, getting close enough, he called out, and when Tbolt turned he made a center shot, hitting him in the head. The jury brought in a verdict of guilty. It was the crowd itself which set the penalty, which was immediate hanging.

At this sobering news, Ives approached Sanders. "Colonel," he said, "I am a gentleman, and I believe you are. Now, there is a favor I would like to ask. If our places were changed, I know I would grant one to you." He acknowledged that he had been pretty wild since he'd left home, but he had a mother and sister in the States, and he wanted a stay of execution until the next morning so he could write them, and arrange his estate.

Sanders had had cordial enough relations with Ives since their first meeting the spring before in Idaho, and it was a difficult request to turn down. Furthermore the crowd, after having pronounced his doom, was by then disposed to a little mercy. Aleck Carter, Bill Hunter, and partisans of the road-agent bunch had been very active trying to stir up sympathy, and George Lane—"Clubfoot George" of border legend—had been dispatched to Bannack to summon Plummer to the rescue, a summons the worried sheriff would ignore. Sanders did not know that, but while he hesitated and the crowd stilled to hear his answer, short, black-bearded X. Beidler, standing guard on the low roof of a cabin called across, "Sanders, ask him how long he gave the Dutchman!" It steeled the crowd against Ives, and the verdict was ordered carried out forthwith.

He hurriedly composed a few lines of a letter, and left it unfinished. Having vowed not to die with his boots on, he removed them. Later, his feet became cold when the execution was delayed, and someone lent him a pair of moccasins; in these he was hanged.

Two days after the hanging of Ives a group of Virginia's leading citizens met secretly and formed a vigilance committee. There had been communication with Bannack, and an allied group was formed there about the same time. On December 23, the Virginia force rode out to look for Aleck Carter, one of Ives' confederates. The weather had turned very cold, and there was deep snow. They rode to the Big Hole, the large western tributary of the Jefferson, and turned northward across the pass within five or six miles of Butte Hill. Coming to the present location of Warm Springs they met Erastus "Red" Yager, who was helpful, or seemed to be, volunteering that Carter and a number of his friends were at Cottonwood, the settlement south of Gold Creek later called Deer Lodge City. Yager knew they were at Cottonwood because he had been entrusted with a message from George Brown, the gang's secretary, warning them that the vigilantes were on the way.

Not finding Carter and his fellows but learning that Yager apparently had warned them, they turned back and scouted for his trail. It snowed heavily, and the cold deepened. X. Beidler was not with the group, having set out some days before to scout the situation of an overdue wagon train. He later found it stalled in snow at the foot of Monida Pass, but before reaching it he spent the coldest night of his life, saving himself from freezing by building a fire and keeping in almost constant movement around it. The cold probably prevented Yager getting to Bannack and warning Plummer, in which case the vigilantes' task would have been more difficult. They traced him to a shebang called Pickett's Lodge. He confessed, divulging the gang's whole membership, establishing Plummer as the leader, with a Bill Bunton as second in command, and added such interesting points as the password, "I am innocent," and the peculiar sailor's knot used in tying the road-agent cravat. With George Brown, a former wagon scout turned bartender and spy, he was taken to Laurin's place near the road fork to Virginia City and hanged on a cottonwood tree. Red Yager's last words were "Good-by. God bless you. You are on a good undertaking."

Plummer knew that the vigilantes were busy at Virginia,

but his own camp of Bannack was situated 75 miles away, across the Ruby Range, and he did not suspect that a Bannack chapter of the secret organization had been established. He was being watched, however, and when horses arrived indicating that he contemplated an earlier-than-planned departure for Salt Lake City, the group closed in.

Since the departure of his young wife, Plummer had been living at the boarding house of Mrs. A. J. Vail. He was awakened and told to dress. Outside he found that his deputies, Ned Ray and Buck Stinson, were also prisoners. He denied his guilt and begged for banishment. However, when it became obvious that nothing could alter the determination of his captors he resigned himself to his death, asking only for time to pray. By one account he was hanged from a tree, according to another from a scaffold he had himself constructed for the execution of a horsethief. Under the rope he stripped off his cravat, which, fastidiously, he had delayed at Vail's to put on, and tossed it to a young fellow boarder as a memento. "Give me a good drop, boys," he said. They obliged, lifting him high in the air and letting him fall. He died without a struggle. In the course of six weeks a total of 22 men were hunted down and hanged.

In a later tribute it was said the "trails were safe for honest men" after the vigilante work was done. They were far from safe if for no other reason than other vigilante organizations, lacking the purity of purpose attributed to the original, roamed the land hanging anyone they felt like. History, or at least romance, has placed a stamp of approval on the Montana vigilantes. Such universal fervor was not shared by the pioneers. A usual comment from these went, "They started out all right, but—" It was unfortunate that the first vigilantes were closely bound with the Freemasons, because when bands went through the country hanging honest prospectors, and a disproportionate number of the victims were Irish Catholics, the obvious conclusions were drawn. Chinese were favored victims, also, and friendless people in general.

The vigilante warning sign of 3-7-77, dimensions of a

grave, were said to have scared the lawless element into flight when posted on doors, gateposts and sidewalks in the early camps. This warning that summary justice would be meted out, hanging without trial, was recently chosen as a symbol for the Montana State Police force, its Highway Patrol. A good, hardworking, understaffed body of law officers, nobody has ever accused them of hanging people without trial, yet they are obliged to go around with 3-7-77 on their shoulder patches and the sides of their automobiles. It was suggested by sincere people who wanted to pay a tribute to state history and failed to recognize the insulting implications.

When this writer was a young man in Bannack the old residents, pioneers of 1863, were not even unanimous in their condemnation of Plummer. Often they would set forth on an account of people who were worse. No doubt his image was helped by recollections of later vigilante bands who posed the masked and midnight terror of the knock on the door and the quick hanging.

Had Plummer gone East when he first intended, shortly after Thanksgiving, there is little doubt he would have received his U.S. Marshal appointment. It came through posthumously. It is an interesting speculation whether he would then have returned to exercise his authority. Probably he would. As U.S. Marshall the vigilantes might have hesitated going for him. And could any charges against him have stood up in court? Certainly not after all the witnesses against him were executed! As U.S. Marshal he could have become a political power in the territory, and a rich man. Even as sheriff he would undoubtedly have reaped larger monetary rewards than as a bandit leader. Such offices, even though conducted with the most scrupulous honesty, were highly lucrative. Mining claims were generally held to small size, often a couple of hundred feet only, yet miles of gulches, rivers, benches, and even mountaintops were staked. Placer claims ran to the thousands, and even greater areas were taken by the hard-rock or quartz claims which came later. In the Helena Mining District alone there have been 1700 mining claims patented—which means they have been developed, surveyed, advertised and handed over by the government. Many times that number were held on simple claim, and the same is true of all the mining camps. By federal law, which was modified according to local agreement or custom, a certain amount of work was necessary in order to hold an unpatented claim. In the early years anything except actual possession and active operation was deemed abandonment, hence there was much relocating, preempting, amending, and the like. In instances where claims were held by groups of men, somebody was always abandoning the partnership with the resulting preemptions of his share. There continually arose problems of encroaching tailings and dumps, rights of way for roads, tunnels, and ditches, and the multiple encroachments of off-angle claims, resulting in mountains of legal work. Sheriffs, recorders, judges, and other officials generally had no regular pay, there being no provision for taxation, but they were given the privilege of keeping part or all of various fees. When John Manning, later of Butte City, was sheriff at Deadwood he became wealthy through the collection of fees which ran to as much as $75,000 per year. The take for the wide lands of Plummer's jurisdiction as sheriff would have been large and as U.S. Marshal would have been even larger. As a former law officer in California, he could not have been unaware of this. Yet he chose to align himself with men who could not help but destroy him. It was as if he had a compulsion to violence and the violent as some have to the bottle, or the gambling tables. A man of strange complexities, he has been a favorite with writers and readers for a century.

Although Alder Gulch continued to produce, stacking up a total greater than its three closest rivals combined, the main excitement moved northward. In the late summer of 1864 Last Chance and Orofino gulches were discovered, and Helena became the center of a great new gold region. At Confederate Gulch in the Big Belt Mountains, miners doing the minimum of work because of easy accessibility and shallow gravel staked some of the richest ground ever known. A single shovelful of gravel at Montana Bar, a terrace just north of Diamond City, yielded two and a half pounds of gold. Miners later writing of their experiences told how when the water was first shut off in the sluices they were found to be clogged with the yellow metal. In Cement Gulch, where the road climbed toward the Smith River divide on its way to Fort Benton, the richest claims yielded $1000 per running foot. In the autumn of 1866 a single cleanup on Montana Bar yielded a cargo which required three wagons and as many span of mules for transport to Fort Benton. An armed cavalry accompanied it. It was loaded on a steamboat and safely reached St. Louis. Not so happy was the experience of some miners who found what they thought to be one of the world's greatest deposits of coarse gold in a small tributary of Beavertown Creek south of Helena four years later. They freighted a barrel of nuggets to Fort Benton and thence to St. Louis before learning they were nuggets of native copper worth about $50 rather than gold worth $25,000. Hard at work they had what they believed to be $100,000 worth of metal under guard when the bad news reached them.

When Lieutenant Mullan built his road westward from the Deer Lodge Valley, he had passed a gulch mouth called The Bear. Although colors were washed from the Clark Fork River at its mouth, the gulch diggings and the rush to Bear waited until 1865. Claims were restricted to 200 feet along the stream, so there was room for quite a number of miners along the twenty-odd miles of the Bear and its tributaries. The gold was nearly all concentrated within a couple of feet of bedrock and perhaps a foot or so of the bed itself, generally a creviced and softened limestone. This lay at depths of 35 to 50 feet and made a channel about 15 feet wide. Since the miners did not wish to treat any more gravel than was necessary, they sank shafts to bedrock and hoisted the pay by bucket windlass. The gravel was sodden, so generally they worked in muck and water to the knees. In poorly consolidated ground they ran the continual danger of having the roof fall on them, and it had to be worked by a system known as forepoling. This consisted of driving sharpened poles over a prop or false set, one length beside another, and then digging the gravel from beneath, leaving the poles as a roof. Later cap and post timbers were set permanently, and the work proceeded.

When the individual workings became connected it was possible to walk up the bedrock bottom of the Bear for 10 miles without coming to the surface once. The men who labored to build this dark and winding passage were said to have assumed, one and all, a bearlike appearance, with thickened shoulders, spread feet, and bowed legs, and a habit of holding the head low and squinting because of the drip of sand into the eyes. The term Beartown Tough became territorially synonymous for all massive, brawling, saloon-wrecking men of subhuman appearance, and Beartown was renowned as the toughest camp on the gold frontier. At one time it was the center for 5000 men, with other populous camps at Reynolds City, Top o' Deep, Springtown, and Bearmouth. Despite the Mullan Road nearby, potatoes in Reynolds City cost twelve and a half cents a pound in 1866; salt 50¢, sugar 75¢, nails 25¢, and bacon 80¢.

Bear Gulch was one of the last of the placer discoveries. By 1867 the cream had been skimmed. Miners who took the coarse gold and nuggets and tossed the light stuff away as too much trouble were already on their way north. Bill Fairweather, finding the gulch he discovered grown too crowded for him, prospected up the mountains all the way to Alaska, where in 1865 a Russo–American company was surveying a telegraph line to cross at the Bering Straits, the entire territory to be purchased by the United States two years later. Soon a trickle of gold was finding its way out to Wrangell or to ports on the Yukon River. Due partly to the Alaskan climate, but mainly to the gigantic volumes of earth to be prospected, paystreaks lying much deeper in those parts than in Montana and Idaho, the main discoveries did not come for another thirty years, but when they did those interested in mining-camp records have found many names reappearing in Circle, Forty Mile, and the Klondike which earlier were known to Virginia City and Last Chance Gulch.

Most of the placer miners, however, turned to the nearby mountainsides and looked for the mother lodes. At Williams Gulch, one of the northern branchings of the Bear, miners followed the exceptionally rich and shallow paystreak uphill until it ended on the forested mountainside. They didn't bother to investigate why it stopped right there. It was not until 1874, eight years later, that Sam Ritchey staked his famed Nancy Hanks claim on the mother lode directly at the end of their working, and twenty years more were to pass before he was encouraged by discoveries east and west along the ridge to sink forty feet necessary to tap the "red ore" which was to make his fortune. A camp named Garnet for the nearby conspicuous reefs of that mineral came into being and briefly, around 1897, furnished Montana its chief gold excitement.

The hardrock rebirth of the Bear came late. At most camps, miners set out looking for the mother lodes as soon as they saw where the placer paystreaks seemed to be pointed. At Bannack, the Dakotah Lode was being worked by a rude stamp mill fabricated from old wagon parts even before water could be brought to some of the richest placer claims, and in later years twin pipes of ore, rotten with gold, called The Shotguns, were dug out under the eye of company guards, watchful that miners would not augment their $4.50 daily wage by dropping selected portions of a $10,000-per-ton high-grade into their dinner buckets. In Helena, Last Chance and Orofino gulches were followed upstream to mother lodes in the granite with the result that Unionville came into existence at the Whitlatch-Union group of claims during the early winter of that same year, 1864. By 1872 the mine was closed by litigation, but by that time it had produced $3½ million in gold, more than any corresponding area in the gulch.

The association of rich placer with as rich or richer

mother lode was, alas, not the rule. People searching for the quartz lodes whose erosion furnished the gold for Alder Gulch found them numerous in the gneissic country rock but only spottily worth the drilling, blasting, and crushing. The rich gulches of the Confederate area reach like octopus tentacles to enclose a mountain of diorite, large volumes of which constitute a gold impregnated subore, but the best of it, staked by old-timer "Blind Mike" Schabert, grossed him less for a lifetime of work than a single season at one of its better placer claims.

The best hardrock mines of all lay at the ends of gulches that contained gold in sparing amounts. Butte Hill had decayed enough of its veins to supply moderate amounts of gold to Silver Bow Creek, and was an early fair-to-average gold camp. The largest of the hardrock gold veins, the Drumlummon at Marysville, the Jay Gould nearby, and the Southern Cross near Philipsburg, had skimpy placers. Few of the lodes paid out as long as equipment had to be brought in by steamboat and freight wagon. The gold veins required heavy capitalization, and capital, because of the spectacular fortunes then being reaped at the Comstock, was chiefly interested in silver. In the years between 1868 and 1885 it was silver which furnished most of the excitement in the mountains, while the supply of its camps and mines, and the transportation of its ores, furnished much of the tonnage on the Salt Lake Trail.

Placer mining stakes seldom ran to more than a quarter-million dollars. Anyone taking $25,000 from the gold fields was considered to have struck it rich. The kings of the country from 1863 to 1880 were its suppliers, the big men in wagon freight. As they became large owners of livestock, their need for pasturage put them in the ranching business. Freight stations were established at the best crossings, the best water, and best natural pasture. As a result, the freight owners found themselves with the best townsites. Early freighters hauled for the pioneer established merchants. It

wasn't long before they built warehouses and became merchants themselves—haulers, wholesalers, retailers. Later they
invested in railroads, mines, and smelters, but that is a
story beyond the range of this book.

The men who drove the wagons for these kings of the
road were a hardy lot. Why is it they have been so neglected
by the historians of the West and those who collect its lore?
One sees books of gold miner, cowboy, and lumberjack
songs, but none recounting the romance, travels, and travails
of the wagon freighter. The rough, self-reliant, and on the
whole well-paid freighters were a special breed, but they live
in legend only for their profanity.

Freighters were not esteemed for their manners, and
some have compared them with wolfers and buffalo-skinners,
but this is unfair calumny. There are tales of freighters sew-
ing themselves in their underwear in preparation for the
winter season, not to come forth until spring, in the belief
that clothing attained warmth with its ripeness. But they
were not alone in this. All along the frontier men genuinely
believed it was debilitating to bathe in cold weather.
Freighters, particularly in winter, were forced to sleep in
vermin-infested bunks, and there is some evidence that the
body accumulates an essence which either repels lice or ren-
ders them dormant. However, as a group they were probably
cleaner than most frontiersmen, if for no other reason than
that their day-to-day struggles with creek and river crossings,
braving currents to their armpits, and their life outside in
sun, wind, and summer deluge kept them at least as clean as
their animals.

One of the most rugged of all the northern freight bosses
was A. V. Brower, yet a photograph of his outfit shows him
and most of his men posed in neckties. This does not mean
they wore them in their daily work, but it does mean they
possessed them. Brower had the reputation of being a marti-
net, ruling his train with the dictatorial power of a captain at
sea. A favorite anecdote of the Montana–Alberta border

country concerned Brower and may give a brief insight into the character of at least one freighter and substitute, let us hope, for a ballad or other lore:

A. V. Brower had come west from upper New York state as a boy, and, though unable to read and write, had with the help of friends kept up a correspondence with his relatives, and was the support of a sister much younger than himself. He sent money regularly to pay for her education, and was known to have centered on her all the hopes that a more settled man might for his family. One day when his outfit was pulling the road up from the Missouri River, on his way to Fort Walsh across the Canadian boundary, the mail wagon passed his train and left him a letter. As soon as the noon dinner stop was made he took it to his cook, Charlie Nightlinger, and asked that it be read to him.

Charlie, called "Blind Charlie" because of an old whip-lash scar in one eyeball, prided himself on his learning. He was a tall man, with a drooping rusty-red moustache, and like many cooks and redheads, contentious. When Brower approached him he was pounding steak with the butt of his six-shooter, his other hand occupied with a mixture of pepper and flour, a favored way of preparing steak from beef driven along with the train to be butchered as needed, their newly fallen and cut-up flesh tending to be tough. It was not usual for even the boss to interrupt a cook in this important work, but Brower was anxious to hear what his sister had written, so he made the request. Charlie said all right, to put it down, he would read it while pounding the steak. After, one supposes, the usual formalities and news of relatives, the girl asked if he would send some extra money needed for new clothes, as she had decided to enter a certain seminary, which she named.

"Hold on," said Brower. "What is that?"

"What's what?"

"What's a seminary?"

"What do you care what it is?" asked Blind Charlie, not wishing to undermine his position as an educated man by admitting he didn't have the slightest idea. "She needs new clothes to enter a seminary. Send her the money. You can afford it. You make more than any three men in the whole outfit."

"Of course I'll send it to her, but I want to know what a seminary is."

"You won't find out from me because I'm not going to tell you."

"By God, you will tell me, or this outfit will be needing a new cook."

Blind Charlie knew that the boss meant it. He still had no inkling of what the girl intended to do, but he knew it was necessary to come up with something very impressive to justify his refusal so he said, "Well, all right, but remember I didn't want to tell you. A seminary is nothing but a high-toned name for a parlor house."

By this time, teamsters being a hungry crew at mealtime, quite a number were within earshot of the cook wagon, so there were numerous accounts of the incident when they reached their next stop at Big Sandy Crossing. All agreed the news hit Brower very hard. He nearly broke into tears, and beat on the side of the cook wagon with his fist saying, "No, I won't do it. I won't send her a cent. If she wants to do that she'll just have to do it in her old clothes."

Fortunately there were a number of men at the Crossing who were educated in the simple lights of the time, and one of them approached Brower with the true facts of his sister's request. Undoubtedly relieved, he hunted out his cook, who was drinking at one of the local saloons. However, the crowd which tagged along to see the killing was disappointed. No shooting took place, even though Blind Charlie doggedly refused to acknowledge ignorance or error.

"That may be so," he said, "but the kind I had experience with weren't one bit better than high-toned parlor houses."

The first freighting center of Montana was Fort Benton,

where connections were made with the St. Louis riverboats. Later Virginia City became important, its gold furnishing capital to extend the lines. With the decline of Alder Gulch in the late sixties most of the companies headquartered in Helena. The district to the south was rich in silver which the pioneer smelters and mills were unable to extract successfully, and a profitable traffic developed, the sacked, hand-sorted highgrade going first to Fort Benton and downriver to smelters in Omaha and the east coast, and when their service proved unsatisfactory, down the Salt Lake Road to the Union Pacific at Corinne, Utah, thence to San Francisco, and by sailing vessel around Cape Horn to the smelters of Saxony and Wales.

Some difficult freighting jobs cost as much as 50 cents a pound for the Utah-to-Montana haul. When the Hope silver mine at Philipsburg installed a pan amalgamation mill the heavy iron pans, ten stamps weighing 650 pounds each, and a Leavenworth steam engine and forty horsepower return-flue boiler all came by bull freight, requiring most of the spring and summer and costing the consignees slightly less than $1000 per ton. At one crossing of a stream the heavier pieces sank out of sight in the quicksand. Undaunted, the freighters camped and waited for dry weather, digging them up again and moving them to their destination in good shape.

As the road improved, rates went down. By 1876 freight rates from Butte to Corinne averaged $51 per ton. The service speeded, also. Although the bull teams customarily took more than a month, there was a fast freight which made the journey from Butte in six and a half days. Express by Concord coach made it in four.

In 1871 ground was broken for a railroad up from Brigham City. By 1874 it reached Franklin on the Idaho–Utah line. After being bogged down there for another three years it was purchased by the Union Pacific, which built it to the Beaverhead in 1880 and completed it to Butte in 1883. Its guage was three feet, and it was at that time the longest narrow line in the world. The excitement of its arrival was dimmed by the final completion of the Northern Pacific that same summer. Both lines celebrated by driving silver spikes, a tribute to what they believed to be the chief wealth of the territory. Elsewhere horse freighting continued to be big business because of outlying mines and the Army supply, but long-distance hauling was taken over by the railroads.

Chapter 8

In the mid-nineteenth century there was no animal which meant more to Americans than the horse, and the one who knew more about horses than any man alive was Professor Othniel C. Marsh of Yale University. "The most wonderful thing I ever saw!" wrote the great Thomas Huxley on being shown his superb sequence of equus fossils, demonstrating the horse evolution from a tiny, clawed animal not much larger than a fox to the Clydesdale engine of power to be seen pulling the brewery wagons of that day.

Marsh had already attained some celebrity in the national press when, late in 1869, he branded as a fake the Cardiff Giant, "a petrified man ten feet four and a half inches tall weighing 2090 pounds," which had been carved out of gypsum by George Hull, a Binghamton, N.Y., cigar manufacturer. Even earlier, al-

171

though it had not been given much publicity, Marsh pro-
pounded the theory that the horse had evolved from the
small clawed animals and was a product of North America.
Although extinct in all the Western Hemisphere when the
first white men came, he believed it had migrated, using a
trail which ran up the Western mountains, and had crossed
to Asia and Europe by an ancient land connection at Bering
Strait.

Marsh had turned his attention to the fossil horse, to
the West, and to the Great North Trail as the result of a fortunate accident. He was in Chicago attending a scientific
meeting when the newspapers carried accounts of some peculiar bones which a well-digger had found at a place called
Antelope Station, about 15 miles from the Nebraska–
Wyoming boundary, on the line of the new Union Pacific
Railway. Then, by chance, he was offered a free trip west on
that very line, and accepted it in preference to a vacation in
Canada.

To his annoyance, he learned after the long, wearying
journey, that Antelope Station was not a regular stop.
Marsh, however, was a hard man to turn aside. He finally
bulldozed the conductor into halting the train for a few minutes by promising otherwise to make a full, adverse report to
General Snider, head of the U.P., who was a friend.

The conductor grudgingly said he would stop for five
minutes. Antelope Station proved little but a boxcar dumped
from its wheels for a depot, a log store, and some sheds set
out on the prairies of Lodgepole Creek. Marsh had no trouble
finding the well, which had been dug by the railroad. A
large heap of whitish Nebraska dirt stood beside it, undisturbed since the hoisting. To his delight he found it shot
through with bones. Most of them were in splintered fragments, but he was rewarded with a relic of *Equus parvulus*
—he named it on the spot—the long-suspected but previously undiscovered three-toed horse. Full-grown, it had been
about the size of a shepherd dog. The train was tooting for

him with short, impatient blasts. He signaled to wait, wait! and kept digging. Indignant passengers shouted from the open windows, but he dug deeper. At last, slowly, the train started out. Stuffing his *Equus* bones in his pockets and carrying under his arm the shinbone of an extinct American camel, he ran and caught the last coach. He had spent less than half an hour at Antelope Station, but it was the turning point in his career. All the rest of his life his chief devotion was to Western paleontological exploration.

Marsh was an immediate success with his three-toed miniature horse. The country was at that time in a fever over evolution. A decade had passed since Darwin's publication of *The Origin of Species,* and though few in America had read and understood this massive work they had had plenty of contact with a conclusion drawn from it, and its oversimplification—that the Bible was a lie, and man came from the monkey. From a thousand pulpits *Origin* was attacked and Darwin scourged as a representative of the devil.

In 1856, three years and a few months before Darwin's cataclysmic book, quarrymen at the Neanderthal, a vale near Düsseldorf, broke into a limestone cave and found some peculiar fossilized bones. These and quite a number of earlier human relics were viewed with new interest in the light of Darwin's theory, and in Europe one scientist started arranging such bones in progression, linking man with the lower animals. There were certain gaps which needed filling, and when this was announced it came to be believed that the evolutionary chain of Darwin was lacking one crucial skull. If this skull, this missing link, could be found, then the Darwin theory would be the winner over the Bible. If not, then the Bible was winner over the Darwin theory. Nowhere was the missing link so branded as ridiculous, and the idea of its existence so condemned, as in America. Yet nowhere was it so eagerly sought. It was this death wish of orthodoxy which accounted for the success of George Hull's gypsum giant. It attracted cash customers numbering the hundreds of thousands for years even after it was known to be a hoax, and a competing giant at Barnum's Museum also did good business.

From the largest dailies of the great cities down to the boiler-plate sections of the smallest weekly papers, paleontology was big news. As missing links appeared all over middle and south Europe, America dug in vain. The only thing found in the New World was the Calaveras skull in California. As one of the principles in this controversy will later play a prominent part in these accounts, it will be summarized here:

In June 1866, Professor Josiah Dwight Whitney was chief of the California State Geological Survey. He had already won acclaim as a leading geographer, geologist, and paleontologist. Two years before, he had enjoyed the distinction of having named for himself the highest peak in the nation. He had every prospect of a continued celebrity from the mountain mapping of California, and of a succeeding career filled with wealth and fame. He could not suspect that sitting in his office at that moment was a subordinate, a dapper young geologist named Clarence King, who would soon travel to Washington, D.C., pull various political strings, and supplant him as the premier mapmaker of the West, or that the package which a legman for the express company carried through the door was to render him either one of the world's most celebrated anthropological pioneers or else one of the sorriest dupes of the century, depending on the point of view.

The package was wrapped in ordinary brown grocers' paper, and came from William Jones, M.D., of Murphys Camp over in Calaveras County. Murphys, Angels Camp, and Altaville were then important places because of their position solidly in the middle of the great Mother Lode mining region. Dr. Jones, a popular physician of the area, was like Whitney a part-time paleontologist. They shared the opinion that man, when science had the facts, would be proved much older than the figures then heard from the evolutionists. And both held America to be the most likely cradle of the human race. The proof of their mutual convictions was what Jones sent to the Director in his express package.

Whitney opened it and found a skull, obviously of great antiquity. It was opalized, raising its specific gravity far above that of any recent bone. Time had encrusted it with a limy material in which gravel and shells were embedded. He immediately set out for Murphys to ascertain all of the conditions surrounding its discovery.

Murphys Camp was already known to archeologists. In 1857, Paul Hubbs of Vallejo, later the State Superintendent of Public Instruction, had picked up a portion of human skull from the dump material of the Valentine mine shaft at Table Mountain only a few miles away. Hubbs had given it to a medical doctor named C. F. Winslow in October of the same year, and Winslow, knowing the rivalry which existed between Boston and Philadelphia scientific groups, had sawed it in half and sent one portion to the Boston Society of Natural History and the other to the Philidelphia Academy. Whitney had been too late to see the skull, but he had talked to Hubbs and was convinced of its authenticity. The Hubbs skull had been only one of a whole succession of curious finds from under Table Mountain, which was really a layer of basaltic lava overlying some ancient gold-bearing stream gravel. At Sonora, another nearby camp, a Dr. Snell had made a collection of such bones and artifacts, labeled them "From Under Table Mountain," and had displayed them in his office. The collection, which included a stone mortar and a human jawbone, had been examined by Whitney, but unfortunately it had been destroyed when Snell's office burned in 1866.

On his arrival at Murphys, Whitney learned that the Jones skull was not one of the Table Mountain relics. It had come from beneath Bald Mountain, a similar lava-capped layer of gravel at Altaville, which adjoined Angels Camp on the north, and which in turn was 7 miles down the road from Murphys. The actual discovery had taken place six months before. Since then the mine workings had proved unprofitable, been abandoned, and allowed to fill with water. However, with Dr. Jones' help, Whitney located the miner who had dug it up. The miner, a man of excellent reputation whose name was Mattison, recalled every detail of the find. The mine, he said, was entered by a vertical shaft which pierced black lava rock for a distance of 40 feet. With overburden, volcanic ash, and the thickness of gravel added, the depth of the entire working was 132 feet below the present surface. A drift had been turned at bedrock, which was actually the bed of an ancient river. The river gravels had become somewhat cemented during the centuries, and sunken driftwood had tended to petrify through the absorption of silica. On that memorable day, he had descended and gone to work at the end of the drift noticing not a thing out of place or unusual. The gravel was entirely cemented and undisturbed. The skull, when he came to it, was firmly embedded. He first took it to be a grayish burl of petrified wood. Using his pick, he pried it loose. The skull still bore marks of this. As soon as his candlelight fell on it he realized it was a human skull.

Wisely, Mattison decided not to try chipping off any of the material which encrusted it. He laid it aside and that evening carried it down to the express office and gave it to the agent, Mr. Scribner. Mattison told Scribner that some collector might find it of interest, and if Scribner cared he could send it to one of them, express collect. Scribner showed it around for an hour or two when somebody suggested that the person who ought to get the skull was Doc Jones at Murphys Camp.

Jones was known up and down the Mother Lode as an exponent of the Darwin theory. A professed atheist, he was one of those who espoused the new Huxley text that man was descended from the apes, or at least from a common ancestor. The suggestion that Jones receive the skull was greeted with cheers. So off it went in care of the stage driver with a sizable delegation from Alta and Angels Camp, on horseback and racing behind the coach on foot, to see how he would receive it. They were not disappointed. One look at the fossilized skull and they had a wild man on their hands. "Boys," Jones was quoted as saying, "this just knocks the hell out of old Moses!"

For the next several months Jones hardly let the skull out of his sight, carrying it with him in his bag and showing it everywhere, even in camps as far away as Amador, and it was described in several newspaper stories. Indeed it was an arresting sight, staring out with one eyesocket, the other scabbed over with lime, shells and gravel, and the bone, where exposed, streaked brown from iron oxide. However, there were stories going around which impugned the skull's authenticity. Some of these Jones traced to the clergy he had long ago named the worst liars in creation. Other tales, more reliable, seemed to originate in Angels Camp. People there were saying a trick had been played on him. Instead of being "at least 994,134 years older than Adam"—a figure Jones arrived at by subtracting the time a celebrated Irish divine had placed on the Biblical creation of the world from the estimated minimum geological age of the Bald Mountain capping of lava—they were saying the skull was actually that of a prospector whose skeleton had been brought in from the hills and whose skull had disappeared from an Angels Camp saloon where it had been on display. Because of this and several other pieces of gossip, Jones sent it off to the supreme California authority, the Director of its Geological Survey, and awaited verification.

The results more than fulfilled his expectations. Whitney was as wild as Jones had been, but whereas Jones had been more or less bounded by the southern Mother Lode, Whitney was enthusiastic on a transcontinental scale. With Whitney's name to back it, the skull was on the news telegraph all over America, and in England and Europe as well. Most newspapers in their accounts also made mention of Mt.

Whitney, 14,501 feet in height, thus giving the skull considerable added eminence. Soon it was being called Calaveras
Man, and many artists' reconstructions were printed.

Whitney was not long in California after the discovery.
He traveled with the skull to Harvard University. There,
with the help of skilled paleontologists, the coatings were
removed and the bone tested. It was determined to contain
only a minute remnant of animal substance. By comparison
with Neanderthal and Gibraltar skulls, this seemed proof of
its greater antiquity. As a further check, its metamorphic
state was compared with the petrification of wood fragments
in the ancient Bald Mountain gravels, and proved contempo-
rary. These gravels had already been dated by the foremost
geologists of the world as of Tertiary age, sealed more
tightly than the tombs of the Pharaohs by 40 feet of solid
lava rock; Calaveras Man, Whitney said, must therefore be
of similar antiquity. As further substantiation he pointed
toward the finds beneath Table Mountain, where the skull, a
jawbone, and a mortar had been unearthed, proving not only
that man did exist in those remote eras, but that he had a
tool-making culture as well. In all this Whitney received
considerable support. Many scientists regarded Calaveras
Man highly, and some do still.

However, Whitney, like Dr. Jones, was embarrassed by
a number of rumors. Newspapers in the Mother Lode belt,
and later in San Francisco, suggested that he had been made
the victim of mining-camp hoax. The skull, according to a
new version, had originated at an Indian burial cave on the
side of a nearby mountain. Authority for this was a man of
the cloth, a Reverend Brier of Alvarado. According to the
Reverend Brier, his brother, a hardrock miner and prospector, had been present in the cave when the discovery of the
skull was made. Other Indian skulls had been found under
similar circumstances, he said. On this occasion someone got
the idea of coating it with lime plaster, shells, and pebbles,
baking it several days in the warming oven of a cookstove
until the proper hardness had been attained, and wedging it

in a prospecting drift under Bald Mountain, where it could be authentically discovered before presentation to Doc·Jones as the one and only genuine missing link.

The controversy thrust a terrible choice on the·California press. On the one hand it very much wanted to promote California as the birthplace of man, and on the other to be in on *the know,* and show up the experts of Harvard University. The latter temptation proved the stronger. The high point of the detraction was reached when Bret Harce, one of the most notorious spendthrifts in history, who had just been named Secretary of the California Mint, lampooned Calaveras Man in rhyme in the columns of *The Californian.* But Whitney stuck with his skull. If a hoax, he said, how about the similar skull halves in Boston and Philidelphia? Or the jawbone, the pestle, or any of a host of relics dug from nearby lava-capped gravel? The real error seems to have been unsuspected, and it was the same which weighed so heavily in favor of another anthropological anachronism, the fraudulent Piltdown Dawn Man of England. In both the Calaveras and Piltdown instances, geologists had dated the formations incorrectly. The Piltdown gravels of England were assigned the Tertiary period, when in reality they were wash from glacial moraine. In California, much volcanic material, and the gravels they cap, are more recent than was once generally imagined.

It was into this missing-link controversy that Professor Marsh introduced his horse. The horse was at that time as important in man's everyday life as the automobile is today, and if a man could not discover an apelike progenitor of Adam, far and away his best substitute was the ancestral horse. Steel-engraved illustrations appeared in newspapers all over the land showing Marsh standing beside a table with a reconstruction of the dog-size horse. Later, when some fossil lemurs were discovered in South America and incorrectly identified as small humanoid missing links, a newspaper artist showed Marsh's horses with monkey-size missing links riding on their backs.

Marsh was too excited about his finds to take much notice of national publicity. He made hurried preparations and the following spring found him on the train for Wyoming with wagons and camp gear. He unloaded in the desert country of the Green River plateau, and headed south. He braved unfriendly Indians, had a brush with horse rustlers, suffered short rations, alkali sickness, and other hardships, but his ultimate take of fossils weighed several tons. He then turned to Salt Lake City with some trepidation, fearing the receptiveness of that Mormon stronghold to an expedition out to prove the Darwinian theory. To his amazement he found Brigham Young and the bishops assembled in his honor. In the East Marsh had been attacked from numerous pulpits for teaching godless evolution; in Salt Lake City he was received as a defender of the faith. It turned out that the *Book of Mormon* was being held up to disdain in some quarters because it had horses in early America although well known they had been introduced by the Spaniards. Hence the discovery of *Equus parvulus* proved the *Book* to be correct.

Although gratified by his reception, Marsh showed some hesitation in endorsing the Mormon concept of the American horse. He pointed out that *parvulus* was no larger than a dog. In fact, outside in the wagons were bones of adult horses no larger than jackrabbits. However, Young and his bishops brushed this aside. They put the question, yes or no, did horses exist in America previous to the Spanish conquest? To this his answer was yes, and he enjoyed the prodigality of the city. Quipping afterward: "I was not prone to look a gift hippus in the mouth."

Marsh was a nephew and chief heir of millionaire philanthropist George Peabody. In obtaining a large grant from Peabody for the establishment of a museum of science for Yale, he in no way hurt his own academic security at that institution, where be became Professor of Vertebrate Paleontology. His capabilities were without question, but the recognition might not have arrived so early without his connections. From the firm base of the Yale Museum, and with a sizable inheritance, it might seem that he would have clear sailing as America's leading paleontological explorer. However, a rival had made his appearance. This was Edward Drinker Cope, of Philadelphia.

Like Marsh, Cope was a young man of wealth, and he was even more an infant prodigy of science. At the age of six young Edward had written his grandmother, "I have been at a Museum and I saw a Mammouth and Hydrarchas, does thee know what it is? It is a great skeleton of a serpent. It was so long that it had to be put in three rooms." When Marsh, in his early thirties, returned from studies in Germany to take over his Yale professorship, Cope, in his early twenties, had already become the scientific rival of Professor Joseph Leidy, University of Pennsylvania, the great man of American anatomy and paleontology.

At that time English and French scientists had turned up the bones of several extinct reptiles of Mesozoic age they called Dinosauria, a name arrived at by combining the Greek *dinos,* terrible, with *sauros,* a lizard. It happened that the Philadelphia Academy of Natural Sciences already had in its possession a large, unorganized collection of such bones which had early been gathered from the coal regions of Pennsylvania and southern Illinois by Parker Foulke, an amateur at science. Leidy had supplemented these with fossils of his own, taken from Iowa, Nebraska, and even the Judith River of Montana, enough to keep most paleontologists busy for years.

Cope, however, was not held long by the bones in the Philadelphia Academy. He traveled in Europe, which for him meant rushing from one museum to another, seeing what they had, and spotting the errors they had made. Returning, his attention was called to an area in New Jersey where some peculiar remains were reported in a greensand quarry. He immediately turned up with the bones of an 18-foot flesh-eating member of the Dinosauria which he named *Laelaps aquilunguis.* A good man with an artist's pencil and a descriptive phrase, Cope gave the public a fiercely fanged creature which roved on powerful rear legs, carnivorous and rapacious, the terror of the saurian marshes. It was an immediate hit. Soon Cope was hauling tons of bones to Philadelphia. He traveled through Maryland and western Pennsylvania, and even Ohio and Virginia, and his monographs and articles came rolling off the press.

Meanwhile, at Yale, not yet dreaming of the West, Marsh was a very unhappy man. He was itching to put his uncle's museum in the forefront, but it had not been built. He visited Philadelphia and found Cope's discoveries overflowing the museum. He heard that even greater treasure was hidden behind locked doors at the Cope mansion, and in his stable. And at every report, Cope was ranging farther, buying up private collections, and putting crews of his own diggers to work. Marsh was alarmed that Cope would succeed in gobbling all the truly significant fossils in the country, eventually leaving Yale with the finest of museum facilities and nothing really first-rate to put in them. He made a trip into New England, a poor choice. All he found there were a number of fossil footprints by extinct birds standing 20 feet high.

It was then that Marsh took his free trip on the U.P. and discovered the West. When he published his findings in regard to the three-toed horse and mapped its migration route —to Asia, Europe, and back again via the Great North Trail, public interest being the greater because of recently acquired Alaska, it was Cope's turn to be alarmed. The next he heard, Marsh had set out with his wagons for Wyoming and Utah, and when he returned, his finds secured in heavy plank boxes furnished by the Mormons, the scientific world was filled with rumors. The West, from Missouri to the deserts of Oregon, was reported to possess ancient boneyards exceeding in size and variety of species anything known to paleontology. So, in the following spring of 1871, while Marsh was still busy with his finds of the season before, Cope was moving through Missouri, locating fossil fields and searching out private collectors.

According to scientific practice, to receive credit for a new species one had to publish its description in an approved manner, or deliver a paper on it before one of the learned societies. Private collectors were seldom able to do these things. Cope solved their problem for them. He would obligingly identify the species in their collections, place each new one in the system of biology, name them suitably, and describe them in print, thus taking credit as discoverer. Cope was a charming man, witty and amiable. People took to him at first sight. He was a Quaker, and never completely lost his Quaker manner of address, but otherwise he might have played a French count in sophisticated comedy. Even after he had rooked some poor backwoods teacher or regional historian of credit for his discoveries, he seldom left any real bitterness behind. Instead they were likely to serve as his scouts, or perhaps ship him their new finds, only to be beaten out of the scientific credit all over again.

Marsh was equally without scruple. However, when he raided collections he won wrath and unforgiving outrage. In later years Dr. Thomas Condon of Oregon State University would not allow Marsh to enter the room that housed his fossils unless accompanied by a sharp-eyed guard whose job it was to make sure he slipped nothing into his pocket.

The differing reactions to Cope and Marsh piracy no doubt went deeper than mere personality. It might have been due to their objects, which somewhat differed. To Cope, discovery was all. He did not really care so much whether he ended up with every bone of an animal provided he received credit as the discoverer of that species. Most people were collectors. Marsh was a collector. He wanted possession of a thing, every bone complete. So he competed with more people. Marsh was to beat Cope by perhaps a trainload of fossil bones, but Cope consistently beat Marsh at discovery. Time and again Cope staked his scientific reputation on some creature which he projected entire on what others would have considered the most trifling evidence, and all but once came out unscathed. In the badlands of the Judith, Cope once classified twenty-one dinosaurs by means of their teeth alone.

Cope's unscientific blooper, which Marsh never let him forget, took place on his expedition west from Missouri in 1871. His course took him through Abilene—where Wild Bill Hickok was then town marshal—Ellsworth, and Hays City, leaving the train to form his expedition at Twin Buttes near the Colorado border. Heading up Butte Creek, he discovered, projecting from a cutbank, the bleached skull of a monstrous creature which he immediately identified as a relative of the Mosassuria, a genus of large marine reptiles whose remains had originally been found in rock beds bordering the Maas River of the Netherlands.

Only a relative, however. This, because of size and other features, he determined to be not only a new species, but a new genus as well. The reptile had fallen in death to the bottom of a shallow sea. In subsequent ages the sea had been uplifted to become Kansas prairie. Gullies had turned its resting place into the spur of a bluff. The vertebrae in fact led directly across the spur a distance of 75 feet. Size alone made the find sensational. Its form was more sensational yet. Its most notable feature appeared to be a long, snakelike neck. The neck, in fact, seemed longer than all the rest of its body, tail included. He named it *Elasmosaurus platyurus*— flat-tailed, platy saurian. He sat down by his campfire and wrote a monograph with sketches. Later he described it in a magazine article. He returned and mounted it for display at the Philadelphia Academy, and made a speech on its evolutionary significance. But Elasmosaurus rose to haunt him. In this one instance he had slipped. In his rush to get into print, and in premature awe at the saurian's long, snakelike neck, which distinguished it from all other reptiles since the beginning of time, he had made the mistake of putting its head on the wrong end, so what he thought was a snakelike neck was in reality only a long tail.

Cope was most enthusiastic about the possibilities of

the West, and that winter made plans to visit the Bridger Basin, where Marsh had been two years before. This area, in the extreme southwestern corner of Wyoming Territory, had yielded a number of gigantic skulls, some of them with horned protuberances of arresting ferocity. The basin was named after Jim Bridger, who operated a nearby "fort" on the trail to California, where thousands of emigrants stopped for supplies, repairs, and a needed rest, and where the nearby Arapahoe and Shoshone Indians could supply themselves with guns and ammunition. The Indians would not touch the great bones. They called them "thunder horses" and held them inviolate by command of the Great Spirit. Mountain Men and emigrants had been picking them up for years and bringing them to Bridger. "Old Gabe" was one of the most celebrated liars in the West, an accomplishment rated among frontiersmen roughly on a par with crack marksmanship and the capacity to hold strong drink. The gargantuan remains served Bridger not only as inspiration, but also as visible proof of his veracity. There was really little danger from such animals, he reassured the emigrants, for they were likely to keep away from the beaten trails. Only once had he been driven by hunger to hunting the terrible beasts. That had been during the year of the two winters, when the whisky froze solid in the jugs and all the buffalo retreated south of the Arkansas. If anyone doubted the severity of the year, said Bridger, or the famine of that season, he had only to step outside and see how clean the bones had been picked. Such stories served the good office of steeling emigrants against the hardships which lay ahead, while encouraging them to lay in an extra-heavy supply of powder and ball at stiff Fort Bridger prices.

Bridger's old fort had been burned by the Mormons in the late 1850s and his relics scattered, but the first geological parties found others on every hand. With so much at the surface, it was anyone's guess what would be found in the mother lode Cretaceous strata themselves. However, when

Cope got off the train at Green River, he learned to his dismay that Marsh had returned and was in the field ahead of him.

The town of Green River was then outlet to the Sweetwater gold-mining region which lay 80 miles north. At least 10,000 miners had stampeded into the Sweetwater five years before, establishing the camps of South Pass City, Atlantic City, and Miner's Delight. In 1872, South Pass City rivaled Cheyenne as the territory's foremost metropolitan community. It was the only town in Wyoming with five hotels, one of which had three rooms. In 1872 the camps were on the downgrade, and disheartened miners filled Green River, looking for jobs. From among these refugees both Cope and Marsh recruited their labor force.

Marsh had no legal claim on the Bridger Basin. However, when Cope showed up, he had possession. Marsh simplified their relationship by telling his men that Cope was a claim jumper. He made no recommendation as to procedure, but up on the Sweetwater it had been the custom to shoot claim-jumpers on sight. Cope got out of range and lodged complaints with the Army, but without success, Marsh having told the commander that Cope was a Department of Interior man out to undermine the military jurisdiction.

Argument was useless. Cope gave up on the Basin and headed eastward, more or less following the old Overland Trail, although in the southern basin areas a wagon could be driven almost anywhere. It was not a friendly land, however. In Cope's course lay such drainages as Salt Wells Creek, Sandy Creek, Alkali Creek, and the Burnt Fork of Bitter Creek, all surrounding or intersecting an area of badlands. On a later, more northerly, journey he passed in succession two Sand Creeks, two Salt Creeks, two Dry Creeks; as well as Little Dry Creek, Poison Spider Creek, Poison Spring Creek, Poison Creek, Badwater Creek, Alkali Creek, and Water Creek. Water Creek, like most of the others, proved to be dry.

Turning south Cope camped in the Washakie Basin,

where he found good fossil digging. There word reached him that Marsh, over in the Bridger, was violating all professional ethics by releasing his new species to the newspapers immediately on discovery, rather than waiting for the presentation of papers before the learned societies. Cope had been doing it for years, but when Marsh did it after driving him out of the Bridger Basin, he was outraged. He added an extra crew of diggers and established a courier service between the badlands near Haystack Butte, where his camp was located, and the telegraph line, to rush his claims to new species. He carried a small Greek lexicon in his pocket so he could whip it out and furnish suitable names such as *Loxolophodon, Dicornutus, Bifurcatus*, and *Expressicornis* right on the spot. A telegraph operator, who had just listened to a dispatch from Marsh, precipitated one of the bitterest disputes of the century when he made the error of sending Cope's Loxolophodon as a repeat of Marsh's Lefalophodon. In the end, Marsh accepted credit for both. He said Cope's fossil was only his own Tinoceras discovered the year before, anyway. Cope was furious. He countered with the charge that Marsh was publishing the names of species projected from his imagination and then using them to claim priority when anything likely showed up anywhere. Cope challenged Marsh with *Timitherium rostratum,* related to the monkeys, and perhaps an ancestor of man, the most ancient of missing links. He also rushed his dispatch rider away with telegraph particulars on Bathmadon. Marsh countered with Orotherium. Cope came back with *Hadrianus octonarius,* and with the entire new order of Proboscidia. And so it went. Despite his late start, Cope turned up 100 species, 60 of them new to science, and claimed a numerical as well as a moral victory.

It was Marsh's turn to yell foul. He said Cope's papers were so error-filled they held American science up to the opprobrium of the world. He said that no claim for a new species was valid without a scholarly paper being presented to the Philosophical Society, and Cope had not been within

2000 miles of the Society all summer. This charge, leveled by a man making claims from Fort Bridger, 2075 miles from the Society, drew only jeers from Cope. He called Marsh a good administrator but a sorry scientist. "I have been beating him in the field for years," said Cope, pointing to his finds in New Jersey, Maryland, North Carolina, and Ohio. Marsh countered by charging that Cope had stolen some North Carolina fossils which were his private property. He also enumerated several instances of fraud. To these charges, Cope responded by asking what could a person expect from a man who got his professorship through a rich uncle's endowment? As for being a scientist, Cope said that Marsh would be out of business if he didn't have Cope's writings to fall back on. He referred to him as "The celebrated professor of Copeology at Yale."

Word then came to Marsh from Colonel T. H. Stanton in Cheyenne that prospectors sneaking into the Sioux lands of the Black Hills had been coming out with fossil bones of a very peculiar appearance. Further inquiry placed the source of the bones somewhere near the Red Cloud and Spotted Tail agencies.

It was late autumn, the poorest time of year to launch an expedition into Dakota. Winter temperatures in Dakota sometimes dropped to 56 degrees below zero. Settlers in Dakota strung lines from their sod houses to their dugout barns to serve as guides during the blizzards which roared down unimpeded from the Great Barrens, two thousand miles north. However, Marsh did not dare delay. Cope was temporarily in New Mexico, collecting with the Wheeler Survey, but his scouts were almost everywhere. It was a question of only a few months at best before the Dakota fossils came to his attention. And another thing spurred him on: Cope had been sending large quantities of bones to Philadelphia, and although these had remained crated at his residence and none of Marsh's contacts at the Academy could find out what they consisted of, word had trickled up from New Mexico that Cope was in a virgin field of profligate richness, and that his reports of the next winter would startle the scientific world.

(It was true. The Torrejon and Puerco formations in the Trail area of New Mexico were to prove the most important diggings of Cope's career. These beds, immediately overlying the dinosaur beds of Cretaceous age, contained in great variety a world of extinct mammals never dreamed of before. For months, practically every bone and tooth Cope picked up could be identified as a new species. Then, in addition, he discovered a great mammal horizon in the Santa Fe marls, yielding numerous stages in the evolution of rhinoceri, camels, mastodons, and a startling medley of the smaller carnivores.)

The Army could offer Marsh little protection, but he was allowed to proceed to Red Cloud agency with one of the supply units. The Indians were restless, and it was reported that they were secretly storing away arms and ammunition with the intention of going on the warpath with their allies, the Cheyennes—which they did two years later, to the sorrow of Custer.

It was freezing when Marsh arrived. He asked for a military escort into the badlands, but the commander felt he had scarcely enough men to protect his own cantonment in case of attack. He advised Marsh to get out of the country with haste. Instead, Marsh hired an escort from among the nearby Sioux. These were mostly warriors who had taken part in the Red Cloud War six years before. On observing Marsh's equipment, they became convinced that his story of ancient bones was a subterfuge. They believed that he had got wind of some gold discovery and was secretly out to investigate it. After holding a powwow on the matter, the warriors decided to string along with him until they could discover where the gold deposit was located, then kill him for his arms and supplies. But, day after day, Marsh moved through the badlands, digging for ancient bones and making no move whatever toward prospecting the creek bottoms. The weather grew very cold, and the shivering Indians built shelters by stretching their robes over frameworks of brush. They would crouch all day over a fire and watch Marsh as he tirelessly searched the rock and dirt faces of the badlands. Bones accumulated in camp; these he roped to the backs of packhorses like bleached faggots. Sometimes the bones were so friable that they fell to pieces, and Marsh sat by the hour cementing them with wet mud which froze to iron hardness under subsequent wrappings of burlap. As this went on, and the weather grew colder, the Sioux became convinced that he was possessed by the demons which were reputed to have residence in the badlands. They associated his appearance with the legends of the thunder horses. The thermometer dropped to 20 degrees below zero. It was so cold that in the morning Marsh was unable to pull his boots on until they had been softened over a fire. Finally a blizzard swept the area, covering it with snow except for the perpendicular cut-bank faces, and Marsh was forced, reluctantly, to discontinue his search for that year. His Sioux escorted him back to the Agency. His exploit became legend, and to the end of their years they referred to him as Big Bone Chief.

It was not yet deep in winter, but already he found the tribe close to starvation. Buffalo were growing scarce, and the Army had orders to fire on any Indian caught straying off the reservation. Congress had made an appropriation for food which should have seen the tribe through the winter, but it was the administration of U. S. Grant. The Indian Service, always a stronghold of grafters, had reached its all-time low. Marsh examined the food which he saw Indians carrying home to their families and was appalled. The meat, when thawed out, proved to be carrion. Taken as a whole, the allotment, he said, was garbage. He was incensed. He inquired of the tribesmen who told him it was "all same like last year."

The graft proceeded as follows: First the successful bidder was put to great expense in taking care of the officials. Nevertheless he was bound to furnish the Indians with a certain tonnage of foodstuffs. The only way to do this was by lowering the quality and misbranding it. It was a good chance for manufacturers to empty their warehouses of stuff that could not be sold through regular channels. In the case of beef, which was generally driven in on the hoof, steers and crippled cows, too poor to warrant the shipping from Dodge City, appeared at the reservation. It was a joke that such beef was "jerked on the hoof." Everyone expected a piece of the graft. Wagon freight outfits were paid by the ton mile, and hence distances were exaggerated. In this the Army cooperated because it did not want its appropriations cut, and the command liked to point to the vast areas which it had policed with insufficient forces. Anyone with a pencil and paper could have proved by road miles that the West from Kansas to the Pacific was larger than Siberia. Even so, the freight companies stood to lose because they were caught in the bidding and kickback, too. Hence, if anything of marketable quality happened to be included in their Indian cargo, it would likely be swapped with some storekeeper for enough wormy flour, rancid cornmeal, or bulged canned goods to make up the weight. Indians were told that wormy flour was better because of the meat it contained. Bulged canned goods, the freighters always claimed, had frozen en route. It was with the cooperation of such hearties that the Western Indian won his reputation for preferring rotten food. "Thank God for the American Indian," was the toast of the Department of the Interior in Washington. "May his numbers increase, but let his gourmets be few in number."

As soon as Marsh got back East he blasted the Indian Service. He traveled to Washington and called at the office of Mr. Columbus Delano, Grant's Secretary of the Interior, a political hack from Ohio. Delano refused to see him. This was a mistake. Marsh soon showed that he was not a person to be brushed off. He carried his outrage to Grant. Grant saw him.

By this time the Indian supply had become big news. A delegation of newspapermen called on Delano. Alarmed that the professor might drive him off his fat preserve, the Secretary fought back the only way he knew how. He said that Marsh might be well-meaning, but he did not know what he was talking about. He said Marsh wished to pamper the Indians and interfere with Interior Department policy, under which they were rapidly becoming provident farmers and industrious tillers of the soil. Marsh should stay in his classroom, Delano suggested. Professors and busybodies did more harm than good. Marsh had been hoodwinked in the West. The Indians had made a fool of him. When Marsh answered by another blast of charges, Delano accused him of being a mugwump, a Democrat, a Southern sympathizer, and a plain liar. Delano suggested he was also an enemy of religion and morals, out to corrupt the youth of the country through teaching them that the Bible was a lie and that everyone had evolved from the apes.

Marsh, thriving on controversy, called Delano the things he usually reserved for Cope, but chiefly he simply went on repeating his accusations over and over. Grant, who admired wealth and successful people more than anything else in the world, was very upset. Marsh was after all a man of position, gladly received in the aristocratic circles which would have snubbed Delano at the front door. He tried to hush up the furor, and when that failed, he was driven to the utmost extreme of his entire career—he fired one of his crooked friends. The Indians continued to get the same wormy pork, as they have, in one guise or another, to this day. But Marsh had licked the racketeers. It was a signal achievement. Memory of it was to have an effect on his future dealings with public officials.

Actually, Marsh had brushed Delano out of his way with his left hand. He had been occupied all along with matters which to him were more pressing. At that time he had no fewer than twelve groups of diggers in the field. Bones were coming by freight train to Yale faster than he could classify them. Yet he was unable to take too much time away from the field in view of the bonanzas being turned up by

Cope in the Torrejon, the Puerco, and the Santa Fe marls. Unsatisfied with these biological riches, Cope had crews of diggers invading Kansas, a territory to which Marsh believed he had prior claim, and he was making yearly attempts to get established in the Bridger Basin.

The field groups of both Cope and Marsh were more or less autonomous units headed by some scientist who was willing to suffer hardship and small pay for the privilege of working at the science he loved. Other members were mostly men who had been hired around cow camps and mining camps. Such uneducated scouts, cowboys, and prospectors, if they developed a real taste for bone-digging, became sharp practical paleontologists. The best-known of Marsh's unschooled pioneers was Sam Smith, who called himself "Sam Smith of the Rocky Mountains." Marsh sent him a rifle from New Haven, and he wrote back, "I never mist a shot yet. This fall I will get you a grisly or bust." Poor Sam was drygulched during the eighties. "Cope got him," went the word from Deadwood to Green River. Although Sam had engaged in some bitter osteological feuds, there was nothing about his death to indicate that science was in any way responsible. No one knows how many species bearing a name such as *Hesperornus Marsh* or *Regalis Cope* should in truth give some small measure of credit to the Sam Smiths of the West. Money seemed a secondary consideration to everyone. Cope and Marsh sank their fortunes in paleontology. The Sam Smiths gave years of their lives knowing they would never profit more than a grubstake, without complaint forsaking the chance of fortune in the Montana and Colorado silver mines. They learned to recognize fossil signs, just as a game hunter or a gold prospector learns to recognize animal and mineral signs. They looked for pockmarked strips along strata of rock, knowing that bone and rock seldom erode at the same rate. Some rock was favorable to fossils, as some was favorable to gold. Practical paleontologists learned to look for thin, irregular, and impure layers of sandstone, mudstone, conglomerate marl, and sandy shale. These rocks had likely been laid down near the shore of the ancient Cretaceous sea which had once covered the country all the way to the Rockies. Cope referred to it as "The American Mediterranean." At first it was thought to have been a freshwater lake, and thus it was that Marsh described it to his guide, Buffalo Bill.

The shallows and shores of ancient seas were always the best places to look for fossils of the reptilian age. True, the creatures might have fallen anywhere, and many were able to survive in deeper water, but if they died in the open sea they were devoured by the fish. On the shore, with its storms and sudden sandbars and fluctuations, they were much more likely to be interred and preserved. Sick dinosaurs sank in mires and quicksands. The thickness of some fossil boneyards indicate that miry lagoons had existed as deathtraps for ages. Hence the Rocky Mountain front, a repeated shore of the middle American sea, provided not only the land passage to Alaska and Asia, it was also the supreme evolution and burying ground of the continent and probably, through many ages, of the world.

The Bear Paw Mountains in north-central Montana Territory were known to be one of the most ancient of shore areas. During the Cretaceous, thick layers of sand and mud gathered around the slowly sinking, eroding shores of the Bear Paws. Later the sediments, consolidated as yellow sandstone, gray shale, and black coal beds, had been pushed up as mountain flanks an average of about four thousand feet. When in the ice age the Missouri River was dammed off in the north and forced to seek an outlet eastward, it cut a channel a thousand feet deep across these beds, while rivers such as the Judith and the Arrow eroded rapidly to grade, and a thousand coulees sliced the rock in crazy patterns, revealing knife-clean faces of the Cretaceous strata for the examination of the prospector and the fossil-hunter. The prospector was mostly disappointed, but not the fossil-hunter. Leidy had been there briefly and reported fossils in abundance. Cope set out for the Bear Paws in the spring of 1876.

He was accompanied by a celebrated assistant, Charles Sternberg. For funds in that frontier area, Cope had $120 sewed in a trouser leg, and some orders against Virginia City (Nev.) and Ogden banks. Road agents, according to reports, were at that time busy in Montana Territory. The Utah & Northern had come to its stop at Franklin on the Idaho boundary, awaiting rebirth with U.P. capital. There was no hotel in Franklin. Cope and Sternberg slept on the depot platform and caught the northbound coach at six o'clock in the morning. It was a fast trip. By means of relays, six drivers in all, and a new six-horse team every 12 to 16 miles, they reached Helena after a continuous four days and three nights, with only time out for what was referred to as "food" at the stations.

One of Cope's drivers, a man called "Whisky Jack," was very drunk. Cope objected to him and demanded a relief driver. He was unsuccessful in obtaining one. The coach company was not even apologetic. Whisky Jack, said the station tender, was *always* drunk. Jack was, on the other hand, one of the concern's fastest drivers. His performance for a time was spectacular. However, he fell asleep near the end of his run, and Judge H. N. Blake, on his way to Helena to convene the supreme court, was voted the important task of sitting beside him and keeping him awake. "His breath scared the road agents off," said Blake. For some years Whisky Jack had the run commencing at Watson's Station, where the stage road crossed Beaverhead River south of present-day Dillon, and swung over to Bannack. In the early 1930s certain old-time residents of the mining towns thereabouts still remembered Whisky Jack. His prowess with bottle and six-horse team was legendary. He was known to get so drunk he had to be tied to the seat, but he never allowed a substitute on his run. Each time the superintendent came through from Salt Lake City, the rumor followed that Jack was about to be discharged for drunkenness. Jack promised to shoot dead any superintendent who dared fire him. One time he started out from Watson's, drunk as usual, fell off the seat somewhere beyond Badger Pass, and was not missed until the team came galloping through Argenta driverless. After a man on horseback had captured the coach and brought it back, a severely shaken passenger said he had heard gunfire, and it was surmised that Jack had been shot off his perch while attempting to outrun road agents. He was briefly a hero, but he showed up on foot half an hour later, unwounded. Later he claimed to have jumped off on purpose in order to demonstrate the unusual training he had given his lead team. Although unchallenged by superintendents to the last, Whisky Jack was deposed a couple of years after Cope's experience when the Utah & Northern was built through Beaverhead Valley.

Popular everywhere, on his arrival at Helena Cope was feted by the territorial governor, a one-time general, Benjamin F. Potts. Cope then traveled on by coach to Fort Benton, which he found in a state of excitement over news that Sitting Bull had destroyed Custer and all his command on the Little Bighorn. Sitting Bull was then reported moving northeast toward Canada. Army units were out to intercept him. No one in Fort Benton expected the Army to accomplish this, but there was general apprehension that Sitting Bull might be driven to the Benton area. A most likely route would be at the Judith, goal of Cope's expedition. There was some talk of raising a force to protect Benton not only from Sitting Bull, but from an estimated 15,000 Blackfeet, Assiniboins, and Crows reported roving the riverbanks between Benton and Fort Lincoln, firing on steamboats. One report had Madame Moustache, the lady gambler, on her way up from Nevada to captain the militia. Madame Moustache, described by contemporaries as "a raven-haired beauty," was a sort of Fort Benton Joan of Arc, having been credited with saving the camp from the ravages of smallpox when she drove a pestilence-ridden boat away from the levee with two .44 caliber Colt Army pistols. She was also said to have "kept a watchful eye on the young and inexperienced."

With Montana's gold placers on the downgrade and the cattle ranges barred by Indians, Cope expected hard times at Benton, but he found it booming. There was a big business in buffalo hides, and it had been found easier to supply southern Alberta by way of the United States than across the breadth of Canada. Prices were high. He needed horses; wild broncs, the only ones available, sold for $65. But the hard thing was hiring men. Because of the Indian scare, Cope's offer of $100 per month wages waited several days for takers. At last, however, he set forth.

Guided by a part-Indian hunter named Jim Deer, Cope's party traveled northward to the mouth of the Marias. Fording that stream they climbed the Loma Hill along a route first scouted by George Brown, later "secretary" of the Plummer Gang, and swung eastward to cross the wide valley where the Missouri once flowed, to the Cow Island Trail. Across-country it was no more than 50 miles to his destination on the mouth of the Judith, but the route, holding to the moraines and benches in order to skirt the coulee crossings, took them twice that far. The country, wrote Cope, "abounds in buffalo, antelope, deer, wolves, Indians, etc." They came down on the river near the mouth of Buffalo Chip Coulee at what was later the Lohse ranch and ferry. The Judith flowed in on the other side. They had made the journey in four and a half days.

They crossed over to the mouth of the Judith, there to found a trading post called Fort Claggett. It stood at the site of Fort Cooke, which had been abandoned by the Army in 1869.

At Claggett the prices were even more outrageous than those in Benton, although it was supplied as cheaply from the steamboats. The reason for this might have been seen in the added danger of doing business in that locality, which was the domain of warring Indians. While Cope was at the store there arrived a number of Piegans who wanted to trade horses for firewater and firearms. "I shoot Sioux," the chief of the group assured the trader, indicating that he had heard of the Custer business and was strongly on the white man's side.

Cope traveled up the Judith three miles and camped while making some preliminary explorations of the area. He reported that there was good hunting for mountain sheep, the flesh of which was deliciously tender. There was an abundance of berries, some which he called *garambullos* after the name common in Mexico, probably bullberries, while chokecherries ripened and bent the bushes. Squaws braved the grizzly bears to compete with them for the fruit, and chokecherries were spread on buffalo hides to dry in the sun preparatory to being mealed for making pemmican. Cope estimated no fewer than a thousand Indians within an hour's ride of the Judith. He counted 110 lodges in the largest camp. There were River Crows, Mountain Crows, and a few Piegans. Their ponies grazed the river bottoms for miles. An encampment of about thirty lodges of Blackfeet stood near Claggett. There were also some Gros Ventre camped near Teton Creek.

All of the Indians proved to be in an agitated state. Great stories of Sitting Bull's victory 150 miles to the south had reached them. Far into the night could be heard the beating of tom-toms and whoopings as the Crows and Blackfeet, old enemies, united in jubilation at the prospect of all white men being evicted from the country. Cope slept well on his camp mattress, but arose to find that his Fort Benton employees had all sought greater privacy in the bushes. As a result, he faced his day refreshed and ready for work while they were heavy-eyed and jumpy. They advised immediate flight to Fort Benton, or at least moderate safety of the trading post. Cope laughed at the idea. He carried gifts to the Crow chief, Bear Wolf.

Bear Wolf was instantly taken with Cope. Before the day ended they were practically cronies. He returned with reassuring news. "Why, this is the safest place a person could be," he told his men. Their fear of the Crows he tried to counteract through application of logic. He had learned from Bear Wolf that his warriors had just been successful in lifting twenty-six scalps from the Sioux. They had also conducted a series of successful horse raids which netted 900 animals. Most of these also came from the Sioux. Since a Sioux considered it less disgraceful to lose his scalp than his horse, the horses were considered far and away the greater triumph and proof that a state of war existed between the two nations. The Sioux, Cope triumphantly pointed out, were the Indians who had wiped out Custer. Therefore the presence of the Crows in such overpowering numbers was the most fortunate of coincidences. "We are safer," said Cope, "here in the badlands than we would be inside the very blockhouses of Fort Benton."

When his employees failed to respond to such reasoning he visited the Blackfeet camp, made friends with the chief there also, and carried back *his* personal assurance that he was "very big friends of all white men." But they still wouldn't listen to him. That night, under cover of darkness, most of them took to the hills, not even staying to collect their wages, and were never seen by Cope again. The loss of Austin Merrill he particularly regretted; he was a first-class cook. Cope, a gourmet, also valued highly the skill of Jim Deer, who had kept the camp pot supplied with fat antelope, mountain sheep, calf buffalo, and similar delicacies. After the flight of Merrill and Deer the expedition was reduced to a diet of pickles, bacon, hardtack, and such jerked buffalo as could be purchased from the Indians.

Cope did not consider turning back. With two wagons his bobtailed party headed up an intermittent stream called Dog Creek into the badlands.

Cope had been ill during the late winter and spring. Before setting out for the north even the slightest exertion had tired him and left him shaky, his forehead beaded with sweat. His recovery started in Franklin sleeping on the depot platform. After four days and three nights of being hammered by the stagecoach en route to Helena, he was in such excellent fettle that an all-night wining-and-dancing party at the Governor's did not faze him, and on Dog Creek, as others weakened, he gained in strength. When even the pickles ran out and the party was left with nothing but hardtack and cold bacon straight, Cope continued to improve. He even professed to thrive on alkali water, which in the Dog Creek sinkholes became very strong and acted as a violent purgative.

September came with heavy rains, relieving the water situation but forcing the wagons to the ridgetops. The badlands ridges were often very sharp. The preceding year George Bird Grinnell and Edward Dana had visited the country from the south, following ridges which became so sharp they had to be straddled by the wagon wheels with the horses perilously on opposite declivities. Grinnell and Dana merely went to the mouth of the Judith and out again. Cope traveled the country as no man has since. He crossed it from ridge to ridge, across the grain, as the Western saying went. Even today no roads come close to Cope's course. He was forced to raise and lower his wagons by way of windlass. In some places even his horses needed assistance. He traveled along one of the main spines of the country called Whisky Ridge. A dirt road follows it today. There is a chance he also followed Oil Well Ridge, about twelve miles northwest of present-day Winifred.

Much of the area was covered by the Bearpaw shale. While numerous tiny fossils were found in the shale, it was barren of the saurian remains which formed the chief interest of paleontologists at that time. But high on the ridges the Bearpaw shale was overlain by yellow Claggett sandstone, and near the base of this, Cope found saurian fossils in abundance. Some of the sandstone was actually layered with bones. Here and there they had weathered out until they could be scooped up with a shovel, although by then generally too shattered to be of any value. Only the teeth were resistant. It was on this occasion that Cope brought about his storied accomplishment of identifying twenty-one different dinosaur species by their teeth alone.

Although in America the dinosaurs live today only in the little horned toads of the Southwest, the midpart of the continent was once the great reptilian area of the world. Nowhere did the dinosaurs thrive, branch out into so many species, and attain such a size as they did in America. In the Judith, Cope found for the first time in America examples of the horned dinosaurs, Monoclonius. On one of his red-letter days he sat down to a writing table made of a wagon endgate on a pickle keg to describe, with drawings, the saurian *Monoclonius crassus,* a beast with a horn over each eye and a third vicious one atop his nasal bone. The iguanodonts were also well represented. They were shaped after the manner of kangaroos with large hind legs and small front ones. In the barren badlands fronting the Bearpaw Mountains, Cope found hadrosaurs which resembled giant kangaroos crossed with crocodiles. Even when they were of the same genus and species of those in the East, the Judith fossils had developed on a more kingly scale. Cope identified creatures quite similar to his Laelaps and Dryptosaurus of New Jersey, but larger and in greater variety. Later he found them with unusual, heavy armor. The Trionyx and the Adocus had teeth arranged in magazines, one below another, so that when one set wore out, the next would come up and take its place. One skull had a total of 400 teeth, a hundred of them in actual use when the reptile died. Palaeoscincus had teeth shaped like a closed fist. Another creature, a raylike fish, *Myledaphus bipartitus,* had teeth arranged solidly on the upper and lower surfaces of its mouth like the bricks in a pavement, and these operated in the manner of a mill, one section grinding back and forth across the other so that everything indiscriminately would be reduced to a pulp for passage down its intestinal tract. The enamel of the bricklike teeth was peculiar in that one side was white, and the other black.

With bones in such abundance he had to pick and choose, taking only the most significant portions of each skeleton, but even so when mid-September came there was almost a ton of bones. With these carefully packed they decided against retracing all the terrible self-made trail and struck out for the Missouri, coming down just to the east of a steamboaters' hazard called the Dauphin Rapids.

By wagon and then by mackinaw boat, Cope got 1700 pounds of bones as far as the steamboat landing at Cow Island. Most years, he would have been stranded at that point for the season. The Missouri was often navigable to Fort Benton only during the weeks of high water from melting snows in the Rockies. This crest usually came around June 20th. After August 1st steamboat passage downriver from Fort Benton was problematic. Some years the boats did not get to Benton at all. In order to supply gold-wealthy Helena with the luxuries which had dazzled Cope on his visit, a landing called Carroll had been built about three fifths of the distance from Benton to the Dakota border, and from there, via a road 250 miles long, Helena could be reached by bull freight in a matter of seventeen days. This extended Helena's river season to about six months, but its champagne prices remained distressingly high, and it was practically impossible for a person to walk into one of the city's restaurants and get a really good oyster, lobster, or fillet of plover Benedictine until the train whistles of the Northern Pacific "awoke the echoes of Last Chance Gulch" in June 1883.

Despite the season, Cope was in luck. Early autumn rains and high Indian-scare prices had encouraged the steamboat *Josephine* to chance a quick run to Benton and return, and he got himself and his fossils aboard on the seventh of October. Later, when the *Josephine* was commandeered by General Hazen for use in the pursuit of Sitting Bull, he transferred to the steamer *C. K. Peck*.

Beyond Fort Buford at the mouth of the Yellowstone, the river became very low, and the *C. K. Peck* made headway by a process known as "grasshoppering." Grasshoppering consisted, essentially, of windlassing forward by means of tackle mounted on masts, an arrangement which lifted the boat as it was pulled. The whole procedure could be likened to a boat on crutches. Doing this, the boilers consumed one cord of fuel every hour, with the result that all aboard were drafted into chopping crews which ranged the banks for cottonwood. Things finally got so bad that the crew concluded a hex had been put upon them. Their attention became directed to Cope's fossils. What particularly alarmed them was the skeleton of an Indian he had brought in from an old burial site. The captain, torn between the crew's threat to mutiny and Cope's promise to sue the steamboat owners for everything they had, was finally saved from decision when the more violent laid hands on Cope and gave him his choice of being tossed overboard or taking his skeleton ashore there to "bury it in a decent, Christian manner." He chose the latter.

The war between Cope and Marsh went on. A year after Cope's return from the Judith, Arthur Lakes, onetime Oxford University student and a teacher at a Golden, Colorado, religious school, found the vertabra of an enormous animal on a hogback ridge near Morrison. Further search resulted in other interesting discoveries, among them a femur which measured fourteen inches across the base and was as tall as Lakes himself.

Excited, Lakes hauled his femur and vertebra down to Morrison, where he stored them in a borrowed shed whose door was fitted with a padlock; then he got off a quick letter to Marsh and hurried back to the ridge, setting up a semipermanent camp. In almost no time he had a ton of monstrous bones. Although he had not heard from Marsh, he decided to ship the bones. He went back to digging, coming down from the hills once in a while to see if there was any mail. When weeks passed and still no answer he decided Marsh lacked interest, so he shipped his next fossils to Cope.

Marsh was not uninterested. He merely had the bad habit of letting his mail stack up. Apparently he did not inspect the box of bones, either. With so many diggers in the field, such boxes arrived all the time and had to wait their turn. Sometimes years passed before he got around to them.

Marsh, however, never failed to keep day-to-day tabs on the activities and publications of Cope, and when his rival, then at home in Philadelphia, began announcing his Colorado fossils he remembered seeing the letter with a Morrison, Colorado, postmark. He read it, opened the crate, saw what it contained, and got off a telegram to Lakes. HAVE NO MORE DEALINGS WITH COPE, he said. FURTHER COMMUNICATIONS FOLLOW.

The telegram was not delivered. Marsh had addressed it to Lakes' home in Golden, a place he had not seen in weeks. Despite this mixup Marsh was finally able to get a sort of tenuous control over the area and to buy title to the fossils Lakes had sent to Philadelphia.

Cope let the Morrison diggings slip, and was willing to release at least some of Lakes' Philadelphia shipment, which he had identified and named after himself anyway, because he was after bigger game. At almost the same moment Lakes was making his initial discovery, another Colorado educator, W. O. Lucas, Superintendent of Schools for Fremont County, found similar fossil remains near Garden Park, outside Canon City. While Marsh was dealing with Lucas and leaving the details in the hands of David Baldwin, a vertebrate paleontologist in his employ, Cope was quietly purchasing Lucas' claim to Garden Park.

As luck would have it, Marsh had returned East when rumors of the Canon City finds reached him. There was nothing definite, but he sent a telegram telling Baldwin to go down and have a quiet look around. Baldwin arrived incognito as representative of a pickle manufacturer. He did not need to use such caution. Canon City, a former gold-rush town, had been reborn as a resort and health center, and strangers were everywhere. One of the first things Baldwin saw was the skeleton of a miniature dinosaur, no larger than a fox, on display in a gift shop. The owner thought it was the skeleton of a peculiar bird. He purchased it for $3 but he was too late for the main diggings, 9 miles to the northeast. SECURE ALL BONES POSSIBLE, wired Marsh. He added

COPE IS VIOLATING ALL HIS AGREEMENTS, obviously intending that the telegram should be shown to Lucas.

Marsh named his fox-size dinosaur *Nanosaurus victor* but it seemed a sorry consolation when compared with the truly gigantic and peculiar remains Cope was soon hauling from Garden Park. Cope's quarry quickly relegated Morrison to the second class. The Canon City bones were running a quarter to a third bigger than those above Morrison, with such giant saurians as Diplodocus still waiting to be unearthed.

The world at that time was enthralled by the sheer appalling size of prehistoric life. That something which looked like a lizard could rear 30 or 40 feet in the air and attain a length in excess of 70 still had the power to grip millions of newspaper readers. Great distinction devolved on the scientist who came up with the largest species. In vain did Marsh point to his tiny *Nanosaurus victor* as the only one of its kind in the entire world. Even scientists who should have recognized its importance merely wagged their heads and went grabbing for the latest paper which announced that Cope, in Canon City, had identified a sacrum vertebra which was 3 feet and 1½ inches in diameter, that Cope had found a humerous as tall and as thick through as a 200-pound man, and that on the evidence of a giant centrum, 14 inches in diameter, Cope had predicted an assemblage of sauropod bones which would prove the prehistoric existence of a reptile no less than 78½ feet long.

Obviously Baldwin had failed utterly. Marsh went himself to Canon City. He found Lucas and asked to see the contract he had signed with Cope. "You have been robbed," said Marsh. "If you had only written to me first you would not have been a victim of this shabby outrage. Do you realize that you have sold out the paleontological find of the century for a sorry pittance?"

Marsh assured him, however, that all was not lost. Obviously, the Cope agreement had been perpetrated through false pretenses and fraud, and hence not worth the paper it was written on. Besides, what the agreement actually said was that Cope was buying not the quarry, but "the remainder of the fossils." According to the Marsh interpretation, this meant that Cope had purchased only those bones which would bring to completion the skeletons of which he already had a portion. In other words, Lucas owned any new ones which happened to show up. These were what Marsh wished to purchase. Lucas, a strict Presbyterian, hesitated over the matter of ethics, but finally Marsh was able to force payment on him. The next problem was to determine just where the discovered specimens ended and the undiscovered ones began, because the bones seemed very much scattered and mixed up. Cope simplified this problem by never recognizing Marsh's agreement. He had possession of the diggings; he held it by means of a crew of miners he had hired up around Central City; a number of them were armed with repeating rifles, and when the Marsh forces tried to come up the hill it was Cope's turn to cry claim-jumper.

Marsh tramped the bottom of the hill in a rage, but there was nothing he could do except prospect around and find a digging of his own. This he succeeded in doing, but whereas Cope's fossils lay in a mudstone formation which broke in a mellow manner, exposing the bones undamaged, the Marsh quarry was hard sandstone which on breaking was likely to shatter the delicate remains beyond repair. One rare skeleton of a Diplodocus more than 50 feet long was in fact consigned to the dump, a rubble, although men of a more patient nature later put it together. Marsh continued to cast around for some way of evicting Cope from the mountain, but Lucas finally solved the problem for him by signing another contract with Cope, giving Cope two bills of sale to Marsh's one, a clear legal advantage.

Marsh departed Canon City, visited his diggers in Kansas, and returned to New Haven. The exploration and exploitation of the West was moving at an ever-accelerating pace. Scarcely a week passed without the report of a discovery of minerals, of a new kind of clay, of a peculiar form of wildlife, or of strange bones at some town that nobody had ever heard of. A depression had struck the land, but it caused only a brief hesitation in the great period of railroad expansion. At a thousand water tanks and flag stops, in stations made of unwheeled boxcars, with an office and a clicking telegraph sounder at one end and living quarters at the other, a thousand young men in sleeve-protectors and eyeshades had been marooned by their employers to stand vigil over segments of rail line which ran off through the sagebrush to shimmering infinities of mirage, and through days as endless as the horizons they had nothing to do.

Sheepherders in similar situations traditionally went mad trying to ascertain the long side of a soogin, a cheap cotton quilt made absolutely square. Station agents, however, were for the most part adventurous young fellows from back East who had answered institute ads reading *"Earn Big Money as Railroad Telegraphers."* They found more imaginative ways of passing their time than by trying to find the long end of a square quilt. Many of them tamed local animals, particularly the badger and coyote. One station agent suckled kittens to a mother jackrabbit, and the sight of the friendly cats and rabbit on an N.P. platform was memorable to numerous early-day passengers on the North Coast Limited. A favored story in the West was of the station agent who taught his tame rattlesnake the Morse code. Charles Baker, onetime cook on a C.B.&Q. work train, reported a station agent who had learned how to mummify and shed his skin yearly by means of the sun and massage, with the result that it was later displayed, mounted by a taxidermist, as one of the stellar attractions of the St. Louis World's Fair of 1904. In far-off Australia, a lonely stationmaster discovered the famous Broken Hill mine because he could think of no pastime better than sinking a shaft in a nearby hillside. The agent at Como, Wyoming, discovered the West's greatest bonanza of dinosaur bones.

Como was listed on the maps of the time as having a population of "25 or under." The only resident one could count on was the depot agent, but sometimes he was fortunate in having visitors, cowboys from the Medicine Bow ranges who liked to loaf along the platform and wait for the trains to go by.

When a cowboy makes a brief stop he generally turns his pony to graze merely by letting the bridle reins drop. This restrains most horses so they can pick their way only a half-mile or so in the course of an afternoon, but some of the very intelligent broncs of the Wyoming plains master the art of traveling front-sidewise, nimbly avoiding placing a hoof on the reins, and these are best grazed at the end of a drag. At Como an ideal drag was provided by a peculiar object which looked like a cross between a weathered cottonwood burl and a buffalo skull. A rope could be tied on it without slipping off, and the large hornlike protuberances which on every side dug in the earth were enough to restrain a bronc without limiting him to a single patch of grass. This drag turned out to be the tail weapon of a Stregosaurus, a fantastic dinosaur with gigantic armored back fins, the headlessness of a mole, and a tail which served as a natural slung shot, a limber-handled battle club, with which Stegosaurus could smite its enemies.

When the Como agent realized that the thing was actually a fossil he had something to do in the long waits between trains. He went up the track to the east to 300-foot high Como Bluff and prospected where the railroad dirt-movers had sliced the bank away. More bones were found, sticking from the rock-and-dirt layers and mixed with the grade itself.

He had heard greatly inflated reports of money being paid for dinosaur bones. He wrote to Marsh, but caution was almost his undoing. Not wishing to use his true name, for fear it would be traced down in the U.P. books and the deposit stolen from him, he signed a false one. When Marsh came to terms and mailed him a check, it was made out to a fictitious person, and he was unable to cash it. Thus the deal remained unconsummated, and Cope, hurrying toward Como on the U.P., all but snatched it for himself. He was too late, however, and was met at Como Bluff by Marsh's armed guards. Later he was also dealt out at Bone Cabin, where a sheepherder had built a cabin of cottonwood logs with dinosaur bones as its foundation.

Marsh was now at the top of his career, reaping all the triumphs that had eluded him in the Colorado. Wyoming produced Atlantosaurus 60 feet long; Allosaurus, a fierce, reptilian carnivore with terrible claws and teeth; and finally *Brontosaurus excelsus,* whose footprint alone measured a square yard and whose skeleton today dominates the Great Hall of the Peabody Museum in New Haven, standing 67 feet long, his head rising to look high across the gallery. Bones were arriving at Yale by the boxcar, a flood that far exceeded any facilities for their classification. Some were not unpacked for years. Some are said to be stacked away in the basement to this day. In all, these Wyoming bone quarries yielded Marsh 1115 ton-size, plank-built boxes of bones. Reporters referred to the Wyoming activity as "Marsh's three-ring dinosaur circus."

In Wyoming, Marsh gave himself over to the public fancy for the huge and terrifying by starting his species out toward scientific celebrity with names such as the already mentioned Atlantosaurus and *Brontosaurus excelsus,* and also Titanosaurus and *Morosaurus grandis.* (Cope maintained that he had already discovered Morosaurus at Canon City and named it *Camarasaurus supremus.*) A mouse rated the name of *Hesperomys loxodon.* The idea of ferocity was continuously played up. Even Marsh's Diplodocus (which Cope claimed under the name Amphicoelias), a huge, sluglike mass of flesh which had wallowed in the ancient shallow seas, a reptile grown so soft and unwieldly it was probably unable even to propel itself on dry land, and which used its long tail to sweep water plants to its mouth and thus eat from a wide area without having to stir its sedentary tonnage—even Diplodocus was referred to as "the great, whip-tailed dinosaur," and readers pictured it as a sort of saurian Simon Legree.

Thus Americans, denied anything which even resembled a missing link—Calaveras Man having failed to stand up as anything but an old Indian—found their country preëminent in the giant and the terrible, its West along the edge of the mountains furnishing reptiles and mammals in a profligate abundance unrivaled anywhere on earth. After the novelty of size and ferocity wore off, people became intrigued by the basic incongruity of the great animals. The idea that a creature 70 feet long, weighing 40 tons, would have a brain no larger than an ordinary baseball is a staple scientific wonder to this day. Marsh, investigating his sauropods, or herb-eating dinosaurs, noticed that they possessed a vaulted chamber in their sacral vertebrae. This, he pointed out, was obviously a nerve center for the pelvic region, or a second brain. What was more amazing, its rear "brain" was several times larger than the one in its head. The newspapers, and soon the music-hall comedians, seized on this with delight:

> *The only animal whose mind*
> *Is located in his behind . . . .*

With his victory in Wyoming, Marsh was willing to settle down to digging, but the war with Cope again blazed. When Marsh, after unearthing a particularly fine specimen, which he named Morosaurus, discovered that Cope had already claimed it under the name Camarasaurus, he lost his temper and accused Cope of predating his reports. Cope responded that if there were any dishonesty it was the other way around, that by using his influence Marsh had been able to get Cope's reports pigeonholed and his own tardy ones published ahead of them. Marsh repeated the predating charge, and demanded that the Academy of Natural Sciences appoint a committee of inquiry. He put it in the form of a resolution, which was defeated. Cope then charged that *The*

American Journal of Science, founded at Yale by the elder Silliman, famed pioneer scientist, long one of the most highly regarded scientific periodicals, had been corrupted by Marsh to his own uses, and he warned one and all to beware sending any material to Yale because it would be offered to Marsh for editing and piracy before its acceptance or rejection. Cope said Marsh had built his reputation by hiring impoverished scientists and putting his own name to their discoveries and their written reports.

He pointed to the instance of David Baldwin. Baldwin, said Cope, was a scientist of the highest probity whom Marsh had sent to Canon City, in disguise as a pickle salesman, to gain illegal title to the quarries discovered by Lucas, and when he failed, Marsh, in angry retaliation, had refused to pay him the $1400 which was his due for collecting 34 large boxes of Permian fossils, an entire season's work. He pointed to the record, which showed that Baldwin had been forced to go to court to collect, and even then Marsh was able to beat him out of $400, the judgment being for only a thousand. To the truth of all this Baldwin vouched. He was by that time employed by Cope.

Also, Cope was ranging farther than ever, and luck seemed to be with him. Through Professor Thomas Condon of Oregon, who disliked Marsh after lending him a number of fossils which he never got back, Cope received valuable tips on a virtually untouched part of the nation. When ex-Governor Whitaker, a part-time archeologist, discovered the Fossil Lake locality, it was Cope who received the news first. Charles Sternberg went to Fossil Lake and found it strewn with the bones of extinct North American llamas, ancient elephants, primitive horses, and giant sloths. Even more interesting were the evidences of early man. Sternberg quickly gathered a cigar box full of teeth, flint weapons, tools, and unidentified artifacts. He sat down the same night, and by the light of a sagebrush fire wrote Cope a letter concerning his discovery. He immediately dispatched the letter by Indian messenger; Cope, on receiving it, published it as an arti-

cle in his *American Naturalist,* a magazine he had purchased
to counter Marsh's virtual control of *The American Journal of
Science,* doing little but change the signature from "Chas.
Sternberg" to "E. D. Cope." Cope also struck paydirt in
Texas. Called in by the Lone Star Geologic Survey he found
to his delight—and to Marsh's dismay—the transitionary
forms between fish and amphibians: fish with fins enlarging
to rudimentary legs with which to drag themselves up the
shores of the sea. And he hit Marsh where it hurt most, in his
preëminence with the five-, four-, three-, and two-toed
horses. Cope's "Blanco Beds" of the Southwestern Staked
Plains were rich in the life of Pliocene times, just before the
ice ages. Geologically they were as recent as the Texas Permian was old, and they proved to contain certain very recent
stages of horse evolution. The Blanco horse skeletons Cope
correlated with discoveries in both South America and Southern Asia, and he was led to speculate with new authority on
the grand migrations of the continents, up across the Isthmus
of Panama, through Central Mexico, along the mountain
front of the Western states and provinces, the Valley of the
Yukon, across the land bridge formed when so much of the
ocean's water was sucked away in forming the great ice
domes. He saw evidence of the same route for the elephant,
the musk ox, the camel, deer, and even man.

Cope was now running with the bit in his teeth. With
such a flood of fossils, his genius stood him in good stead.
Marsh, the meticulous perfectionist, was forced to play
Cope's game in order to keep up. Marsh, too, often gambled
on incomplete evidence, and without a doubt was forced to
become a greater scientist. His most famous, although disputed, feat was his early discovery of the "flying dragon," the
Pterodactyl, or bird-with-teeth. This creature, with a wing-
spread of twenty feet, a long-sought missing link between the
birds and reptiles, Marsh claimed to have projected, Cope-
wise, on the evidence of a single bone six inches long and an
inch thick, which he had picked up while followng a gully
through the Kansas chalk beds.

Pterodactyl notwithstanding, as a scientific genius Cope could have taken care of Marsh in one hour of his day. But whereas Cope was dominant out in the field, Marsh had steadily established his influence among the directors and financial supporters of the museums and the universities. No world is more racked by bread-and-butter fears than the academic, and in the great institutions it became understood that no one ever lost his job or was denied a full professorship because of his partiality to Marsh. As a result, uncertain whether to credit the discoveries of an erratic and spectacular Cope or the slightly later but solidly respectable ones of Marsh, decision generally went to the latter. Even after the passage of two thirds of a century, Marsh wears the orthodox mantle of a man with whom it is honorable to associate, while Cope's name calls up the vision of a dangerous radical. Even the brilliance and charm of Cope's scientific writings seemed to violate the sensibilities of the pedants. No one wants flashes of wit in his encyclopedia. Marsh was so dull it seemed inevitable that he had to be right.

So, while Cope was dashing around the West, triumphantly beating Marsh to whole transitions of animal kingdoms, Marsh remained more and more in the East, working among the regents and politicians, setting his deadfall for the kill. The definitive instrument proved to be the U.S. Geological Survey. Until an act of Congress in the late 1870s, what was called the U.S. Geological Survey was actually only a series of government-financed expeditions, mostly in the West, some under the Interior Department and some under the Army. Dr. Hayden, the surveyor and geologist with whose expeditions Cope associated himself while doing much of his early work, largely owed his success not to scientific skill but to getting appropriations from Congress. His real purpose was to explore the West geologically and geographically, but when he went to Washington he always stressed the profit possibilities in the new lands, ready for the plow and the railroad, waiting to be tapped for gold, iron, coal, and petroleum. So large were some of Dr. Hayden's appropriations that Cope was able to print at government expense his early works, one volume of which ran to 1000 pages

There had undoubtedly been a great deal of useless rivalry and injustice under the old system. Under the new act a Geological Survey was planned to unify all the surveys under a man to be appointed by the President. Cope went to Washington and plugged for Hayden. But at politics Cope, the charming and witty dinner guest with such a gift for popularity, was no match for the dour and dedicated Marsh. In Washington, Cope discovered a thing or two about politics. He found that politics turned a dedicated face outward toward the electorate, but at work it was a cynical, horsetrading business conducted without any gratitude, or much honor, and alas, by a group of mediocre people.

Marsh's choice for Director was Clarence King, the celebrated California mountain climber who had played a minor role as Josiah Whitney's assistant in the early days of Calaveras Man. Since then he had won celebrity as a surveyor, explorer, and the author of a geological history of the West. Although suspect because he liked to appear in public in velvet knickers, King knew all the right people. The fact that he had made a fortune in Wyoming cattle and as a highly paid witness in the multimillion-dollar mine litigations then wracking the West was strongly in his favor. In vain did Cope point out that King had long-standing commitments to the big mining interests. He was named Director of the Survey by President Hayes in 1879.

The worst Cope had predicted for himself under the Marsh–Cope Geological Survey came to pass. He had already with the government printers his *Vertebrata of the Tertiary Formations of the West,* the first segment of his monumental work under the Hayden Survey. Volume two was never printed. In private, many scientists were willing to admit that it was without doubt the great paleontological work of the century. But the fear of Marsh's influence was so strong that Cope was left with scarcely a voice but his own crying for publication. King was Director of the Survey only briefly, but the Marsh group did not let his successor, John W. Powell, forget for a moment how he received his appointment. Cope neglected his fieldwork and went to Washington trying to get the remainder of his work published. He buttonholed congressmen. Office help in the capital were treated to the spectacle of the great scientist cooling his heels in the offices of political hacks. The Secretary of the Interior made an appointment to see him, then let him wait for five and a half hours and finally sneaked out the back way.

Cope fought on for years, but his only victory came at one session when he pointed out to economy-minded Eastern legislators that nearly all the Survey money was spent in the West, and succeeded in getting its budget cut so low it was temporarily out of business, but at the next session the funds were restored.

There was a saying in the West that all faro dealers will shoot craps. This means that every sure-thing gambler is also a grade-A sucker. The latter nineteenth century saw this apply to the geologists. Men such as King and Cope had no trouble, when they wished, reaping handsome fees from a mining industry which was then in its Comstock–Butte–Leadville stage of development. On every hand these men saw evidence of idiotic mining practice. One mining concern was guided in its underground explorations by day-to-day consultations with a Gypsy fortune-teller who got mixed up in her directions and brought the main working, a tunnel, to the surface within a few feet of its starting point. Mining tycoons of the West were men such as H. A. W. Tabor, a loafer and storekeeper; Winfield S. Stratton, a carpenter; and Marcus Daly, practical miner. The only mining king who started out as a geologist was F. Augustus Heinze, the Butte copper king, and Heinze made his fortune chiefly by ore raids in the claims of others 1000 feet underground, after first buying the local courts. King and Cope both tried their hand at mine promotion and operation and were failures. King went to the ancient Sombrerete silver mines of Mexico where he sank a great deal of money, including his own.

Cope, needing money to pursue his paleontology, now that he was cut loose from all government support, looked at antiguas all over Mexico while employed by that government, and on his own traveled by stage through the American West, examining mines for investors and for himself.

At last Cope seemed to find what he was searching for at Lake Valley, New Mexico. There a layer of limestone contained irregular bodies of silver ore, rich but unfortunately at unpredictable places. One ore pocket called the Bridal Chamber, less than one hundred feet from the surface, had yielded other miners an almost-solid mass of silver chloride weighing 125 tons. Like other rich finds in the area, the Bridal Chamber had been found by a lucky drift in the Lake Valley limestone. As the ore shoots were "blind"—might occur anywhere in the favored horizon—Cope placed the percentages directly in his favor by exploring with the newly developed diamond drill. Ore was encountered, and for a time Lake Valley looked as if it would become a permanent camp —"with ore sufficient to last for a hundred years," as the editors were fond of predicting. He appropriated enough of the corporate profits to build a Unitarian church, and improve the school. But the ore played out, the drill failed to develop new tonnages, and the enterprise collapsed.

With the failure of Lake Valley, Cope had to disband his paleontological field parties. He was forced to sell his home in Philadelphia. However, he was not yet quite defeated in what newspapers called "the great dinosaur sweepstakes." Shunted aside in the United States, he looked toward Canada. For many years the Dominion had courted his attention. Made an untouchable in Washington, Cope was feted by Canada. He entered the Canadian Geological Survey, where he was given unrestricted access to the fossils gathered by Dr. Alfred R. C. Selwyn and Dr. George M. Dawson in their northern and western explorations, still largely unclassified or even taken out of the crates. He found himself presented with a wealth greater than any he could have realized from his own costly field parties. He was also, at Canadian expense, allowed to travel widely and extend his system of Cretaceous geology through investigations of the Swift Current beds and the strata of the Cypress Hills. The Plains area, which a decade before had been considered a Cretaceous lake, was now shown by Cope to be a salt sea of vast extent, stretching from Mexico to the Arctic.

The final battle between Cope and Marsh came about as the result of an order, dated December 16, 1889, from John W. Noble, Secretary of the Interior, directing Cope to deposit his Tertiary and Cretaceous fossils in the U.S. National Museum.

Cope had collected the fossils while he was geologist on the Hayden Survey. However, he had financed himself from his own bank account. His chief advantage in being designated U.S. paleontologist was that of publication. Even that had been taken from him when the second volume of his "bible" had been suppressed. Powell, then Director of the Survey, knew this quite well. Whether Secretary Noble knew it is a question. At any rate, Cope knew whom to blame. Marsh had the Survey loaded with his men, and through them was able to keep the National Academy of Sciences under control, too. Cope in his outrage had only one place to turn—to the public. He called on a friend, William Hosea Ballou, then a reporter on the New York *Herald*, later to become editor of the New York *Dispatch*. Ballou listened sympathetically to Cope's long tale of scientific triumph and political defeat. On Sunday, January 12, 1890, the story was on page one. There, and in later blasts, the U.S. Geological Survey was described as a sort of mutual back-scratching club devoted, at least paleontologically, to the celebrity of Professor O. C. Marsh. Not satisfied with this, said Cope, Marsh was using a legal technicality to seize Cope's property for his own personal benefit. Cope pointed out that his fossils had been dug at his own expense. In contrast, since his appointment as Survey paleontologist, Marsh had been collecting at government expense, yet he had taken all the fossils home to Yale and would not allow the public to view them. The reason for this, said Cope, was so he could keep the real inventory a secret and retain the best as his own personal property.

Cope enumerated Marsh's errors and perfidies. Marsh had once mistaken a horned saurian for a primitive buffalo. Marsh's proudest work, on the evolution of the horse, had been stolen from previous work in Europe. His celebrated "discovery" of the Odontornithes, birds with teeth, had been done by his assistants. (According to Henry Fairfield Osborn, successor to both Marsh and Cope as America's greatest paleontologist, his birds with teeth had not even been done by his assistants. The truth, reported Osborn, was even more damaging. Marsh's birds with teeth, the long-sought evolutionary form between the birds and reptiles, had been discovered by Professor B. F. Mudge of the University of Kansas, and Mudge had fully recognized their importance. He had collected a box of these fossils and was ready to send them to Cope in Philadelphia, but Marsh got word of it and secured them instead for the Peabody Museum. With these Marsh was able, in 1872, to announce the most important discovery of his career. "Discovery of a Remarkable Fossil Bird," Marsh wrote in his title. He told the story of how he had picked up, while walking along a Kansas chalk bank just at twilight, a single bone which he put in his pocket—later to become interested in its hollow lightness, which, incongruous with its saurian character, led him to project the creature in its entirety—poor Mudge forgotten.)

Marsh answered quickly. He said he had made every sacrifice a human was capable of in the attempt to keep on a friendly basis with Cope. He had persisted in this attempt, he said, even when his rival's conduct had become by turns petty and outrageous. Cope, he said, had actually gone to the length of attempting to enter Yale Museum unannounced in order to gain access to Marsh's fossils and to his unpublished writings. For a long time, Marsh said, he had overlooked such things because he knew that Cope was not really responsible for his actions. He said he had first met Cope twenty-five years earlier when he, Marsh, was a student in

Berlin. Cope had then told him his troubles, and Marsh confessed that his heart had gone out to the poor fellow. He resolved then and there, he said, to do all he could for him as he had severe doubts as to his sanity. During the next five years they met often, and they remained friends although Marsh became more and more convinced that he was a mental case. The realization of this affliction, Marsh indicated, prompted him to overlook Cope's underhanded activities and violations of scientific ethics of which he was the chief sufferer—even when, Marsh said, it approached the biblical limit of seventy times seven.

To show how in the past he had tried to help Cope, Marsh cited the instance of Elasmosaurus. Cope had come in from Kansas with the bones of an extinct reptile which he gave this name. He read a paper on this creature, which was made to seem like the most remarkable animal of all time. In a communication published by the Boston Society of Natural History he placed it in a new order, Streptosauria. In the *American Naturalist* he published a restoration as it was supposed to be in life, swimming the sea, its neck so long it bent like a giant figure 8. Later Cope arranged its skeleton in the Museum of the Philadelphia Academy of Natural Sciences. Marsh happened to be a visitor at that time, and when Cope led him around to show him some of its peculiarities, Marsh noticed that the articulations of the vertebrae were reversed. To save Cope embarrassment, Marsh quietly told him that he had the whole thing wrong end foremost, that the head was where the tail ought to have been, accounting, of course, for that remarkable figure-8 neck. His friendly suggestion, said Marsh, far from being appreciated, threw Cope into a rage. He insisted that the articulations were correct. Even when Professor Leidy found that the error had been made, Cope would not admit it. That, said Marsh, was the reason for his lifelong campaign of vilification, ending to the detriment of science, smeared across page one of the Sunday papers.

In public, the scientific world was almost solidly against Cope. Even those scientists who privately admitted that he

had received bad treatment waited in line to state their outrage at what he had said, and the intemperate publicity with
which he had said it. On leaving Canada he had obtained a
professorship at the University of Pennsylvania, and it looked
for a while as if the public quarrel would cost him his job, but
the fearful president of that institution delayed action and
the storm finally abated. Cope won a partial victory relating
to the Survey fossils which Marsh had carted home to Yale.
Marsh at last acknowledged that they were public property.
He did not go so far as to release them from the museum,
however, or allow any but a chosen few to view them, but he
did sign a paper acknowledging that the United States had
the right to claim its property after he was dead.

Cope also successfully prevented the Interior Department from taking *his* fossils. He died in 1897 at the age of
fifty-seven. Lying in delirium, his friends were amazed to
hear him deliver, with all his excellence of manner and dic-
tion, a complete lecture on Felidae, the cat family, enumerat-
ing in order all of the major evolutionary discoveries, their
relationships, and their correlations with zoology in general.
Marsh followed him in death two years later; he was sixty-
seven.

A map of the favored Cope and Marsh diggings shows
them scattered along the region of the Great North Trail,
but because so much of their effort was directed to the resur-
rection of the reptilian age what is chiefly marked are the
western shores of the midcontinental Jurassic and Cretaceous
seas. There is evidence that reptiles of many species passed
from Alberta to Siberia across parts of the continents now
mountain, and shallows which have sunk to cold ocean
depths. A better case can be made for an Atlantic passage
roughly by way of Ireland. It has already been noted that
many European species turned up in slight variations in Kansas and the Judith.

Although the main age of the reptiles was still millions
of years in the future, their successors, the warm-blooded

land creatures, had probably split away as early as Permian times. Cope may have found the mother strata of all warm-blooded, young-suckling, land-traveling creatures in middle New Mexico where Permian rocks run from the Guadalupe escarpment northward overlooking the old Mission Trail to the region of Santa Fe; or in Texas, where they commence near Abilene and pass upward through Oklahoma. Fossils from similar beds in Russia have also been advanced as the birthplace of the first warm-blooded creatures, as have remains from the Karroo formation of South Africa.

There are those who hold that the triconodonts of Wyoming, named for the peculiar form of their molar teeth, were the first clear severance from the reptiles. The Wyoming

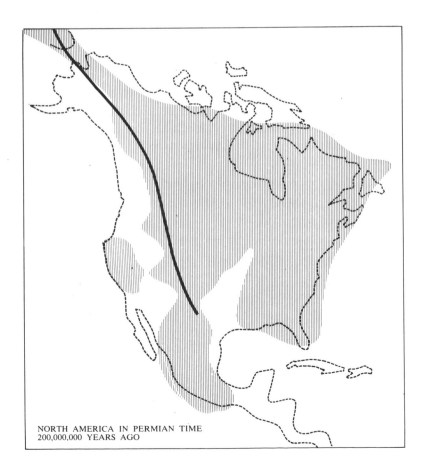

NORTH AMERICA IN PERMIAN TIME
200,000,000 YEARS AGO

triconodonts were about the size of house cats and lived in
Jurassic times, but they may have been merely the offshoot of
an earlier form. Apparently they left no descendants. Como
Bluff in Wyoming also furnished numerous jaws, teeth, skull,
and leg bones of the Ctenacodon, a gnawing creature the size
of a large rat. Its appearance in England at approximately the
same age indicates it had some means of migration between
those two widely separated points, so probably it, too, was a
traveler on the Great North Trail. The marsupials were once
deemed the basic transitional stage between reptiles and
mammals. The most ancient of all marsupials, believed to be
the ancestor of all the opossums and kangaroos, came from
the Cretaceous strata of Montana. The marsupials developed

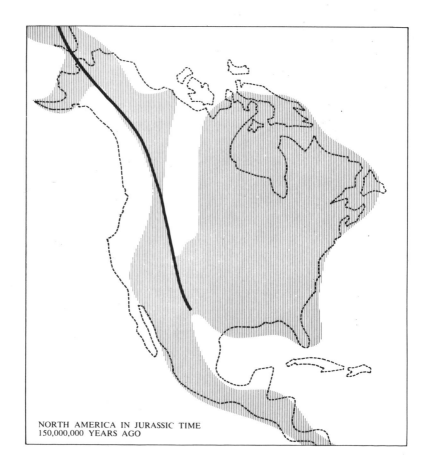

NORTH AMERICA IN JURASSIC TIME
150,000,000 YEARS AGO

in abundance from New Mexico through Wyoming, Montana, Alberta and across into Asia, and for a time they seemed destined to be the dominant creatures of the land, but they fell behind when faced by competition with the new placental orders, and only in isolated Australia were they able to continue their evolution, developing into kangaroos, dasyures, and bandicoots. The American marsupials are today represented only by the opossum, one of the most primitive extant warm-blooded animals. The first link on the human chain may have been discovered in Wyoming, later to appear as the ape and lemur forms of Asia, Java, and Africa. One of Cope's greatest Wyoming finds was *Timitheium rostratum*, which he dug from the rocks of the Washakie Basin. The

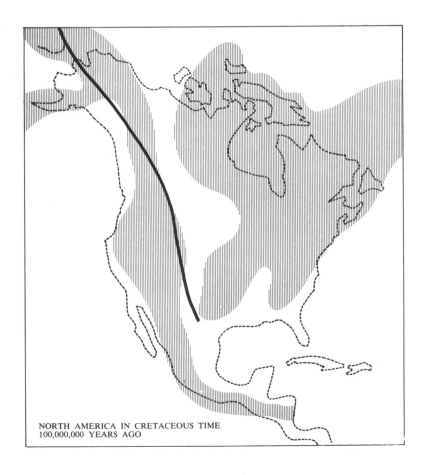

NORTH AMERICA IN CRETACEOUS TIME
100,000,000 YEARS AGO

creature, first of a new order Quarrumana, he put forth as the ancestor of all the primates on the face of the earth.

Credit for the original placentalia is widely disputed. Recent exploration in Mongolia has turned up a placentary group of insect-eaters which have been named the first of the mammals. These came from Eocene strata which is more than 100 million years later than Cope's Permian. The Mongolian insectivors can be shown to have had many descendant species, and these have been found abundantly in America. Others traveled in a westerly direction and developed in Europe. Often it is impossible to decide whether the European form, the Mongolian form, or the American form was the

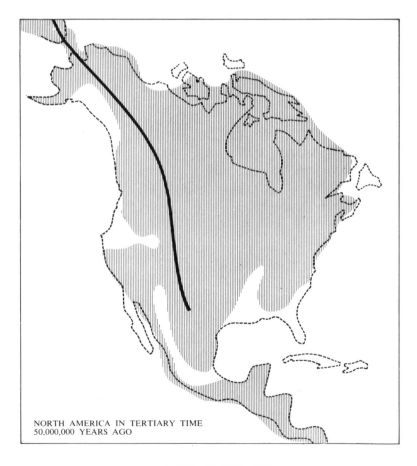

NORTH AMERICA IN TERTIARY TIME
50,000,000 YEARS AGO

ROUTE OF PAST AGES

original. When the same species, or species very closely related, appear at apparently the same age in Europe, Asia, and America, it is a speculation whether they traveled across the world by some convenient route or developed independently as the result of a tendency toward a similar environment. Most paleontologists believe in their mobility. Deep in the rocks they mark the route of the Great North Trail.

THE CATTLE TRAIL
—NORTH FROM TEXAS

Chapter 9

In 1871 when Edward Drinker Cope was making his first journey across Kansas, there were long stretches through which he kept his train windows closed against the stench of buffalo carcasses preceding marksmen had left along the tracks. In those days buffalo were still so numerous that conductors, passing through one of the great herds, often stopped to give their passengers the opportunity of killing one. Grand Duke Alexis of Russia chartered a private train to use as headquarters on his historic buffalo hunt, with Buffalo Bill Cody—the onetime guide of Cope's rival, Professor Marsh— serving as his guide and gaining thereby some of his earliest international publicity. From all over the world sportsmen came to shoot numbers of buffalo and take back their salt-embalmed heads for mounting, with no thought but that the herds, like the herring of the sea, were endless. Their imminent danger of extinction did not occur to Professor Marsh, although he was the foremost authority on the horse and he could see everywhere the evidence of its sudden disappearance from the hemisphere. Cope did not consider it, either. Yet three years later the Kansas herd was a thing of the past, diminishing from four million to a stray few thousand.

But farther to the west the buffalo still roamed. In 1874 there were probably ten or twelve million of the original sixty. The Army that year estimated the Montana herd, centering at Judith Basin, at four million. Some reports had the buffalo growing scarce, but, urged on by higher prices, the Blackfeet and other Indians of northern Montana brought unprecedented numbers of hides in to Fort Benton. Baker Brothers alone shipped 75,000 robes from Fort Benton in 1876. At that time the Canadian government became alarmed at the kill and tried to put game laws into effect. These were designed to prevent the wholesale slaughter of animals for their hides and the killing of all animals under two years of age. Due to famine among the Indians, however, the law had to be repealed. In 1878 the range was very dry, and Indians, attempting to drive buffalo, set fires which swept the Canadian border, driving large numbers south to slaughter.

In 1872 Congress tried to restrict the hunting of buffalo, and followed the attempt in 1874 with another, stricter statute, but neither bill seemed important enough to President Grant for him to sign. Granville Stuart of Gold Creek fame, by then looking to cattle ranching rather than gold bonanzas, wrote saying a great many influential white men welcomed the extinction of the buffalo as the only cheap and easy means of subjugating the Plains Indians. Most white men in official position who argued for the buffalo's rapid extinction pointed out that they had only the Indians' good in mind. Once the buffalo was gone, the Indians would learn to be peaceful, productive farmers, a credit to the country. Many people, even in the states most afflicted by warlike Indians, however, were concerned about the buffalo slaughter, and this was expressed in a number of laws. The Kansas legislature in 1872 passed a law to prevent the wanton killing of buffalo, but the governor vetoed it. The legislatures of Idaho, Wyoming, Montana, and Nebraska all took some action to impede the slaughter. New Mexico, South Dakota, and Colorado passed laws after there were no buffalo left. Colorado passed its law protecting the buffalo in 1897.

By 1880 the buffalo was finished. For a thousand miles in the heartland of the old domain only his bones and droppings were left to show that he had ever existed. The bones rotted clean and white and Indians gathered them for shipment to the charcoal plants. They also hunted out the horns, scraped them smooth with bits of broken bottle, polished them, mounted them against backgrounds of cheap plush on slabs of wood, and sold them for parlor hatracks—the Indians' final utilization of the buffalo.

The grass did not long flow in the prairie winds, or cure brown and nutritious on the ground with nothing to graze it. The great cattle boom was at hand. A large number of things in addition to available grass combined to bring this about.

It has been noted that in 1849 the nation had fewer than a million wage earners and that they averaged less than a dollar a day. After the Civil War, and particularly after 1878, their numbers and rate of pay went up sharply. While the U.S. population doubled between 1849 and 1880, the nation's urban population multiplied eight times over. Most of the city growth took place in the North and centered around its labor-hungry new industries.

While the industry of the South was being destroyed by the war, that of the North grew to supply the needs of the military. In mid-April 1861, when the first shot arched across the water at Fort Sumter, several ships were nosing into the ice-clot of Lake Superior, anxious to reach the canal which had been built around the torrent of Sault Ste. Marie with cargoes of iron ore and native copper. The natural destination, particularly of the iron, was Pennsylvania's Lake Erie shore. By war's end the traffic had become a big one, and the Pennsylvania furnaces and foundries began looking around for a new market now that no more guns and armor plate were needed. They found it in the railroads.

Other industries boomed also. Although Confederate partisans had freely predicted the destruction of the New England textile industry, it emerged from the conflict with the ability to put more spindles in action than at any other time in history. The petroleum industry, barely making a start with a 2000-barrel production in the year before the war, was producing 2½ million barrels per year at the war's close, and by 1869 had stepped up its production to the 4 million barrel mark, and to 11 million by 1874.

With the demand for labor, shipowners hurried to supply it. Immigrants from the poorest sections of Europe poured into the Eastern ports. A few were recruited in labor gangs before leaving the old country and were immediately taken to their jobs, but most of them were simply dumped on the docks. Moving a few blocks, they took over the poorest sections, formed slums, and furnished the sweatshop labor and the tuberculosis mortality which so shamed the nation during that era of the very rich and the very poor.

Fortunately, most of the immigrants did not know how badly off they were. They tended to compare their slums with the dugout quarters they had occupied in the old country, and found them an improvement. Although they took the worst jobs at the longest hours and poorest pay, that was better also. In Russia the serfs had been freed only in 1861, and well into the 1880s many worked in some degree of bondage. In much of central Europe the lot of the peasant was just as bad. In the old country America's immigrants had made out on unbolted flour bread, root vegetables, and cabbage soup. In America a man could earn around two dollars a day and could buy meat. Many of them had scarcely tasted beef in their entire lives. They were not a discriminating buying public, and Texas had just the thing for them.

During the war Texas was an economic island. Some of its cotton was brought eastward through Louisiana and down the Red until the Mississippi was taken. Other shipments ran the blockade from Galveston with moderate success, but Texas' cattle had no market. They roamed the chaparral, becoming lean and wild and sharp along the backbone, and as able to shift for themselves as any animal on the continent. When the war was over, men with no means of livelihood started chasing this wild stock to such markets as were available, to the hide-and-tallow plants set up along the Gulf Coast, to New Mexico for the Indian allotments. Some started for California, but they didn't get there; Texas cattle reached the Union Pacific and competed with buffalo in the commissaries.

Several railroads had been started into eastern Texas, but they were impoverished spurs by the end of the war. It was the seventies before a line was built as far as Fort Worth, and it went bankrupt with the general hard times of that decade. Closest railroad to the cattle-raising end of Texas was the Union Pacific, but its nearest point, Kearney, Nebraska, was about as far away as Springfield, Illinois. However, there was a demand for beef in the East, and Texas tried to supply it. The first big northern drive was attempted in 1866. That year a quarter of a million cattle, in herds of many sizes, driven by a small army of Confederate veterans, started out with a general idea of getting to Missouri. It was not to be. Forewarned, the farmers, fearing destruction of their crops, organized and met them along the Neosho River, at the northeast corner of the Indian territories. They could not continue, yet driving cattle back to Texas was too preposterous to be contemplated. For weeks the herds stacked up along the river bottoms, held from straying by cowboys, bawling over the rail fences at farmers and their staunch sons who rode the line armed with guns, pitchforks, and long bullwhips. Some benefactor arrived with a wagonload of whisky and a tent. The little town of Baxter Springs found itself placed strategically in the midst of the excitement and boomed to become the forerunner of Abilene, Dodge City, and Cheyenne. Eventually most of the Baxter herds either got through or found owners who bought them cheap for fattening, but the Texans had learned their lesson, and no more cattle went to Missouri by the corner route.

The Kansas Pacific Railroad had by then laid its rails as far as Salina. That town was put forward as a shipping point. Hearing of it, farmers from the rich valley at the juncture of the Salina and Smoky Hill rivers objected. No Baxter Springs hell-town for them. They stood ready to tear down any loading pens the railroad might attempt to build, and so informed the management. However, up the track about 23 miles was a siding, a depot, and a cluster of shacks called Abilene. . . .

Abilene had been laid out as a city and its lots offered for sale, but the sale had languished. At present it had three business establishments—a store, a saloon, and a feed stable. The valley around was still largely unsettled, hence no one objected when its businessmen welcomed an increase in trade in the form of Texas cattle. A crew soon arrived, doubling the town's population, and started to build stock pens and loading chutes. Soon after came an entrepreneur to start a second saloon. Several herds were already on their way north from Texas, mostly without more than a general destination. One, according to the moccasin telegraph of the Plains, was headed for California via the South Pass of Wyoming and the deserts of the Humboldt. Scouts were sent out by the shipping interests to inform it and all others of the new facilities.

To the California herd, an exploit of Colonel W. O. Wheeler, the Abilene boosters arrived in good time. They found him, his cattle, and his armed force of cowboys halted by the news of warlike Indians in the border area of Nebraska and Colorado. Abilene received the Colonel's herd of 2500, fat from being delayed in good grass, almost before the chutes were completed. About 33,000 more were shipped that first year. Winter allowed the little community to prepare for the flood that was to follow. By 1871 its pens handled upwards of half a million head per year. Since it required about five cowboys to trail-herd a thousand cattle—a number which did not include cooks, wagon flunkeys, wranglers, scouts, owners, and those free souls who strung along for the action—a trail-herd population of at least 2000 arrived in the boom years. Added to these were clerks, yard hands, bartenders, gamblers, soldiers, and the residents of the surrounding Kansas prairies.

Abilene had at its crest a population of almost 5000, although scarcely more than a thousand could be counted through the winter. The town's main thoroughfare became a solid bank of hotels, stores, saloons, and miscellaneous establishments. A location in the hell-roaring center of town was very important, and a man might make a fortune in a single season simply by erecting a building and renting out the liquor, faro, monte, and restaurant concessions. Lots became spectacularly valuable.

Seeing the fortune in Abilene real estate, boomers arrived at sidings all along the Kansas Pacific, purchased land, built pens and loading chutes, organized townsites, laid out streets and alleys, and tried to sell city lots. With yards and sidings ready, promoters' representatives rode the trails to inform the Texans of the new and improved facilities, including an inducement of untouched grass, a virgin area where herds could wait in lush abundance, putting on valuable weight for the market. Abilene responded by sending representatives even farther, supplied with lists of the buyers who would actively bid for the beef at their yards, the greatest assemblage of meat-packing money in the West. Abilene also named its great saloons to appeal to the Texans. Its most famous, boasting the largest mirrors and longest bar in Kansas, was The Alamo. It also had the Lone Star, the Longhorn, and the Applejack, all named to suit the Southern fancy. Its red-light district was named Texas Town. To stave off competition, particularly from Wichita and Ellsworth, the businessmen of Abilene did all they could to give the visitors the kind of a wide-open environment they hankered for.

Soon the honest settlers from the surrounding Smoky Hill Valley became embittered. The herds devoured their range and were always bursting through into fields with wild cowboys chasing them, and they were afraid to go into town. The women of Abilene, most of whose husbands depended on the Texans for their livelihood, became outraged at the flagrant prostitution of Texas Town, and organized a march one hundred strong, demanding the abolition of the oldest profession. In Abilene, girls were so much in demand that the operators of the better houses regularly met the trains from Kansas City looking for likely recruits. The city council, knowing they could not drive away the girls without having the Texans follow them, segregated the district to an area which became known as Mud Town, then moved it outside the city limits where they could lay the blame for it in the laps of the county and state authorities. Another move toward appeasing the farming and female contingents had been to hire a marshal and build a jail. The marshal was soon dead and the jail demolished. The councilmen then decided to hire as town marshal a former Indian scout, exhibition shot, and gambler named James Butler Hickok, known to one and all as Wild Bill. Bill came to Abilene recommended by a recent performance in Hays City where, on the preceding New Year's Eve, he had shot three men stone-dead in a single engagement. The accomplishment was rendered the more remarkable by the fact that Bill's eyesight was failing at the time. In Abilene his eyesight diminished still more and the best he could do was kill two in a night, one of them by mistake.

Wild Bill Hickok did not satisfy the law-and-order element. He lined himself solidly with the saloon and red-light crowd, looking with suspicion on lawyers, ministers, and people in the dry goods business. In Abilene his most celebrated association was with Mattie Silks, a courtesan who was later to reign over Denver's night life. In the end he was sent packing, and the good people next sought to eliminate the prime reason for his being there. In revulsion from its summer of greatest violence, they met and drafted a notice which was sent to Texas newspapers stating that Abilene no longer welcomed the cattle trade. They were shooting at a dead wolf. A shorter, better-grassed route had already been established to Ellsworth in the West. But Abilene for all time had won its spurs as the first great trail town. It seemed destined for wickedness from the start. Its name had been selected by the wife of an early settler for its biblical meaning—city of the plain. Albert Griffin, a temperance lecturer, likened Abilene, Ellsworth, Wichita, Newton, and Dodge City to Admah, Sodom, Gomorrah, Zeboim, "and Bela which is Zoar."

Dodge City, which had known the tramp of Spanish horses when Coronado passed that way, guided by a renegade Indian up the main eastern course of the Great North Trail, had a history older than any of the others. But even trail-centered Dodge could not stand against the forces which had destroyed its predecessors. More and more of Kansas came under fence, some of the land claimed legally, but much of it simply preëmpted. Trail drivers could not stop and sue those who had fenced them off, however illegally. Ground not fenced was held by resident cattlemen who met the herds with armed force to protect their range. Routes all the way to the Texas border were interrupted. The Kansas legislature passed a quarantine law barring diseased cattle, a handy legality to back up all those who wanted to bar sections of the old trails. Cattle still got through, but grass along the open routes was very scarce. Texans who once were able to spread their herds near Abilene and Dodge and put on some tallow before offering them to the buyers now wondered whether they could keep their critters alive to the shipping pens where hay was available. Then too, more and more of the cattle entering Kansas were not destined for the railroad, but were being driven through to Nebraska and Wyoming. From these cattle Kansas received no benefit at all, unless a few cowboys happened to stop in at Dodge for a spree on their way home in October. Finally, in midsummer 1885, the governor issued a proclamation barring the state's borders to all the through herds. As nobody could prove he intended to ship his cattle from one of the Kansas railheads rather than drive to Nebraska or Wyoming, the order meant all herds could legally be barred, and generally they were. However, cattle had become a business on a national and international scale, several new factors having appeared in addition to the cheap stock of Texas and the hungry market of the booming cities. . . .

In the early 1850s the oyster fisheries of the East Coast began using refrigerator cars to transport their catch to points as far away as western New York. Refrigerator cars appeared on the Union Pacific and were used to haul meat to the the work gangs. Refrigerator cars were not needed to get cattle from the ranges (it was cheaper to haul on the hoof), but they allowed large central packing plants—the meat industry of the Midwest. The next development came when the Bates refrigeration process permitted ocean vessels to turn themselves into gigantic coolers and carry fresh meat across the seas to England and Europe.

With a demand that grew by the day, it is not recorded that any Texas steer was turned away at the slaughterhouses of Kansas City because of its low quality. They were lump-jawed, blind, and half-alive after having fallen and been trampled in the cars; some were even deliberately crippled by their drivers to render them more tractable on the trail. But all were beef. The longhorn was not famed for its steaks, but it carried a lot of meat. One Kansas City packer estimated that the average Texas steer produced four steaks, four roasts, and 900 pounds of good, durable stewing beef. However, such lean beef did not hang and age well, and it did not please the patrons who were used to the well-larded meat of the Eastern farms.

At the outset a longhorn was worth only $2.25 per hundred at the shipping pens. In a few years demand had pushed the price to $6, and more for beef of the better sort. In England, a cry arose from the local producers, the fisheries, mutton growers, and distributors of Danish bacon. Tick fever was common among Texas cattle, causing embargoes to be raised against them in other places besides Kansas, and the English interests became alarmed for the public health, predicting that epidemics would result from a continued importation of "sick American beef."

Although perhaps few upper-crust Englishmen would be served American beef when the excellent local cuts were available, the clamor interested them. Inveterate readers of the market quotations from all over the world, they took note of the astounding rise in beef at Kansas railhead, and talked less about the possibility of England being swept by Texas fever than of who was getting the extra $3.75. They reasoned it unlikely that Texas steers had ever been sold at a loss. However, assuming $2.25 to be the break-even point, then $6 beef was selling at a clear profit of 62½ per cent—or figured the other way around, on the original investment, some lucky fellow was picking up a clear 266 per cent profit.

Already England had a large number of gentlemen who had made investments in American mines, railroads, and industry. For fifty years it had been considered fashionable to visit America, travel up the Mississippi, see Niagara Falls, venture an estimate as to the rate with which it was eroding its way to Lake Erie, and shoot a buffalo on the Plains. Englishmen of the better class settled in Colorado in such numbers that Colorado Springs became almost an English city. In 1880, it is safe to say that the average upper-class Englishman knew more about the American Great Plains than did his counterpart in Philadelphia. Englishmen more than Americans were aware that both the Indian and the buffalo were on their way to extinction. The stage was set for one of the most natural speculative opportunities of all time:

One purchased lean Texas cattle at a very low price. Texas was the greatest breeding ground for cattle known in the world. Its climate was dry, and healthful, and warm all winter long. However, although excellent for calves, it lacked the long grass of the northern regions where steers waded to their bellies and put on the meat which paid off in quality as well as weight at the market. So one purchased young stock in Texas—yearlings for $5, two-year-olds for $10.00 and three-year-olds for $15.00. Any of these animals would double its weight in a single year on the tall grass of the northern ranges recently abandoned by the buffalo. The drive from Texas could be made in a single summer. The chief expenses were for herdsmen's wages, an average of about $25 per month and grub, cow ponies at about $40 each, plus a number of wagons and other equipment. Ranch buildings were practically without cost; satisfactory ones could be made of timber felled from the valleys near the ranch. The grass was endless and free, no taxes, no rent— nothing. One had to expect a loss of stock to predators, accident, thieves, cold weather, and the like, but those with experience in the country estimated this not to exceed 12 per cent. Make it 15 per cent to play safe. Expenses and losses would cut the profit from 100 per cent to something like 60.

But wait! Another factor had also to be considered: the Wyoming poundage commanded almost double the price of the Texas poundage because it was grass-fat and market-ready. This in turn added to the profit, which now became around 120 per cent. It seemed a bit of all right. Soon some members of Parliament, who had taken no action to save the health of its people from sick beef, sent representatives to America for a look around. What they reported in public and in private started a rush to invest. British capital poured into the American Plains. The market for Texas stockers boomed. The age of the feudal cattle ranches and of the cattle barons was at hand.

The most famed of all the cattle barons was located in New Mexico, where there also took place the most celebrated encounter of an Englishman with the Wild West.

John Chisum, a Texan from Tennessee, came to New Mexico shortly after the Civil War, liked what he saw, and next year, 1867, returned and set up a ranch. Soon the sites where Clovis man had butchered and cracked the marrow bones of the giant bison were being trampled by Texas cattle, and his lost flints were becoming overlain by a cultural level of tomato cans and empty cartridge cases.

Chisum brought in an initial ten thousand head of long-horns. The country was encumbered only by land grants of Spanish and Mexican origin, which could safely be ignored. The Pecos River, running from north to south, offered the western fourth of the state its most dependable water. Chisum established a home at Bosque Grande, named for the groves of cottonwoods which spread up from the river. A tough, likable man who had previously been successful mainly in talking others into investing in enterprises which for one reason or another went broke, Chisum this time borrowed with better results, at least for himself, bringing in herd after herd until he controlled the Pecos range for 150 miles south to north, and from east to west as far as a steer could graze from water. The old Chisholm Trail was named not for John Chisum but for Jesse Chisholm, who established the route from Fort Worth northward through the Indian nations to Abilene and Dodge. John Chisum, however, had a Chisum Trail of his own. It went up the Pecos, over Folsom, and through the Cimarron Pass to Las Animas, Colorado, and the Kansas Pacific built a spur line to meet it. One of the things John Chisum was best known for was his part in the Lincoln County Cattle War. His rival in this celebrated un-pleasantness was Major, brevet grade, Lawrence G. Murphy.

Unlike Chisum, whose heartiness and hospitality caused even his enemies to like him, Major Murphy was imperiously cool to those not fully his peers. At one time he had seemed destined for the priesthood, but worldly ambitions inter-vened. During the war he secured a commission and joined the California Column, the Union force sent to counter Con-federate moves in New Mexico and the farther Southwest. After the peace, he stayed on for a while, assigned to Fort Stanton, westward about three days' wagon travel from Chisum's Basque Grande. They were neighbors as distances were seen in that sparsely settled land.

Fort Stanton's main purpose was the control of the Mescalero Apaches who ranged the hill and desert country south to the Guadalupe Mountains. There was a treaty of sorts according to which the government was obligated to supply the Apaches with beef, flour, sugar, and other commodities, and in this arrangement the restless and quick-witted Murphy saw a chance to make money. Upon being mustered out, as a major, he stayed on at the fort, got the backing of Colonel Emil Fritz, U.S.A. (Ret.), one of the German officers who had given such an imperial flavor to the Union Army of Missouri, and opened a store.

The store prospered. Markups of several hundred per cent had been usual in the West since the days of the fur traders. Murphy sold at high prices to the local ranchers and soldiers, and ingratiated himself to many of his former fellow officers by extending them credit for gambling and booze. He was well acquainted at the territorial capital in Santa Fe, where the officials learned that by favoring him they were not likely to suffer in a financial way. All this made his expenses large, but he expanded into ranching and the Indian supply. He obtained beef contracts and increased his margin of profit on one hand by purchasing at cut rates from the cattle rustlers and on the other by shorting the Apaches on the count. For a while the ranchers from down toward the Rio Grande were chief sufferers, but later, with his knowledge, or without it, some of the cattle were supplied by Chisum.

Chisum's *Long Rail* brand, a single straight line burned from flank to shoulder across an animal's side, was supposedly impossible to alter. At any rate, nobody fooled Big John for long, and in a few months he was tracing his stock to the rustlers and to Murphy. Murphy said that if any stolen stock ever found its way into his Indian beef issue it was because he had been fooled completely, but Chisum put on extra guards. At about that time certain Army men were becoming suspicious of him, too. Under the date of July 22, 1873, a Captain Randlett of the Eight Cavalry wrote of Murphy & Co. to the Secretary of War:

"... This firm I know to have been defrauding the Government since my arrival at the post. Their contracts with Indian agents have been fraudulent to my certain knowledge. So powerful is the ring to which they belong that I am able to prove this firm has even attempted to force upon officers of this post contract goods inferior to samples from which they were bought. I consider that L. G. Murphy and Company's store is nothing more than a den of infamy and recommend the removal of the firm from the Reservation."

Not all the officers agreed with Captain Randlett, but Murphy did not mind leaving Fort Stanton. He moved down to the new county seat at Lincoln and built himself a large adobe brick store. The depression of the seventies was drying up credits and stopping the western-bound railroads cold in their tracks, but Murphy, by bold enterprise and the still-expanding nature of the cattle business, continued for a time to profit. He had the only store of any size for miles around; ranchers were forced to pay his prices; he extended credit and when they failed to pay took over their holdings. His friends in Santa Fe were a great help. The Carpetbagger era was just closing; federal appointees and other officials were chiefly Northerners who wanted to grab what they could and get out. With their help, and through tax deeds, water-rights conflicts, and adverse claims, some of the latter dating to the days of Old Spain, it was not hard to gain titles that would hold up in a friendly court. And there was still the Apache trade. Despite Randlett's complaint Murphy was not excluded from the bidding, and by now he had a force of gunmen and rustlers in his employ that made others hesitant to bid against him.

The Indians on the Mescalero and Sierra Blanca grounds were down on the books at 1100, but such a population was not to be found. Four hundred was the most ever turned up by actual count. The Army never acknowledged this and stuck to the larger figure, lest the importance of the fort diminish and appropriations be cut. Care was shown never to have any goods, Indian or other, left at the close of the year, and Murphy helped them out of their difficulty. Lacking suitable storage for the Apache goods, much of it was freighted down to Lincoln to the big store on loan, but it was never paid back. Although there was no proof that the arrangement benefited the officers at Stanton, Murphy was always good for a loan, never pressuring for his payment, and he lent sizable sums to the governor at Santa Fe.

If Chisum was king of the Pecos, Murphy was king of western Lincoln County. His store was the center of the community, containing the post office, a saloon, a pool table, bar, some commodious offices with leather chairs, and the Masonic temple. But despite outward appearances, he was not getting rich. His credits weighed heavily on him. He was in his turn getting to be a bad risk. His suppliers in Santa Fe, St. Louis, and New York started demanding cash with order. It was a time to cut back his operations, but he could not. He had to control the country or he would lose everything. And Chisum started to make trouble. A herd of Long Rail cattle had been traced to Murphy—or to some of his men, which was the same thing—and Chisum was talking legal action. He wanted some arrests.

Then there was a further complication. Colonel Fritz, Murphy's silent partner, had been taken sick and went home to Germany. Word came of his death. If the Fritz money was now taken out of the firm, Murphy would have to make an accounting. People commented that Murphy did not look so healthy as usual; he had lost weight; his sparse beard and mustache, so carefully careless, had become thinner; and they were likely to find him in a brittle, falcon-eyed humor.

At about this time a lawyer arrived in Lincoln from Atcheson, Kansas, and hung out his shingle. He was cultivated, well educated, and, like Murphy, he once had had ecclesiastical ambitions, although with an approach to the Diety by a Presbyterian route. He had with him a newly acquired, handsome wife, molten of hair with a disposition to match. Murphy greeted them cordially, they became friends, and he put in the lawyer's hands the collection of Colonel

Fritz' $10,000 life insurance policy. Later he asked him to defend the men who had been taken with Chisum's cattle.

There McSween—the young lawyer—drew up short. The men were guilty and religious principles would not allow him to defend a guilty man pleading innocent. (They did not prevent him trying to take a $7,500 fee for collecting the $10,000 insurance policy, but that was at a later date and quite a few things had happened in the interim.) Some people believed his religious scruples had less to do with the defense than his reluctance to go against John Chisum. At any rate, he made an enemy of the ailing Murphy. Then in 1876, with the big store only four years old, competition arrived.

John Tunstall was a young Englishman of a good and wealthy family who came West in the search of profitable investments and adventure. He was a solidly built man, personable as were the other principals in the unfolding drama, and of staunch character. He stopped in Santa Fe to inquire into what opportunities the country afforded, and someone told him about Lincoln County. The surveyed lines of the Southern Pacific and the Atlantic & Pacific had been run close to that county south and north, and property values, temporarily down, were bound to boom when the railroads were built. He arrived on the stage, and Murphy tried to sell him a ranch he had acquired without much of a title. For a while Tunstall found Murphy very cordial, the storekeeper seeing in English capital an escape from his financial dilemma.

Tunstall, however, went south of town to the Felix (or Feliz) River and bought a ranch there. To make it more galling, he stocked it with cattle for which Murphy had made a competing offer. Next he came into Lincoln and built a store of his own.

Tunstall's store was roughly on a par with Murphy's, having as an added feature a bank. The bank was backed by himself, McSween, and John Chisum. It has been said that Tunstall was a very innocent young Englishman who believed Murphy would stand still in the face of this challenge. However, he must have had the notion it would lead to trouble because one of the first men he hired, in an unspecified general capacity, was a smooth-faced, polite, graceful, and arrant young man by the name of William H. Bonney, better known in those parts as Billy the Kid.

Billy was at that time only seventeen, but he already had quite a history behind him. Having left the mining camp of Silver City, where his mother ran a boardinghouse, he had drifted to Arizona and become a horse thief, prospector, and monte dealer. Lacking anything better to do and hearing about the big action in Lincoln County, he joined a group of young fellows as lawless as himself and headed back through his old stomping grounds, across the Rio, the old Mission Supply Trail, and the lava deserts, arriving one day at Murphy's big, thick-walled store, where he spent some time loafing around, staying sober, and making timely investments in the card games. He was on the Murphy payroll for special jobs, but he met Tunstall, took a liking to him, and made what was to be a permanent alignment with the opposition. Quite a bit has been made of their friendship, and apparently there was something to it. The two young men were as far apart in background as one could imagine, but Billy was brighter than average, as those who played cards with him well knew; he admired the Englishman, and was flattered when Tunstall gave him a special rifle and a fine horse.

About this time, having had a former fellow Army officer, Major William J. Brady, appointed sheriff, Murphy decided to settle accounts with Tunstall. Brady, with a "posse" and some sort of legal document, headed for the Rio Felix ranch, met the Englishman and a small party in the road already headed for town, demanded and got his surrender, and disarmed him. One of the posse then shot him, and another, detecting some life remaining as he lay in the dust, placed a bullet in the back of his head. They also shot his horse, and one of the men, picking up Tunstall's hat, put it under the horse's head. It was the type of humor appreciated in New Mexico at that time.

Billy the Kid was watching from a distance when Tunstall was killed. Partisans of Billy maintain that he was filled with wrath and became therefore the vengeful terror of legend. Perhaps, but not right away. He was too good a card player to go against the house odds, and that afternoon on the road to Felix the odds were hopelessly in the sheriff's favor. He retreated to the home ranch and bided his time.

Murphy's health had gone steadily downhill. Leaving his affairs in the hands of a young partner, James Dolan, he went to Santa Fe. The day Sheriff Brady took care of poor Tunstall, Murphy was in a Santa Fe hotel room being treated by a doctor.

Tunstall was barely in his grave when Murphy & Co. moved by attachment to take over all his property. The Rio Felix ranch was placed instantly on the delinquent tax rolls and later bought up at a small fraction of its value. The store, Murphy claimed, was a partnership venture of Tunstall's and McSween's, and it was attached as part of a claim derived from the handling of Colonel Fritz' insurance.

All of this, of course, bears the stamp of some more than friendly courts, and Murphy, who was not too popular at home, had to go some distance to find them. He probably hoped that with Tunstall dead McSween would leave the country. The lawyer was a tougher man than he thought. Although his backer, Chisum, remained safely in the wide, shady house at Bosque Grande, McSween struggled against a series of arrests and court actions, and managed to mount a fight of his own. One advantage was having most of the Lincoln people on his side. He found a justice of the peace and a constable not afraid to issue warrants and name deputies. The identity of Tunstall's killers were known, and a posse with this competing authority set out after them. Two were taken into custody, "escaped," were ridden down by Billy the Kid, and killed.

Things were moving fast. Billy and some of the boys next rode in to Lincoln, found Sheriff Brady and a deputy named Hindeman near Murphy's store, and shot them down. Brady died at once, but Hindeman lay with a bullet through him, suffering in the hot sunshine, while Billy's and Murphy's forces, behind adobe walls on opposite sides of the street, dared not show themselves. At last a local resident heard his pleading for water and carried him some in his hat; and Hindeman, after gulping a little, expired.

The county authorities then named a sheriff friendly to McSween, but he was put out of office by the governor, who appointed one of Murphy's gunmen. In the meantime another of the Tunstall killers, a Texas desperado called Buckshot Williams, entrusted with the task of assassinating McSween, was himself run down and killed at a sawmill, but not before killing Dick Brewer, manager of the Tunstall ranch, shooting the trigger finger off one of the Coe boys of desperate fame and inflicting a number of wounds in a resistance that was said to have won expressions of admiration from Billy the Kid himself.

Neither side would surrender the town. People cautiously went about their business. Both stores remained in operation. The weeks passed. Dolan and his sheriff tried to get the Army to intervene and clean out the McSween forces, who were, they said, opposing the duly constituted authorities and bringing in gunmen, most of them Spanish-speaking, to challenge the authority of Washington, D.C.

In command then at Fort Stanton was a General N. A. M. Dudley—actually on the payroll as colonel, but he had been breveted a general. Dudley was frequently at Murphy's store. To him, particularly after the killing of his old comrade Major Brady, it must have seemed that it was an insurrection of outlaws and foreigners—McSween as well as Tunstall had been born a British subject—aimed at America and her former Army officers. He longed to help, but his superior in Santa Fe had warned him to stay out of it. Finally, with about fifty men holed up across the town from one another and the McSween home under long-range fire, somebody fanned a couple of bullets past a soldier. Dudley assumed the shots came from McSween's camp. At any rate it gave him the pretext he needed to bring troops down from the fort, "give backing to the constituted authorities," and also "protect the lives of women and children."

Dudley was already acquainted with McSween. Some time before, a group of McSween's witnesses had appeared at a hearing to testify against some Murphy men and were arrested by the Army without warrants. This day he told Mc-Sween to surrender. "Do I surrender to the Army?" asked McSween. If so, he was willing, but he pointed out that surrender to Dolan and the sheriff would mean death. Would the General guarantee their safety? This Dudley would not do. He answered that protecting them was the sheriff's task. Dudley, backed by his troops and Gatling guns, then ordered all the nonresidents of Lincoln to depart.

By enforcing this he tore the heart from McSween's forces, most of whom were Spanish, which made them easy to sort out. Also, although there is no indication that it was prearranged, Dudley created a diversion which gave the sheriff a chance to set fire to McSween's house. It was burning when the soldiers pulled back. Dudley bivouacked and had his tent set up. Under its sunshade he could see the smoke as the fire progressed from room to room through the long, low Southwestern-type structure while the Murphy men, posted with rifles ready, watched all the exits.

There was no water to fight the fire; what little dirt could be thrown on it was ineffective, and it crept on and on through the hot afternoon. McSween sought solace in his Bible. He refused to touch a gun. Darkness at last settled and a man named Romero decided to surrender. He came out with his hands lifted, crying "I surrender," and was met by a volley of rifle bullets. He lay dead in front of the house and then Susan McSween came out. Nobody shot her. She walked under the rifles to General Dudley's tent and demanded that he intervene and save the lives of her husband and the others in the house. Dudley responded that he was there to protect women and children and back the civil authorities. He advised her that her husband and his men should surrender. She pointed to the body of Romero, who had tried to surrender, but Dudley informed her that their interview was over.

Finally, that night, when the fire progressed to the last room, the men made a run for it. Most of them were cut down by the waiting rifles. McSween, unarmed, clutching his Bible, was riddled. As he lay in the yard in the dark with the fire casting long shadows, one of the deputies named Beckwith ran up, calling out his claim to a reward that Murphy had evidently offered for McSween's death. In his eagerness, in the dark, with the flames in the background, he failed to notice a man already bent over the lawyer. It was Billy the Kid. Beckwith's reward was a shot from each of the Kid's pistols. According to a coroner's report Beckwith was hit by both bullets, one taking effect in the head and the other in the heart.

At this point it may have seemed that the Murphy enterprise was triumphant, and the good old days of easy living on the Apache supply would resume. But in Santa Fe, after some reports of improvement, Murphy's health deteriorated. Also, the officials were becoming alarmed. The East, always partial to Western violence, was reading all too much about the trouble in Lincoln County. Down in Texas, the Carpetbaggers had finally been expelled. Rutherford B. Hayes had been elected President, but only after large segments of the vote unfavorable to him had been tossed out; it troubled him to be called Ruther*fraud* B. Hayes, so, anxious to be a good President, he fired the New Mexico territorial governor and looked around for a worthy successor, picking lawyer-soldier-author Lew Wallace. Wallace was an organizer of the highest attainments, as proved by his recruiting activities after Lincoln's first call for troops; he was a leader at Fort Donaldson and Shiloh, and his had been the distinction of saving the national capital from capture when, outnumbered at Monocacy in July 1864, he delayed a Confederate thrust until reinforcements could be brought up. He had served on the commission which tried the persons accused of shooting President Lincoln, and the one set up to investigate Andersonville Prison. With all that behind him, Wallace turned his hand to

writing, and before his appointment as territorial governor of
New Mexico published *The White God*, a historical tale of
the Aztecs.

When Wallace took office, Major Murphy lay dying in a
room a few hundred yards down the street. Young Dolan
came up from Santa Fe by stagecoach, accompanied by a
party of mounted guards until he got out of Lincoln County,
and found Murphy already in his coffin, his hands like porce-
lain and his beard and mustache as thin as gauze. Not many
attended the services. Dolan conferred with the old capital
gang. They were wary, waiting to see what the new governor
would do. It was widely believed he would do nothing. They
assured him that Wallace was only a passing phase. Things
would return to normal. Wallace had taken the governorship
with romantic notions, but his real interest was in writing
books, and as an indication of his character it was noted that
his latest work concerned a young Jew named Ben-Hur who
made numberless obscene advances to Gentile women.

Dolan returned to Lincoln and busied himself trying to
stall creditors and hold the Murphy enterprises together. He
took over the Tunstall ranch on tax deed, but he was range-
and cattle-poor. There were warrants out for everybody, issued by competing officials, some of them from distant counties; but word came that all had been washed out by order of
Wallace, that he had declared a general amnesty. General
Dudley was suspended and General Hatch, Commander of
the Department of the West, headquartered in Santa Fe, de-
tailed five officers to a board of inquiry, three to serve as
judges, one as prosecutor, and one as judge-advocate. Driving to bring Dudley to justice was a lawyer named Huston
Chapman, who defied the threats of Dolan and his men but
was murdered before the board of inquiry met. His killer was
probably Jesse Evans, former pal of Billy the Kid, but the
stories conflicted and no arrests were made. The board of inquiry listened to the evidence, retired, deliberated, and
whitewashed General Dudley just as everyone knew it would.
He had acted, they said, as befitted an officer, protecting

women and children and backing the established authorities. Dudley was not returned to his post, however, and in the future Dolan's calls for Army assistance went unheeded.

The 1870s ran their course, and with the eighties came new people and new alliances. Billy the Kid, hired by Chisum after McSween's death, was unable to collect his wages and threatened the cattle king with violence. Chisum offered a reward for him, amount not specified; nobody risked his life on the poor chance that the baron of Bosque Grande would give him more than a hearty handshake after the deed was done. A tall Texan named Pat Garrett, who had recently been a saloon proprietor in Fort Sumner, ran for sheriff and was elected, perhaps because so many of his opponent's supporters were not qualified to vote. Although popularly supposed to be a Dolan man, he proved to be a good sheriff. He captured Billy the Kid on a charge of murdering Sheriff Brady, stood up to those who wanted to lynch him, and delivered him safely to the jail in Santa Fe. Realizing it would be impossible to get a conviction in Lincoln County, the case was moved to Dona Ana County to the southwest. Billy was found guilty and returned to Lincoln under sentence to hang but made his escape, killing his two guards, and ultimately was shot by Pat Garrett in a night-dark bedroom at Fort Sumner.

"*Quién es?*" said the Kid on entering the room, not realizing that Garrett was standing near the head of the bed. He was shot at point-blank range, falling dead with a bullet through the breast. Garrett later became a rancher, a collector of customs, saloon hanger-on, hard-luck poker player, and perennial seeker for political appointment. He was killed in "self-defense" in 1909 by a shot in the back. Murphy's holdings were attached for debt soon after his death, but Dolan carried on and became prosperous, strangely escaping retribution from his enemies, who were legion. Chisum outlived the war by only a few years, dying in Eureka Springs, Arkansas, in 1884.

The Lincoln County cattle war was fought along the

southern anchor of the Great North Trail, and many of its place names became famous in scientific circles for their archeological remains. The second most celebrated cattle war was fought along the Trail in Wyoming. But whereas the southern war ushered in the age of the princely ranches and the cattle boom, the one in the north came at its close. Quite a number of things happened in the few years between. . . .

Anchored in Texas and in the Pecos River of New Mexico, the cattle trails led northward, shifting according to the grass, the shipping and economic situation, and the fences erected against them. The Kansas embargo against herds bound for the northern ranges and Colorado, adding to Kansas a quarantine barring Texas cattle, deemed the probable carriers of fever ticks, if enforced would have made a solid wall, but the grass was there, and the British and Eastern capital, and so a way was found.

Many of the herds followed a route up the boundary lands where Kansas and Colorado joined, tightroping it, ready to move to one jurisdiction or the other as the temper of the residents demanded, and Trail City came into being. It was in Colorado, within rifle range of the Kansas border. The cattle trail there became main street, "wide and spacious," walled by false fronts, and nobody objected much when cowboys drove their herds down the middle of it, bringing their thirst and their money with them.

The era of Trail City was brief, but it stood long enough against the trample of Texas hoofs and the shifting tides of economics for old Print Olive to go there and be shot in a gunfight. Print—short for Prentice; his mother pronounced the *e* as *i* Texas fashion—was the toughest cattleman who ever came up the trail, and his death there in a shooting match was a great feather in Trail City's cap. Print had gone north to Nebraska and become a cattle king in the best Murphy tradition by overunning the country he wanted and killing the people to whom he objected. The career of Print Olive was to inspire a whole generation of Western novelists.

All the fictional tough, range-grabbing fathers with families of rawhide sons driving herds across the grain fields and garden plots of poor homesteaders are patterned after the Olives. Old Print and his sons rode them down, shot them down, hanged them, dragged them dead on the ends of lariat ropes, and burned their bodies afterward. Even men such as Doc Holliday and Wyatt Earp were offended by the Olives, who killed not cleanly, within reach of a good undertaker and news coverage, but out on the range like wolves, leaving their victims to desiccate in the sun. Old Print at last became too tough for his own family, who avoided him. When he was finally laid low in a Trail City saloon, it was a relief to all. No one went looking for his killer, a man by the name of Sparow, who was reputedly no great shakes as a gunman. Instead, the men who might have been his avengers hauled his body over to Dodge City by a complicated route via the K.P. to Kit Carson Junction, the branch to Las Animas, and the A.T. & S.F. to the cow capital, there to bury him amid great pomp under direction of the Odd Fellows Lodge.

From Trail City, in a stream a hundred miles wide—or rather in a hundred little streams, which like the Platte at low water followed a wide, branching course—the cattle moved to the area where Colorado, Wyoming, and Nebraska joined. Cheyenne became the new cowboy capital. There the stream parted, some of the herds moving north through Dakota Territory, some heading around the Laramie Range toward middle Wyoming. But the main trail was the natural one, as it had been for millions of years, northeastward toward the wall of the Big Horns, and the deep-worn ruts of the Bozeman Road were pounded out by the hoofs of cattle. They rolled through Montana and eventually across the Canadian border, and their range mingled with the range of the woods buffalo of the North, but that was years away. Meanwhile the main cattle excitement took place in Wyoming. . . .

Chapter 10

There were small native herds of cattle in the mountain valleys of the Northwest long before the first Texas drives. The Mormons brought cattle across the plains, and cattle went with their apostate and colonizing groups when they moved from the Salt Lake. Many of the early fur posts kept cows, pigs, and sheep. Cattle in fact were driven to the Green River rendezvous in 1830. Father DeSmet, who established an early mission among the Flatheads, had the first herd in western Montana, and Johnny Grant, the trader at Fort Hall, left those parts after a tragedy to his family and settled in the Deer Lodge Valley, turning rancher with 600 head which he had accumulated trading with the Oregon immigrants. The Smith River Valley, over Benton Pass from Confederate Gulch, was a ranch country long before anyone got the idea of driving cattle from the Pecos.

252

The first herds lived in the lush and protected mountain valleys. The windy plains were found to be cattle country by accident. In 1858 a force under General A. S. Johnston was ordered to the "State of Deseret" to quell the Mormons, who had established a warlike barrier to California travel, and the year before had shocked the nation with the massacre of a California-bound immigrant party at the Mountain Meadows. The freighters Russell, Majors & Waddell contracted for Johnston's supply by wagon from Fort Leavenworth, but due to the lateness of the season, and quite a number of mishaps, winter caught their main train in eastern Wyoming. It was useless to attempt a crossing of the Wasatch Divide in the deep snow, so it was decided to make camp for the winter. Short of feed for even the best stock, the cattle were simply driven up Chugwater Creek to make out as best they could. The winter of 1858–1859 was very cold and little hope was held for the stock, but when spring came a scout found three head in fine condition, prompting a wider search which turned up the entire herd, fatter than when they had been released the autumn before.

The first herds which spread across Wyoming and Montana flourished and put on weights of beef which exceeded all optimistic predictions. In many cases they followed the buffalo closely, and cowboys actually "whopped" the buffalo away from some choice valleys. Indians watching this process believed the white men had gone mad. They could not imagine driving off the buffalo which provided abundant food with no care whatever, replacing them with other animals that had to be tended. Once the buffalo were gone and the cattle had replaced them, Indians staged cattle drives, riding them down on horseback and killing them with rifles and arrows. They were attacked by whites for their actions, and some of them were hanged as cattle rustlers. But except for the Bloods and other Blackfeet who raided down from the protection of Canada, the Indians gave little trouble. The chief problem in the North, as it had been in Texas, was one of transportation. Stockers could be driven great distances, no care needed. But when carrying tallow from the good grass, drives of more than a couple of hundred miles were made at a real cost in weight and grade. Wyoming was lucky in that the Union Pacific had to swing north to avoid the Colorado Rockies, and hence pass through the heart of its best grass. Con Kohrs, an early Montana stockman, with stock derived from the increase of gold-camp cattle, had to drive from his Sun River range in Montana 800 miles, a route plagued by Indians, and his stock, on arrival, were too lean to command a good price. The Tingley interests made one of the first big killings in Montana beef by driving to Deadwood and selling at gold-boom prices, but it was a hair-raising gamble, the Sioux having all summer held the Black Hills camps in a state of virtual siege. Other early Montana ranchers drove eastward to the Northern Pacific, which had come to a delayed halt at Bismarck, Dakota Territory, because of financial troubles.

The first Wyoming ranches were small affairs, antedating even the drives to Dodge City. Disappointed prospectors from Colorado and wagon-freight men cut adrift when their employers were put out of business by the railroad raised small herds. Men came out on the first Union Pacific immigrant trains and took up land under the veterans' homestead law—generally those places blessed with permanent water. Print Olive and his kind drove many of these folk off their claims in Nebraska, and Wyoming offered some kind of haven in its greater expanse and desolation. They survived with a bobtail herd of cattle, a potato patch, and a supply of strychnine to bait for wolves in the winter.

Clarence King, whom we have already glimpsed as Whitney's assistant in California and as Cope's chosen enemy on the Geological Survey, was perhaps the first to call Wyoming's bonanza potential to the attention of eastern America and the world. King was able to occupy a particularly choice parcel of range in the midst of hostile Indian country, his safety assured because it was deemed accursed, a nearby Indian village having been wiped out by smallpox.

In addition to being an explorer, surveyor, geologist, and adventurer whose hobby had been reaching some of the most remote crags and deserts of the continent, King was a Delmonico gourmet and Brahmin intellectual. When he went East looking for investors in his ranch, which lay along Owl Creek near the Wyoming–Nebraska border, he attracted a celebrity roll including Henry Cabot Lodge, Mayor Edward Cooper of New York, Alexander Agassiz, and Frederick Law Olmstead; and he received the favorable notice of the poet Longfellow. King was regarded as an authority on the Comstock Lode, but he told his friends in the East he saw a better chance of doubling one's capital in Wyoming cattle. His own investment at Owl Creek amounted to $8380, and although he seldom visited his holdings, preferring when in Wyoming the comforts of Cheyenne with its celebrated cattleman's clubrooms, he ran it up to the point where he once profited by $120,000 from a single transaction. His investors also did well by following his advice, realizing yearly returns of 20 per cent or more, and he traveled to England looking for well-heeled men of the more impeccable sort over there. King got out at the top of the boom with a respectable fortune which, as has been accounted earlier, he lost at silver mining in Mexico.

Most of the corporations were not so lucky as King. He got his land for nothing, while most of them had to buy. They didn't buy the range, it was free, but they had to buy the key locations which contolled it. These, generally the creek bottoms, the springs, and the best hay land were in the hands of squatters and homesteaders. As it often happened the original small claimants sold out to medium size outfits, these to large ones, and the large ones to gigantic ones, the prices multiplying. As there was nothing much of tangible nature to put down on the deeds, only a few acres of land and the sheds and shacks on them, prices were based on cattle. The cattle were out on the range. Nobody could count them. The inventory on the tally books hence was accepted. It was a seller's market, and the buyer who procrastinated generally found his ranch bought away from him. There was one tale of the Wyoming rancher looking disconsolately out at a blizzard whitening the Cheyenne street, worried about the fate of his stock on some frigid range, saying, "Thank God, the tally books won't freeze!" All he needed to do was sell out before the spring and he could reduce his losses to zero; indeed, even figure a normal calf increase into the price.

Westerners with experience went around appraising ranches for corporate buyers, and soon there were newcomers from England who felt able to do the same. Many of these men were accused of accepting commissions from both buyer and seller. Although the inventories might show double the number of cattle on the range, the buyers were likely to add a few more. It broadened the base of their capitalization, and made their debentures seem more secure. Yet despite all this water in the cattle stocks, the investors expected quick dividends. Not any mere six or eight per cent, either. King's investors, some of the most articulate men in America, made no secret of their solid 20 per cent, and large capital gains besides. Shareholders in the new companies expected as much. Some of the corporations accomplished this simply by floating new issues and dividing up the proceeds. A greater number of them, however, honestly played the game of producing beef. The more conservative outfits stocked the range with cows, raised calves, and tried to improve the breed. The importation of shorthorn bulls became common. Cows half shorthorn gave a great deal more milk and immediately raised larger calves. The trouble was, they did not forage like the longhorns, nor was it feasible to drive them so far across country.

Increase through brood stock was much too slow for the sensationally promoted outfits. Their success depended on quick profits, and the only way of securing these was by buying lean Texas cattle—the leaner and cheaper the better —driving them north to spend a year or two, and harvesting the beef. This worked fine as long as every horizon was a

new sea of grass. That the grass was indeed a sea, and endless, became the geography of the cattle boom. There were
those who warned that the sea of grass was not endless, that
actually it washed up against the Indian treaty lands of
northern Montana, and even if those treaties were modified,
on the shores of the Saskatchewan River. A glance at the map
could prove that the greater part of the available range was
occupied.

Such talk, however, was considered defeatist and trea-
sonable, particularly in Wyoming. Beef ranching was a form
of agriculture, and agriculture, it was pointed out, never was
known to lower the productivity of the land. Cyrus Thomas,
a Lutheran minister turned agricultural expert, recently associated with the Hayden Geological Survey, had printed a
booklet entitled "Agriculture in Colorado" which seemed to
prove that as population increased the amount of precipita-
tion increased also. Old-timers of the Cherry Creek diggings,
he said, had seen this firsthand. When they arrived in the fif-
ties the area was known by its few Spanish residents to be
little better than a desert, but it was seasonally deluged after
the heavy settlement of the gold rush. In fact, the early
houses of Denver were washed away by floods, and the land
around Fort Collins became established as some of the most
productive in America. The Thomas principle became crystallized in the dictum that "rain follows the plow," an ace in
the hole of the land promoter for the next sixty years. They
said the new-turned earth attracted moisture like a blotter
attracts ink. In Wyoming nobody spoke highly of plows, but
many believed that grass stooled out better when mowed off,
as by the cropping of cattle. It was pointed out that the agricultural income, having increased an average 100 per cent
per year since the arrival of the first large ranchers, would, if
allowed to expand unimpeded make Wyoming the wealthi-
est agricultural state or territory in the mountain West by
the late 1890s.

By purchase of small ranches and preempting the range
all around, some of the spreads became small kingdoms, and

they were run as such. In Nebraska the most famous ranch was the Bay State. With a basic herd of 150,000, Bay State's holdings spread across today's Banner, Morrill, Kimball, Cheyenne, Duel, Keith, and Scotts Bluff counties, an area larger than some of the Eastern states. But this was only the home ranch; Bay State also held large areas in Wyoming, and intended eventually to establish a kingdom which would stretch from the forks of the Platte all the way to the Big Horn Basin, a distance of 350 miles. Its ranch house was an Eastern mansion dismantled and shipped west to be reconstructed on the flatlands of Lodgepole Creek. Trail herds were not welcome in the heartland of Bay State's domain, so it was generally avoided to the west, but Texas cowboys returning home often rode some distance out of their way to sample the Bay State's bunkhouse hospitality and view the mansion. To it came a succession of the fanciest dudes ever seen in Nebraska. The opulence of Bay State even awed old Print Olive, who settled on Plum Creek to the north. Olive carefully skirted the prized Bay State holdings while raiding lesser owners to the east and south.

In Wyoming the big ranch was the Swan, named for Alexander H. Swan, and was the culmination of a life of vision, enterprise, promotion, and skulduggery unique even in the West, the land where everything was bigger than anyplace else. Funded in Scotland, in its heyday the Swan claimed both banks of the Laramie River for 130 miles, and its herds ranged much farther, from Ogalalla, Nebraska, to Fort Steele, Wyoming, a distance of three hundred miles, although this latter could not be considered a solid range. It occupied the Chugwater, where the abandoned oxen of Russell, Majors & Waddell wintered and grew fat, and extended there for a hundred miles north and south, or from Colorado to the old Oregon Trail.

Swan was born in Pennsylvania in 1831, the great-great grandson of a plantation owner in Bowie, Maryland. His grandparents traveled over the mountains near Cumberland by packhorses before the American Revolution, settling on Indian treaty land. That soil, however, did not long hold Alex, a tall, powerful, irrepressible young fellow, who exercised on people of all stations a peculiar magnetism. Going to Iowa, he helped establish the Council Bluffs Stockyards, the Union Stockyards of South Omaha, and a number of ambitious land syndicates. From stockyards and packing interests he moved into cattle, and took the first Hereford beef stock to Wyoming. Associated with his brothers, who were of a similar temper, although lacking his physical size and grandiloquence, he founded a number of cattle companies including the Tomahawk, near the future mining town of Encampment, the Wyoming Hereford Ranch, the National Cattle Company, and the Ogalalla Land & Cattle Co. These were mostly based on former ranches which he purchased without haggling over the stock tally. By every action Swan let it be known that he was in on a good thing, so good in fact that the most optimistic estimate was always outstripped by future developments, the West being bigger than the poor mind of man could comprehend. In 1883 he brought off his greatest promotion, the Swan Land & Cattle Co. organized in Edinburgh, Scotland, at £600,000, or approximately $3 million. Directors, in addition to Swan, included a number of Scottish manufacturers and financiers, and Lord Douglas Gordon. Bankers for the corporation were the British Linen Co. Bank of Edinburgh and London, the Importers' & Traders Bank of New York, the First National Bank of Omaha, and the First National of Cheyenne. To the original ranches, most of them tossed into the corporation by himself and his brothers, Swan added more, purchasing the Muleshoe, the TY, the 40 Bar, and the M Bar. Needing money almost immediately, the capital stock was raised to a total value of $3,750,000, $1,870,000 of which was fully paid. On paper the holdings seemed gigantic, but it owned only 6037 deeded acres, and by its own count only 89,167 head of cattle. With the new money Swan moved to remedy this, purchasing more than half a million acres from the Union Pacific and bringing in one trail herd after another from Texas.

Although he was seldom seen at any except a couple of his favored ranches near Cheyenne, Swan was fond of touring his holdings by means of a private car on the railroad. It was his fancy to take favored guests, entertaining lavishly on fancy meats from his own feedlots, or shellfish rushed in ice from the Atlantic Coast. To all appearance his fortune was secure, "as firmly based as the Rockies." The idea that Swan might run into financial difficulties was too far-fetched for anyone even to consider. He turned his hand to politics, was elected to the territorial legislature, and ran for Representative to the national Congress, to be defeated by twenty-five votes. He was one of the founders of the American Hereford Cattle Breeders' Association, and pleased his investors by bringing in herd bulls of that English breed, his enthusiasm being dominant in making them the almost universal cattle of the West. Plagued by paper inventories and expanding obligations, he was forced into ever larger corporate manipulations. The shareholders were not collecting dividends, but the future, with the U.P. lands in its control, seemed full of hope. Basing computation on an imaginary inventory, he printed figures to show that the expense of running a cow was only 56¢ per year.

Other concerns used the same arithmetic and tried also to expand. Since there was little new range short of the Indian lands beyond the Missouri, the only way to do it was by putting more lean trail stock on the range. For a time even the Rio Grande supply was insufficient. In Oregon a cattle business had been flourishing for forty years. By 1883 the main movement along the old Oregon Trail was from west to east as herds came 100,000 strong across the treacherous Snake River and the desert rocks of the Idaho Plateau.

Rain did not follow the plow in Wyoming Territory, where the plow was the hoofs of cattle. No longer did grass blow in the winds, yellow-green in June and brown in July, much of it to shrivel so the cattle could paw to it through the snow, a concentrated food which brought them out heavier in April than they had been in November. Much of the range was seriously overgrazed. Grass clumps were cropped short and left as little eroded islands by the runoff of rain, and by the melting snow which took place much quicker than it used to. Hungry cattle had taken to eating clumps so short that the crowns and roots were destroyed.

There was drought over much of the country in 1885, but the winter was a mild one. This was considered fortunate, because the price of cattle was down, and many of the ranches had decided to hold more than the usual number for an expected rise the following spring. The mild winter was nevertheless not in all ways a blessing. It helped many thin cattle get through the year in tolerably good shape, but the snows melted early and passed off into the atmosphere. As a result, the range was dry in the spring, and the prairies were cured brown before June was half over. Low beef prices were having an adverse effect on company dividends, hence the next harvest, despite poor range, had to be greater. Cheap cattle were becoming increasingly hard to find. One of the largest absentee landlords had taken over in Texas, the hated XIT, which even published a little book of rules and regulations for its cowboys. The XIT decreed that hereafter its men would no longer carry pistols, drink whisky, fight, or use profanity. No longer were its bunkhouses to be opened to the use of visiting cowboys, nor were women to be permitted anywhere. There were no cheap cattle at the XIT. Northern buyers took to going beyond Texas into Mexico. There they turned up some of the scabbiest stock ever put on the trail. Poorer to start with, the Mexicans had to be driven farther, and over worse country. Mexican cattle bound, as some herds were, for the Milk River country of Montana, high against the Canadian border, had to travel about 1500 miles. Starting as early as March those poor, footsore dogies had a hard time making it by fall.

The drought held. Dust blew from the ranges where it

had been unknown. The sunsets were the most brilliant anyone could remember. The Indians, whose last treaty lands
were being overrun, viewed the sunsets and said that the
Great Spirit was in a vengeful mood. They predicted that
with fire and thirst he would purge the white men for destroying the buffalo. Some of the northern ranches tried to
drive cattle north into Alberta but they were stopped by
mounted policemen with the demand that they pay a 20 per
cent import duty. Con Kohrs leased land on the Canadian
side, but still he could not drive his stock across without
forking over $72,000 in charges. Twelve hundred of his cat-
tle "strayed" across and were impounded, and the Canadians, to teach him a lesson, forced him to travel all the way to
Ottawa to pay up. Montana ranchers started registering
their brands in Canada. With stock branded the same on
both sides of the border, the harassed Mounties had the
problem of proving that a steer wandering across the line
was not Canadian in the first place. The authorities then
ruled that the Canadian brand had to be different and distinctive. But all regulations notwithstanding, in the summer of 1886 a quarter of a million Montana cattle were herded
across the border.

No rain fell, and fires burned in the mountains, but most
cattle growers were optimistic. There had been a fine, open
winter the year before. Statistics showed that mild winters
generally came in cycles of three. But November opened
with bitter north winds from Canada to Kansas. A blizzard
struck, carrying heavy snow. At first it was not cold, and
native cattle easily dug to feed. However, the Mexican stock
was already in trouble. Sorefooted from the trail, they huddled in the coulees, slobbering over one another's backs, and
looking wall-eyed at the terrible land they had been driven
into. Cowboys tried to chase them up the coulees and back
again, and in that way uncover the feed. It was futile. Even
before the first real cold there were reports of fallen Mexicans. Native cattle, on the other hand, were still doing satisfactorily. The heavy snow in some places brought life to the

grass. People talked of an early chinook. The chinook wind, characteristic of the country, would blow gale-strength from the southwest. Chinooks came without warning except for leaden colors in the sky, and often blew for days at a time, shaking the line shacks and singing through the wire-hard twigs of the box elder trees, stripping the snow everywhere except in the coulees, which then lay like ribs of white in the brown and mud-gray country.

The chinook came in December. Snow sank ahead of it, and for a time, it looked as if all would be well. Then suddenly the southwesterly wind turned about upon itself, becoming a northern blast which dropped temperatures forty degrees in the space of two hours. The water-saturated snow froze. The land was glazed with ice. It was a crust that cut the legs of cattle when they tried to walk. Digging for feed was impossible. Their noses bled when they tried to root for grass. January came with the country locked in a terrible cold. Ranchers in log houses, cowboys in line shacks, and residents of the towns all had trouble procuring fuel to keep their stoves going. In the mining camps wood went up to eight dollars a cord, about double the previous year, because of the deep snows which made hauling impossible. After the near slopes were denuded, woodcutters supplied the mining camps by means of muletrains. But, in the midst of the timber, they were lucky. There was a lot of heat in pitch pine, and the chief problem was keeping supplied with post and cap timbers for the mines, or going without work if some of the stamp mills had to suspend. Out on the prairie it was tougher. There was little heat in cottonwood even where enough of it could be found. Cottonwood is a tough, stringy wood, favored for boat ribs and hard to chop. Filled with sap and frozen hard, it broke more easily, but in the stove it melted out with a steam that carried away almost as much heat as the wood eventually produced. Miles City had just installed a steam-operated electric plant, and ran into fuel trouble despite the nearness of coal, but it was kept going most nights, the town's lights shining bright through thickening window frost, giving the cow capital a deceptively festive appearance. Miles City was fortunately on the railroad. Towns on wagon-freight and coach lines found themselves isolated, without news for weeks. Often in the very midst of disaster they did not know as much about general conditions as did the shareholders in England.

Winds, sweeping across the prairie, carried snow for miles without an obstruction, and dropped it ten feet deep in the little wind-riffles of coulees. Line shacks became buried, and cowboys had to dig their way out. When the snow crusted they could walk across the roofs, as could wolves and coyotes. Cowboys in line shacks and at the lonely ranches, ready to lose their minds from cabin fever, sometimes started out and rode forty or fifty miles to town, arriving wrapped to the tops of their heads in dogskin overcoats, icicles hanging from the ends of their mustaches, faces circled by hoarfrost, feet and legs kept from freezing by gunny sacks full of hay which were hung like tapaderos. These men brought the only real word from the ranges. But even their information was scanty. Pilgrim cattle, particularly the late-arriving Mexicans, were reported to be a total loss. The consensus, however, indicated that the native cattle were wintering without more than the usual bad-season losses.

Many local editors ignored the range situation or professed optimism. Loss of the Mexicans, some said, might well be a blessing in disguise, and they quoted their own warnings against the importation of inferior cattle. Ranch, village, and Army-post thermometers kept turning up with early-morning readings of sixty below zero. Most of the editors were reluctant to print such news for fear it would be picked up by the out-of-state press, placing the country in an unfavorable light, inimical to growth and progress. Occasionally the temperature readings were printed, but with comments of a jovial nature, implying that cold snaps were merely among the trifling inconveniences one must be willing to accept in order to live in that abundant country. The Army, however, regularly reported such information, and it made the Eastern papers, particularly those in New York and Boston, where so many influential people were involved in the cattle business. The Army also reported herds of roving cattle invading the land of the various posts, attempting to get at the hay which had been put up for the mules and horses. The Army news had a sound of disaster, and many of the Eastern shareholders wrote to the ranch managers, but these men for the most part were wintering in town and knew little of real conditions either.

In January it was generally agreed, on the basis of all information, that a good early-February chinook still would keep the losses well below the disaster level. February dawned blue from cold. The sun shone with no life, and the smoke rose white from chimneys to hang congealed in the air. When the wind blew it became impossible to heat all of a house, so the occupants remained mostly on the windward sides of their stoves, or they moved from the more exposed rooms and blocked off the entrances with buffalo robes and blankets. Some stockmen on the smaller streams tried to cut holes in the ice and found them frozen to the bottom. Cap Nelse on the Marias took some of the poor beasts, including a pet ox, into his house and lived with them. He reported that the presence of animals cut down one's fuel problem. Starving and freezing cattle gathered in ranch yards. Seeking warmth, they pressed against the houses, chewed the tarpaper covering off shacks near the Great Falls, and had to be driven away with pitchforks. Drifting with the wind, many cattle wandered far off their home ranges. Cattle wearing unknown brands turned up in Kansas and furnished tough stew meat on the reserves of Indian Territory. But chiefly they stacked up along the drift fences which everywhere cut the old migration route. Baffled by the strands of steel, they staggered on until they dropped of starvation. Sometimes they froze standing, their legs braced and turned hard as stone, and so remained until spring. Cattle by the thousand piled up in coulees, at first for shelter, but later, when the coulees drifted full, they tried to cross and found them deadfalls. In the spring, some of the smaller streams were dammed by the carcasses of cattle, and they rotted with a stench unknown since the days of the buffalo.

At last the chinook came, but it was March and too late. Cattlemen went out to appraise their losses and were sickened by the sight and smell. Turkey buzzards gorged themselves in the southern regions until they had trouble lifting themselves off the ground. Many of the cattle on Montana ranges proved to have Canadian brands. Near the Great Falls cattle driven southward late in the season had gathered on the Missouri River ice until it collapsed, and their hairy, beaten carcasses accumulated as islands below the rapids. There was a spring roundup, and following it the beef skinners. Hides were the chief harvest of 1887. Many of the northern ranges reported losses of 90 per cent. Some outfits were so completely wiped out that their managers sold the residue, whatever it was, for a lump sum, and got out of the country.

The disaster struck the old-time outfits as well as the get-rich-quick corporations. Granville Stuart, whose experience dated back to the early 1850s, was surprised by the terrible winter, and estimated his losses at two thirds. Con Kohrs counted only 3,000 of an estimated herd of 35,000. In Wyoming it spelled the end for Swan. Already forced to juggle his assets, putting here and taking there, his corporate structure was unable to stand the cataclysm of the hard winter. He failed in May. He was the leading livestock figure in the West, and his failure undoubtedly caused many others to toss in their cards. He resigned, and the Company managed to continue. He went to Ogden, tried to recoup at new promotions, but he had lost his touch, and died there in an asylum in 1905.

The hard winter, disaster falling heaviest on the pilgrim cattle, spelled the end of the trail herds. The trail was about finished anyway. It might pay, here and there, to fatten Southern cattle up north, but it was becoming increasingly difficult to drive them through the barbed wire. Railroads, looking for north-south tonnages, believed for a while it might be feasible to load cattle in the region of Cheyenne for transport to the Yellowstone, but nothing came of it. The hard winter marked the end of the open range, although there was a struggle to perpetuate it in Wyoming. It led to the Johnson County Cattle War.

In 1866 Captain H. E. Palmer, late of the Kansas Cavalry, got together four wagons with teams and harness, most of it purchased cheap from one of the Western Army depots, laid in a stock of trade goods, and headed up the Bozeman Road to start a store. He found a place which suited him on Clear Creek, only five or six miles from the steep rise of the Big Horns, and built a hut, chiefly of sod, in size 12 by 12 feet. His first visitors were 25 Cheyenne warriors who took his store down and replaced the sod where he had dug it up, whereupon Palmer left the country. Later the Army established tragic Fort Kearny eighteen miles up the road.

Although the country, after Kearny's abandonment, was returned to the Indians, outlaw freighters and immigrants continued to use the Bozeman Road, and gold-seekers, uniformly unsuccessful, kept probing the Big Horns, the wealth of those mountains being one of the most persistent myths of the frontier. After Sitting Bull's retreat to Canada and the collapse of Sioux and Cheyenne power, trade along the Bozeman Road increased to the point where a freight station appeared profitable, and one was built, of logs rather than sod, near the site of Palmer's old store, and the town growing up around it was called Buffalo.

Buffalo prospered. All along the Big Horns the mountain valleys opened out rich in grass, and were blessed with permanent streams. While the rest of Wyoming was being chopped up into ducal domains and exploited by corporations, the valleys of the Big Horns were attracting settlers from the wagon outfits who built rail fences, practiced small-scale irrigation, and raised crops. The longhorns of Texas came bawling up the trail, dust-coated and tick-infested, and found the red and brindle Eastern stock of the wagon outfits already established around the Big Horns. The bosses were obliged to take to the alkali plains east and ford Powder River, "a mile wide and an inch deep," near its fork with Crazy Woman Creek.

In territorial days Buffalo was part of Carbon County with administration in Fort Casper 120 miles to the south. It was closer to Montana. When the Northern Pacific was built, it was half again closer to that line along the Yellowstone than to the Union Pacific in far-southern Wyoming. The Northern Pacific, before its arrival, mapped a branch down from Big Horn station through Fort Custer to Buffalo to encourage that source of cattle revenue, but nothing came of it.

In 1887, preparatory to Wyoming's admission as a state, Johnson County was formed, with Buffalo its seat. Cut away from Casper, it started administering its own affairs in its own independent way. It became one of the few counties not run by the Stockgrowers Association. But independence didn't come easy. Johnson County had to fight for it.

Many small ranches went into business after the disaster of 1886–1887. Cowboys without jobs got herds together one way or another, filed on homesteads, and had brands registered. When the big outfits tried a comeback most of these men preferred staying on their land rather than go back to their old jobs at $40 a month. This annoyed the big outfits, as did their occupancy of the range, and the way some of their herds seemed to be increasing. The powerful Stockgrowers Association took to calling them rustlers and Buffalo the rustlers' capital. There was some legal substance to the accusation.

According to Wyoming law all mavericks, or unbranded strays, were property of the state. Whenever a man put his iron on an unbranded calf he was a rustler. The big outfits all did it; few indeed were the mavericks surrendered to the state anywhere, but when no maverick herd came from Johnson County there was outrage. Roundups were set for certain dates in certain areas so the state could have brand inspectors on hand. This sounded fine, but the state was controlled by the Association, hence they were the inspectors, and none of the recent brands were honored. Johnson County did not take to this. It staged its own roundups, and the brand inspectors attended at their risk if at all.

To show how ridiculous the state maverick law was, here is a quotation from the second annual report of the Swan Land & Cattle Co. in 1885: "The severe spring storms, as for example that in April, 1883, killed not only young calves, but sometimes newly calved cows, and . . . ranchmen have come to be aware that outside branding does not, as they have hitherto imagined, compensate for these losses. During the years 1881 and 1882, when herds on the Chug and the Sybille were in the hands of the native Corporations, from whom they were purchased by this company, no allowances other than outside branding was made for losses . . . ." By 1889, however, the big outfits were acting as if the sideburned maverick was the invention of Johnson County. Ignoring the fenced trail and the raped public domain, they pointed to the "rustlers" as the one thing preventing a rebirth of the industry. Their estimate of stolen cattle grew until it was claimed that whole herds were being lost. Such losses, however, were never substantiated. Rustled cattle might be hidden for a while, but eventually they had to be sold. They could not be sold at the shipping points to the south because of Wyoming inspection, and their numbers never showed up on the records of the Northern Pacific.

What really troubled the large cattlemen was not loss of stock to rustlers but loss of water and grass to claimants under the homestead law. Concerns such as the Swan had purchased many miles of land from the Union Pacific which had been granted it by the government checkerboard fashion, in alternate sections. This alternation was at first regarded as a good thing, allowing purchasers to fence the entire area, but homesteaders began taking up the government sections, demanding access under the law, and letting their stock trespass where they would. Some of the big ranches tried to purchase choice pieces of the public domain at bargain prices, but a cry went up which was heard in Washington, and most of the really favorable deals died like bacilli brought out into the air and sunshine. In retrospect it is easy to see that the cattlemen were caught up in the inexorable process of Western settlement, their position somewhat reminiscent of the Indians' a couple of decades earlier. But it was not obvious at the club down in Cheyenne in the late eighties and early nineties. There it seemed that if the landgrabbers of Johnson County could be rooted out, those of the lesser centers would take the hint and move on, and the good old days might come back again.

As it happened, the big cattlemen were goaded into striking closer home, and it proved to be a bad thing. Down on the Sweetwater River a homesteader named James Averill, later turned storekeeper, postmaster, whisky dealer, and justice of the peace, committed the shocking heresy of sending a letter to the editor of the Casper Weekly Mail, condemning one of the large cattle concerns for what was obviously an attempt to swipe some public land legally. Averill had no cattle, but he had staked a girl friend, Ella Watson, into the bagnio business, and in the conduct of this, by taking pay in kind as well as in money, she had accumulated a small herd. Some of the animals may have been rustled from the big spreads; it was never proved. However, the situation sufficed as an excuse. Ella (nicknamed Cattle Kate) and her backer, who had the temerity to attack the big interests in the press, were captured by ten of the ranching crowd and hanged. The lynching of a woman was something new for the Eastern fans of Western doings, and it received wide coverage in newspapers and magazines. A coroner's jury turned up with two witnesses who were willing to name the participants in this sorry business, but neither was on hand when time came for the trial. One was dead and the other had deemed it advisable to leave the country.

The hanging of Averill and Cattle Kate was the most sensational, but there were other hangings and bushwhackings, and the exact number who were simply drygulched and buried under the caved sides of cutbanks will never be known. Wyoming, particularly that part east of the Big Horns, was in a state of guerrilla warfare for a couple of years.

In 1891 the State Livestock Commissioners, armed with a list of what were said to be outlaw brands, moved to confiscate the cattle wearing them, all bills of sale and other proofs of ownership to be disregarded. The Commissioners were unable to do this on the range because of the physical difficulties, but there was nothing to stop them from seizing the cattle at the scheduled roundups, or when they were driven to the railroad shipping pens. As almost all the small ranchers, or at least those without influence, were put on the list, what it did in effect was allow the Association to take over the property of any outfit it didn't approve of. A great many people, formerly sympathetic to the Association and its problems, were repelled by this brand of arrogance, and some of them said so. However, the Association went ahead with its plan.

In many sections, small owners were immediately faced with a hopeless situation. Their stock was on the range, mixed with that of Association ownership. They were unable to round it up, not having the riders, and even if they had it could not have been done legally. Most of them were members of roundup associations and had agreed that any prior, independent roundup was an act of rustling. All they could do was wait for the regular roundup and have their herds confiscated.

Johnson County, however, was in a better position. Its owners had never boggled at early roundups; on this occasion they called one unusually early, and the Association's inspectors were informally advised not to attend. Afterward, they could drive straight up the trail into Montana and the N.P. where they could ship without trouble.

Faced with this the Association decided to raise an

army and invade. It was to be a quick thrust, without warning. To keep all preparations secret, no local gunmen were hired. Smooth, dandified, ruthless Frank Wolcott, a cattleman and former Army officer, was put in charge of the operation. He sent a representative to Texas to recruit the body of the force. They were brought north on a special train after being assembled in Denver. Even the supplies were purchased in Denver to prevent some clerk or freight handler from getting suspicious and talking too much. The acting governor of Wyoming, Dr. Amos Barber, gave the expedition his blessing, and provided it extra guns.

On April 4, 1892, the train pulled into Cheyenne on the Denver Pacific. Unfortunately for Wolcott, Cheyenne was small enough that the arrival of trains were big events in its day, and unscheduled ones were particularly noticed. Texans alighted and showed their backs to local people who tried to be friendly while having a few quick ones at a nearby bar. Cheyenne recognized them for what they were and an attempt was made to send a warning telegram to Buffalo, but the lines had been cut.

Fortunately for the invasion, Casper had been linked by rail with Cheyenne a little more than two years before, so the train rolled on ahead of the telegraph repair, and the Texas gunmen luxuriated on the plush and played cards while their horses rode up front in a baggage car.

About twenty cattlemen were along. Here and there the train stopped for an added recruit. In Casper some of the cattlemen retired from active participation and left for Goose Egg Ranch, a temple of pleasure maintained for the kings of the land fourteen miles to the southwest, but enough of them, and their representatives, went along to bring the invaders' number to fifty. It was hoped that the force would be doubled through enlistments on the way. The cattle barons' army called themselves the Regulators.

In two days, without increase in strength, the Regulators arrived at the southern border of Johnson County. They were at the edge of enemy territory, but not *all* enemy.

Johnson County had several large Association ranches. At the first of these, the Tisdale, they camped for the night, and a number were waiting with rifles and ammunition to join. There they heard the first reports from the north. One was that two of the "rustlers," Nate Champion and Nick Ray, were holed up at the K.C. Ranch, a small holding just east of some timbered hills on the Middle Fork of Powder River. Champion had exchanged gunfire with a group of cattlemen vigilantes a few months before, and since had been let alone until the odds could be brought more overwhelmingly against him. Johnson County considered him and Ray honest homesteader-cowboys, but the Association had placed them high on its list of rustlers. The Regulators decided to hang them before moving on north for the capture of Buffalo.

An April storm came up, but they set out with hats bent against the driven snow and arrived on the morning of the ninth of April at the K.C. Ranch. Its headquarters consisted of a three-room log cabin, a barn, and the usual corrals. They surrounded it, crawling up through a brushy draw and over a low hill.

There were more men at the ranch than they expected. Two strangers, who turned out to be wolfers spending the night, came down to the barn while breakfast smoke rose from the cabin chimney. The wolfers were captured without trouble or alarm, and managed to talk the Regulators out of hanging them. After a long wait a tall man, recognized by the Northern recruits as Nick Ray, came a few steps from the door, apparently wondering what had happened to their guests. The Regulators opened fire. He fell but was able to crawl. They kept shooting until he was apparently lifeless, face-down in the snow. Champion then suddenly appeared, grabbed him, and amid a tattoo of bullets managed to drag him inside. He closed the door and returned the gunfire.

None of the Wolcott forces wanted to get killed, so they stayed under cover and proceeded to cut the cabin to splinters with their ample supply of ammunition. Champion remained inside and passed the time by jotting an account in his notebook:

> Me and Nick was getting breakfast when the attack took place. Two men here with us. Jones and another man. The old man went for water and didn't come back. His friend went out to see what was the matter, and he didn't come back. Nick started out, and I told him to look out. I thought there was someone at the stable and would not let them come back. Nick is shot but not dead yet. He is awful sick. I must go and wait on him. It is about two hours since the first shot.
>
> Nick is still alive. They are still shooting and are all around the house. Boys, there is bullets coming in like hail. Them fellows is in such shape I can't get at them. They are shooting from the stable and river and back of the house.
>
> Nick is dead. He died about nine o'clock. I see smoke down at the stable. I think they have fired it. I don't think they intend to let me get away this time
>
> It is about noon now. There is someone at the stable yet. They are throwing a rope at the door and dragging it back. I guess it is to draw me out. I wish that duck would get out farther so I could get a shot at him. Boys, I don't know what they have done with them two fellows that stayed here last night.
>
> Boys, I feel pretty lonesome just now. I wish there was someone here with me so

we could watch all sides at once. They may fool around until I get a good shot before they leave. It is about three o'clock now. There was a man in a buckboard and one on horseback just passed. They fired at them as they went by. I don't know if they killed them or not. I seen lots of men come out on horses on the other side of the river and take after them.

I shot at the men in the stable just now—don't know if I got any or not. I must go and look out again. It don't look as if there is much show of getting away. I see 12 or 15 men. One looks like Frank Canton. I don't know whether it is or not. I hope they did not catch them fellows that run over the bridge toward Smith's. They are shooting at the house now. If I had a pair of glasses, I believe I would know some of those men. They are coming back. I've got to look now.

Well they have just got through shelling like hell. I heard them splitting wood. I guess they are going to fire the house tonight. I think I will make a break when night comes, if alive. It's not night yet.

The house is fired. Good-by boys if I never see you again.

The Regulators took a wagon abandoned by a rancher who had happened along the road and fled the shooting, loaded it with hay and wood, set it afire, and rolled it into the cabin. The cabin took fire all along one side and at last Champion came out running, trying to make it to the coulee. He was carrying a rifle. He turned to fire but a bullet knocked him off his feet. He fell and the Regulators, from their places of cover, riddled him until a later check of his body left the number of wounds in controversy. They searched him and found the notebook. They talked of destroying it. Instead, Canton's name was cut out, but witnesses supplied it later.

Champion was dead, and Ray was dead, but the alarm had been carried to Buffalo. Red Angus, the sheriff, swore in 100 deputies and rode out to meet the Regulators. An Association spy hurried from town with this news, and Wolcott, believing that "he who hits and crouches low will live to strike another blow," decided on a retreat to the friendly T.A. Ranch 14 miles south of Buffalo. The alarm had now spread, and armed men joined Angus from all along the Big Horns. No longer was it fifty to two, the sort of odds favored by Wolcott, but fifty to perhaps two hundred. He was entrenched at the T.A. when the Army from Fort McKinney came to his rescue. The commanding officer had refused to move when Angus asked for help against the invasion. In this he acted in the opposite manner to the commander at Fort Stanton in New Mexico. One officer abetted the civil authorities, the other what, technically, were the insurgents. However, they were alike in their backing of those with the most influence. Johnson County was one of the final, sad chapters of the record of the Army in the West.

The Regulators were herded down to Cheyenne and held under technical arrest, free to come and go on their own recognizance. Johnson County was assessed $100 per day for their expenses. Gladly would Johnson County have taken them in charge and tried them, at least their leaders, for the murder of Champion and Ray, but the state authorities would not surrender them, holding it would be impossible to obtain a fair trial. No serious attempts were made to try them elsewhere, and finally, when the per diem was no longer forthcoming, they were all turned free. Most of them left Wyoming. The scars of Johnson County remained, however. Years later men were being killed in the feuds which lingered after that last of the cattle wars.

With the coming of the Northern Pacific Miles City for a time became the cow capital of the West, but the center again moved northward. When the Montana Central Railroad was built to connect Butte and the mines around Helena with Jim Hill's westward-coming Great Northern, the large domains of the Blackfeet and Gros Ventre shrank and cattle covered the last free grass in Montana. This could best be called the Milk River country. Fort Assiniboine had been built in 1879 on the bottoms of Beaver Creek, a few miles south of the river, and a freight road came into being for its supply. The road as generally followed ran north from Fort Benton to the mouth of the Marias, not far from old Fort McKenzie and up the Loma Hill, crossing a windy high prairie with one of the widest views in the West to drop down on the pre-ice-age Missouri River, dry except for tiny Big Sandy Creek which meandered with what seemed endless futility across the great bottoms.

Despite its insignificance when measured against its Arctic-bound predecessor, Big Sandy Creek, trickling from boghole to boghole, presented freighters their major obstruction of the journey. Quite a number of roads and crossings were tried, but most favored was the one discovered by "Big Sandy" Lane. Whether the creek was named for Big Sandy or he for the creek is not certain. At any rate the crossing, and the town which followed, bore his name. The first establishment at Big Sandy's Crossing was a saloon, started when some wagoner with a cargo of liquor unloaded with the intention of pulling the deep mire by stages with light cargoes and found business so good that he never had to load up again.

Business was indeed brisk, and soon he had competition. At certain times of the year, when the crossing was a quagmire fifty yards across, freight outfits would be forced to spend entire days at Big Sandy, with business improving as a consequence. Tons of rock and logs were carried to the crossing, but they failed to improve it, and the saloon owners came in for some hard words, it being generally suspected that they dug out the ballast as soon as it was put in, and even went upstream and blasted out beaver dams to provide little flood surges in times when drought threatened to discourage trade.

The present town of Big Sandy stands not athwart the crossing but high and dry on the plain. This came about through saloon competition when one owner, claiming trespass on his lot by the building of another, hired a teamster late one night to skid the offending establishment to its proper distance. For a joke the teamster did not stop until he had skidded it a mile and a half to the south, dropping it on a knoll with its back to the road. Undaunted, the displaced entrepreneur erected a sign reading THE FIRST CHANCE and was rewarded next day when the northbound teamsters caught sight of it and started a new road to his door. One after another the competing establishments were skidded to the new site, and when the firm of Broadwater, McNamara & Co., later McNamara & Marlow, moved to Big Sandy from Fort Maginnis, the swerve of the road was acknowledged in the placement of its pioneer general store. By that time C. A. Broadwater, one of the state's freight tycoons, had moved into the bigger field of railroad promotion, and when his (and Jim Hill's) Montana Central came through, it recognized the swerve also, as does the highway of today.

When the main line of the Great Northern arrived, joining the Central at Pacific Junction near Assiniboine, Big Sandy found itself in the big cattle business. It quickly counted a depot, the McNamara & Marlow store, a railroad section foreman's house, nine saloons, and the biggest stockloading yards north of the Missouri. In the nineties, pioneer conductors on the Great Northern main line, noticing that fully half of their stockman passengers owned Palace car tickets to Big Sandy, concluded that it was a city roughly the size of Duluth, Minnesota. Its permanent residents numbered three hundred. It was the last of the cattle towns to appear on the Great North Trail. Situated on land newly won from the Indians, it marked the last stand of the open range.

Chapter 11

To an Indian, medicine was a spiritual commodity. It was a power given by the supernatural, often revealed in a dream. What was called an Indian's medicine was often only its symbol—a bundle of feathers, perhaps, to impart the speed and eyesight of the eagle, or a tuft of hair to invoke the power and bravery of the silvertip bear. The Catholic missionaries, or Blackrobes, were accepted by the Blackfeet because their ceremonies and trappings promised a powerful new medicine. This was substantiated by Indians who accompanied them from far to the rising sun, attributing fearful potency to the Blackrobe incantations, or "big prayer." The big prayer made priests an initial success. Later the Blackfeet were disillusioned when their priests refused to use it to promote anything important, such as warfare and horse-stealing. The priests in fact might have been driven away or executed but for fear they would retaliate by conjuring up smallpox. One priest said that the Blackfeet attributed the great bravery of the Flatheads to their baptism and wanted some of the same medicine. The Blackfeet, armed and prosperous, had already driven the Flatheads beyond the mountains. When it got to the point where the Flatheads did not dare emerge through the passes to hunt buffalo, their medicine was lightly regarded. Finally the priests gave it up as a hopeless job and abandoned the Blackfeet mission. Even the Flatheads returned to their pagan ways, and their priest in discouragement retired for five years to California. The Protestant missionaries did not have even the outward success enjoyed by the Catholics. The Blackfeet called them Shortrobes, considering them a sort of shavetail variety of Catholic, a second team, denied the possession of incense, holy water, candles, beads, medals—in fact, any medicine whatsoever.

One of the most powerful white-man medicines was a line nobody could see that ran along the ground. Starting at the northern toe of Bear Mountain in present-day Glacier Park, it continued into the rising sun for many sleeps, some saying it terminated only in the country of many waters, northern Minnesota. Indians had been riding back and forth across the line since the oldest man without knowing it was there. The white men, however, had recognized its existence almost from the start. The Hudson's Bay traders and the Longknives from the Missouri both were careful about going over the invisible medicine line. Later, white men with whisky for the Indians sometimes were chased by other white men, but in such instances the medicine line was a mighty, invisible barrier, and on crossing it the whisky traders were able to stop and thumb noses at their pursuers. Some Blackfeet argued that only certain chosen white men could make the medicine line work for them. Others said this was not so, that the medicine line worked for that white man who crossed it first. Whatever the secret, there was not the slightest doubt that its power became particularly pronounced after the arrival in Canada of the Redcoat police. These new white men would sometimes chase other white men all the way from Belly River southward, but the medicine line stopped pursuit as abruptly as a glass wall. Soon the Blackfeet got to experimenting with the line to see whether its medicine would work for them, and they found that it did. For example, they could engage in daring horse raids on the south side of the line but once to the north of it, its powerful influence was a bar to pursuit.

There was the time when two Bloods were killed in Fort Benton, and a party under Calf Shirt started out to ascertain the reason and to collect a generous peace payment in the form of whisky. On their way southward, following the Marias River to a point near the present village of Loma, they encountered a party of white woodcutters getting out timber to build a town. This town was to have been Ophir, or North Ophir, located on the north side of the Marias River, at its juncture with the Missouri, downriver from Benton, and in a position to get first shot at the booming gold-rush traffic. Next year the Fisk Wagon Road from Minnesota dropped down from the bare dirt hills almost on top of the site, and its backers might have made a fortune if that day their woodchoppers had not opened fire on Calf Shirt and his Bloods.

Calf Shirt was not looking for trouble. But he was not turning back from it, either. He was a tall, powerful, roistering and violent man, the terror of his own tribe. He was, in fact, considered by many the toughest man, Indian or white, on the Northern frontier. His band had the white men at Ophir outnumbered. Once in action the Bloods made a clean sweep of it, killing all twelve of the woodchoppers delivering to the budding city a blow from which it never recovered.

After scalping the victims, Calf Shirt and his Bloods headed home. Had that home been on the south side of the medicine line, the Bluecoat soldiers would have taken a substantial revenge. As it was, the Indians did not even have to go into hiding. All Calf Shirt had to do was wait in safety on his own grounds until things cooled down.

Historically, the whites who made best use of the medicine line were the whisky traders from Fort Benton . . . .

In 1866, the Hudson's Bay Company was prevailed upon by the Canadian government to release its sovereignty over southern Alberta. For whisky traders on the U.S. side, this was particularly opportune. U.S. laws prohibiting the sale of whisky to the Indians had been on the books for thirty-five years; as a practical matter, they could be enforced only through the inspection of upriver boats. As the country was settled and traffic by both boat and road became heavy and the whites demanded substantial alcoholic supplies, such inspection became impossible and the whisky trade flourished. For years the Indians had been hunting buffalo and trading hides for whisky. When settlers drove the herds away from many of their native haunts, Indians, to keep themselves in whisky and all the other trade items on which they had learned to depend, stole horses and traded them, or they took a leaf from the road agents' book and waylaid travelers for their goods. Some Indians even tried their hand at washing for metal, but bending the back did not suit their rapacious, equestrian culture. They preferred to locate some remote gulch or hillside where miners were busy and fall on them when the season was over and the harvest in. Even ordinarily peaceful tribes, such as the Crows and Nez Percé, were not to be trusted when they got to feeding a whisky habit.

One fine example of Indians mining the miners took place in Montana near the northeast corner of Yellowstone Park. In 1869 four trappers—Adam Miller, J. H. Moore, Bert Henderson, and Jim Gurley—were robbed of their horses by the Crows near Cache Creek, but managed to escape with their lives by hiding in the brush and working their way northward on foot across the divide into Montana. Dropping down on Republic Creek and finding they had given their pursuers the slip, they rested, provided themselves with game, and did some prospecting. Rewarded with good showings, they went outside for grubstakes and led a small rush back to those remote parts. Later, when the gold in the creek thinned out someone started tunneling in an outcrop heavily shot through with black oxide of manganese. At twenty feet or so the stuff became weighted with lead and silver. It was staked as the Republic Mine. Another rich find was the Black Warrior on a saddle between Miller Mountain and Crown Butte, about three miles to the north.

The miners at the Black Warrior ingeniously constructed a furnace, fired it with their own charcoal, even improvised their own fluxes, and labored throughout the summer extracting metal. Unknown to them their activity was noted daily by a war party of Nez Percé Indians who took their ease, feasting on fat deer and trout from the Goose Lake country nearby, until the autumn cleanup. Then, when the white miners were finished for the summer and had their silver-lead ingots loaded for a pack trip out to the old Bridger Road, the Indians attacked, put the miners to flight, and carried off all the bullion, ultimate destination unknown.

Rightly or not, the whisky dealers were blamed for most of the Indian trouble, and when the cry against them became loud enough their posts were put out of business. But the Hudson's Bay Company had relinquished control north of the boundary. As yet the Canadian government had sent no agency to take its place. The medicine line was protection against the U.S. Army. So in 1869, a prospector and town promoter, John J. Healy, left Fort Benton with a wagon train headed north "to prospect the government lands, and launch a scientific and economic exploration into the adjacent land of Canada."

The expedition was equipped by I. G. Baker, one of the leading merchants of the Missouri River country. Alfred B. Hamilton, a nephew of the boss, went along. Its value was on the books of the company at $25,000 wholesale, and included some cases of Henry lever-action rifles and a substantial gallonage of 180-proof grain alcohol. "Don't let 'em whoop you up" was the admonition shouted after the departing caravan by its backer, I. G. Baker, who understandably enough did not want his representatives wiped out by drunken Indians. The road therafter was called the Whoop-Up Trail.

Traveling westward and then almost straight north, their course paralleled the Old North Trail but did not touch it until reaching the Oldman River, near its confluence with the St. Marys. There they unloaded, put together some rude shanties, mixed a supply of whisky, and were in business.

The Hudson's Bay Company had always given out a little high wine (watered alcohol) to stimulate the trade, but never as much as an Indian wanted. As for guns, H.B.C. made it a practice to trade the cheapest, most old-fashioned pieces available. It was with reluctance that they traded modern percussion caps, feeling it safer to keep the Blackfeet armed with the then-obsolescent flintlocks. If there was anything for which a Blackfoot would trade more head-and-tail buffalo robes, beaver pelts, and saddle horses than whisky, it was a repeating rifle. Healy and Hamilton had arrived with plenty of both, and the old Company, at its posts in the North, found itself without customers.

It was the start of a new era for Fort Benton. Cope had heard that the town was depressed because of slumping gold-camp business. He arrived to find it busy, and the reason lay in the trade initiated by Healy and Hamilton. Almost two decades were to pass before the treaty lands north of Fort Benton were thrown open to cattle. The trade with Canada was its salvation in the seventies.

Healy and Hamilton made a rich first season's haul in furs and hides. Next year they left earlier, with a larger caravan. The found their first rude fort burned, but they had arrived with a labor force to build permanently. Healy chose a new location a few miles southwest of present-day Lethbridge and laid out a fort which was to be first-class in every particular. He hired a skilled carpenter who had been an employee of the H.B.C. to direct the crew, and erected buildings in a rectangle, bastioned and solid. A number of brass cannon were put on prominent display. Grape shot in 25 pound sacks stood ready for emergencies. The walls were loopholed and the windows fitted with iron bars. All the trading was done through a barred wicket. The popular name for the fort—Fort Whoop-Up—lacked dignity and made the place sound disorganized, an outlaw hangout even, but such was not the fact. Under Healy, Fort Whoop-Up was as rigidly organized as the Hudson's Bay posts to the north. There was plenty of law, and it was all Healy's. He was a tough Irishman, a man who kept his promises, but was at the same time smart and ruthless, let nobody be fooled by his charm with an anecdote.

Little business was expected through the winter. The crew at Whoop-Up settled down for a long, lonesome wait while the days grew short, the strong cold settled, and moisture was driven from the damp cottonwood logs to form efflorescences of frost, turning the interiors into crystal caverns. But the directors at the fort were surprised. Business continued. The Indians moved their winter camps nearby, and some of them traded off all they owned, down to their blankets and moccasins. American settlers had complained that the whisky traders rendered the Indians dangerous. Healy's were left little to be dangerous with. Father Scollen, a missionary among the Blackfeet, complained that he had never seen the Indians so destitute. Although at that time it was still possible to hunt buffalo for food and trade, he reported that the Indians were reduced to rags. He said they had even traded off their guns and knives for whisky, but old-timers branded that an exaggeration.

The success of Fort Whoop-Up brought a rush of competition. Even while it was being pioneered, other traders were preparing to invade the north. By this time the federal authorities in Montana Territory were alarmed. Fort Whoop-Up was too well established to be interfered with, but they decided to stop the less influential traders from going north. Numbered among these was Joe Kipp, twenty-four-year-old halfbreed son of the old Fort Union trader. Getting financial backing in Fort Benton, Kipp tried to escape notice by procuring his goods in Helena, floating down the Missouri to the mouth of the Sun, just above the Great Falls, then ascending that river to its crossing with the Old North Trail, thence going by packtrain. When U.S. Marshal Charles D. Hard learned of this ruse, he set out to intercept Kipp short of the Canadian border.

It was high-water time, with the tributaries of the Marias booming full. Hard, trying to make his crossings farther downstream, was delayed more than Kipp on his Indian trail in the foothills, hence, even with the advantage of a cutacross via Healy's Whoop-Up Road, he did not catch sight of the packtrain until it was on the high prairie against the Lewis Range. All day the pursuit went on with the parties in each other's view, but far out of shouting or rifle range. At last Kipp crossed the North Fork of Milk River, which at that point curves across the boundary and back again. He believed it marked the boundary, and that its far shore was Canada. So he stopped and waited.

"It's the Marshal, all right," he confirmed, studying the party through a telescope. "We might as well wait here and stand them off."

Hard, riding his dripping horse up from the river, ordered the caravan to turn around to be escorted back to Fort Benton. Kipp refused. "You're just twenty minutes too late," he told him. "We crossed the boundary at the North Fork." Hard believed him and turned back empty-handed. Later the boundary was surveyed and the spot was found to be just three hundred yards inside the United States.

Kipp went on to Belly River and built a fort near the mouth of the Waterton which became known as Fort Stand-off in honor of his encounter with the marshal. The first year's trade proved a success. Kipp returned to Fort Benton that autumn with 3000 buffalo robes and a fine tonnage of smaller pelts. In the meantime, he also managed to be in on the first discovery of gold in the Sweet Grass Hills. It profited him less than the whisky trade.

Other forts called Slideout, Robber's Roost, Spitzee, and Solomon came into being. Most of these facilities were on the skimpy side. The later traders generally had poor whisky and nothing else. Their "forts" were seldom more than dugouts or cabins, and they stayed only as long as their supplies held out, or until they had to flee from Indian violence. Existing beyond the reach of any effective jurisdiction, the whisky forts became the most notorious places on the frontier. Eighty-eight of the northern Blackfeet were known to have died in camp brawls during the single year of 1871. In the winter they got drunk and staggered away to freeze to death. A number were said to have been deliberately poisoned when they had bankrupted themselves and became warlike in demanding more whisky. Of this there was no proof. The term *poison* was in use for all Indian whisky. The vile nature of the traders' concoctions has often been described. However, they did not add such ingredients as red pepper, ginger, tobacco, molasses, and horseradish to make anyone sick, but merely to stretch the alcohol and lead their customers to believe they were getting good, strong drink for their money. Few traders wished to kill off their clientele; the object was not even to get them drunk. In fact, it was policy, once things were going well, to cut down further and further on the alcohol in order to keep the party going full cry with the encouragement of further trade. In later years, old-time whisky traders held their audiences with tall stories of their mixtures, and claimed to have added such ingredients as loco weed, cactus juice, and snake venom, giving the formulation of Indian whisky a Paul Bunyan flavor.

Oliver Tingley, whose family held most of the range near the cow capital at Big Sandy, recounted meeting a trader named Grovon (Gros Ventre) John on his way with several demijohns of liquor to trade with an Indian village in the Judith country. Grovon John, after standing treat from one of the containers, took occasion to lecture young Tingley on the evils of drink. It had ruined, he said, many a good man. "Now I make this stuff myself," said John, "and it's as good as any, but I'd be first to admit that there's not a thing in it that'll do you a bit of good, except maybe the horse urine."

(Grovon John was named for his association with the tribe of Indians rather than for his girth—*Gros Ventre* meaning "big belly" in French. French breeds pronounced it "Grovont." The Crees, who were considered shifty sneak thieves by the Gros Ventre, in turn considered them dirty, treacherous, and depraved, and the name Gros Ventre was always pronounced with contempt. However, by the second decade of the twentieth century the name was so romantically lodged in the folklore of the region that a Great Falls, Montana, women's club, wishing to honor their American heritage, decided to call themselves The Gros Ventre. People who adopt the pioneer French designations apparently do so at considerable peril; another group of women, these in the town of Choteau, 50 miles to the northwest, near the Teton Mountains and on the Teton River, decided to name their square-dance club the Teton Twisters. Teton, in reference to a woman's breast, was a favorite of the traders who fancied a resemblance in many smoothly contoured and top-nippled hills.)

The most celebrated of all drunken Indians was the Blood chief Calf Shirt, leader of the band which wiped out the woodchoppers near Fort Benton in 1865. He was a very large Indian, well over six feet tall, tremendously powerful and with a sudden violent temper which rendered him uncontrollable when crossed. Before the arrival of the whisky forts he had already killed three of his fellow Bloods in camp quarrels. Calf Shirt claimed that his medicine had been given him by the grizzly bear, and nobody among the Indians doubted him. The Blackfeet called him *Min-ix-see*, which translated into something like Wild Man. It characterized him better than Calf Shirt, but it is as Calf Shirt that he had gone down in the annals of the high border, the toughest Indian of them all.

Calf Shirt was wealthy in horses, robes, and wives. It made him a valuable customer at Fort Benton and accounted for the fact that he still dared make occasional appearances south of the line even after the slaughter at Ophir. As long as whisky was only occasionally available to him, Calf Shirt maintained his position of affluence. However, when an unlimited supply came to his neighborhood, he lapsed beyond all control. He traded off everything he owned, and everything he could bully from his fellows. At Fort Whoop-Up, shout and beat on the iron bars as he might, he could not get inside, and Healy gave out no liquor on credit. Other forts were not so well protected; in these the trade rooms were open, and Calf Shirt could usually get himself a bottle gratis, provided he promised to go home and make no more trouble.

Among these lesser posts was Kipp's Fort Standoff. One winter day a number of wolfers had gathered at Standoff to get in out of the cold and were playing poker in the bunkhouse, leaving Kipp alone behind the counter of his trade room next door, when Calf Shirt entered. He advanced on Kipp, and in a violent mood started beating the counter with his fist and demanding whisky. Tired of being bullyragged for whisky, the manager of Standoff told Calf Shirt that if he wanted free whisky to go down the river to Solomon's. At this, Calf Shirt drew an old-time muzzle-loading pistol. Kipp, however, was ready for him. Hidden by the counter he already had a gun in his hand, and when Calf Shirt drew, Kipp shot him in the breast.

The bullet knocked Calf Shirt back on his heels but he did not fall, nor did he drop his gun. He turned and walked outside and across the snow. Hearing the shot, the wolfers hurried out, and seeing an Indian with a gun in his hand, they opened fire. The range was short, not over thirty or forty feet, and wolfers were not in the habit of missing. They pumped bullet after bullet into Calf Shirt, but he made no sign of feeling them; it was as if they vanished before reaching his body. He kept walking until he came to a depression where some sods had been lifted for the purpose of chinking the buildings, and there he fell. He was dead when they came to the spot. Pulling up his shirt they found he had taken sixteen bullets, most of them exactly where they had been aimed.

Although a bull buffalo could hardly have taken the weight of lead Calf Shirt did, his death in Blackfeet legend took on an even more heroic cast. In Blackfeet lore, all white men feared the mighty Min-ix-see, and, unable to meet him in combat, they decided on poison. "You are giving me poor whisky, O white brothers," said Min-ix-see, but he drank the potion anyway, and it had no effect on him. The white traders then decided to shoot him. They emptied their guns at him, but the bullets could not enter his body; they only made small, blue marks. Walking away, he stumbled into a hole, and there they set on him with axes. Still unable to kill him, so strong was his bear medicine, they chopped a hole in the ice and held him underwater with poles. There, after many minutes, the struggles of Min-ix-see ended.

It was true that the men at Standoff got rid of Calf Shirt's body by pushing it through a hole in the ice. Two days later it was found washed in among some driftwood, and the Indians hauled it ashore. There his wives waited for him to arise, because he had assured them that in case of his death, or apparent death, he would arise at the end of forty-eight hours. Arise he did not, although it was said that he responded with one hard kick when whisky was forced down his throat.

The whisky forts' corruption of the Indians was a fact deplored by most right-thinking people. However, they were at times contradictory in stating the facts. While missionary Father Scollen, as we have seen, had the Indians trading themselves out of both clothing and weapons, the Hudson's Bay Company accused the whisky forts of endangering the white settlers by lavishly arming them with rifles of the most modern type. In the United States, one group cried out that the traders were killing the Indians in vast numbers by use of poison whisky, while others claimed that the Indians were more aggressive and hard-riding than ever, a scourge to be eliminated. On any of these counts the whisky trade was a bad thing. Healy had still another version. Far from corrupting the Indians, he said, he had given them a lesson in law and order. As founder of Fort Whoop-Up, a stronghold in the wilderness, he claimed to have made the roads safe for white settlers to travel, establish homes, and rear children. "We had the best brand of prairie men that the world produced doing legitimate business scattered through the various posts," he said, "and taught the Blackfeet, Bloods, Sarcees, and Crees to behave." Healy always contended that he was run out of business not to save the Indians but to save English profits for Englishmen. "We gave the Indians a money's worth while the Hudson Bay didn't want to match," he said. The Old Company, however, regarded this as arrant nonsense. In calling on Ottawa for assistance the factors pointed out that H.B.C. had been prevailed on to relinquish sovereignty over the country on the reasonable assumption that some effective jurisdiction would be set up to replace it. Now as a reward for their cooperation in the matter, they found that their trade had been undermined. Indian groups which had been their customers for a century had now moved south, where they could get whisky in abundance as well as all the modern guns they could pay for.

The wolfers on the U.S. side of the boundary constituted the group most affected by the Blackfeet acquisition of modern arms. The Indian hated no one as he did a wolfer, who shot buffalo, pumped the carcass full of strychnine, and awaited results. It was an easy way to acquire wolf hides, but many Indian dogs also fell victim to the poison bait. Hence Indians killed wolfers at every opportunity. When the Blackfeet started riding the land with Henry rifles, a group of wolfers, calling itself The Spitzee Cavalry, set out for Whoop-Up to teach Healy a lesson. Their resolve was dissipated by his adamant personality, and by the abundance of wet goods he later placed before then. A wolfer's thirst was known to exceed even that of an Indian.

But the day of the whisky fort was about over. In 1873 the Canadian government decided to take action. It had heard the complaints of the Company, and of the general lawlessness, but chiefly it had become alarmed at imperialistic sounds from the United States. Fearing that a large-scale movement of settlers northward would mean the loss of prairie Canada, a military force was organized and named the North-West Mounted Police. Adventurous and jobless men flocked to its colors, and it was trained in record time. A major problem was getting west. On Canadian soil there was no transport beyond Lake Superior. However, the United States laid aside whatever imperialistic intentions it had and allowed the foreign military force to proceed via Duluth and Moorhead, provided their arms were kept in sealed cases. Many of the arms had been purchased in the United States originally, and as it was obvious that the NWMP were to be dependent on United States merchants for supply, their welcome was enhanced correspondingly. They arrived in the region of the South Saskatchewan after the first frosts, promptly got lost, but after some wandering reached Fort Whoop-Up. Healy, warned well in advance, had time to bury his liquor inside the fort enclosure. A search revealed nothing unlawful and the MP commander, Colonel Macleod, did not at that particular time feel his position strong enough to bring much pressure to bear. He traveled on and established winter quarters on an island in the Oldman River.

The Mounties had a hard time of it. They were ill-clothed, short of food, their cabins were mere dirt-roofed wickiups, and the choice of an island situation was unfortunate. It seemed at the outset a place of safety from attack, but in the strong cold the ice crystallized through the ground and the floors of the cabins. Later the thickening river ice buckled and made an approach perilous to horses, while there was fear it might break up suddenly in the spring and sweep away the post.

The adventurers who had flocked to the banner were bitterly disaffected with the place they had been led into, and one frigid day a party of twenty-one set out for Montana, fifty miles to the south. They were on foot under the leadership of a Crimean War veteran named George Frasier, remembered along the frontier as The Old Fusileer. Without his leadership, the deserters would have scattered and perished. Freezing, he drove them on through the deep snow. When a pursuing force under a Captain Crozier overtook them, The Old Fusileer turned his men and prepared to fight. The forces were about even; capture of the deserters was an obvious impossibility; Crozier was in fact afraid that his own men would seize the opportunity to head for the south also. He wisely retired. The deserters crossed the boundary and were herded by U.S. cavalry to Blackfeet Agency. They were disarmed, fed, and some had their frozen toes and fingers amputated. Later, set free, they scattered southward toward the cattle country and the mining camps.

(For years deserter mounted policemen were commonplace in the camps of northern Montana. Often setting out in the dead of winter without food or any more clothes than they had on their backs, they arrived, if at all, with frozen feet. All along the high border, peg-legged and stump-legged men were likely to be RCMP deserters, just as men without thumbs were likely to be cowboys who had lost them between rope and saddlehorn while lassoing steers.)

With the arrival of the Mounted Police, traders such as Kipp and Healy got rid of their remaining stocks and departed across the border. The few who remained were mostly captured, fined, or given terms in jail. A whisky trade continued for years, keeping the police busy, but for the most part it was a small, packhorse, back-trail operation. Even John Healy, best-known of the traders, had failed to grow rich. Later he became one of the pioneers of the Yukon country. An associate at Whoop-Up, D. W. Davis, became Alberta's first representative in Parliament. Kipp was honored when a Montana State Park was named for his pioneer family.

Fort Benton did not suffer when the whisky forts were abandoned. Arrival of the Mounted Police signaled the first broad development of the southern Alberta and Saskatchewan areas. The trail pioneered by Healy and Hamilton soon became a busy wagon road, shown on many of the early maps as the Whoop-Up Trail. Within a short time it was carrying many times over the freight of the old whisky-trade days. The Carroll-to-Helena wagon road had cut deeply into Benton's traffic during years when the river was low, and soon the railroad from Utah to Butte was to divert substantial tonnages from the river entirely. Coming when it did, the Canadian business was a godsend.

Like most other roads, the Whoop-Up followed an ancient trail of the Indians. One could start it on the Yellowstone at Billings, trace it to the town of Cushman, through the Judith Gap, between the Little Belt and Big Snowy mountains, to the Shonkin and a river ford below Fort Benton. The river bottoms near this ford offered abundant camping spots to Indians, and the original post was built there in 1846 but later moved a couple of miles downstream to a better boat landing.

The Whoop-Up Road commenced near the ford and swung off the direct course northwestward to ford the Teton River and find an easy way through its gumbo and badlands, either of which could be a well-nigh impenetrable barrier in times of rain. Pend Oreille Springs and old Fort Conrad were stopping places along the way. Fort Conrad, like Fort Whoop-Up, had nothing to do with the military; it was built by I. G. Baker & Co., the Fort Benton and St. Louis trading firm, and named for Charles Conrad, who ran it for them. Later Baker sold out to Joe Kipp, who had been driven from Standoff by the RCMP. Located at a natural crossing of the

Marias River, it became a small town with Kipp its "mayor," but only a few of the original sill logs remain today. From Fort Conrad the road curved northward, and when Jim Hill built his main line through from Minneapolis, he honored the crossing of the Whoop-Up Trail with an expendable box-car which he unloaded from its trucks and marked with a sign reading Shelby Junction. Actually the road ran a mile or two to the east, but both lay between the rims of a broad, parched coulee. The road went on to the north and crossed the Canadian boundary about where it touched Red Creek, a northward-flowing tributary of the Milk.

Favored stopping places in addition to Fort Conrad were Pend Oreille Springs, Yeast Powder Charley's, and the Cap Nelse Ranch. Hospitality of the last-named became one of the grand chimeras of the road and provided its favorite anecdote: A frequent visitor at the saloons in Fort Benton, Nelse, a French-Canadian squawman, never failed to invite his acquaintances to a ranch table which, according to his description, sagged beneath a lavish abundance of the finest foods, including pie. Since it was known that the culinary competence of Cap's wife had never advanced beyond the slumgullion stage, his invitations were accepted in spirit only. Not understanding this, a St. Louis gentleman once dumfounded Cap by driving up at the appointed day and hour in a hired rig. Undaunted, Cap met him opened-armed and with effusive cries of delight. However, he owned to being chagrined by an unforeseen circumstance. Some old squaw, he said, had slipped into his home by the rear door, and before anyone could stop her, had devoured all the pie. In fact, Cap said, the old squaw could even then be seen escaping into the brush downriver, and he pointed her out. The squaw was his own wife who always went into hiding whenever a well-dressed white man came to her home.

The Whoop-Up Road ceased to be important when the Canadian Pacific started supplying Alberta in 1884. Its first string of freight cars cut into Fort Benton's total business by one third. At about the same time the Northern Pacific took over a large piece of its territory in the south. For a time the rising cattle boom made up part of the loss, but fewer and fewer steamboats braved the rapids and bars of the Big Muddy. In the summer of 1887 Fort Benton boomed with the arrival of an estimated 9,000 men, all of whom were in some way involved with building the Montana Central Railway. By September they had moved on to the Big Sandy Flats. The Montana Central delivered the final blow to steamboating on the upper Missouri, and to Fort Benton as a commercial center.

THE ROAD NORTH —KLONDIKE

Chapter 12

Nearly all the placer gold of the United States lay to the south of the Blackfoot River of Montana, roughly on the 47th parallel, but nobody knew that in the 1860s. The wilderness of peaks, timber, snows, and thundering torrents which extended northward apparently to the edge of the world were confidently expected to hold gravels as rich as any yet found. Coarse gold was discovered on Libby Creek, a tributary of the Kootenai in northwestern Montana, in 1867, but the prospectors were driven out by Indians. The Cedar Creek diggings close by the high Bitterroot range west of Missoula drew a rush numbering ten thousand to some quickly exhausted gravels in 1869, and there were other discoveries in the mountains, but the more adventurous had traveled much farther, and some of the Alder Gulch pioneers reached Alaska.

In 1867, when the Indians were driving away the first prospectors on Libby Creek, an exploring party for the Western Union Telegraph Co. found gold on the Seward Peninsula. The party did not follow up its find. It was there to map a transcontinental telegraph line, all by land except Bering Strait, a project discontinued upon news of the Atlantic cable. There were tales of Russian diggings in the early fur-trade days also, and an authenticated find by Peter Doroshin, a graduate of the Imperial Mining School, who in 1849 was sent from St. Petersburg by the Russian government to investigate the possibilities of developing a northern coal supply for the steamships which then were plying the Gulf of Alaska. Hearing about the California gold discoveries, he strayed from his original purpose long enough to wash several ounces of gold from a stream subsequently called Russian River. It was only a diversion. Soon he was developing a coal seam on English Bay at the tip of the Kenai Peninsula, importing a great variety of expensive machinery and later a crew of staunch German coal miners to teach their art to the local Aleuts, but with a payroll of 125 and a daily maximum of 30 tons, his coal cost 1½ cents per pound to produce, and it was, moreover, a poor grade of fuel.

The first sizable rush of miners reached Alaska in 1872. These were not attracted by Alaska's gold, which as yet lay unsuspected beneath the tundra, but to the panhandle port of Wrangell, a short cut to the Cassair district of northern British Columbia. From Wrangell one could take a steamboat up the Stikine, a booming, treacherous stream, as far as Telegraph Creek (named for another party of telegraph-cable explorers, these planning to reach Siberia and Europe via the British Columbia short cut of the Great North Trail), only a week or ten days by trail and lake from their destination.

The Stikine itself had been mined for surface colors since 1861 by wanderers from the Fraser, men who had simply gone on and on through the wilderness, and found a refuge among the coast Indians. Other prospectors had drifted more to the east, finding small amounts of gold on the Omineca. The Cassair discovery was made by Harry McCulloch and Henry Thiebert, who started out from the Edmonton region on the false report of a gold discovery beyond Fort Nelson, and finally, so deep in the Liard River country that there seemed little chance of getting out before the freeze, they just kept on going, following an unknown stream across to the Pacific side. They were in the Cassair Mountains, the range forming the western boundary of the British Columbia Trench. The streams over a considerable area showed gold, but it was too late to pause more than briefly. They continued and came upon a party of miners from Wrangell who were utilizing the low-water period to mine some bars on the Stikine. With their news and a small sack of color, McCulloch and Thiebert had no trouble grub-staking themselves, and everyone joined the rush to the Cassairs.

In 1874 word of the Cassair strike reached the outside world and precipitated a rush almost as great as that to the Fraser. Some of these gold-seekers took the canoe-and-horse trail up from Prince George, but most of them arrived from Wrangell. Figures regarded as reliable show that 25,000 stampeders passed through that port between 1874 and 1877, and nearly as many came back again, disappointed. The gold of the Cassairs was not bonanza stuff. It lay in fine division, deep under the soil. However, a few diehards stayed on, toiling in the shafts and drift mines that rarely yielded half an ounce per shift, and men are working there today. Some of them stayed only a season or two and drifted north, up the Teslin to the Lewes, past the mouth of a swift, cold, roily stream called the Klondike, and on into U.S. territory, where pockety gold kept showing up in the Yukon's vast, frozen bottoms or could be washed from its bars after the bleak and oceanic floods of summer. There they re-mained, living more like Indians than whites, having found the Ultima Thule of the wilderness.

In that era the Alaska Commercial Co. was the only organized business in operation, and generally the only effective government in all the unknown land Seward had obtained from Russia. Prospectors wintered near its posts on the Yukon, brought their small moosehide pokes of gold in for trading, and occasionally rode the company steamboat which plied the river from St. Michael.

One of the few men who deliberately set out for Alaska, instead of just finding it at the end of north, was Jack Mc-Questen, who tried to reach it by the Liard River route, changed his mind at Fort Nelson, and instead went north by way of the Mackenzie and the Porcupine. The journey took him a year and a half. His experience proved that the route of the three-toed horse and early American man was not really a broad highway or a beaten trail, terms which were favorites of the archeologists. Another man who explored much the same route was named Harper, and his experiences were equally rugged.

The easiest way to the upper Yukon, if one excepted the Commercial Company's steamboat, was by ocean vessel up the drowned glacial channels of Chatam Strait and the Lynn Canal to Dyea Inlet, and over the Coast range which rose as a snowy backbone a few miles inland. By this route, the headwaters of the Yukon were only 30 miles away, crow's-flight distance—although a generation of Northerners were to remember it as the longest 30 miles of their lives.

For as many years as anyone knew, the route inland via the Dyea Inlet had been controlled by the Chilkat Indians. They guarded it jealously, for it allowed them to control the trade just as the Arikara had controlled trade by holding the bluffs of the Missouri. And like the Arikara, they were tough fighting men. Even the Russians, who destroyed whole tribes as a matter of policy, left the Chilkats alone. The U.S. traders who moved up the islands of the Inside Passage at the time of the Alaskan Purchase gave them wide berth when they objected to the establishment of trading posts. They did not drive the American traders away; they wanted their goods, but it was their determination that nobody else should use the pass—or passes, for there were three of them: the Chilkoot, the Chilkat, and the White. In the old days, the Chilkats exchanged fish for moose meat or ivory for sinew, but with the source of supply at nearby Douglas Island they were able to add manufactured products to their stock in trade, getting more furs from the interior to trade for more goods, and were on their way to becoming wealthy, at least by their tribal standards.

George Holt is credited with being the first white man to cross Chilkoot Pass. It is believed that he had a companion along, but if so, his name has been lost. After a summer of exploring and prospecting they returned by the same route in the autumn, or claimed they did. Holt did not advise anyone else to try the pass, although he said it was safe enough for him because he had mastered the Chilkat tongue and was, he maintained, regarded by those Indians with simple awe. He went down to Sitka by skinboat, or oomiak, and tried to promote an expedition to the interior, claiming to have discovered gold in the rolling plateau country beyond the mountains. True, he had only a few colors to show, but that was because he had sent its main weight, coarse gold and nuggets, down the river to the Alaska Commercial Co. by friendly Indians.

Telling and retelling his story, he got the reputation of being one of the North's worst blowhards. It was noticed that the story became embellished, the country, adventures, and gold all proliferating in the retelling. If one thing more than the rest stamped it as a fabrication, it was his insistence on the coarse gold and nuggets. All old-timers agreed that the gold of the interior was fine leaf and flour off the bars. However, although most of the real miners laughed, he found some people who would listen, and one of these was the commanding officer of the U.S. troops then located in Sitka. This young man busied himself with preparations for a reconnaissance of the interior, which happened to be Canadian soil, but an unexpected order calling the detachment back to the States prevented his making the history books.

Holt attempted to find backers elsewhere. He went to traders, shipowners, miners, and prospectors' camps, trying to promote an expedition. Over the pass, he said, were natives who used gold nuggets as fishing sinkers and arrow points. He claimed to have been on one of the richest treasure troves of the ages when hostile tribesmen had turned him back. Still looking for a grubstake, he was killed by an Indian near Anchorage in 1885.

It was inevitable that Holt's geography would be discounted along with everything else. When his description of the interior did not agree with that of men who had penetrated the country from the Stikine, it was taken as proof he had never been there. When later information tended to prove it was Holt and not the Stikine miners who was correct, his detractors said he had gathered his information from the Chilkats. Later still, the doubters were given something to think about when a quantity of gold, containing a couple of nuggets, turned up in the hands of the Alaska Commercial, Holt having indeed entrusted it to an Indian trader. Where he had found it was never learned.

As it turned out, no armed force was needed to subdue the Chilkats. As soon as the natives found they could make more carrying freight and collecting toll from the white travelers than they could by themselves, trading with the poor tribes of the interior, the pass was opened.

In 1880 Fred Cushman and nineteen prospectors sailed up the Lynn Canal, accompanied by a small U.S. naval force, and went ashore for a council. The officer in charge of the sailors prudently remained on his ship, but he did send a letter setting forth that it would be most pleasing to "the Great White Father in Washington" if they invited their white brothers to prospect in their domain. None of the Chilkats could read, but they were reported to have been impressed by the message. However, what really brought them around was an offer of money, a few cents per hundred pounds, if they would serve as packers over the summit.

Months later, the friendship was formalized by a sort of treaty. There was no naval officer available on this occasion, but the miners enlisted the aid of Gouverneur Morris, then U.S. Collector of Customs at Sitka, who came up and impressed the chiefs by donning his old Civil War uniform.

So opened the famed Chilkoot Pass, and in a little while the White and Chilkat passes nearby. By mid-June a party was at Bennett Lake, across the Canadian boundary, whip-sawing lumber for boats. They followed lake and river tributaries of the Yukon and walked the old Chilkat trails, reaching a country known long before by the H.B.C. and by Peter Pond's traders from Athabasca. Most of the prospectors made it back over the pass before winter, but some stayed. Gold had been found on the bars of the Big Salmon and the Hootalinqua.

Next year quite a number of prospectors arrived, enough to make a small settlement at the head of the inlet while waiting to be packed over. The Chilkats charged 25¢ per hundred and at that rate even the poorest prospector felt like a king. While their men were away, bending their backs under the hundred-pound loads which were considered standard, many of the women added their bit to the family horde by practicing prostitution. With everyone earning, many Chilkat families saw as much as $3 a day during the season, and they became the richest Indians on the coast. They soon developed a fondness for the more sophisticated trade goods available at Dyea's first business establishment, a saloon and trading post—John J. Healy, late of Fort Whoop-Up, Proprietor. Healy, since leaving Whoop-Up, had failed in flour milling and in the hotel business, and had served a term as the sheriff of Chouteau County. Defeated for re-election he was now come to the North to repair his fortunes.

Business increased for Healy when gold was discovered on the Stewart River. Unfortunately, the Stewart was a long journey, and many of its gold-bearing bars were not exposed until late in the summer. Hence most of the miners were wintering there and trading their gold with the Commercial, or with the semi-independent traders who carried its goods to the Canadian side. Healy, who had guessed right about the interior and placed himself at its main entrance, was unfortunately trying to do business with people when they had the least money to buy.

Inside, the chief trader was Jack McQuesten. This early explorer of the Great North Trail was still looking for his stake, although for the past decade not so much as a gold-seeker but as a fur trader for the Alaska Commercial. Then, about the time of the Stewart River finds, an unexpected opportunity came his way.

A few years before, Edward L. Schieffelin, an Arizona prospector, had gone out in the desert and staked a pair of claims which he named the Tombstone and the Graveyard, soldiers having warned him that the area was certain death because of Apaches. The famed camp of Tombstone grew at the site, but Schieffelin was smart and sold out for a fortune before it was learned that the bonanzas were superficial. Wealthy and with his vision as a mining man proved beyond any reasonable doubt, he turned to global geology, theoretically projecting the silver belt of Peru to the even greater belt of Mexico and to the Comstock Lode. He did the same for the Mother Lode and the rest of the California gold belt. Then he noticed, that the two belts, if projected farther, intersected in Alaska. He then purchased a good, small steamboat, had it towed north, and set out up the Yukon to locate the spot. He predicted the greatest concentration of precious metals in the hemisphere. (People of the North long joked about poor Schieffelin and his scheme, which indeed came to naught. However, J. E. Spurr, the great man of American mining geology, in 1923 published what was essentially the same theory. Spurr mapped a "Great Silver Channel" for 6660 miles slicing across Bolivia, Peru, Mexico, and the Western United States. He also mapped a gold zone from Montana to Nome, and his Great Silver Channel, if projected, would have intersected it just where Schieffelin said it would. The gold camp of Ruby was found in that approximate location, but it set no records for abundance.) Schieffelin in his new boat steamed up the Yukon, looked at the low shores, the bedrock everywhere hidden beneath the accumulated dirt and muck of a million, or a hundred million, springtime floods, grew discouraged, and decided to sell his boat for any price he could get. McQuesten, Harper, and Mayo formed a partnership and bought it.

Some say the three were backed by the Alaska Commercial Co., which wanted to send them into British lands at the head of the Yukon, that area having been abandoned by H.B.C. since the discontinuance, many years before, of its Liard River brigades. Gold, however, rather than furs interested the new company. They were soon supplying the Stewart River diggings. There were no bonanzas, although two men with a rocker made as high as $150 per day during the brief season, and miners who could bring water around by flume ran small sluices at an even greater profit. A minimum estimate of the Stewart diggings gives them a total of $75,000.

The first solid discovery of the North was made in the summer of 1886 when a prospector named Howard Franklin crossed over to the Fortymile, a river which flows into the Yukon near the Alaska–Canada boundary, and turned coarse gold and nuggets. The Stewart was deserted within a day after the news arrived. Harper, who had charge of the trading post at the Stewart, followed with all his stock, and set up at the present town of Fortymile, just inside Canada, at the mouth of the river.

In the normal course of events he would have been well supplied. However, news of the strike traveled unexpectedly far. Prospectors came from all over the Yukon, and moccasin telegraph informed those on the outside as well. There was a new demand for Chilkat packers, and a squawman, "Siwash George" Carmack, formed them into a union, served as their agent, and stiffly increased the pound rate until many of them saw a dollar a day, and he himself made enough to set up a shanty trade store among the Tagish Indians inside.

At Fortymile, Harper had supplies on hand to last the winter, but he knew that a continued flow of prospectors would mean famine the following year unless word could be sent to Jack McQuesten, who was in San Francisco, unaware of Fortymile and the rush, buying only as usual. A meeting of miners was called. Tom Williams, a former riverboat man, and a halfbreed called Indian Bob volunteered to carry a message to Juneau, where a regular winter boat schedule was maintained with the States. They set off by dogsled along the winter trail, past the future site of Dawson City, to Wounded Moose Camp, down the ice of the Lewes and Nordenskiold rivers, across the Little River divide to White Horse and Bennett Lake. They reached the ridge east of Chilkoot Pass in January, starving. Too weak to travel, Indian Bob left his companion in an improvised camp and made it alone over to Healy's post. A rescue party brought Williams across. Williams was dying, but news of the Fortymile finally reached Jack McQuesten.

The Fortymile diggings were extensive but seldom rich. Many prospectors worked hard for a grubstake, then moved on. Discoveries followed on Mastodon Creek to the northwest. Again the main camp was not at the diggings but on the Yukon. Because this camp was believed to stand on the Arctic Circle, it was named Circle City. It was located just upriver from the Flats, where the ancient migration route crossed over, skirting the swamp and island country, heading westward past the Ogilvie Mountains to the Mackenzie.

Circle City, besides being placed advantageously to the river and trails, was a celebrated grazing area for moose and caribou. The busy fishwheels of the Siwash Indians turned night and day, in the season, dipping salmon from the current. Although the old-timers told of hardships when the supply boats failed to get through, there was never starvation. Circle became the favored wintering capital of the Arctic Brotherhood, the far-north aristocracy. In future years no one could claim to be a real pioneer unless he was a veteran of Circle. The winter temperatures at Circle City became legendary. Because mercury solidifies at slightly less than forty degrees below zero, common thermometers of that era were considered by Circle City to be of use only on its more balmy days. To furnish miners a truly serviceable thermometer, Jack McQuesten, then the leading local trader, was said to have devised one from bottles which he filled successively with kerosene, hundred-proof whisky, and Sagwa bitters—liquids of various freezing points. When kerosene thickened to the consistency of syrup, the wise Circle City resident stayed off the trail and favored the south side of a stove. Later such winters were recalled nostalgically as "the good old days," and celebrated for the close personal relations and good fellowship which prevailed. Although the prices of goods were necessarily high, with freight rates running around $50 per ton, no trader expecting to remain long in the country could turn a flat-broke miner from his door to starve. McQuesten, and later John Healy, who entered the Yukon trade, never refused credit for basic supplies. Although occasionally a miner died in their debt, their collections were excellent.

In 1889 the Alaska Commercial had put in operation the first large steamboat on the Yukon, its 140-footer *Arctic*. John Healy, leaving Dyea, raised capital and built a competing boat which he named the *Portus B. Ware*. Miners liked to call it the *Partners Beware*. The Commercial, solidly backed by San Francisco money, had long been a monopoly, not greatly challenged by McQuesten, Harper, and Mayo. Healy was a different matter. It was not long before the old king of the Whoop-Up was fighting them for dominance of the river. Opposing him was Edgar Mizner, a mining engineer and scion of a prominent California family, and it would have been interesting to have watched the battle—but the lines had barely been drawn when new events produced more than enough business for all.

After serving briefly as a contractor for the Chilkat packers at Dyea, George Carmack moved to "Carmacks," where the Yukon Trail forks to its British Columbian and Liard River branches. He had no white neighbors—only Indians. This suited him fine. He got on very well with Indians, many of whom were his in-laws. They brought him their furs and he traded them grub and whisky. In 1896, as was the summer practice, Carmack with his squaw and a number of the nearby band moved to a summer fish camp at the mouth of a small stream called the Klondike—*Trondiuck* to purists, Indian for "small water." Because catching salmon was considered a woman's work and Carmack did not wish to violate the tribal customs, he found himself with little to do. After idling around for a few days, news came that some white men had found hopeful showings at a place called Gold Bottom. So, accompanied by two Tagish friends, Skookum Jim and Tagish Charley, he went over to see what the rumors amounted to.

Arriving at Gold Bottom, Carmack was made welcome and invited to stake a claim, but his companions ran into racial prejudice. No Indians were welcome, they were told. Carmack, resenting the slight to his wife's relatives, said he wouldn't bother to drive stakes into such poor scratch gravel anyhow, and headed back toward the river.

They were in no hurry. It seemed to be a fair gold country. All the bars showed strings of color. The grub began to run low and it looked as if they would have to give it up and return to the main camp when Skookum Jim had the good fortune to shoot a moose. He had the further good fortune to drop his moose on Rabbit Creek, which was later to be called Bonanza.

When Carmack panned $12 worth of coarse gold from a false bedrock close to the surface and showed it in Fortymile, the great rush to the Klondike was on. Fortymile and the Yukon country to the west were quickly emptied. Word got to Dyea and there was heavy movement over the pass. All winter parties fought the deep snow to the Klondike. Yet at Gold Bottom the miners worked on, oblivious to what was happening so close at hand. Prospectors from as far away as

Seattle got to the Klondike in time to stake claims, if not on Bonanza, at least on one of the adjoining creeks. Later Carmack went to Seattle on a holiday, taking his wife and a couple of his Indian friends along, and while enjoying the role of Northern nabob and hero, amusing himself by dropping nuggets from his hotel window to the crowd gathered below, he was accused of double-crossing the men who had offered to share Gold Bottom with him. It is not recorded that he ever showed the least remorse.

Few on the Klondike itself realized that first winter how rich the diggings really were. Except for a foot or two at the surface, the ground there never thawed. Miners chopped through rubbery muck and moss and tried to melt it little by little by building fires and lowering red-hot stones. Here and there a bit of the icy stuff was taken for testing, carried to the cabins to be thawed on the stove and washed in a tub of water. But mostly they just guessed at the paydirt and hoisted it by hand windlasses which could be heard for miles creaking in the cold. The days were short, and the little sun was obscured by a heavy layer of smoke which hung from the thawing fires. Candles ran out, bacon grease was at a premium for lighting, and some got along on the worst-smelling lamp ever devised—the burning oily flesh of smoked salmon. Gravel built up in long windrows, hard as iron, awaiting the spring thaw. There was great anxiety over the first sluice runs. They exceeded all expectations. Klondike gold, typically in oatmeal-size flakes, promptly "clogged the riffles."

After cleanup, quite a number of the new-rich left for a fling in the States. A TON OF GOLD was the newspaper headline which heralded the bonanza. First Seattle, and later San Francisco, was swept by the fever, as ships docked carrying men from the North, unshaved and roughly garbed, who staggered off carrying small parcels of great weight. Stevedores who saw powerfully built men in the prime of life struggling with suitcases of moderate size dashed off, leaving their ships half-tended to outfit themselves for immediate departure. One Klondiker got off in Seattle using both hands to tote a small cowhide valise and was subjected to the embarrassment of having its handles tear out by the roots. Refusing all offers of assistance, he went reeling away with the treasured burden clasped in his arms. Word of mouth outraced the newspapers. All over Seattle men claimed to have witnessed the scene, or had close acquaintances who had talked confidentially with this or that Klondike miner, and had themselves hefted the metal. The newspaper estimate of a ton of gold soon became regarded as ludicrously conservative. Furthermore, the gold in suitcases was deemed to be mere pocket money. The real tonnage was said to be locked up in the insured storage below decks. It was pointed out that even the insured cargo represented only that small portion of the season's take that various of the miners had decided to carry out the hard way, over the White and Chilkoot passes, and that the major shipments had gone by river steamboat down the Yukon, and were then in St. Michael waiting an ocean vessel. Some of the Klondike claims were individually said to have yielded more than a ton of gold during the past season alone.

The Klondikers were only briefly taken aback by the excitement they had occasioned. One of them tipped a hack driver with a nugget estimated to be worth ten dollars, but the driver profited more, selling it to a nearby saloon for $25, and there it attracted crowds when displayed in a glass case. A wide eyed claque followed the Klondikers from one saloon to another and their simplest North-country witticisms occasioned a merriment that would have been the envy of Joe Weber and Lew Fields. Plied with questions, they answered in the manner most likely to give satisfaction to their listeners. The Klondike was pictured as an area roughly 60 miles across, containing from 70 to 80 gulches or small streams, each from 12 to 30 miles in length, almost all of them showing gold. However, the people were warned that the gold was not to be won without difficulty. It was a hard country, and some of the sourdoughs claimed to have seen the thermometer drop to 80 degrees below zero. Furthermore, the gold lay at bedrock beneath permanently frozen muck and gravel, sometimes as much as 60 feet thick. And not all claims were uniformly rich. Sometimes it was necessary to sink as many as three shafts from 30 to 60 feet deep before tapping the paystreak, and there were some hard-luck miners who had realized no more than $10,000 or $15,000 for an entire season's work.

The Klondike rush was perhaps second to California's half a century earlier, but it was very large. There were a number of reasons for its size. First, it was the real thing. There was evidence of that from the outset. Then, it came at a very opportune moment. In 1893 a panic had swept the financial world. Banks folded, and there was a flood of bankruptcies, some of them the largest and most respected companies. The price of silver collapsed from previous levels of over one dollar an ounce to an average 1894 price of 55¢, closing mining camps all over the West. By 1896 not only America, but also much of the world, had suffered three years of hard times. Men with nothing to lose were waiting to go anywhere.

The excitement of the Klondike was immediate, world-wide, and vitalizing. Seattle, whose sawmills and fisheries had been three years in the doldrums, felt prosperity over-night. Arctic outfitters suddenly appeared in a hundred of its vacant locations. The price of neglected ocean vessels boomed. In Central America, banana boats changed destination and steamed northward. Some, hearing that horses were in exceptional demand for transport over the White Pass, dumped their bananas on the beach and took on cargoes of ten-peso ponies. They arrived to find Seattle happily stripped of horses, many of the cabs out of business, and the draying prices up 50 per cent. To supply the Alaska demand horse buyers ranged eastward as far as South Dakota, buying any sort of draft stock they could find. Four cowboys rode into Glasgow, Montana, and were stunned by an offer made for their broncs. They sold them and used the money for tickets on the Great Northern to Seattle. Some communities, particularly in Washington, the Coeur d'Alene of Idaho, and in Montana, took on a deserted air as upwards of one third of their predominantly male populations raced for the Klondike.

The Klondike fever spread. All over the Northwest, chambers of commerce and commercial groups saw the bonanza being reaped by Seattle and sought to get a portion of the business for themselves. Some advertised themselves as staging points where argonauts were advised to supply themselves at low, regular prices. Others offered alternate routes. Kamloops, British Columbia, got out a shadow relief map of the Canadian West showing the town as entrance to a great mountain trough running straight to the north, along which the gold-seeker would be guided to the Klondike by the opposing walls of the Rocky Mountain and Coastal ranges just as surely as a river would be guided by its banks. Looking at the map one might assume that a virtual highway ran all the way to the Cassair country, where the town of Telegraph Creek was prominently shown, suggesting that it would be nice for the travelers, after reaching that settlement, to send a message of safe progress to the folks back home.

Spokane, Washington, publicized itself as southern anchor not only on the Kamloops or Okanagan Trail but also on the more westerly Purcell and Rocky Mountain Trench to Summit Lake, and the "river highways of the great north" via the Parsnip and Fraser, but it is not recorded that the city enjoyed any increase in business as a result. The land route which attained most notice was the Great North Trail. Edmonton was its jumping-off spot.

Although by 1897 Edmonton had been for almost a century one of the most important outlets to the fur trade of the North, it was apparent that something more would be needed to make it into much of a city. At that time it could claim only 700 inhabitants, and quite a number of those

were Indians. It had a bank, a hardware store, a hotel, two
blacksmith shops, a part-time milliner, and several general-
merchandise establishments. There had been attempts at
railroad promotion, all unsuccessful. Some tar sands far up
the Athabasca were believed to be a huge source of fuel,
chemicals, and petroleum, but the distances were prohibi-
tive, and so far they had provided only canoe calking, and a
medicine said effective against intestinal worms. Twenty
years later, Edmonton was to attain quite a romantic celebrity in the writings of Mr. James Oliver Curwood of Owosso,
Michigan, whose lonely red-jacketed Mounted Police ser-
geants looked toward Edmonton as a Western Montreal, but
in 1897 the chief claim of its chamber of commerce was that
it owned the most northerly bank in the Dominion. As for
the Klondike, it was a place reached by ship from Seattle,
and a long distance off.

However, unknown to Edmonton, the attention of the
world was already being turned its way. This came about
when a professional English tourist and free-lance writer did
an article about an all-Canadian short-cut route to the gold
fields, mapping the great trail of Professor Marsh, with
Edmonton and Dawson City its southern and northern an-
chors. The article was a masterpiece of clarity, conviction,
and definitiveness, based not only on a solid historical and
archeological competence, but on personal observation
gained by the author when he had journeyed through Western America by railroad several years before.

The article became big news immediately upon its appearance. It was sent all over the world by cable and was
read everywhere except, apparently, in Edmonton itself. Its
success led to follow-up comments by the author, and other
writers were soon busy laying out the trail with an even
greater authority. Before long they stopped calling it a trail,
and made it a *road*. By some accounts it was an excellent
road through most of its length, but the more conservative
warned that it was on the whole an unimproved road and
suitable only for the more rugged type of vehicle. Fortu-

nately, the writers pointed out, it passed through the great North Woods, which, while suffering from heavy snow and protracted cold during the winter, in the summer flourished abundantly, teeming with deer, caribou, moose, and mountain goat, while the streams abounded with trout, including the famous native speckled trout, or cutthroat. As a result, it had a strong attraction not only to gold-seekers, but to many of the better type who did not feel that wealth was everything and brought along their flyrods and fowling pieces, ready to enjoy a summer's trek away from the grime and bustle of city life, a body conditioner preparing them for the hard winter's work of digging frozen gravel in the gold fields.

Unwarned, Edmonton woke one morning in the summer of 1897 and found itself full of strangers. Every room in town was rented. A tent city sprang up along the Saskatchewan. The merchants quickly sold out everything they had at steeply rising prices and then were faced with the problem of supply from Calgary. Calgary, on the Canadian Pacific, was the closest rail connection, and its wagon transport was at a premium, in demand by the argonauts who disembarked from every train. Some of the arrivals had their own horses and wagons, but many arrived planning to outfit themselves with Western animals, writers having informed them that Calgary lay at the northern end of the greatest horse range in the world, and hence taking their own stock would be like carrying coals to Newcastle. Many freighters merely sold out, pocketed the money, and left for the southern range to purchase more horses. But by paying a price, the Edmonton merchants got goods to their stores and did a booming business.

Although nobody in Edmonton had been over the trail in its entirety, few seemed to doubt that it existed just as described. When people asked for information concerning its exact course and condition, it was only a question of time before Edmonton began supplying it. By the autumn of 1897, although no travelers had set forth toward the Klondike by the "Back Door Route," as it became known, news of the trail was passed around Edmonton almost daily, making it sound like a busy thoroughfare. Gold was said to have been discovered on the Liard, with miners making $50 a day. The caribou herd was reported being driven south by unusually heavy hunting in the region of Dawson City, news greeted with cheers by the gold-rush population, for with good hunting assured it meant they could risk lighter cargoes, and hence make greater speed to their destination.

Edmonton had around 10,000 people when the winter of 1897 closed in. Some, looking with alarm at the migration due to start with the first dry ground of April, talked of substituting sled runners for wheels, estimating they could be in Dawson City by Yuletide. An old-timer, said to have both trapped and prospected in the North, warned that the time for winter travel soon would pass, because with deepening snows and thick, late-winter ice, one might find both his sled impeded and his supply of winter fish rendered skimpy. Another termed this nonsense. He said that the Klondike could be reached in the dead of winter by dog team, and in fact it was the best time to go, the cold serving as protection against spoilage of the food supply, and at the same time providing the good tracking so prized by hunters who wished to replenish their larders with wild meat. It was easier to travel 30 miles per day by dog team than 15 miles per day by horse and wagon. Also, the snow, when it attained its midwinter crust, would be able to support the weight of men and dogs, smoothing over the rocks, deadfalls, and underbrush which caused such a waste of time in summer.

There is no record that anyone actually started out for the Klondike by sled. For one thing, the land beyond Sturgeon River was an unbroken sea of white, and nobody could tell where the road went. A few grew impatient and left for Vancouver via Calgary and the C.P.R., however, and the town, alarmed that an exodus inimical to business would occur, warned that those who went by sea, either from Vancouver or Seattle, would of necessity have to pass through American territory in Alaska. Crime, so notably absent in Edmonton, was reported rampant in Skagway and Dyea. American gunmen were said to be terrorizing the trail over the White and Chilkoot passes, while, it was pointed out, the Back Door Route was patrolled by Her Majesty's Royal North-west Mounted Police every single step of the way.

Meteorology was also cited in Edmonton's favor. For instance, those taking ships to entrances via the Chilkoot Pass and Valdez, while seeming by the map to be closer to their destination, still had to contend with mountains, would be forced to wait longer for the spring thaw, and then have to fight their way through dangerous glacial streams. Those choosing the Back Door Route, while admittedly having farther to travel, would have more time in which to do it, and could expect to arrive in the Klondike well ahead. Comparative meteorological information served to bear this out, for an average of only 24 inches of snow fell in the Liard drainage, protected as it was by the moisture-catching peaks of the Rocky Mountains, while snowfall in the Chilkoot area had been measured at 40 feet. To indicate the comparative flood conditions that might be expected by those using the Back Door Route and those who chose to go via the Alaskan ports, it was also pointed out that the tonnages of Pacific snows were exactly that, heavy because of their high moisture content, while the snows of the eastern slope were dry and powdery, progressively evaporating much of their original moisture because of the dry, invigorating atmosphere.

Although the actual couriers from the North were never in evidence, word of discoveries right on the route of the road brought repeated excitement. To the report of gold on Liard River was added one of finds on the Fort Nelson. Next, a copper deposit assaying richer than Butte Hill was said to have been exposed by a squaw digging potatoes in the Copper River Mountains. This was regarded as particularly significant because it not only substantiated all reports as to the unlimited mineral wealth of the North, it gave the lie to stories of the awful arctic cold, showing it was actually a climate in which thrived the potato. When the thermometer in Edmonton dropped to 50 degrees below zero, people were assured that it was not necessarily colder in the North; quite the opposite, the weather tempered northward as one passed the bulge of the globe and got closer to the sea winds. It was pointed out that the Liard River was no farther north than Stockholm, Sweden, or southern Alaska than Belfast.

The Royal North-west Mounted Police was not flattered to find itself extolled as guardians of the trail. The Mounted issued a statement saying that it seemed inconceivable that sane men would even think of trying to reach the Klondike by an overland route at all. The statement caused general consternation among the taxpayers of Edmonton. Many refused to believe that men who were supposed to be public servants could level at the community—aye, at the prairie provinces themselves—statements that could only interfere with their future development. Later, however, cooler and more cynical heads pointed out what was bothering the police. Already they were suffering from severe drains on manpower and budget, and from this narrow view it was to their advantage to eliminate new routes as far as possible.

The police did not bother to answer such charges directly, but repeated what had been said already, adding that they knew of no *road* except the ones close to Edmonton. Beyond the Athabasca they knew of no road at all, and beyond Peace River little that could be considered a continuous trail. As for the maps which were everywhere, they were constructed on archeological theory and not worth the paper they were printed on. But they were shouting into the wind. To many the Mounted was already discredited. By their own admission they had never been over the trail, so how could they say it did not exist? Anyhow, that "Mounted" business was a joke. Seldom using horses in the North, they traveled by canoe or shanks' mare. So it boiled down to whose word one wished to take, that of the scientists and the people who had been traveling the trail, or that of some inspector in

Regina who would like to see the land emptied of white people and turned back to the Indians so his job could be simplified. To people who had already made up their minds, all this was good logic. To many it became simplified on even more petty human terms—they thought the RCMP was knocking the road simply because somebody else had found it first.

Although the Edmonton boosters had won their argument in that almost nobody was discouraged by the police, there is evidence that they had some uneasy moments, and a former schoolteacher was set to researching, that the facts might be determined. He could find no individual who had himself actually been over the route farther than Fort Nelson, and though it was agreed that wagons could be driven over considerable distances, the route was a trail rather than a road. Aside from that newly in print, the literature of the country contained little information. Histories recounted how, during the 1840s, the Hudson's Bay Company had penetrated Alaska by way of the Liard and had established posts named Fort Halkett above its lower gorge, Fort Selkirk at the main forks of the Yukon, and Fort Frances at the crest of the Liard–Pelly Divide. However, all had been abandoned and the Company had pulled out of the country, leaving no published maps or descriptions. Farther west, from the Cariboo diggings north to White Horse, the country had been mapped by a government geological expedition under George M. Dawson. Dawson himself had never been through the Liard, but he had sent a party into the country under geologist R. G. McConnell, who had mapped the middle portions. McConnell, unfortunately, had not indicated the trail. The Edmonton group, therefore, subscribed $1,500 and hired a man by the name of Taylor to blaze the route as far as the Pelly River. He managed, suffering extreme hardship, to get as far as Fort Nelson, about 500 miles as the crow flies, although more like twice that distance by the winding route that the rivers, muskegs, and mountains forced him to follow.

Taylor's experiences came too late to discourage anyone from leaving, and nobody was able to follow the blaze marks he made on the trees. To blaze a good trail one must be familiar with it in the first place. In this case, his marks were too widely spaced, while numbers of them were almost immediately obliterated by the bark-chewing of porcupines attracted by fresh sap.

However, nobody lacked for instructions on how to reach the Klondike. Dozens of maps, books, pamphlets, and news clips were available. "All one needs is a good constitution, some experience in boating and camping, and $150 in cash," said one authority. Guidebooks marked towns at Athabasca Landing, Fort Assiniboine, Fort McLeod, Fort du Tremble, Fort Nelson, Fort Liard, Fort Frances, and Fort Pelly. One of the most popular maps had a place called Chinatown midway on Liard Canyon. As nothing weighs against the value of a map like areas of blank space, the one containing Chinatown was particularly popular, its purchasers feeling an added security in the prospect of being able to hire cheap coolie labor, as well as Indian, in the event some impediment made wagon travel hazardous or difficult.

Although most talk was of the trail, or the wagon road, a second group came to Edmonton intending to reach the Klondike by water. Theirs was to be the old fur-trade route, by canoe via the Athabasca, the Great Slave, the Mackenzie, and up the Peel. Others, more imaginative, sported amphibious vehicles, mostly of their own design, fitted to face up to a variety of terrains, and hence to institute short cuts, traveling here by land or there by water, ice, or snow. Some were sailing craft and others were steam-powered. One was referred to as a land locomotive. Another rolled along on pontoon wheels made of wine barrels, suitable for dry land but giving the needed buoyancy to support it on the mossy muck of muskeg. One steam sled utilized not only traction; it also had paddlewheel appendages designed to power the vehicle through any snow which might be encountered in the farther mountains. One of the boats had, in addition to sails, a set of forged steel skates which could be clamped to the bottom in the event winter caught its owners somewhere on the Mackenzie. The wagon outfits were also at times on the fanciful side: one titled Englishman came with an entire retinue including servants, shooting companions, cricket bats, and a brass bed with folding legs which was designed to be set up in as little as 2½ minutes while on the trail.

Two hundred miles to the south, Calgary was busy freighting all this heavy equipment north. It also tried to get as much of the outfitting business as it could. Situated on a transcontinental railroad, Calgary advertised itself as the true end-of-trail, trying to make Edmonton appear its suburb, a handy frontier outpost where a person could pick up, at high prices, those last-minute essentials which were always being forgotten at the true point of departure. Even in the United States, towns tried to get in on the windfall. Great Falls, Montana, advertised that it was end-of-trail for all those who wished to launch forth under the Stars and Stripes, but Helena, the state capital, pointed out that Great Falls was not even on a main-line railroad, and one of her hardware stores printed a batch of handbills headed HO! FOR THE KLONDYKE! advertising gold pans, mineral jigs, picks, shovels, quicksilver, giant powder and fuse, portable stamping mills, and water wheels. In Dupuyer, a small cattle town, the leading saloon changed its name from the *Grand Hotel and Bar* to *The Klondike*, and celebrated Christmas by giving away Yukon Toddy, a hot whisky sling with lemon.

There were two routes to Peace River. The shortest of these was about 300 miles long, leading straight across to old Fort Assiniboine (not to be confused with Montana's Fort Assinniboine to the south), there to ford the Athabasca and drive on toward the Smoky Fork of the Peace. Although direct, it had more difficult crossings, and was poorer in grass. The second route kept to a better grass and game country by making a wide swing to the north, passing

around the flanks of Wallace Mountain. The Klondikers preferring the water route also had several choices. During the
winter they swelled the population of Athabasca Landing,
90 miles to the north, to an estimated thousand. Most of
them proposed to sail north by river and lake to the mouth
of Peel River on the Mackenzie, thence to reach the Klondike by boat and portage from the northeast. As this was
from 2,500 to 4,000 miles in length, depending on whether
one wished to take the straight river and lake distance,
or figure in the meanderings, many decided it could not
be made in a single season, and plotted other water routes.
One of these would take them *up* Athabasca River to Lesser
Slave Lake, instead of *down* it to Lake Athabasca. After a
crossing, by sail, they planned to portage the 75 miles to the
Peace. Thence they believed it possible to travel by boat to
the Peace headwaters at Finlay Forks, up the Finlay to
Sifton Pass, and across to the Kechika, one of the forks of
the Liard, where the main trail would be encountered. And
there were other courses, all of which looked perfectly reasonable on the map, designed to use water transportation, but
to short-cut the gigantic northward swing which led almost to
the Arctic Ocean.

While the boatmen impatiently waited for the Athabasca
to clear of ice, wagon outfits were already setting out, anxious to be first on the road. Their eagerness got them nowhere. Most of them bogged down on the Sturgeon River,
whose every tributary was in flood. They soon learned
there was no actual road—or rather, no single main one.
Even the wagon groups who had employed guides experienced trouble, for the tracks of Red River carts often could
be followed for days across the country, at last to end at an
abandoned ranch, an Indian village, or some shack trading
post with its roof caved in. Parties fell to arguing with their
guides, who generally had promised too much in order to get
the advance fees, fired them, and went on using maps and
hearsay information. What one day was a good road would
the next be a poor one, and the day following become a deer

trail with just clearance enough for a good spread of antlers. There the wagoners had a choice of chopping their way or turning back. Eventually they learned to send scouts ahead to locate the trail. Even so it became necessary in many instances to chop a passage forward. Two miles per day often became good progress. Some of the roads were cut off where windstorms of recent seasons had passed through the forest, hurling down wide swaths of timber. Such windfalls were hopeless barriers. Even men on foot found passage virtually impossible across the deeply laid windfalls where one misstep would likely mean a broken leg, and a broken leg eventual death in the wilderness.

Muskeg was an even less predictable obstruction. In the early summer one could distinguish muskeg by the uneven pattern of water lying across it. Later its surface dried and took on the appearance of gray-brown turf, a natural deadfall. Even old-timers could be fooled by muskeg, although generally it gives off a characteristic vibration and drum sound under weight and impact. Railroad builders have been cost fortunes when stretches of line, laid during cold weather, later disappeared into muskeg without a trace. When the Alaska Highway was being pushed northward during World War II, whole bulldozers, power shovels, and Caterpillar tractors broke into muskeg, were left where they were, used as fill, and had gravel heaped over them. Some of the Northern muskeg lies frozen and unsuspected until a house is built on it, and then it thaws selectively under the warmest parts, the result being a dwelling broken in the middle, or tilted at an angle, so its owner needs hobnails to keep footing in his own parlor. Many Klondikers tried to cross muskeg and lost their entire outfits. Without warning, horses would break through knee-deep, lunge out streaming black mud on the clean-washed moss, only to break through again and even more deeply. With their struggles only miring them, other horses were hitched on to pull them out, but at considerable peril, for what often seemed to be solid ground would fail from the additional weight.

As early as July, discouraged men with depleted outfits were stringing back into Edmonton, and the road promoters found it advisable to leave town. But most of the travelers, despite all difficulties, went on. Things had to improve at the edge of the mountains. They built trail and bucked their way forward. Feed remained scarce. Everyone was far behind schedule. Fear of being caught by the Northern winter drove them to greater effort and further reduced the stock.

The Edmonton literature had mentioned "trifling insect pests," much like a recommendation, as if they formed some minor inconvenience one should be glad to put up with so as not to feel guilty about reaching the gold fields so effortlessly while his misguided brothers were struggling up the ice of Chilkoot Pass. In June, mosquitoes became a plague. The mosquitoes of the North were beyond anything of the travelers' imaginations, an actual hazard to life. Some of the swarms cast shadows, could be heard humming from a stone's-throw distance, and stuck with a savagery that caused men to flee and cast themselves into water for protection. Men ran high fevers and lay jouncing for days in the wagons getting over a severe poisoning by mosquitoes. No meal could be eaten except in the protection of smudge fires. Later, in the gold country, a shocking punishment for cache robbers and murderers consisted of stripping the victim to his waist and floating him downstream to be devoured by mosquitoes. Horses got to running from mosquitoes, crashed through the brush, and their owners were days in finding them. A concoction of kerosene and axle grease was found to help against the pests, but nothing kept off the bulldog flies which were a bedeviling nuisance.

Some of the hazards were unforeseen even by the most experienced woodsmen. One of them happened to be porcupines. These animals, among the stupidest known to nature, possess an insatiable appetite for salt, and, rendered fearless by their quill defense, will go anywhere to obtain it. Dirty shirts were eaten out at the armpits, harnesses chewed to pieces for the accumulated salt left by drying sweat. Even the handles of axes and shovels were gnawed to ragged uselessness by porcupines. Travelers awoke to find their harness so chewed that they gave up trying to mend it, transformed its usable portions into packsaddle gear, and abandoned their wagons.

Then there were the Indians. The tribes of northern Alberta and British Columbia had been described as both peaceful and cooperative. The Edmonton chamber of commerce had recommended them as a source of cheap labor, the bearers of burdens, the willing performers of those small camp tasks which the travelers might require during their passage across the terrain. Most of them were Athabascans of the Beaver and Sikanni tribes, and it was true that they had never been as warlike as the Blackfeet, their neighbors to the south. This changed when a scourge of travelers suddenly invaded their country, shooting the game ahead of them, driving it out of the region, destroying traps and snares, and appropriating dugout canoes at every river crossing for use as wagon pontoons.

Desperately the Indians sought ways to stem the invasion. Some of them harried the advance with long-range gunfire. Generally the resistance did not take so positive a form. The Indians preferred to descend suddenly with shouts and waving blankets on the camps where stock was out to graze, chasing the animals, capturing or butchering them. A more tricky practice was that of hiring out as guides, leading the wagons into impenetrable sinks in the forest, and then simply disappearing after borrowing heavily against future wages.

The trail became strewn with broken and abandoned wagons. Years later, when the country was opened to homesteading, people drove up from Montana and found that good wagon wheels could still be purchased from the Indians for as little as 50¢ each. Near the rivers nearly all the wagon wheels were ruined when Indians removed the steel tires and covered them with mesh to make hoop nets. All over the area a favorite exhibit of cabin handicraft was the porch rocker made by lashing a wagon seat slightly below the center of gravity between two wheels. Wagon iron was removed by burning the boxes and refashioned it into everything imaginable, a forest resource of scrap. The axles were prized as heavy gate and barn hinges above any the H.B.C. traders offered. Many endgates became the doors to houses. Wagon tongues were preferred over local wood as clothesline masts while the whippletrees, ready-bored, end-shod, and ring-mounted, made excellent cross-members. The spokes of wheels from which the tires had been removed for hoop nets can to this day be seen gracing the old cabin porches as balusters.

In spite of all obstacles, some of the wagons were taken across the Kiskatinaw and even beyond the Peace. The most undaunted even managed to roll to the other side of Fort St. John, but finally the wilderness of jackpine and aspen became impassable. Scouts returned to the camps and reported that the woods seemed endless. There the last wagons were abandoned and the last harnesses cut up into packsaddles. Loading what they could onto their horses' backs, shouldering packs themselves, the travelers headed into the forest wilderness. It was a hilly country, but there were no important summits and one might walk for days without very steeply climbing or descending—and without seeing more than 50 yards in any direction. One of the main lines of travel passed along the lowlands of Halfway River which, even in August, were treacherous from muskeg. A better route followed higher land to the east between the Halfway and the Beatton. After days of travel this route attained a low divide and descended to the headwaters of the Sikanni Chief River, and in more days, or weeks, a second divide, where at last the timber parted and the travelers had a view of the country. Ahead stretched the declivities of Prophet River. To the northwest, the west, the south, around 180 degrees of the compass, were mountains, range upon range stretching in blue-and-white infinity, apparently to the end of the world. To the homeless and trail-weary, with winter coming on and ice freezing nightly across the water buckets, it was a frightening magnificence.

None of the mountains then bore names. Twenty years later, responding to the patriotic urge of the first world war, trappers and prospectors in the Finlay River country named one of the jagged summits Mount Lloyd George, and short chains of mountains west of it were christened the Joffre and Kitchener ranges. Almost fifty years were to pass before anyone was to get around to naming the closer peaks to the north, and once more a wartime fervor was evident. The three highest are today known as Mount Churchill, Mount Roosevelt, and Mount Stalin.

At that stage, few of the Klondikers had more than a general idea of their geographic positions. Their maps had proved next to useless. Place after place marked in bold letters on the maps was found to be nonexistent. Three hundred miles still separated them from Fort Nelson which appeared on the guide maps as large as the city of Winnipeg. Fort Nelson was one of the most celebrated places in all Canada, an anchor of the Hudson's Bay Company in the West. Supplied by canoe brigade from Edmonton via the Athabasca and Great Slave Lake, it drew trade from an area which was about equal to New England and the Middle Atlantic states. It turned out to be in fact a log store, some elevated cache houses with flattened tin cans nailed around their pilings to resist the claws of marauding packrats and wolverines, and a number of Indian shanties.

For many days the travelers had looked forward to their arrival at Fort Nelson. All were low on food. Their shoes and socks were worn out, and many of them were out of ammunition, having shot at too much small game with big rifles. But although their needs were great, their funds were generally small. Everything in Edmonton had cost twice what they expected, but at Fort Nelson they learned what high prices really were. And, starting high, they quickly went up with the demand, the factor being forced to preserve at least a little of his stock for his own needs and those of the trappers who would come in for outfitting that autumn. The broke and needy failed to move him at all. Edmonton publicity had made much of the camaraderie of the North, "where the cabin door is never locked, and each man takes as he needs but always leaves the woodbox filled on his departure." The stampeders asked: What about this? Bitterly they recalled the old Canadian jest which had the Company initials H.B.C. meaning "Here Before Christ." This got them nowhere. The only free thing the factor had to offer was advice—that they get busy whipsawing boats, building rafts, and using any other floatable means of getting downriver to some Indian village before the big freeze, or, before Christ, he promised they'd be here permanently, with the wind whistling through their ribs.

Few if any took the factor's advice and went down the river, which was the Fort Nelson and would have taken them to the lower Liard, and with good fortune to the Mackenzie close to Great Slave Lake with its numerous trading posts and Indian villages. Although the aspen-filled valley around Fort Nelson was already turning bright yellow from frost, they started the long climb to the Liard Divide. The divide stands at 4250 feet where the Alaska Highway crosses it today. Summit Lake formed a good camping place at the crest. A village of pole shanties and canvas sprang up, continually augmented from the direction of Fort Nelson and melting away toward the Liard.

Liard means cottonwood in *voyageur* French. They pronounced it Lay-*ar*. Most English-speaking people, and particularly those who live on the Alaska side, call it the *Lee*-ard. The upper tributaries of the Liard are still only half-known, branching like the legs of a spider into the mountain country of northern British Columbia and Yukon Territory.

Liard River was first explored by the Nor'westers looking for a route to the Pacific. After amalgamating with the Hudson's Bay and negotiating a treaty which allowed their penetration into Russian America, it served as a route to the

Yukon headwaters and the chain of posts were built—not for trade, for there was little there in the way of furs, but as places of shelter and supply for the brigades which carried trade goods to Alaska and the Western furs out again. Liard Post was established on the lower reaches of the river, then Fort Halkett on a navigable stretch of water above the Grand Canyon; a summer post was built near the confluence of the Dease and the Frances; Fort Frances was built on the Liard–Yukon Divide; and finally Fort Selkirk, the main post on the source of the Yukon.

Fort Selkirk proved only intermittently profitable. The route to it was considered the most hazardous the Company had ever established and the Liard the worst river in the North. Men were drowned in its rapids, swept away by its unpredictable currents while wading near shore, and they slipped and fell to their deaths on the canyon portages. The Rapids of the Drowned was named for an entire *bateau*-load of *voyageurs* who were carried to their deaths in its pulverizing rocks and currents. Even the placid stretches of the Liard could be dangerous. The current was always deep and swift. The river was forever undercutting acres of forest, washing out the trees and stacking them, roots and limbs intact, in jams which were as much as a quarter-mile long and a hundred feet thick. Sometimes only a narrow strip of open water would be available to the boatmen, the whole power of the river concentrated in a sucking, silent current where it passed beneath the jam, and the unwary who ventured too close were likely to be carried down as into the maelstrom, never to be seen again.

Starting out with the spring break-up at Chipewayan, the Company found that its brigades were hard put to reach Selkirk before the autumn freeze. Thus the brigade which went in with trade goods one season came out with furs the next. The *voyageurs* on the Liard River route usually had two squaws and two families, one in Selkirk and one in the region of the Slave. The Company encouraged this because it was easier, once such a state of affairs was established, to keep men on the brigade—they were anxious each year to see whether they had a new child at the other end of the route. A few of the *voyageurs* were originally from York Factory or Lake Superior, and hence they had wives there, too, but by no amount of traveling were they able to keep all three in anything like full production.

The Company, no less than the Indian wives, was greatly concerned by the time element. Ten per cent was not, in that era, an unusual rate of interest, even on well-secured investments, yet every shilling tied up in rifles, traps, woolens, and other trade goods had to bear at least four years of interest before a single beaver or fox fur arrived at the warehouse in Montreal. Often it proved easier to reach Fort Selkirk by way of the Mackenzie and Porcupine rivers than by the terrible Liard, and eventually its posts were abandoned in favor of Fort Yukon, far to the north.

"The road up the Liard is in the main steep and primitive," read the guidebook. The "road," where it could be found at all, was a foot trail. Its most clearly marked stretches were the portages which had been used by the *voyageurs.* Some of these clung to the canyon sides with the black-walled, white-frothed Liard rushing below. There was little feed, and the hoofs of horses quickly gave out on the rocks. They were urged along as far as possible and then butchered for food. Game proved very scarce. Few caribou or moose strayed into the sparse feeding grounds of the Liard. There were some grayling and trout in the river, but fishing required much time. For days the Liard flowed through a gorge, and the travelers walked in thirst within its sound. Even rabbits were scarce. The Indians hunted siffleurs, a small species of groundhog, skinned them, dried them near fires, and stacked them like mummified bats against the hungry time of winter. Some winters the Indians were reduced to chewing the underbark from pine trees for a syrupy nutrient it contained, with the result that old village sites were marked miles in advance by clumps of dead pines, stripped of bark and left standing.

The travelers' most dependable food supply, after their horses gave out, were the porcupines which had so bedeviled them back at Peace River. The animals' love of salt was now a human lifesaver. There were hot springs along the Liard, and some of them had saline encrustations which attracted porcupines by the hundreds. Porcupines were easy to kill. With a club, one could stand beside a porcupine trail and kill the single-purposed animals as they plodded by. Half-starved men stumbled onto a plenty of porcupines, killed them by the dozens, gorged on the oily meat half-raw, and were rendered violently ill. They recovered and were sickened forever after at the odor of fat meat in the least remindful of porcupine, but that autumn they ate more porcupine when faced with starvation. At last, even porcupines became scarce. There were no more siffleurs. They hunted lemmings and packrats, and they got by for a time by roasting low-bush cranberries from the infrequent muskegs.

Some of them tried to find the Chinatown marked on their maps. It did not exist. The closest thing to a Chinatown ever found on the Liard was a "Dead Chinaman Rapids" where a boatload of Chinese prospectors had been drowned some years before. These Chinese, having come over from the Cassair, were said to have located rich diggings on the Liard. In the 1930s a sharp eye was still being kept, during periods of low water, for their lost gold, said to be contained in small moosehide sacks and to have a total value of $70,000.

The travelers passed such places as the Hell Gate, the Grand Canyon, the Chutes, and the Devil's Portage. When their shoes burst they made moccasins of rawhide, filled them with grass or dry moss in place of socks, and kept going. There were few Indians, but some of the travelers succeeded in trading guns, ammunition, and extra knives for food. Many wasted all their 30-30, .44, and heavy .405 ammunition on small game and then threw their rifles away to get rid of the weight. They were now only about halfway to Dawson City, and winter set in.

At Liard Post, far down the river, garden vegetables could be grown and the first frost did not generally come until mid-August, but in the canyon there were frosts all through June and July. The mid-August frost of Liard Post became, above the canyon, a solid freeze. In September, with snow gathering around the rocks, the Klondikers were still struggling up the gash of the valley. The river in its quiet stretches froze solid. At least in one particular the Edmonton promoters proved correct—the snow was light. Whereas on Peace River the snowfall ran as heavy as two feet by Christmas, on the Liard there were only a few inches. The thin snowfall permitted some of the travelers to keep going until December, or until they bogged down in the deep snow of the mountains.

It is not known that any of the travelers got over to the Yukon drainage the first season. Of the total distance from Edmonton to Dawson City, the most anyone covered was about two thirds. The vanguard managed to climb the Yukon Divide near old Fort Frances, where the Simpson and Campbell ranges toe out into the eastern plateau, but further progress was checked by the deep snows. They built cabins and brush wickiups under the shelter of Teton summit and most of them managed to survive the winter.

Those, such as the group at Frances, who were lucky enough to be near a lake could sometimes chop holes through the progressively deepening ice and catch fish. Some of the parties learned that once they had camped, game started appearing, and they were able to kill bear, moose, and caribou. Deeper snows drove mountain sheep down from the high country. The lucky ones had to chew pine and gather frozen cranberries, thus tending to escape the scurvy which was a worse killer than starvation. Those who had thrown away their cooking utensils were driven to eating the game, including glands and organs, in a relatively uncooked state, and this also helped them escape the deficiency diseases. No one will ever know the numbers who died on the Liard, the numbers who managed the following year to stagger on to Dawson, and the numbers who turned back and reached some downriver post. Probably no more than a couple of hundred reached Dawson. Some of the travelers walked up the Liard, missed the turnoff up Frances River, wandered across the divide southwestward onto the headwaters of the Tuya River and there met other lost parties who had traveled northward from Kamloops, on the old telegraph trail. One party kept going until they reached the Dease Lake country and were taken in by miners who had staked claims during the Cassair rush.

When it was learned that hundreds of men were marooned in the mountains, too weak to get out of their makeshift camps, the Dominion authorities fitted out rescue expeditions, but they did not attempt to reach them by the Back Door Route. A Mounted Police expedition which set out to test the trail was no more than the other travelers able to reach the Klondike the first season, their time being fourteen months. Rescue was sent via Wrangell, the Stikine River, and the Cassairs, and a hundred or so were brought out on muleback too weak to walk.

Those who tried to reach the Klondike by way of the Mackenzie River fared little better than those who fell victim to Edmonton's "road." None of these arrived at the diggings that first season, either, but a number managed to reach the Mackenzie and there hole up for the winter, crossing over by way of the Peel River and Seela Pass next year. Some of the boatmen got on the Mackenzie and floated down its broad, gray waters all the way to the Arctic Ocean, not knowing, in that bleak and featureless land, which of the western tributaries to follow. Cast up on shore, they wandered from one Indian village to another begging fish, not getting to the Klondike until the third summer, and many took Indian wives, never getting there at all.

Derelicts of the Back Door and the British Columbia Trench routes also were taken in by Indians, and many were satisfied to remain. For many years, such towns as Prince George, Hazelton, and Prince Rupert were visited by men who had started for the Klondike and became residents of a country that could be lived in easier than crossed. They trapped through the winter. In summer, after the torrents of the big thaw resorted new volumes of glacial moraine, they managed to recover a few ounces, or occasionally a few hundred ounces, of gold from the river bars. They raised summer gardens. In autumn they guided hunting parties of wealthy Americans and Britons for moose, mountain sheep, and goats. Such men never complained that a Kamloops or an Edmonton chamber of commerce had lured them into a mountain *cul-de-sac* of disaster, but owned that their life was a good one, and they could ask for no better.

Chapter 13

An estimated 1500 wintered on the Klondike in 1896–1897. Three thousand got
through to the district the following
summer. The real rush arrived in 1898.
By autumn of that year, Canadian records showed 35,000 in the district. Sixty
thousand were believed to have actually
set out from Seattle, Vancouver, San
Francisco, Edmonton, and other staging
points. In the winter of 1897–1898 the
Mounted Police counted 28,000 who had
crossed over Chilkoot and nearby passes.
Many took a look at the icy Chilkoot
and turned back. Quite a number were
stopped by the Mounties because they
lacked the minimum of supplies or because they were deemed morally undesirable. Many thousands more went
north to St. Michael at the mouth of the
Yukon and upstream by paddlewheel
steamboat. This proved to be on the
whole the easiest route, although they

were jammed aboard the boats in a manner which would
have raised objections from a cattle shipper, and often they
had to help chop wood during the journey. Some boats unfit
for southern rivers such as the Columbia were towed north
and found unfit for the Yukon also, and one group arrived
with tools and machinery intending to fell local wood and
build their own transport.

From the Pacific no less than from British Columbia
and Edmonton there were a number of routes chosen because of misinformation or from study of the popular maps.
One of these led from the Russian anchorage at Cook Inlet
straight north to the Tanana, a route followed by the Alaska
Railroad today. It was logical although few got over it, and
those who did still found themselves a long way from the
Klondike. The Richardson Highway now follows an old
stampeder's trail from Valdez to the Tanana, but even fewer
reached their destination by this course than those who disembarked at Cook Inlet. Approximately 5000 decided to go
by way of Wrangell. This, for the first lap, was the old route
to the Cassair diggings. It had the advantage of offering
steamboat transportation to Telegraph Creek, approximately
a sixth of the total distance. From there anyone with a map
could see he had only to cross over the relatively low divide
between Tuya and Teslin lakes, and he would have clear,
broad sailing up the Teslin, Lewes, and Yukon rivers straight
to Dawson City. A company was organized to build a railroad there, and sold tickets. The line remains unbuilt although one ticketholder was said to have forced the concern
to furnish him alternate transportation, with the result that
he arrived in Dawson paddled in a dugout canoe by two Indians. Wrangell's railroad stands in gold-rush lore beside
Soapy Smith's telegraph company in Skagway, which had no
wire strung but nevertheless accepted messages to anywhere
on earth for a basic $5, and always had an answer back, col-
lect, within the hour.

Some travelers sailed deep inside the continent by following the Portland Canal along the southern boundary be-

tween Alaska and British Columbia, reaching the town of Stewart where they took the Bowser Lake Trail, crossing over the Iskut River headwaters to Telegraph Creek, making a summer's work of what the Wrangell travelers accomplished by boat in a few days.

Students of maps who formulated their own short cuts got into the most preposterous situations of all. One of the "short cuts" led about 500 to go ashore at Yakutut Bay, sealed by mountains and the Hubbard Glacier. Maps indicated that after a steep climb and descent the traveler from Yakutut was far ahead of those choosing the Chilkoot, and furthermore he would bypass the White Horse rapids. Some of them actually did manage to cross the Hubbard to Alsek River. There they found themselves on a glacial torrent bounded by cliffs of ice. They had brought along their saws, intending to whipsaw lumber for boats, but the Alsek had no wood larger than willows. They attempted to bind willows together into bundles and the bundles into rafts, and in these get down the ice-water flood. When downstream passage proved impossible they ascended the canyon. Winter overtook them. Next summer, those who survived starvation, cold, and scurvy made it down to tidewater and found that they were a day's canoe travel from Skagway, at Pyramid Bay.

Many Klondikers had left the gentler climes because of economic depression. There was no depression in the Klondike, if they managed to reach it. True, no large percentage struck it rich, but nobody able and willing to lend a hand suffered from unemployment. Prices were very high, but so were wages. Eggs, potatoes, fresh vegetables, and sometimes even whisky were in short supply, but gold was abundant. Muckers shoveling in at the sluice boxes made as much in three days as they would have made in a month back in the States. Tradesmen were particularly fortunate. Men skilled at carpentry, barbering, dentistry, blacksmithing, and any number of other skills earned far and away better than the going wage back home, and some of them came out with bigger stakes than if they'd had claims on Bonanza. The gold country expanded with strikes in new gulches. The bench diggings of ancient streams high on the hillsides were developed. But although the Klondike gold country proved of greater extent than anyone had a right to imagine, an end of it all finally came, and the flow of gold-hunters set in the other way, moving back down the Yukon into United States territory. They reprospected the streams which had yielded gold to the men of '86, and new finds were made. The camp of Woodchopper, 60 miles southeast of Circle City, became a boom town, miners at one spot finding gold settled among layers of mastodon bones. A number of discoveries were made along the Tanana, but the bedrock was very deep, so that mining required heavy capitalization, and waited for a later era and the installation of thawing rigs and bucket dredges. By far the biggest excitement was near Cape Nome, on the distant Seward Peninsula.

It is fitting that the last gold rush should lead to America's final peninsula, and Cape Nome, which might claim—together with Norton Bay, Deering, and Cape Wales—the distinction of being the terminus of the Great North Trail.

Cape Nome is a geographically unprepossessing lump of ground, a beach surmounted by a low headland, projecting slightly from Seward's southern coast. Early explorers indicated the cape, but gave it no name, and a cartographer wrote *name?* wishing to have one supplied. His *a* resembled an *o* and Cape Nome was born. The nearby town was first called Anvil City for the gold diggings on Anvil Creek a few miles inland. In the summer of 1899 about 3000 miners were there from the Yukon, the Koyukuk, and across Norton Sound from St. Michael. Claims were staked, but the area lacked a land office. The country was flat-lying, much of it under muskeg; no one had a very good idea where the pay gravels were likely to lie; and the claimants, in order to play it safe, staked everywhere.

According to mining law, the claimant of a placer or lode claim is required to show valuable mineral of some sort, and to make the excavation necessary to show it in place. Few bothered to do more than stake the ground on Anvil Creek, and latecomers of only a few weeks, arriving and finding the entire country jabbed with stakes and notices of location, but nobody holding the ground, adjudged it abandoned and staked over again. Some of the ground on Anvil Creek ended up with as many as ten claimants. However, it was not only a problem of which was first on a parcel of land. According to law, placer claims had to conform to the Public Land surveys and could not exceed 20 acres each. There was no survey on Anvil Creek, so claims were laid out every which-way according to the crazy compasses of that far Northern latitude, with corners set accordingly. Associations of people could take up proportionately larger claims. Some individuals in the Anvil Creek region simply staked the maximum area of tundra and went to town to sell shares, giving the transaction a tardy semblance of legality. As a practical matter, nobody owned ground which he did not control through force. Hence, many early arrivals who were on the paystreak banded themselves into protective groups, some working rockers and sluices, some standing guard.

In Nome an old Idaho miner named John Hummel wished to prospect, but he was rheumatic from the damp cold and unable to travel inland. The best he could do was prospect the beach close at hand. Finding color, he persuaded a young soldier to do most of the work, directed the construction of a rocker, and soon the partnership was profiting $100 a day. Thus was discovered Nome Beach, "The Golden Sands of Nome," soon to sound as a clarion call to Northern wealth and adventure.

Nome quickly emptied its doors onto the new diggings. There was a run on lumber for the construction of rockers. Rockers are much like a baby's cradle, with a screened box at the top, an apron of canvas to catch the coarse gold, and a bottom, where the baby's bed would be, fitted with a couple of riffles for the gravel, sand, and water to swish across, leaving the gold behind. They are one of the best gold-saving devices ever contrived. Even gravel which has been passed over the intricate gold extractors of a modern dredge frequently show colors in a rocker. But rockers with riffled bottoms which worked well enough on Anvil Creek failed on the beach. The beach gold was fine, about sixty colors to the cent, and the black sands, garnet, and other worthless heavy material quickly packed the bottom, letting the gold slide straight through. Hummel had the bottom of his rocker fitted with a copper plate which he coated with mercury, and which built up a gold amalgam. All the copper plate in Nome was soon gone. Copper wash boilers and all the copper flashings in the area were flattened out into plate. Sailors deserted the ships which were anchored offshore, taking all the removable copper fittings with them. When even these sources of copper were exhausted, silver was utilized. Silver is superior even to copper as an amalgamation plate, and after the scanty supply of table silver was gone, rocker bottoms were cobbled with silver dollars, effectively building up thick layers of gold amalgam, but very difficult to handle at cleanup time.

The miners worked in teams for the most part, one shoveling and hauling water, the other operating the rocker and feeding in the pay. Average ground made $50 per day to the team, but a rich streak easily ran it to $500 or more. The paystreak was not at the surface but was three or four feet down; the sand was easy shoveling, however. For a period of two months the beach produced an estimated $20,000 per day. As the wealth was recovered with practically no overhead, it became so much cash and went immediately into trade. No workman would stick to his job unless paid as much as he could make on the beach, and wages boomed. Some men went to the beach and dug gold only until they had supplied their financial need for breakfast, a few drinks, and a stack of poker chips, whereupon they put aside their shovels until the morrow.

The boom was a magnet for miners all along the Yukon.

St. Michael, the Koyukuk, and the gold camps of Ruby and Rampart City saw heavy exodus. Two of the arrivals from Rampart, in the winter of 1899–1900, were Rex Beach and Tex Rickard. Rickard, a gambler and former cowboy, was said to have arrived in St. Michael with $21 in his pocket, jawboned a supply of whisky and his passage to Nome, where he went into the saloon and gambling business. Soon he was able to sell a quarter interest in his establishment, The Northern, for $21,000, multiplying his capital a thousand-fold. Rickard had arrived with some reputation as a handler of deadly weapons. The $21,000 figure became established when Jack McCloud, a placer miner from Anvil Creek, lost his stake at Rickard's, went home, got his pistol, and came back to challenge the proprietor. Rickard was said to have started toward the street with a revolver, but then demurred. "No," he said. "I won't do it. What he wants is to put up the life of a pauper against that of a man who has just banked $21,000. I'm not afraid of him, but I don't like the odds. Go tell Jack to make himself another stake, and I'll shoot it out with him on even terms."

Another Nome saloon and gambling-house keeper of some celebrity was Wyatt Earp, the proprietor of the Dexter Bar. Earp was then controversial not because of his actions at the O.K. Corral, but due to his refereeing of the Jeffries–Sharkey fight down in the States—many finding it inimical to Sharkey and the sums which had been wagered on him. In Nome, Earp, like Rickard, displayed an aversion to gun-play, feeling that it interfered with the orderly flow of money over the faro, chuck-a-luck, and twenty-one tables, the latter then called "Rocky Mountain." Earp, who in his Arizona years was said to have ridden 87 miles to shoot through the hotel room occupied nuptially by a female relative because he disapproved of the groom, had by the time he reached Nome become so peaceful he tried to dissuade a local gunslinger verbally, with the result that he was wounded, and reported by Seattle papers to be dead. He recovered, however, and lived to a mellow age.

The rush to Nome Beach created a shortage not only of labor but of all merchandise. When an expected shipment of fresh vegetables did not arrive, the ship failing to make passage through the Aleutians, carrots soared to a dollar apiece. A Chinese started a bean-sprout nursery, selling his product to salad-hungry miners and making a small fortune. A Nome butcher, shaky at arithmetic, was said to have purchased the camp's only typewriter under the impression that it was a self-computing cash register. The butcher was in big money because the carcasses of wild game purchased from Siberian natives for 25¢ per hundred in Nome sold for a dollar a pound after being reduced to roasts and chops on the block. The high price of meat, like that of all other consumer goods, was attriubuted to costly transportation. The actual cost of transportation was low; only the charges were high. Nome was reached directly from Pacific Coast ports in three weeks by some of the most expendable ships in the world.

Of all the poor man's bonanzas, Nome Beach was the greatest. It lay at tidewater, where legally no claim could be staked. It was free for all, late and early comer alike, and each man with a pan or rocker took as he wished. That was what they believed, and that was the way it ended up, but not without a struggle. At the height of mining the beach was staked, a company was formed, and an itinerant lawyer typed up a legal-looking paper, asking the butcher if he could use his cash register for that purpose. The paper declared all miners to be trespassers on private property and ordered their immediate eviction. It was turned over for administration to a young lieutenant named Spaulding who had been sent from St. Michael with a small detachment of troops, and was at that time the sole authority of the U.S. government on all the Seward Peninsula.

Lieutenant Spaulding knew nothing of the law, but the paper looked extremely legal, and he resolved to back it with the full force of U.S. arms. His men were by that time all in hip boots working on the beach, but he gathered them, got them into uniform, and marched them back again, arresting about 300 "trespassers." There was no jail or other enclosure available, so Spaulding was at a loss as to what to do next; he kept them standing around for an hour or so, then freed them with stern admonitions regarding the sacredness of private property, whereupon they trooped back to the beach and resumed mining, the soldiers joining them. Later a federal court declared void all mining claims within 60 feet of high water. In other words, the golden beaches of Nome were open to all.

In the winter of 1899–1900, Nome Beach caused great excitement in the United States and Western Canada. To the popular mind the sands of the sea have always stood for endlessness. As yet nobody knew how far Nome's gold sands extended. They had been followed, not continuously but with rich diggings here and there, for more than 50 miles, from Cape Nome to Cape Rodney at the northwest. Returning prospectors reported that the strip was only 20 feet wide at the most, but such statements received little notice. The gold was popularly believed to have been washed up by the sea. If so, it came from a reservoir so vast as to be practically inexhaustible. Experts were interviewed by reporters, and their more optimistic statements received wide publicity. It was predicted that those places on Nome Beach which had been worked over during the past summer would be rejuvenated by the gales of winter which acted like a mighty mill, constantly rolling the sands in and back again, concentrating the heavier material. No living person, it was said, would see the exhaustion of Nome Beach, and some concern was expressed for the stability of the U.S. dollar against this perennial flood of metal.

A few years before a successful gold dredge had been put into operation in Grasshopper Creek near Bannack. Similar machines were constructed in Seattle and San Francisco and loaded on ships bound for Alaska. Inventors all over the land worked on contrivances of a more experimental nature and rushed them to the ports. Some were no more than large patent gold pans and rockers. One was a machine designed to pick up sand and recover the gold while its operator furnished the power by means of pedals, riding it like a bicycle along the beach. Rex Beach, the former professional football player and soon-to-be literary historian of the area, had charge of a steam-powered machine which was found to function well in places where gold wasn't, but could not be maneuvered to those places where it was.

No group had more faith in the resources of Nome than the West-coast shipowners who were then feeling a slump in revenue after the lush years of the Klondike traffic. Many old ships were recommissioned. Boats deemed unseaworthy for the coastwise lumber trade were declared just the thing to breast the arctic seas, and their owners printed large blocs of tickets. One group purchased a ferryboat which had been retired from the Puget Sound traffic and sold enough tickets to pay for it in a single trip. A number of men, failing to get passage on the regular boats, purchased shares in their own company, chartered an old schooner, and put it in the hands of a volunteer skipper who set out for the Bering Sea but, due to an error in instrumental computation, made landfall in Kamchatka.

Regular lines charged $125 for the Nome passage. Freight went at 2¢ per pound. Although the fare was not prohibitive, many ships crowded passengers in with cargo, and had them sleeping under tables in the dining room and under awnings on deck. Their ads extolled the safety of the journey, much of it in the shelter of the Inside Passage, "as quiet as the lake at your favorite summer resort." not mentioning the terror of the Bering Sea, where a boat was once caught in the ice and borne almost to the North Pole. Mothers who might worry about staking their sons to passage money were assured that Nome was a law-abiding city, watched over by six policemen and a whole regiment of U.S. soldiers. It had any number of good hotels, the publicity said. Food was plain, but wholesome. The moral tone was pointed up by the fact that it had little night life as such, nor any theatrical shows. It was a good place, the publicists indicated, not only to make money, but to save it.

A great deal has been written about the city misfits and pallid bank clerks who joined the Nome stampede. There were those, but large numbers also came from the mining country. When B. A. C. Stone of Garnet, a Montana gold camp, arrived in Nome on the 18th of June 1900, he found so many friends there it seemed like old home week. Besides Eppel, Eggers, and Michelson, who went with him, Stone reported meeting Becker, Baker, McDonald, Hoffman, Reed, West, Johnson, Carlson, Humber, Sorenson, Dolan, Goudy, Holden, and DeBuhr, all from Garnet, while a number of other friends were prospecting the interior. Two years before, the entire Garnet area had only 258 voters, giving an idea of the exodus from just one small camp.

That summer the population of Nome rose to over 12,000. Although few found gold, the beach having failed to replenish itself, there was a great deal of money in the country and jobs were plentiful. The owners of gold-mining machines, after unloading on the beach, had the task of assembling and getting to work. Many of these were well financed by stockholders back home. Stone reported that hundreds of power machines were already at work in the first days of July but that none of them was making wages for their operators, let alone a profit. Their problems were solved once and all when a storm beat the coast and reduced them to flotsam.

The first ships returning from Nome carried an unexpectedly heavy list of embittered passengers. They gave a bleak picture of a hell-town of canvas and jerry-built shacks planted on the gray and windy moss where no tree grew, and where even at midnight there was no darkness and no rest, but a brawling, tramping, never-ending flux and flow of greed. Even Stone, an old hand around the mining camps, was shocked by the state of affairs at Nome:

> The greed of man went farther here than
> in any other place I have ever known.

Many men, I am told, have claims in the hundreds, yes two hundred or more. The local laws do not require a discovery and no work need be done on the claim for two years. Thus if gold in paying quantities be found on the tundra, it would cause trouble if a tenderfoot found it and tried to hold it. All the creeks and gulches have paper locations, but few of them have, as yet, been prospected and are not likely to be so long as a few men hold country. Just think, the tundra which extends from the beach to the foot hills and from Cape Nome to Cape Rodney, 50 miles in length and 8 miles in width, is all located by paper locations and no work done on it, except by very few men. . . . None of the Garnet boys like the place and we have good reason for it.

Geologist A. H. Brooks estimated that of the thousands who that summer decamped on Nome Beach, perhaps 400 got farther than a day's walk inland. No more than 5000 stayed through the winter. Although the Garnet boys may not have liked the place, all but a couple stayed on. They had in their lives done too much hard digging ever to expect gold to bubble up around their shoetops. B. A. C. Stone had been mining on Stone's Flat, between Cayuse and Day gulches, near old Beartown, a paystreak that lay beneath 30 feet of compact clay and rock fragments which was tough as medium mortar. When the Garnet boys heard that the pay on the Anvil and other creeks was only about 4 feet down, they were greatly heartened. Not even Nome's prices provided them a surprise. The older men among them could remember a Bear Gulch price of $75 per hundred for sugar, and bacon at $10 a slab.

As it turned out, few of the paper locations could be

made to stand. When the interior proved rich on a scale which made the beach seem second-class, nearly all the Garnet boys were on hand, having found the driftwood fires and smoky saloons of Nome quite as good as the winter facilities back home. Many of them claimed ground and made a stake. Quite a number lost one stake and went out and made another. As on the Klondike, where labor was priced out of reach, claim owners developed their ground by leasing out portions of it on shares, and a man with a good eye for placer values might pick a "lay" that would yield forty or fifty thousand dollars. So, while the "pasty-faced bank clerks" had returned home, working at $75-per-month jobs and calling the North a fake and a fiasco, their more stubborn brothers were having quite a profitable time of it. The district produced a total of around $80 million in gold. In the next summer, despite legal actions tying up much of Anvil Creek, the per capita take from the Nome area ran around $1000 per person per month, and the town's proportional consumption of champagne and Cuban cigars was far higher than wealthy San Francisco's.

In the romance of the North, Nome rated far above Dawson, which Americans found too well regulated. By the time the Klondike rush got well under way, the Dominion government had a force of one hundred Mounted Police established, ready to take care of all contingencies. After a stampeder struggled up the steep western side of Chilkoot Pass, the first thing that confronted him was a Mounted Police establishment ready to collect fees and duties, to pass on his self-sufficiency, and to turn him back if he happened to be on its undesirable list, which was a long one.

In Alaska there was no law at all—no sheriffs, U.S. Marshals, magistrates; nothing. Pistols were strapped around every waist as soon as the line was crossed. Even prospectors panning the river bars for color felt it best to weight themselves with a pistol and keep a sharp eye out for bushwhackers. By the time the westward movement reached Eagle, the first settlement on the Alaskan side of the boundary, crime had become so rampant that a vigilance committee was formed, and one of its first customers was the former town marshal of Butte, Montana. All along the river boom towns sprang up and miners' courts meted out rough justice. Banishment was the likely penalty for homicide, while the "stiff Yukon rope" was *de rigueur* for sluice and cache robbers.

In the winter of 1899–1900 it came to the attention of Congress that Nome had attained a high property value, but that it was without legal machinery. As a result, a new judicial district was created. Selected to don the robe as Judge was a Minnesota lawyer named Alfred H. Noyes. He set sail rather late in the season, arriving well after the first bulge of stampeders to Nome Beach, on July 19th. With his official party was his friend and adviser, big, handsome Alexander McKenzie.

They came ashore and Noyes set up temporary judicial quarters in a tent. He found the property of Nome in a legal chaos. The town itself stood on an area contested by many claimants, with some business locations being sold at a thousand dollars per front foot, although nothing approximating a legal deed could be provided. Ownership of placer ground along the beach was still indefinite, but the ownership of bonanza claims in the interior presented the greatest complexities of all. It has already been told how they were staked over and over, overlapping and at off-angles. To add to the muddle, some of the early locators had returned and located them yet again, hoping that their double claim would weigh favorably in the event of litigation. In many mining areas of the pioneer West, miners' meetings had established sets of rules to govern the staking and retention of claims, and these had subsequently been accepted as legal, supplemented by the federal statutes of 1866 and 1873. Nome had not one set of miners' regulations but several, all claiming to be legal. When B.A.C. Stone arrived, he appraised the situation correctly when he saw that nobody owned anything he could not hold through force, and the only ones with force enough were those who had arrived early and had formed alliances with their neighbors.

Noyes proceeded to end this state of affairs by means of immediate, definitive decisions. He scarcely listened to an argument and never went near the creeks, but cut cleanly through the most knotty tangles with a dispatch that the camp found amazing. Within four days the owners of five of the richest Anvil Creek claims were barred from further entry, and a receiver was appointed to take over. The receiver turned out to be no old-timer, but the Judge's friend, Mr. Alexander McKenzie. And not only did he take over, he became the operator. He put a large crew of men to work and washed gold from the gravel as fast as it could be shoveled into the sluices.

The claim owners had surrendered their property in the good faith that their rights would be protected. When they found them being stripped, and Noyes unwilling to listen to their pleas, their only recourse was to the U.S. Circuit Court of Appeals in San Francisco, 4000 miles away. Nevertheless, under the leadership of an old California miner, Charley Lane, they sent lawyers on the journey. The Court of Appeals ordered the claims to be returned to their former operators. Noyes, however, would do nothing to implement it. The matter, he said, had been taken out of his hands. McKenzie kept the claims, and, thinking he now had the long winter in his favor, with further recourse to the California-based court a year off, mined gold faster than ever. The cupidity of the shipowners, however, now worked against him. Ordinarily there would have been no chance to get to California and back at that season, but the owners, anxious for another rich payload of freight and passengers, took a chance on the stormy passage into the Bering Sea and Lane's lawyers managed to get back before the big freeze, this time with a warrant for McKenzie's arrest.

At last McKenzie decided it was time to pick up his winnings and get back to the States, where he had powerful political friends in the Republican Party. He had $200,000 worth of gold in the vault of a local bank, but his getaway was hampered by the physical fact that the gold weighed half a ton. Accompanied by a group of his armed allies, he started out to get it, only to be met at the bank by an opposing force under the leadership of Lane. Before much violence took place, the bank cashier locked the vault and left for the day. Later, Lane got possession of the vault, but McKenzie refused to give up his key. It was broken into by two deputy U.S. Marshals. The $200,000 was distributed mainly for expenses, but the claims were to produce millions. McKenzie later was sentenced to a year in jail, but he was quickly pardoned by President McKinley. Noyes served as Judge for almost another year. Attempting to recoup a little in prestige, he kept handing down decisions even after he had retired for safety to a steamer which was anchored off the coast. These became known in the folklore of Nome as "deep-sea injunctions," and no record has been kept of them, but they were said to have been so contradictory as to suggest dementia. Noyes escaped a jail sentence but was eventually fined $1000. It was generally held that he was a mere tool in the hands of the more forceful McKenzie. The affair later served Rex Beach as background for his novel *The Spoilers.*

In Dawson City even such standard American practices as the rolling of drunks in the brothels led to instant police action. Everything that went on the Barbary Coast in its most lawless days was acceptable in Nome. In Dawson the greatest celebrity was Swiftwater Bill Gates who attracted notice by wearing Buffalo Bill hair, a dinner jacket, fur pants, and a stiff-bosomed shirt decorated with natural Klondike nuggets. Nome attracted a group who swung imposing weight in the sporting world for the next thirty years. Tex Rickard, the fight promotor, has already been mentioned. Nome had the greatest of all fight managers in young Jack McKearnan, later known to the boxing world as Jack Kearns. So anxious was McKearnan to get to the land of gold that, in the cold spring of 1900, he jumped overboard when his ship was a mile out from shore rather than wait his turn in the overworked lighters. He made his first (and last) appearance as a fighter in Nome. Always one to claim a bit of the edge, on that occasion he wrapped his fists in lead foil under the bandages, giving them a stunning power that would have been the envy of Joe Gans, but his opponent, after weathering the first round, came back and gave him a bad beating, McKearnan being too tired to lift his weighted hands. The theatrical world was well represented by Sid Grauman, later of Grauman's Chinese Theater in Hollywood, and Alexander Pantages, the vaudeville tycoon. Rex Beach was its ranking literary personality, and Wilson Mizner, brother of Edgar of the Alaska Commercial Co., later a Broadway playwright, operated a faro game in one of its better gambling houses.

Such men, returning to the States, extolled the North as the greatest experience of their lives. They never wanted for an audience. Although the Yukon country was on the whole dismal and flat, its hardships many, and its entertainments few, to people back in the States its name was the bugle of romance. Tales of hardship, cold, and hunger attracted the readers of 1910 just as tales of comfort, warmth, a roof, and a square meal had attracted their ancestors fifty years before. Popular novelists of the 1890s had found it profitable to choose as backgrounds the drawing rooms of genteel England, and their readers could not get enough of ladies, dukes, and earls. After the Klondike they became fascinated with characters patterned after Diamond-Tooth Gertie and the Dog-Faced Kid. Darwinsim had its day as the survival of the fittest became the most extolled of human qualities. The rivers, mountains, and the awful cold came to be regarded as the forge of character, as sycophants of the States, typically Nordic playboys, redeemed themselves by meeting and conquering the forces of nature.

One newspaper correspondent, after a tour of the Yukon, wrote to his editor in New York saying that the country had no drama, no comedy, and no warmth. He predicted that no one would ever see much in the way of fiction about Alaska and the Klondike. "This country is too drab and dreary." His communication became a classic for all the wrong reasons. Readers, it turned out, thirsted for words about the Yukon. America proved filled with frustrated stampeders who wished vicariously to experience the Klondike rush through the medium of the printed page. Even those who had gone North and lived through its hardships wished afterward to read and talk about little else. The rush to California produced a few semiliterate diaries and a thin volume of short stories, but the men of the Yukon dripped pure rhetoric as soon as they thawed out. The memory of such foods as frozen eggs and sourdough griddle cakes moved them as Sienkiewicz had been moved by the banquets of Nero. Yukon caviar—which everyone soon knew was Northern slang for baked beans—became the manna of romance. Robert W. Service waxed lyrical in his descriptions of the effects of scurvy on the human anatomy. One of his poems was a dramatic monologue in which the speaker ended by being torn to bits by a pack of hungry malemutes which had found the entrance into his lonely cabin. The ribs of a fallen chechakho, picked clean and white by wolves, became an Aeolian harp of the Northern winds, and was widely committed to memory. Jack London made heroes of wolves and malemutes; *The Call of the Wild* and *White Fang* became classics. Everything Rex Beach wrote about the Northland became a best-seller, almost before it was mailed to his publisher.

BARBED WIRE
—THE FENCED TRAIL

Chapter 14

After the hard winter of 1886–1887 ranchers, knowing the need for hay and other feeds, began fencing off all the good land they could lease or get title to. The last stand of the open range was in Montana near the Canadian border, and even this vanished between 1910 and 1914, when the area was thrown open to homesteading.

The Homestead Law allowed a settler to claim a quarter-section of public domain, 160 acres, if he cultivated a certain portion of it and made his home on it. Thousands of homesteaders flocked to Montana, about 1910, anxious to break the prairie sod and raise wheat on land which had heretofore been considered good for nothing but pasture. Looking for greater agricultural tonnages along its line, the Great Northern Railroad hired agricultural experts to study the conditions of soil and climate, and the best means of utilizing them in the production of grain. It publicized the homestead lands from Minnesota westward, and ran immigrant sleeping coaches on which the argonauts of the golden grain could speed westward in luxury at less than day-coach prices.

Settlers quickly filled the little cattle towns and were delighted by the expanse at every hand. "Take me back to old Montana Where there's plenty of room and air," read a poem post card which was sent by the thousands to the folks back home. Often they had tickets to no town at all, only the name of a town. Hundreds of immigrants found themselves dropped at a side track and two-legged sign out on the prairie. James Murphy recalled operating a hotel named The Grand Central beneath canvas which had once housed a one-ring circus. Barney Van Alstyne, proprietor of the historic old Spokane Hotel in Big Sandy, hired a roustabout to meet all trains with a baggage cart, instructing him to call out "Spokane Hotel, best hotel in the city, no place for a lady." Settlers found other establishments typically Western. Mrs. O. C. Tingley on entering the family saloon and finding no bartender, no money in the till, and all the chairs filled with nonspending sodbusters waiting to "get landed," attempted to clear the place by firing three times through the floor with a .45-caliber Colt pistol, and received an unexpected dividend when the cellar trapdoor flew open, and the pale and shaken bartender pushed a sack of money into her hands, saying it had been her husband's idea and not his own to empty the till and hide out each time he observed her approach.

Although many considered the immigrants poor spenders, one group who realized small fortunes were the locators who, for a fee, drove them to available parcels of land and helped them record their claims. Such locators, when nearby lands were all filed on, used high-powered automobiles which they drove at top speed, talking rapidly to occupy the passengers' attention, with the result that many an East-erner, who would have considered 9 miles a long farm-to-market jaunt at home, ended 70 miles from the railroad and did not realize it until he set out in a wagon and was three days and nights reaching his holdings.

The country was quickly chopped up with barbed wire and turned grass side under. In the days of the great cattle outfits, homesteaders were frequently greeted with violence. In an earlier day, old Print Olive as unhesitatingly shot a homesteader on his domain as he did a prairie wolf. Fully half the rustlers hanged during the early days of the West were homesteaders trying to get started in the cattle business. But none of the homesteaders of 1910–1914 were hanged, and few were even shot at. By that time all the big stockmen knew the futility of standing against the tide of sodbusters; they retired to the towns after selling their livestock at good prices, or kept ranching in a smaller way on land which they owned or leased from the state government. Anyhow, they predicted, the fate of the wheat farmer would be disaster.

Almost immediately the prairie bore abundantly. Big Sandy, which in the early nineties had become the world's largest primary shipper of beef, twenty years later became the world's largest shipper of wheat. With the first good crops, the town boomers went to work as never before, and poorer lands were homesteaded. In Havre, Montana, a dwarf news vendor was taken into the country and photographed with the wheat coming to his armpits. All along the Great Northern, embryonic cities advertised that they had good openings for doctors, blacksmiths, shoemakers, and mechanics. The town of Fresno, boasting a total population of 75, described itself as a growing city of 500, its year-end goal. Already possessing a newspaper, restaurant, hardware, general store, grain elevator, livery stable, and saloon, Fresno was prepared to welcome a barber, doctor, bank, blacksmith, shoemaker, and dealer in fresh meats. The town of Casady offered even greater opportunities, having by the summer of 1913 attracted only a merchant, a blacksmith, an auctioneer, a well-driller, and a photographer. The towns of Simpson, Tiber, Toledo, Tonjum, Tosland, Mabel, Laredo,

Trommer, Utopia, Warsaw, Ionia, and Filbert—all in Hill County—offered openings unlimited in that not a single one of them had yet attracted any business of any description whatsoever. But they all offered choice locations and advertised, more or less successfully. Laredo, for example, later attracted two businesses, one of them a large frame hotel which operated as a transient facility for five years, accommodating a total of 23 name-signing guests.

There were lush crops everywhere in the trail country of Montana during 1915 and 1916, and high, wartime prices to go with them. Automobiles of the heavier makes stood in front of the homesteaders' tarpaper-covered shacks. Cap Nelse had realized a windfall from the homesteaders of a slightly earlier day, selling for $85 apiece the locoed horses which had been accumulating on his ranch for years, and had heretofore been considered worth no more than $10 each for hide and fertilizer. But Cap was in his grave, and the farmers of 1916 bought tractors. Some of the tractors were as large as branch-line locomotives and were designed to turn over whole counties by means of gangplows. A popular post card of the time showed one such giant turning over 50 feet of the prairie at a single swath while the farmer drove with one hand and his family stood by, watching. "Breaking Land in Montana, the Country of Big Things," read the legend. Some homesteaders owning 160 acres of land bought tractors which were capable of plowing their entire holding in a single day.

But even the big years were leaving many homesteaders in debt. Soon it became apparent that, although the prairie could in many areas produce wheat, 160 acres could not produce enough of it. A section, 640 acres, would have been a more realistic size for the Montana homestead. Prosperous wheat farmers of today generally work better than a thousand. There was drought after 1916. Inflated grain prices failed to make up for the lack of yield. Most of the homesteaders hung on by floating 8 per cent mortgages. In the early twenties, plagues of grasshoppers were added to the drought, and prices slumped. The prairie was sprinkled with abandoned shacks, many of them sagging away from the prevailing wind. Russian thistles, the "tumbleweed" of romance, which had been unknown in the early West, its seed having been brought over from Europe as a hitchhiker with some useful grain or vegetable (old-timers said in a Russian's whiskers), collected in sagging fence corners and blew deep over the abandoned tractors.

Few of the homesteaders left the country as luxuriously as they had arrived. Those who took the Great Northern were likely to ride in boxcars, or they promoted a free ride on the cattle trains. Some of them left in automobiles, having gleaned gasoline money by means of an auction sale. For the most part, however, they went rattling along the dusty roads in drought-loosened wagons. A few years previously they had arrived with an adventurer's zest for a new life among the cowboys of the Great West. Retaining still some of the old spirit, they painted their vehicles with maledictions of farewell. *In God We Trust, In Montana We Bust*, had served other generations and was prevalent again. More original was the *Goodbye, Old Dry*, painted across the back of a fleeing Dort touring car. One wagon, seen climbing the Loma Hill only a mile from the Ophir massacre, read

> *Forty miles to water*
> *Forty miles to wood.*
> *I'm leaving old Montana*
> *And I'm leaving her for good.*

In Big Sandy, the old-time cowboys and retired ranchers who predicted ruin for the wheat farmers, and were chagrined when the prairie gave forth bumper crops, could hardly contain their delight when at last all their predictions of disaster were seen coming true. Oliver Tingley, now out of the saloon business, partly because of Prohibition but chiefly because he could see no impoverished friend go thirsty, composed and led an old-timer's quartette in "The Harvest Days Are Over, Jesse Dear," speeding the departing guests. Tingley and his friends were entranced by the wagon signs, and took them down in lead pencil on the bullet-scarred pillars of the Exchange Saloon, its false front and famous elkhorns by that time surmounting a bootlegging parlor:

OH I LOVE GRASSHOPPERS
AND THEY LOVE ME
EIGHT YEARS IN MONTANA
NEARER MY GOD TO THEE

and

FAREWELL TO YOU
    BLOODSUCKING BANKERS
YOU'VE FORECLOSED ME
    OFF FROM MY HOME
FROM THE CLAIM AND
    THE TARPAPER SHANTY
WHERE THE SNAKES AND
    THE PRAIRIE DOGS ROAM.

But a certain number of the homesteaders hung grimly on, farming their own land, driving a pickup-herd of hippy mix-breed cattle across the abandoned homesteads, selling cream and eggs, trying to diversify, digging their own coal from the bituminous and lignite beds of the Cretaceous seas which outcropped in the badlands—and a good many of them went to moonshining. Montana acted to encourage this home industry when, soon after the advent of Prohibition, its legislature repealed the state regulations concerned with the sale and manufacture of spirits, and thus left its state and county officials with no authority to help the federal men in the enforcement of "their law." In many communities the Volstead Act, which implemented the Prohibition Amendment, was a boon to the liquor business, wiping out taxes and allowing a greater share of the consumer's dollar to find its way into the cash register. In Big Sandy, in 1922, the town marshal, Jefferson Davis English, made an informal count of the town's bootlegging places and came up with twenty-two, and he was generally to be found hanging around one of them. In the old, tax-paying days Big Sandy had got by with seven licensed saloons. At the Community Fair, the premium list included $5 and a blue ribbon for the farm woman who submitted to the judges the best bottle of home brew. In Butte, at the other end of the rail line on which Big Sandy had so recently been the heaviest agricultural shipper, bootleggers became so numerous and powerful that they founded an organization to raise their own standards, and at one meeting pushed through a resolution banning the sale of liquor to Montana State and Montana University players before the opening whistle of their annual grid classic, hosted by that city; and the *Montana Standard,* a daily newspaper, carried a classified advertisement offering for sale a small hotel "with good bootlegging trade established."

Prohibition was a godsend in many communities. It was a last stand of small industry against the encroaching rule of big business, mass production, and the chain store. On the farm, it was found that even a No. 4 wheat could make a very effective whisky. Farmers experimented with stills of many designs, most of them making use of old-fashioned copper wash boilers, and turned out liquor which could be sold to the saloons for $5 the gallon. Farm moonshining became so common it was a standard joke to ask how many gallons rather than how many bushels a field went to the acre; another had to do with the heavy drinker who came to town to sober up.

Although the first whiskies were very bad—some, in fact, were lethal or induced blindness—competition soon forced the farm stills to turn out an improved product. Charred oak kegs from Arkansas became a volume item in the stores, and some of the whiskies claimed to have mellowed for six long months in the wood. The higher-quality trade was supplied by an extensive whisky traffic across the Canadian border. In near-border towns such as Havre and Shelby, the imperial of Walker's Whisky became standard in the better bars and seriously competed with the local product, with the result that moonshiners commenced calling for more stringent border patrols.

The role of federal officers on the Prohibition scene has become the subject of some dispute. Federal enforcement agents have long enjoyed a reputation for being "dedicated and underpaid public servants." Federal agents during the 1920s, while perhaps dedicated after a fashion, lived not in the style of the underpaid. Whisky runners claimed they spent most of their time trying to grab cargoes of Canadian whisky because of the high value of the product. A favorite newsreel segment of the era showed Prohibition agents dumping beer and whisky into a river, with a closing shot of skidway bums downstream drinking the water. This scene was never shot on the Milk River or the upper Missouri. In court, the valuable shipments of Canadian booze were described as having been destroyed by smashing one bottle against another. The broken bottles and whisky-drenched earth of this spiritous Armageddon were never to be viewed by the public. Although it was noted that some whisky runners operated for years on narrow profit margins right in the teeth of the federal men, others were pursued remorselessly.

The old Whoop-Up whisky routes of the 1870s were again utilized, and many new ones inaugurated. In the 1920s scarcely one good road crossed the border, but there were a hundred poor ones. Or one could take out across the prairie and, by a little maneuvering, go almost anywhere. Without lights, loaded down with liquor, automobiles filtered quietly across the border at so many points it was next to impossible to apprehend them. Most of the federal men therefore retired farther south where the traffic tended to concentrate on the better roads. Driving to the brows of those hills which presented themselves, federal men watched through binoculars, often spotting cars at great distances in the prairie moonlight. The game then was to intercept them. A roadblock might be tried. But moonlight worked both ways. Often a boozerunner would see the distant shine of waiting cars, and, unhampered by modern barrow pits, would speed across the prairie. A daring game of fox and hare was played at wild speeds in heavy, expensive cars. Capture might come when a boozerunner wrecked himself, but generally he was able to elude his pursuers and get back to the road. Police cars in California were by 1922 experimenting with a two-way radio which weighed 280 pounds and filled the back seat, but the police of the border country were generally without so much as a rural telephone at their disposal.

Boozerunners, whether pursued or not, liked to hear the full boom of their cars; they would open the cutouts, and people of the small towns nearby grew used to hearing them miles away in the night quiet of the prairie. Sometimes the sound would suddenly cease, headlights would flick off, and the nightshirted householder, arising, would watch a darkened auto drive into his barn; but he would say nothing, nor crank his wall phone to get the operator out of bed; and next morning he would find an imperial or two of Canadian whisky as the reward of his forebearance.

The elite of all boozerunners' cars was the Cole Eight, last manufactured in 1925. Hudsons and Buicks were more plentiful, however, because they were not quite so conspicuous. Typically, they were touring cars with the side curtains attached. As whisky was heavy, and prohibition agents were on the lookout for cars sagging to the rear axles, most of them were fitted with auxiliary spring leaves. A big car with its rear riding higher than its front was a boozerunner going north for another load. The best market down the North Trail was Denver. There were generally two drivers, one spelling the other off, and the entire journey from Lethbridge, Alberta, was made without stopping except for comfort, food, or gasoline, or to change license plates at the state boundaries.

For several years the booze traffic proved to be a timely contribution to the economies of Havre and Shelby, both close to the Canadian boundary. Havre (named for Le Havre, France, by a female relative of James J. Hill, builder of the Great Northern, who also supplied names for Harlem, Zurich, Toledo, Malta, Glasgow, Tunis, etc.) was particularly blessed. During the worst of the hard times it was not only headquarters for Canadian liquor, but had a large Great Northern payroll. Its gambling houses, and later those at Shelby, have been described as opulent. They were in fact smoky dives physically, but opulent in that there was no scarcity of money. Havre's fan tan game was the biggest north of Butte. On court days Havre would boom with apprehended bootleggers or the men they had hired to take the rap for them, filling the hotels and spending money like Texans come to Dodge. Shelby was less favored, but it left Havre far in the shade when Gordon Campbell, wildcat geologist, discovered oil on the old Whoop-Up Trail 8 miles north of town. Campbell later was sent to prison for some overenthusiastic promotions, but in 1922 he was hailed as the savior of north Montana's sagging economy, and scarcely a community was without a drilling rig, shakily financed, and churn tools pounding down through the strata of the Sweetgrass Arch. Leasers were everywhere, snapping up mortgaged acreage, and some people who had left the country came back again to claim their mineral rights. A moderate production has been maintained until the present, but Shelby was no new Tulsa.

Many of the drought-fleeing farmers of the 1920s went to Oregon, intending to get work in the lumber mills and eventually purchase a little fruit farm; or they headed back to their old homes in Minnesota and Michigan. Quite a number, however, struck out for still another new Land of Plenty —the Peace River Country, northwest of Edmonton.

The Peace River area had been opened to agricultural settlement by a rail line roughly following the first leg of the notorious Back Door Route to the Klondike. Connected with this were a number of roads. In 1925 a man drove his Ford car to Fort St. John. A winter road was even said to exist all the way to Fort Nelson, open to sled and team travel during the months when the rivers and muskegs were solid. There

was also at that time some talk about building a Peace River-
to-Alaska road, and a Prince George-to-Dawson road, connecting with a road along the Yukon Valley, from Nome to
White Horse, the northern link of a Pan-American highway
terminating in Patagonia.

When the Japanese struck Pearl Harbor and threatened
to take control of the Pacific, move up the Aleutians, and
grab coastal Alaska, it seemed suddenly imperative that an
interior supply line be established. Fortunately, a Canadian–
American group had already been hard at work trying to
promote just such a highway, with the result that two of the
projected routes, one via Peace River and the Liard, and the
other up the British Columbian Trench beginning at Prince
George, were both fairly well appraised. The trench route
had been mapped in detail by some old railroad surveys; the
Peace River route was less exact, although some aerial pho-
tography had been done. Because of this work, two days
after the U.S. Cabinet approved an Alaska Highway, the
Army Engineers were able to appear with a general plan for
its location and construction.

The British Columbia route was scarcely considered. It
lay through mountains which in the winter were deep in
snow, and it was too close to the sea. The Peace River road
was a shoo-in winner. It was the old gold-rush route as far as
the Liard; thence it hunted new country and made White
Horse its chief intermediate goal. Dawson City was bypassed. The terminus was to be at Fairbanks. Many, particularly in Canada, felt the Peace River–Liard route was a mistake (they still believe so) but to the authorities it seemed
the best bet at the time.

The project was rushed to Canada for approval. This
did not come until March. By that time the U.S. Army had
bulldozers halfway to Alaska. In the rush, some of the troops
were sent directly from the Mojave Desert, alighting in
Great Falls, Montana, the Highway's U.S. terminus, in 18-
below-zero weather garbed in tropical uniforms. With them
came a trainload of heavy motorized equipment with water

instead of antifreeze in its radiators. This being called to the attention of the major in command by a Butte railroad worker, that officer was quoted as follows: "Thanks just the same, but the United States Army will manage to get along without advice from brakemen." Trying to save something from the chaos of ruptured radiators and cracked cylinder heads, the major urged his men in the task of unloading, but to no avail; his thinly clad charges abandoned the struggle and huddled until daylight around bonfires stoked with railroad ties, then bivouacked in the friendly warmth of several downtown lunchrooms.

The misadventure at Great Falls was only one of a hundred that soldiers and construction workers on the Alaska Highway later recounted, but somehow the road went through. The first race was against the spring break-up. When the vanguard, the 35th Army Engineers, reached Peace River with their long string of cat-drawn equipment, water was found springing from beneath the ice alongshore, and large areas of the middle had turned to mush. A plank roadway was laid across the river ice to distribute the weight, padded against shock with sawdust and forest litter. One after another the pieces of equipment rolled across, a real cliff-hanger being provided by a power shovel weighing twenty-three tons. But the ice held.

When the Peace broke up behind them, the Engineers were cut off from all supplies except for what could be dropped by air. Ahead of them the old winter road was still firm, and the muskegs remained frozen for another month. Only the gulches, filling with slush, were major impediments. Fortunately, the caravan was headed north, more or less keeping pace with the season, and the muck of afternoon turned iron-hard by morning. For weeks their goal was Fort Nelson, still prominently shown on all the maps. It proved scarcely less disappointing to the soldiers of 1942 than to the Klondikers of 1898. It was still only a clutch of Indian shanties and one little trade store. The supply of cigarettes and candy bars was exhausted the first day.

At Nelson the Engineers unloaded and built camp. With heavy equipment they quickly carved out streets and a garbage dump. After that, nobody knew what to do next. The bulldozers had preceded the surveying crews, and nobody at Nelson had more than a general idea where the road was supposed to go. The same situation was to be repeated at other locations time and again, and finally the construction boys just went ahead and built road whether one had been laid out or not, and quite often their improvised segments were more successful than those that had been planned. The surveyors, dropped into a strange country, first tried to get exact information from the Indians. The Indians had been quick to respond to the arrival of troops by selling them parkas, mukluks, beaded money bags, and male totem poles in virile attitudes. But aside from anticipating the artistic taste of the American GI, the Indians proved a grave disappointment. They possessed much exact information about tiny streams where the traplines ran, and they knew the muskeg trails most frequented by the moose which provided much of their food supply, but of the over-all geography of their land they knew nothing. White trappers and prospectors were almost equally innocent of usable information. The surveyors were therefore obliged to rely on the old Geological Survey maps, on air reconnaissance, and on their own ingenuity: often they climbed trees and mountains to wigwag their crews, or proceeded by pure guesswork.

Independent contractors soon moved in. Because the job was so tremendous there were fewer conflicts of authority than might have been anticipated. One and all, they were faced with the same problems that had faced the men of ninety-seven—muskegs, bleak hills, swollen streams, distance, mosquitoes, and bulldog flies.

The first necessity was to build a road, any road, something temporary over which supplies might be brought. Generally the temporary road became permanent; it was merely improved and filled, and it was called the Alaska Highway. For uncounted miles the road of the surveyors remains unbuilt, marked only by a line of stakes winding around the hills, their wood turned dark from the many spring thaws since 1942.

The entire job of building the road was accomplished in less time than was required by a party of tough Mounted Policemen simply to make the journey in 1898–99. True, Alaska could not be defended against the Japanese by means of it; the road as it existed could scarcely provide passage for the trucks to supply its own maintenance crews. In many

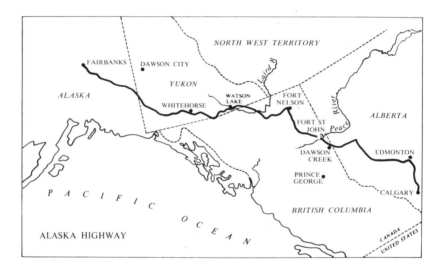

respects, the first Alaska Highway was about equal to the first modest plans for a supply road. But next year the work continued. Segments destroyed or rendered impassable by the Northern winter were moved to new ground, where observations indicated such trouble was less likely to exist. The location became a matter of trial and error. At the end of the second year, a fairly usable supply route was in existence. By that time, few thought that Alaska was in much danger of loss to the Japanese. In any event, the gigantic advances in air transport had rendered the entire project militarily obsolete. With the benefit of hindsight, it can be seen that all those who struggled to beat the Japanese by means of the Back Door passage to Alaska were as misguided as the multitude who tried to fill their purses with Klondike gold via the same route in 1898. On the other hand, it has been pointed out that the Alaska Highway remains the single piece of wartime construction that can be enjoyed by the ordinary taxpayer in either Canada or the United States today. Every year thousands of tourist adventurers see the Klondike, the Yukon, and the North via "the terrible Liard."

Not all Canadians are enthusiastic about their only important north-south highway. They see its ultimate effect as inimical to the principle of "Canada for the Canadians." They feel its main purpose is to connect Alaska with the States, and that doing so will turn the main economic interest of western Canada with it. Many in Eastern Canada would like to abandon the road to the elements. This attitude is not shared by the Prairie Provinces, who see it as their best chance for their commercial and industrial development. Americans would like to make an agreement with Canada for surfacing the highway, but at this writing the leadership at Ottawa is too cagy to talk about it. If the Alaska Highway is allowed to decay, then almost the last vestige of the Trail will have disappeared. In the south the cattle trail is barred by a thousand fences, and the plow has erased the signs of the buffalo. A few roads follow the Trail in a general manner, but each year they are straightened in a manner arrogant of the geography. Fort Peck reservoir, 120 miles long, makes an inland sea blocking the old crossings of the Missouri River, and new lakes have been planned which will fill the river valley upstream almost to Fort Benton. The mountain branches of the Trail may also be flooded. From the Flathead of Montana to the Idaho Panhandle and up into British Columbia the dam builders plan to flood the valleys and the ancient trenches to store water for electric power, one of the largest potentials of the world. Already new roads and railroads are being surveyed along the mountainsides.

The migration of animals has long been cut off. For almost a century the buffalo have been confined to protected parks. The birds, which made the Great North Trail their natural flyway, continue in diminishing numbers, but are falling before the destruction of their nesting grounds, to overhunting in the South, and the onslaught of chemicals. Birds collected by the Montana Fish & Game Department in 1964 showed DDT residues of 6 to 109 parts per million, the safe level for human consumption being, by Food & Drug Administration standards, 7 parts per million. Hunters have been advised to skin all game birds before they risk eating them; and preferably search out and remove all the fat also, that being where the major insecticide concentrations build up. Deer and elk show similar pesticide contamination, so now the hunters of the Northwest eat the game of the forest, heavily sprayed by the Forestry Service of the U.S. Department of Agriculture to eradicate the spruce budworm, at their own calculated risk. The budworm continues to thrive in the imbalance which has killed its natural enemies, and poison levels alarm the cattlemen, whose herds range the mountains and foothills.

So by fence, politics, economics, road machinery, chemicals, and flood, man in the past century has all but obliterated the Great North Trail. The Trail has disappeared several times in the 200 million years of its history, but never before through the power of a species. Our modern age is thus unique. However, because it is ultimately suicidal, it bids to be of shorter duration than those based on geology. A future paleontological intelligence, should one exist, would no doubt discover the biological revolution of the Age of Man and correlate it with the radioactive and chlorinated residues of the rocks. Geologists have trouble dating the systems of geology of one continent with those of another. The poison blanket, thin and uniform throughout all the world, should be invaluable for dating every cape, mountain, plain, and ocean deep to this moment in time.

SOURCES

At the age of fourteen I confessed to my father that I wanted to become a writer, an ambition which so met with his approbation that he ordered, on a free trial basis, the *Elinor Glyn Course in Short Story Writing*. There are two things I remember about the course. One was that it was never paid for. My father had ordered it in my name and letters from New Jersey lawyers were still reaching me years later after I went away to college. The other was a piece of advice Miss Glyn offered. "Write about what you know," she said. "What is dull routine to you may be entrancing to somebody else. If you are a beauty operator, lay your story in a beauty shop. If you are a bricklayer, write about bricklaying."

At that time I was nothing much, but I lived in Montana, in *The West,* land of cowboys, gold and Indians, the most marketable scene a writer could have. As proof of that I did not even have to go to the newsstand and see the flaming magazine covers of the day. I had only to look across several sagebrush-covered lots to the Great Northern Railroad section house where, until very recently, had lived B. M. Bower, schoolteacher, wife of Bower the section boss, and author of, among others, the best-selling *Chip of the Flying U*. And by looking farther I could see the high false front and mounted elkhorns of Barney Van Alstyne's Exchange Saloon where Bertrand W. Sinclair, "The Fiddleback Kid," had tended bar. Fiddleback had made his literary mark also. When Mr. Bower was out working on the section and they were free of nonliterary distractions, Mrs. Bower and Fiddleback had collaborated, the result being novels with the hard-driving Sinclair story line and the creamy Bower dialogue, characterization and syntax. A collateral result was that Mrs. Bower became Mrs. Sinclair, and some of her stories had been signed B. M. Sinclair. But of the time I write she had married yet again, and resumed her old *nom,* while Fiddleback was one of the fixtures of the pulp magazines.

I sold no short stories, but my interest got me on as an apprentice printer at the local *Bear Paw Mountaineer,* and correspondent, at 15 cents an inch, for the *Great Falls Tribune*.

There is nothing that encourages a writer like seeing his stuff in print, and the realization that my accounts of local carloadings, deaths and basketball games were being read all over Montana was strong wine indeed. However, it was not long before the limitations of the news form became apparent. It is not a large acomplishment to answer the five W's—who-what-when-where and why—in the opening sentence and to develop them in succeeding paragraphs, an organization prized for coherence, and because it allows the hurried editor to

369

whack off with a long pair of shears as much of your story as he can use, leaving it complete to that point, but no chance for suspense, no climax. The *Mountaineer,* where I often set up my work directly from the fonts, gave more latitude; but I met what seemed a cloddish lack of appreciation for my finest efforts.

Then I discovered Western history. No land has ever been more avid for its own history than Montana. Montana had a Historical Society organized and collecting dues and materials while many of the pioneers were still using the covered wagons they had arrived in. Its history started in earnest with the discovery of gold at Bannack in the autumn of 1862. By 1875 the Historical Society was so esteemed that W. A. Clark, the banking and mining king, was proud to be its chief speaker at convention. Montana history was very popular in the newspapers. The *Mountaineer's* boiler-plate section, printed in Great Falls by the Montana Newspaper Association, and furnished to it and other weeklies throughout the state, always had a full page of history, often illustrated in pen and ink by Charlie Russell, the cowboy artist. Its history tended to be on the sensational side—Liver-Eating Johnson was a favorite—and highly imaginative, although I did not know that at the time. The "Association" depended on a number of regional historical writers who were faithful to the facts, but on occasion it would be ready to go to press and no article available. In this emergency the editor would construct one on the spot, giving names, places and so much glum detail they were never questioned. Indeed they were dutifully clipped by any number of librarians, catalogued and filed, and today turn up in scholarly bibliographies.

My historical articles were never accepted by the Association. Looking back at them, I know why. I was always trying to be amusing, a completely foreign note, or I strove for the dramatic ending. The *Tribune,* however, was more cordial to my efforts, no doubt because I always used a news-story handle, and tried for less space.

Big Sandy, the old Cowboy Capital, was rich in cattle lore. There were many old freighters there, also. C. J. McNamara of McNamara, Broadwater & Co. was a resident. Our next-door neighbor was "Grandma" Tingley, reputed to be the first white child born in Montana. It seems very distant now, but the career of John J. Healy as sheriff of the county was still a subject of interest, and some bitterness.

One of the most loquacious groups was the Klondikers. Only twenty-five years had passed since the great stampede, and men were still drifting home from the Northern goldfields. Their experiences had been terrible, and yet they wished to talk of little else. And we had veterans of an even older gold rush—men then in their seventies and eighties who had been on Grasshopper Creek, Alder Gulch and Confederate. All furnished material for my articles, few of which, except for those disguised as news, ever saw print.

Although I was aware that a trail ran from Alberta north to the Klondike, and from Montana south to Texas, it never occurred to me that anything like a main passageway, a trail of the ages, existed until I went to work for an oil geologist whom I will call Dr. Downey. He had a Ph.D. and carried his Doctor's cap and gown with him everywhere so he could put it on at a moment's notice in case he was asked to speak. He was a true man of learning, although it often seemed diminished because of the high regard he expressed for himself at all conceivable opportunities.

"Well, I see by the public press that they took my advice," Doc would say. "They finally got around to opening the tomb of Tutankhamen." And he would tell how he had been instrumental in locating the spot through translation of some hieroglyphics in the Cairo Museum when he was in charge of the archeological field group for Oxford University. Or we might be driving down the street past Pep Wilford's saloon in his Packard car, which was on the scale of a Palace Pullman; he'd hear a couple of old, itinerant musicians playing the *Herd Girl's Dream* on the violin and harp, and he'd slam on the brakes and in we'd go. "That's as fine as anything I heard in the great opera houses of Europe," he would cry out, and drop a whole silver dollar in the tin cup. He was a liar, but in the grand style, and practically non-stop. He had read vastly in almost every subject one could think of. The combination of learning and braggadocio was awesome, as those who set out to deflate him soon found out, and he would leave them one and all routed, or in shock.

At that time there was a great deal of wildcatting near Winifred, and around the southeastern flanks of the Bear Paw Mountains. It was Doc who told me that the Bear Paws were particularly interesting to paleontologists, having in all ages formed a shore area of the Western seas. We searched out and I believe located the dinosaur diggings of Edward Drinker Cope fifty years before. There was evidence, he said, that a shallow-water route, a chain of islands and shoals, existed 150 million years ago from Europe all the way to the Bear Paw and Rocky Mountain shores. Not only that, the most ancient of all land routes led down from Alaska. He connected for the first time in my mind the route of the Klondikers with the cattle trail from Texas.

From the high flanks of the Bear Paws one has what surely must be one of the most expansive views of the continent. Doc would drive to one of these vantage points where the Snowy Range, the Highwoods, Judiths and Little Belt mountains were all at our feet, or so it seemed, lying like islands in the sea of Montana, and spend whole afternoons lecturing on the passageways of antiquity. I was enthralled.

Doc left during my junior year in high school and I no longer had a ready means of transportation in the field, but I had learned from him how to supply myself with abundant materials from Washington, D.C. What interested me most were the bulletins and monographs of the Geological Survey. According to the listings these were mostly available at from 25¢ to $1.00 from the Superintendent of Documents. Doc advised me never to pay a cent. Instead, I should write my senator, and if I wanted to mention his name. Senator B. K. Wheeler was an obliging source, as was the late Senator James E. Murray. Even the Out-of-Print asterisk meant nothing to Murray, who mailed what you wanted, and free, free, free!

How many bulletins I read, and how much stuck with me I have no idea, but they certainly formed a major portion of the background for this book.

During the depression, when all other industries were barely hanging on, a boom was experienced by gold mining. It is a simple economic fact that the harder times get, the more can be bought by gold. When round steak in Butte, Montana, fell to 10¢ per pound, gold was still the $20.67 per ounce it had been when butchers were getting a sky-high 25¢. By 1931 gold mining capital started cautiously appearing from hiding, and later, when the price went to $35 and silver was pegged at 77¢ after falling to a low of 28¢ things were very hopeful in the precious-metal country. I went to work for a geologist-engineer whose job it was to find one or two old-time properties worth the re-opening.

Wages for common labor were then around $4.50 per day, with miners at $5.50, but even so it was very expensive to get inside the old, caved and water-filled mines for examination. A person could sample the dumps, trench the outcroppings, and cautiously enter perhaps a few hundred feet of tunnel, but with that done he was put to the expense of underground work at an average of $10 per foot, or core drilling, $1 per foot. The mine maps and assay records could sometimes be found, although as a rule, even for mines which had produced millions, and whose names were famous throughout the West, they were fragmentary, haphazard, and often, I suspect, false. Old residents could be consulted, and former operators. In a few cases there were engineers' and geologists' reports available, but generally the best source existed in the local newspapers of the various camps, and it became my job to go through them. It had to be done page by page, item by item, for one never knew in what story of accident, amusing ramble of the editor, or obituary a key fact might be hidden. I still have in my possession thick bundles of manila envelopes padded with information about the mines, it being my idea that someday they would be worth a fortune. Alas, not so. But they have provided no inconsiderable background for this work where it pertains to the mining frontier.

Later I became a newspaperman, a free-lance writer and a novelist, my interest in the trail continuing. Unfortunately until Mr. A. B. Guthrie agreed with my suggestion that I add this book to The American Trails Series I never bothered to set down the source of a single fact. No doubt I could construct a gigantic bibliography, but not an honest one. Bibliographies on the various areas of history covered by this work are available to students in any good library. However, there are certain works I turned to for verification of facts, and to fill out the portions I knew little about.

The chief geological references were Russell C. Hussey's *Historical Geology, The Ore Magmas* by J. E. Spurr, and *Geologic Structures* by Bailey and Robin Willis. The fault geology of the Montana-British Columbia region is based on R. A. Daly's *Geology of the North American Cordillera at the Forty-Ninth Parallel* which was published by the Canadian Department of the Interior in 1913. The chief Ice Age reference was Flint's *Glacial and Pleistocene Geology.* The ultimate mining reference throughout was *Mineral Deposits* by Waldemar Lindgren.

The general works of history consulted frequently in the final preparation were the Bancroft histories of Washington, Idaho, Montana, Wyoming and Colorado; Coutant's *History of Wyoming,* Brosnan's *History of the State of Idaho, A History of the Pacific Northwest* by George W. Fuller; and the histories of Montana by Sanders, and by Burlingame and Toole.

DeVoto's *The Course of Empire* was consulted steadily in regards to the fur trade and the Spanish penetration of the Southwest, and for the Western fur trade, the standard Chittenden *A History of the American Fur Trade in the Far West. Thirty-three Years Among Our Wild Indians* by Col. Dodge and *When Buffalo Ran* by George Bird Grinnell were relied on in describing the relation of the Indian to the buffalo. *The Blackfeet* by Canfield and the *Old North Trail* by McClintock were used, and placement of the tribes at the coming of the white man is according to LaFarge's *A Pictorial History of the American Indian.*

Margaret Ormsby's *British Columbia, a History* was kept at hand when writing the chapter on the British Columbia trails. The Bozeman Trail material was checked against *The Bozeman Trail* by Hubbard and Brininstool. *Forty Years on the Frontier* by Granville Stuart was heavily relied on for Montana history. Historical pieces in the various books which J. K. Pardee issued under Government imprint should be mentioned. Everyone who writes about the Montana vigilantes goes to Langford and to Dimsdale; this writer also. The recollections of X. Beidler and W. F. Sanders as collected and edited by Helen Fitzgerald Sanders and William H. Bertsche, Jr., were of more than usual interest, and often used.

The most numerous references in the Cope-Marsh story were to *O. C. March, Pioneer in Paleontology* by Charles Schuchert and Clara Mae LeVene; and *Cope, Master Naturalist* by Henry Fairfield Osborn.

The Cattlemen by Mari Sandoz, *The Longhorns* by Dobie, *The Trampling Herd* by Wellman and Dale's *The Range Cattle Industry* all were in a case beside my desk while writing about the cattle trail; William Lee Hamlin's version of the Lincoln County Cattle War impressed the author more than several others, although *The Authentic Life of Billy the Kid* by Pat Garrett was also used; story of the Swan Ranch came from *Wyoming's Pioneer Ranches* by Burns, Gillespie and Richardson; for the Johnson County Cattle War, the classic *Banditti of the Plains,* and Walker and Baber's *The Longest Rope.* Sharpe's

Whoop-Up Country was used for the Whoop-Up trail, and as for the Back Door Route to the Klondike, anyone who reads the books by Pierre Burton will realize that somebody swiped from somebody, and a comparison of copyrights will show who it was.

Maps often differ in their placement of historical points, and in all cases the United States and Canadian Geological Survey maps have been accepted as the authority.

INDEX

Dan Cushman started work at the age of fifteen as a linotype operator and reporter on the Big Sandy, Montana, weekly paper. While in Big Sandy High School, he was also correspondent for the *Great Falls Tribune,* at fifteen cents per inch. Graduating from the University of Montana, he worked first as a miner, prospector, and geologist. His best seller, a Book-of-the-Month Club selection, *Stay Away, Joe,* on which the Broadway musical *Whoop-Up* was based, and his book *The Silver Mountain,* which won him the Western Writers of America Spur Award, are both set in Montana, as is his *Goodbye, Old Dry.* Mr. Cushman's novel *Brothers in Kickapoo* was published by McGraw-Hill in 1962. *The Great North Trail* is his first work of nonfiction.